Christopher Owens

PLAY
DIRECTING

ANALYSIS
COMMUNICATION
AND STYLE

PRENTICE-HALL SERIES IN
THEATRE AND DRAMA

Oscar G. Brockett, *Consulting Editor*

Robert Benedetti
THE ACTOR AT WORK

Charlotte Kay Motter
THEATRE IN HIGH SCHOOL: PLANNING, TEACHING, DIRECTING

Sam Smiley
PLAYWRITING: THE STRUCTURE OF ACTION

Francis Hodge
PLAY DIRECTING: ANALYSIS, COMMUNICATION, AND STYLE

Oscar G. Brockett and Robert R. Findlay
CENTURY OF INNOVATION: A HISTORY OF AMERICAN THEATRE & DRAMA 1870-1970

PRENTICE-HALL INTERNATIONAL, INC., London
PRENTICE-HALL OF AUSTRALIA, PTY. LTD., Sydney
PRENTICE-HALL OF CANADA, LTD., Toronto
PRENTICE-HALL OF INDIA PRIVATE LIMITED, New Delhi
PRENTICE-HALL OF JAPAN, INC., Tokyo

FRANCIS HODGE / *UNIVERSITY OF TEXAS*

PLAY DIRECTING

ANALYSIS
COMMUNICATION
AND STYLE

PRENTICE-HALL, INC. | ENGLEWOOD CLIFFS, N.J.

13–682815–9

Library of Congress Catalog Card Number: 75–143030

Printed in the United States of America

Current Printing (last number):
10 9

preface

For their help in making this book possible, I want to thank two of my colleagues of many years standing, Lucy Barton and B. Iden Payne, from whom I have learned so much about the meaning of theatre and about the artistic dedication and perseverance it takes to make theatre work. I am also deeply grateful to all of my students, from whom I have learned so much in the process of trying to help them. Some people say that directing is a job for the young, and this I believe, for a play is a poem that needs the lyricism and the excesses of youthful spirits. An audience wants to live—to feel deeply, to laugh, to exult. But whether or not a director is young in years, he must always be young in spirit if he is to reach others. Directing is not pinning down a playscript to the ground like a wrestler but releasing it to let it fly with the angels.

I am also much indebted to the following colleagues whose professional work as designers appears in the photographic plates included in this volume: Lucy Barton, Leon Brauner, Herbert L. Camburn, Laszlo L. Funtek, Fred Goodson, Robert Hedley, Joseph E. Johnston, Clayton L. Karkosh, Dan F. Kelleher, David Nancarrow, James A. Pringle, Paul Reinhardt, Ilse Richter, John R. Rothgeb, Leila Sheffield, Bambi Stoll, H. Neil Whiting, and Charles E. Williams. Finally, I want to acknowledge the generous technical assistance of Elizabeth Flack and Sidney McLain in preparing early versions of this work.

design credits
for photographs of scenes
from productions

To the designers whose work appears in the photographic plates included in this book I am greatly indebted. The following list of credits recognizes their personal and professional contributions. Unless noted otherwise, I have directed the productions that appear here. Each entry includes the plate number, the title of the play, its author, and the design credits. All productions, except those especially noted, were staged at The University of Texas at Austin. The photographs appear in this book courtesy of The Department of Drama at the University of Texas and of The Banff School of Fine Arts, Banff, Alberta, Canada.

I *Rhinoceros* (Ionesco). Settings: John R. Rothgeb; Costumes; Paul Reinhardt; Lighting: Dan F. Kelleher.

II *Morning's At Seven* (Osborn). Settings: Joseph E. Johnston; Costumes: Lucy Barton; Lighting: H. Neil Whiting.

III *Outward Bound* (Vane). Settings and Lighting: Joseph E. Johnston; Costumes: Leila Sheffield.

IV *The Shewing Up of Blanco Posnet* (Shaw). Settings: John R. Rothgeb; Costumes: Leon Brauner; Lighting: H. Neil Whiting.

table of contents

PLAY DIRECTING

ANALYSIS
COMMUNICATION
AND STYLE

I

about this book
and its point of view

The process of directing is laid out in this book as a highly sensitive craft involving intensive play-analysis, exceptional skills in communication, and approaches to the making of style. For a long time, people in some quarters have assumed that directing is impressionistic—in other words, that it proceeds largely from a director's strong feelings about plays, coupled with an enthusiasm for making something in the theatre, and that his training consists of coordinating what he has assimilated from diverse theatre courses and learning how to block plays and how to manipulate actors. Such an assumption can be quite misleading, for directing is not merely a director's own doing but his stimulation and arrangement of the doing of others, a very complicated process requiring many exceptional skills of its own. This book therefore rests on the premise that a high level of specialized training is absolutely necessary if a student is to understand thoroughly not only all the concepts which he will use but also how to make them work for him.

To carry out this objective, Part I is a highly developed technical method for examining in detail the structure of a play with the specific purpose of collecting materials and suggesting approaches that can be used directly in communicating with actors and designers. Although

Part II is about the acting process, it does not explicitly teach acting but instead focuses on the ways and the means a director can use in communicating with actors—what can be called *organic communication*. Likewise, the intention in Part III does not teach designing but focuses attention on the director's function as designer—it specifically delineates his options in staging plays—and on his relationship with designers. Part IV again deals with play-analysis but this time on an advanced and much more sensitive level—style-analysis—for the approach is to help a director see how he can express himself in a very personal way by perceiving the individuality of each play he works with and then by finding an individual way of producing it. The director in this book is considered to be at the same time both a master craftsman in the theatre and the dedicated communicator-leader of all those who work with this art form.

The purpose of this book, then, is to lay out the director's job as specifically and completely as possible. If the work seems too extensive, if it seems to invade fields, such as acting and designing, usually discussed elsewhere, if it seems to be based too much on the history of the theatre, you may be thinking of directing in a much too limited way. There are no halfway measures about this job. If you want to think and work as a director, you must face up to rigorous and extensive training. The old saying "Life is short and art is long" is true only because artists have been challenged greatly by the demands of their jobs and then have gone beyond themselves in making their art. If you want to be a director, you must learn it all.

Because of its goal of covering the whole process, this book provides material for a two-year study in directing, although a top-level group might accomplish it in a shorter period. A suggested approach for the first year is to work through Parts I and II within a period of several weeks, with a live directing project (perhaps a five-minute scene from a long play) scheduled as soon as the material has been covered. The remainder of the year can then be spent in the process of intensifying the understanding of Parts I and II through live directing projects of scenes from Realistic plays dating from approximately 1920 to 1960, and in working through Part III with a minimally staged, though fully designed, directing project at the end. Through this plan, the first year can thus be devoted to mastering form and content in both play-analysis and production, and developing communication skills to a high degree. The second year can then be focused on Part IV, with several directing projects first centered on the styles of early Realism (1870–1920) and on departures from Realism, including Expressionism of the 1920s, and then, if resources allow, with experiments on various stage shapes in the interest of defining one aspect of production style. Scenes selected from historical drama and from recent departures from Realism (absurdist plays and plays written since 1960) could also be used on these stages.

A two-year plan obviously has the distinct advantage of permitting intensive exercises to accompany all phases of grasping the concepts. Although it would be pretentious to assume that any instruction in directing could bring about the mastery of form and style in a two-year period, much can be accomplished if emphasis is placed on giving the student a firm basis of techniques through which he can make his own discoveries when future opportunities for directing present themselves.

What can be written about directing is extremely limited simply because it is an activity that is not productive in itself but is entirely reliant on the things other people make—the playscript, the acting, the designs, theatre architecture. This reason is precisely why most of the talk about directing concerns how these things are made and how to use them. What follows, then, is a series of detailed discussions, liberally sprinkled with exercises, on how you can make yourself useful in a theatre that for many centuries did without the director and could very likely do so again in the future unless he can prove he is needed. Directing lies in doing, and you must find out what to do, where and when to do it, and how to do it to the best possible advantage. Therefore, do not look at the exercises as restrictive but as suggestions for the sort you will soon provide yourself, for learning the craft of directing is learning how to *do* and how to *make* with imagination and freedom.

Some will think that the process of study outlined in this book is a too artificial approach to directing, but all beginning education in any field must build from the ground up. You should already be aware that plays are artificial objects, that is, man-made rather than natural, and are works of art if they are greatly imagined. It is therefore pure nonsense to assume that one's natural feelings and responses alone can give life to this artificial body without intensive knowledge of the theatre crafts. We wouldn't think of letting a carpenter experiment with a surgeon's knife on a real body. A playscript is no different, for an uninformed, would-be director can murder it. Making art is a delicate process that requires meticulous care and sensitive skill if it is not to be stillborn.

Remember: Art is a very personal and individual matter. If you are going to succeed—that is, actually to reach a position where you can make art—and if others are to agree that you can, there are no shortcuts, no halfway measures. Everything is hard, dedicated work. Many students drift into theatre training because they have been excited by the stage and want to exhibit themselves on it; they seem to think that being enthusiastic and feeling strongly are all that is really needed, that theatre art is largely self-expression. This reasoning is nonsense. Any work in the theatre, which includes directing as a primary study in communication and artistic leadership, requires the utmost in hard work and personal discipline. Directing is giving to others; it is sharing one's own lifeblood. There are no marbles to give back after the game is over, for the game is always played for keeps. If you lack the stamina, do not try directing.

Learning directing, as with any art, is a process of personal discovery—doing things over and over until they become second nature. How long the learning process will take is a matter of your capability in perceiving concepts, in getting the message in a very personal way. A book of this sort cannot make you into a director, for no one can actually teach you how to direct any more than he can teach you how to act. What can be done is to put you, as a dedicated learner, on the tracks that can lead to self-discovery; the artist in you will do the rest.

2

getting the bull
by the horns: the need
for instruction in directing

The Poet-Playwright and the Director

A play is like a tropical bird—at once exotic in its song and plumage, half-seen and mystical in its darting flight, and illusive and difficult to capture. Our forebears called the makers of these special stories play-*wrights* on the assumption that a play could be made just as another craftsman could make a ship (shipwright) or a wheel (wheelwright), and today we use the same word for almost the same concept. But though the play-maker's status is less elevated in our time than it has been in some other periods, his job is still the same: to be a conscious dream-maker who can, with the appropriate use of basic tools, stir up minds and feelings and cause imaginative flights in others.

The peculiar characteristic of the playwright's making, the thing that differentiates it from other writing, is that his dream-flight, his *improvisation,* has to take into account not only vocal and visual instruments—the actors—but also the particular place around which or in front of which he can gather his audience to hear and watch the story—the stage. He is a rare artist because what he puts down on paper, at its most demanding level, is really not writing at all in the usual literary sense—that is, writing intended for consumption by one person at a time—but is the making of a thing that involves *actors* and *objects* set out in a specific way for seeing and hearing *by a group*. What the play-maker leaves out—the gap for the actors to fill in—is usually as important as what he puts in. French actor-director Jean-Louis Barrault has a good way of describing it: a play, he says, is "interrupted silence." This concept moves us entirely away from thinking about a play as a literary product, as merely conversation written down, for we see that it is far more difficult to leave out than to put in. Many celebrated novelists and poets have tried unsuccessfully to make "interrupted silences," but they abandoned their efforts when they discovered that it takes a very special kind of imagination and skill to devise this sort of complex improvisation and that literary talent is not the basic qualification.

You should not be surprised to learn that playwrights in many ages acted in and directed their own plays. After all, they knew or assumed that they knew, as everybody else did, what their plays were all about. When a dramatic poet composed a play he heard his verses in his mind's ear and saw the actions in his mind's eye. The total thing was the dramatic poem. What the play did to an audience was to arouse its emotions directly: the process was physical and disturbing; and it was only secondarily intellectual, though the experience required a perceptive intelligence—not quite the same thing. When it worked, it reached out to grab and thrill; it could cause tears and laughter, chills and anger; it could also exhaust members of an audience as well as exalt them. Its power was mystical and godlike. As we know, we can retain a well-performed play in our minds for years in the same way that we hold onto an intensively felt personal experience, for characters in plays can seem like exotic friends of many years' acquaintance.

In our day, the playwright seldom directs his own play, nor does he act in it. The pressure of the nineteenth-century world of scientific discovery, of inventions, and of mechanization so changed playscripts, acting, and the stage machine that a coordinating specialist was needed to hold these forces together. Before this new approach to play production was adopted, leading actors with the help of a "stage *manager*"—who was just what his label implied and still implies, a manager of the stage—had given what little direction was considered necessary. In the last quarter of the nineteenth century, the idea of a separate craftsman began to take shape. He would be a skilled coordinator who understood all the crafts of the theatre and could devote his full energies to bringing them together into a single, artistic, rhythmic whole in order to express in the best possible way what the playwright had in mind. Thus was born simultaneously twentieth-century theatrical art and the director as the major theatrical artist.

The need for the sort of study developed in this book is obvious. If the student is to undertake the job of theatrical artist, he must learn as much as he can about the nature of theatrical art.

The Director's Job

It is precisely because he has so much power in the theatre that so much is expected of the director. Yet the curious paradox is that, like the playwright, he is not actually seen *on* the stage but only *through* the actors and the physical staging provided by the designers. In contrast, symphony and opera conductors have a physical presence—they visibly run the performance, with the obvious capability of directly affecting rhythm and mood. But the director's work can be measured only in what happens as the actors and designers work on the audience. In this sense, he is a silent partner, though his work beforehand is anything but silent. To the contrary, the director is a talker, a verbal imagist, for *his primary work is communication*—not directly to the audience but *to actors and designers* who then transmit his ideas to the audience.

The director, then, is a communicator of the highest order. This function is his job, his only reason for being. A person may have very strong feelings about a playscript, but sensitivity, though it will help, will not define his directing capabilities. Because the transfer of his ideas must be made through the minds and feelings of others, the challenge for a director lies in his talent for touching the magic springs in others with what he so vividly imagines and feels himself.

This challenge is the director's paradox. All artists operate within some balance of their subjective-objective selves, but it is the subjective that customarily dominates. The director is an exception, for he does most of his work on the conscious side of the scale. Herbert Blau in *The Impossible Theatre,* a stimulating and soul-searching study of the director's function, puts down this idea in cold print: "The director," says Mr. Blau, "must be a brain." This statement does not mean that the director works only in an objective, intellectual way, for there is no question that he must trust his feelings to react primitively and vigorously to what he helps make on the stage. What it does mean is that the director is the practicing critic in the theatre, and, as such, he must constantly bring what he feels and thinks to the surface so that he can communicate readily with others. The director must perceive; he must evaluate: he must make a diagnosis; and he must devise remedies. His effectiveness in all these actions will lie precisely in his outside-inside responses, his objective-subjective balance. To accomplish this balance, the learning director must become intensively aware of the structures of plays, of the theory and training processes in acting, of the physical use of the stage, and of the visual capabilities of design, for at the base the director is the total designer of a production, the principal "Idea Man," and design is finding concrete form for imagined ideas.

The emphasis here may appear to make the director too coldly analytical, but the intention is to show the need for the extensive training so necessary to equip a director for his job. Without a wide knowledge of the theatre and a keen understanding of its basic concepts, he is simply ineffective. But though his study may be broad and objective, and his development of techniques follow a self-conscious route, unless he has an inherent talent for flight—letting his imagination go wild—he may not achieve much more than did the nineteenth-century stage manager. Like all artists, the director must first be an adventurous soul, eager to cut new paths and capable of soaring on the level of the dramatic poet. He too often may be labeled only an interpreter of the creative works of others; yet if he cannot reach some of the same heights as those achieved by the poet he is attempting to reveal on the stage, he is not fulfilling his function. At his best, he will soar with the angels, but at the same time he must be an engineer-pilot, a professional who is forever landing and taking off. He knows his plane, his instruments, and his flight plan—the limitations that bind his flight yet simultaneously make it possible. The stage is a flying machine that must be manipulated with the greatest skill. By knowing the limitations of his art form, he will know which way freedom lies and thus be able to lead others to it. Flight-in-restriction is his goal.

The Assumptions at the Base of This Book

The approach to directing taken in this book, then, is rooted in five basic assumptions:

1. *Play-analysis is of first importance in the directing process.* Merely feeling about a play is entirely insufficient. Play-analysis (structural analysis) must be mastered as a technique so that it can be used in approaching all aspects of the theatrical art in all plays, historical as well as modern.
2. *The director's core activity is communication.* It is precisely his capability of exact and imaginative communication *with* actors and designers (as distinct from his communication to an audience)—on a sublimated level as well as on a conscious level—that will declare his effectiveness.
3. *The director is a master designer.* A produced play is the "physicalization" of a playscript, and it must be cohesive and integrated in all its aspects, from the manipulation of the actor to the manipu-

lation of the stage space and all the materials used on it. An organic approach to theatre history provides an invaluable working tool for this function.

4. *The director's training must be very closely allied to the actor's training.* Because the director's primary function is bringing out the actor, he must be highly sensitive to how the actor feels, thinks, and works. The approach in this book assumes that the prevailing instruction in acting is some form of Stanislavskian principles, however modified or otherwise identified, and that the director will work closely in coordination with this approach to the actor's training.

5. *The director is a critic and a stylist.* What the director puts on the stage is a direct statement of what he believes the play to contain. Interpretation, as presented in this book, is defined as a sincere attempt at finding an author's ideas in a play and at rendering them honestly and appropriately through theatrical art. The kind of individualization a director uses in this process will declare his style for a particular production.

Improvisation as a Basic Technique

In this book, the development of the directing process, then, will take the route of showing why the assumptions noted above are basic to any present-day approach. To support their validity, throughout this book a technique is used—one that has become very significant in our contemporary theatre: improvisation. In its early uses, improvisation was thought of primarily as Stanislavskian training for the actor, but as its values and possibilities have become more apparent, it has been used not only in the relationship between director and actor but also as a basis for play-making. As a result, not only have a number of experimental moving pictures been made by using this approach, but the experimental productions of The Open Theatre and The Living Theatre in the 1960s have shown us that unusual theatricals can also be developed through this technique.

The approach taken in this book, therefore, assumes that stage direction is the process of freeing the master improvisation—the playscript—by freeing actors and designers to make their own improvisations. The imposition of restriction, of limitation, can take place only *after* the flight and not before. One of the great problems in learning directing is in learning this paradox of freedom and restraint. Both are absolutely necessary: without freedom the imagination of an audience is never aroused; without restraint the telling of a story from the confinement of a stage in a theatre with live actors would be impossible.

The director is therefore an improvisor of the first order. In this sense, he is very close to the playwright, who turns his dreams into forms —all controlled improvisations. The director is forever a game player— always improvising, always making up spontaneously what seems appropriate and honest in a given circumstance.

You will note as you work through this book that many of the exercises require improvisation—*spontaneous storytelling in declared or undeclared circumstances.* If you have participated in such game playing, you will already know that although improvising can make something very much like a play, it is not a play at all but an exercise in releasing imagination. The overall intention is to free those persons who play the game, to let them fly. But in order to do so, several conditions are necessary. Here are a few that must guide you and your class when doing improvisations:

1. The participants are not actors; that is, they are neither acting out a portion of a playscript nor are they performing for an audience. Their intention is to *release each other* through full concentration on each other and the situation. Although some given circumstances may be set before an improvisation begins, the participants work "off" one another, with their imagination dictating what to do in a certain context. There is no preplan of action. What happens will happen only as a participant lets his behavior, in reaction to other forces (other people in the same improvisation), be the result of his response to their pressures.

2. The watchers are not an audience. They are privileged to be there when the improvisation takes place. Therefore, they must not participate like an audience, but watch silently and quietly with no verbal reactions whatever, since this would break the happening by distracting the participants, thus making them self-conscious. Once the participants have become self-aware, the improvisation is lost because they have become themselves and not participants in an imagined circumstance.

3. The place to develop an improvisation is not a stage nor any location that would resemble it, since this kind of setting, because of its artificial nature, would cause the improvisers to feel self-conscious. For this reason, we play this game in a room, defining the space only with what the improvisors find necessary.

4. Only the beginning of an improvisation should be suggested, and that in a barely minimal way. What happens afterward is the improvisation.

It is obvious that a good deal that is playlike can happen in improvisations if the participants and watchers observe the conditions. You can see characters in action, with different moods and tempos, and, as a watcher, you can be moved by the truthtelling and believability of such moments. But you must also realize that "achieving" a complex improvisation is not easily accomplished unless you have participants with experience in playing this game, because learning to release fully takes practice. In working through the exercises in this book you must always give yourself seriously and with full concentration to improvisational exercises. If you do, you will find them most rewarding.

Prerequisites for Training in Directing

What should the beginning director bring to his training? It is obvious that the study of direction cannot begin until the student has first learned a few basic concepts about the theatre and the skills that make them work. To begin with, he should be familiar with a body of plays from both modern and historical periods (at the end of this section is a list of plays cited as examples in Parts I and II), and should know about historical stages as well as about conventions of the modern theatre. He will be able to comprehend more easily the director's function as designer if he has had some elementary study—a basic course in stagecraft or production, for example—and if he knows how stage materials are made, so that he can imagine what to do with them. And acting? He should have studied it in detail, including some technical training in voice and speech, for his work with the actors as the principal instruments of his ideas will be his most important contribution to a production. All his adventures with the physical stage will evaporate like steam if he fails with the actors. Acting and staging are the blood of an interpretation, and without finding their pulse and flow, the body—the playscript—cannot be resuscitated.

The young director will work on some crafts, along with play reading, concurrently with his new study, but unless he has a basic knowledge of what he is coordinating, of what comprises theatrical art, he will wander around in darkness. Directing is not simple manipulation of other people by someone with a dominating ego; it is a mature awareness of how to work skillfully and patiently with others to bring out the life-force of a breathing and pulsating story on the stage. If he is to capture for an audience the wild tropical bird of the play, a director must be a great deal more than a birdwatcher.

Among the first steps in directing is reading many plays. A director who does not avidly read plays, both past and present, cannot go far simply because he will lack a broad knowledge of his most basic tool—the playscript. Therefore get into the regular, weekly habit of reading all kinds of plays and keeping a file card on each play read with brief notations on ideas, setting requirements, story line, characters, and production possibilities. Once you have acquired such a background, you will be able to understand many plays much better because of the comparisons you can make with other plays. However, because Parts I and II are principally for the beginning student, this book does not cite a broad range of plays as examples but confines discussions to relatively few on the assumption that the beginning director probably has not read many plays and will not be able to project examples readily in his imagination. All of Parts I and II, including the exercises, can be accomplished if the student is familiar with the following:

Riders to the Sea (Synge)	*Murder in the Cathedral* (Eliot)
Hedda Gabler (Ibsen)	Any play by Harold Pinter
Ghosts (Ibsen)	*Oedipus the King* (Sophocles)
Candida (Shaw)	*Hamlet* (Shakespeare)
The Little Foxes (Hellman)	*She Stoops to Conquer* (Goldsmith)
Winterset (Anderson)	*The Bald Soprano* (Ionesco)
Desire Under the Elms (O'Neill)	*The Adding Machine* (Rice)

In contrast, the examples used in Part IV range widely, again on an assumption that by the time the student has been in training for a period of time he will have noticeably extended his reading, as well as having greatly amplified his understanding of the structure of drama. Consequently, he should be able to penetrate groups of plays he could not have handled previously with much perception.

EXERCISES

1. What is a dramatic poet? Why is a modern writer of drama in prose also a dramatic poet?

2. Without getting involved in the complexities of the differences between serious drama and comedy, why is the writer of comedy also a dramatic poet?

3. The director is an image-maker. What is an image? Cite images for each of the five senses: taste, touch, smell, hearing, sight. From your knowledge of acting and design, can you see how an audience perceives a play through images? What is the process of transfer?

4. Although there is a major section ahead on director-actor communication, on the basis of your experience as an actor, try to list all the methods of communication between them that you can recall. How do directors "get through" to other people? Simple exposition in words is one of the ways, but it may be one of the poorer ones when it comes to reaching actors. Your answers to this exercise may be largely speculative at this point in your training, but now is the time to call up any experience you may have had along these lines.

5. Make a list of *all* the plays you have (a) read or (b) seen. Take care in dividing your experience into these two categories because they are quite different. Date each one, and then examine your actual coverage of drama. How extensive is your background? Where are you weakest? You must make a habit of reading plays regularly to fill in the weak areas.

6. How do each of the following backgrounds contribute to a student's preparation before beginning directing: acting; designing; the architecture of Shakespeare's stage; the nature of Sophocles' *Oedipus;* what happens in *Hamlet?* a study of phonetics; a study of voice production; an understanding of music and painting?

7. Illustrate the difference between restriction and flight by doing the following improvisation: With the use of chairs, tables, or other essentially neutral forms in the classroom, one student composes a *four-sided* place. The class then tries to guess the *literal* place suggested by the forms and their arrangement by identifying the literal meaning of each form, such as a chair, a bed, a sofa, in the context of other forms. When a consensus has been reached on the literal meaning, the class suggests alternate meanings for the forms, with the intention of arriving at more exceptional locations and contexts. Thus, what might at first seem to be a normal suburban living room could be turned into the mountain hideout of a gangster or the primitive hut of a Basque peasant. Repeat this game with several improvised places. The flight takes place as class members move away from accepted literal meanings of forms in their easily recognizable contexts. (Note: This exercise is not that of making a groundplan for a stage, so do not set up the places with a stage in mind but only as places that could exist in real life anywhere.)

8. Continue Exercise 7 with one student arranging a place and then setting in it two people who have a specific relationship to one another. The class tries first to declare the literal place and its context; it then tries to identify possible flights by suggesting more exceptional places and relationships of the people.

9. Continue Exercise 8 by having the students in the improvisation develop a conflict by using numbers, not words, as dialogue. Example: A says: 1, 2, 3, 4; B says: 9, 10, 20; A says: 2, 3, 6, 7; B says: 4, 7, 9, 10. In this substitute for dialogue, the numbers do not mean anything in themselves, but the attitude behind each group of numbers is the basic meaning behind the line. (The use of actual words in improvisations is very difficult for participants because they must think in terms of word choice. Numbers dialogue is much easier because participants need think only of their attitudes towards other people in the improvisation.) When the improvisers reach an intensity of interresponse, the improvisation can be stopped and the following points discussed:
   a. What is an improvisation?
   b. What are the free circumstances of an improvisation?
   c. How was this improvisation *like* a play and yet *not* a play?

  d. What is a play? (Try defining it as an expert and highly developed improvisation.)

  e. What did the participants add to the suggested beginning of the improvisation?

  f. What are the limitations in the use of numbers dialogue?

I

PERCEPTION:

PLAY-ANALYSIS:
THE DIRECTOR'S PRIMARY
STUDY

The poet's eye, in a fine frenzy rolling,
Doth glance from heaven to earth, from earth
                                to heaven;
And, as imagination bodies forth
The forms of things unknown, the poet's pen
Turns them to shapes, and gives to airy nothing
A local habitation and a name.

THESEUS
in *A Midsummer Night's Dream*

3

the foundation and facade
of the playscript:
given circumstances
and dialogue

Perception: Play-Analysis

Perception as it is used here simply means finding out what a playscript is all about—getting the sense and feel of it.

Many people in the theatre shy away from the phrase *play-analysis* because they think it has a dry, academic ring and implies cold, factual, scientific examination of a playscript that will kill their animal (subjective) feelings about it. They assume that theatre art can be made only if you feel strongly enough about a playscript and that your good sense will carry you the rest of the way. This book does not agree at all with this point of view. Certainly, there are aspects of many plays that cannot be described easily in words, but this difficulty does not suggest that a play exists in a mystical world defying logical examination. Having the right attitude about play-analysis at the beginning is very important.

The use of the word perception is a good one here because it can imply both strong feeling—the subjective flight and freedom in a director—and a basic objective awareness of how a play is made. It implies more than a felt reaction on a first reading: "I like that play. It moves me strongly. But I can't pin down what does it." Perception implies that a penetrating search into a play—play-analysis—is absolutely necessary if the play is to be understood at all. Perception in this sense means that much of a play *can* be pinned down. What a director finds in it will depend on how thoroughly he can take it apart in his own mind and then put it back together again, thoroughly comprehended. Perception is the director's total view of a playscript after he has *felt* it and then *examined* it in detail. If his feelings are strong on first reading, and he knows the job of play-analysis thoroughly, he cannot help but have much greater respect for a play after analysis than he had before. At the least, he will not be left in the gray about it.

This point of view is predicated on the assumption that a play is not life but art. As a form of art it is artificial—a made object that may have a likeness to life but definitely is not life. Even those playscripts that seem most realistic, most like everyday life as we know it, stand this test. You may have heard of Stanislavski's experiment: He asked his actors to perform a scene from a play by Chekhov out-of-doors in a real garden. Before they began, he assumed that the playscript was so lifelike and his players so photographically real in their roles that anyone watching could only think what he saw was actually taking place. He was amazed, and at first greatly disappointed, to discover that the scene produced no such effect, that against the reality of nature in the garden the action and the actors were like wax flowers with only a resemblance to reality. He then began to revise his whole theory of how to make reality on the stage, but it was now based on the realization that a play is a play, no matter how photographic it seems, and therefore cannot be confused with real life.

The nature of art can be defined in many ways, and the young director should try to clarify in his own mind something about this vast subject as early as possible. But though such definitions are highly relevant to any discussion of directing, the intention is not to pursue them at this time except to point out that the more a director knows about the difference between ritual and art form, yet at the same time how they are related, the more he can understand about the origins of dramatic and theatrical forms; and the more he understands about the difference between what is real and what is fabricated on the stage, the more he will comprehend not only theatre as art form but also what he can do as a maker of that art form. Your own definition of art will gradually mature and become part of you as you work in depth with theatrical materials and techniques. Except to get you started, definition can be confusing and complicating. Therefore, you must accept on faith, if you do not yet comprehend the concept, that a playscript is an artificial object you can disassemble and reassemble as you can any other man-made object.

Play-analysis, then, is the director's support *for his feelings* about a playscript. As a technique, it is tied to the primary thesis that directing is not a totally intuitive process but is also an art-creating process in which the director brings the materials (the playscript) of the form to the conscious surface; that is, he becomes *consciously* aware of them, in the interest of finding their strengths and weaknesses, their peaks and valleys, and their rhythms, all of which will serve as a basis for theatricalizing the playscript to the best possible advantage. Adequate play-analysis is no guarantee of success (no one can predict success in the theatre because there are so many factors involved), but it is insurance that the director is at least familiar with his materials. The playscript is the principal machine of the director, and play-analysis is as basic a reason for his job as is helping the actor. Unless he knows his machine thoroughly, he cannot make it work at all. He will be only a stage manager—a traffic organizer and logistical expert. A certain playscript may be a playwright's intuitive improvisation, but the resulting form he makes is not accidental because he brings his own critical awareness to bear on it. The playwright has thus made something that the director, if he understands how it is made, can exploit. The director's study of his job as a theatrical artist will tell him how he can exploit it.

EXERCISES

1. Discuss with other members of the class your experiences with first readings. Do you make a practice of reading a play in one sitting? Why is this procedure good? What did you *feel* about a particular play after the initial reading?

2. What do we mean when we talk about the dramatic imagination in a reader? How does it improve as he reads more plays? Why does such a reader have more capabilities than others who do not read and study plays regularly?

3. Discuss the dangers of impressionism if carried out literally—that is, if the student director moves *solely* out of his feelings. What will it do to his capability to communicate? What will be his problems with actors who also feel very strongly but perhaps differently about a play?

4. Bring some definitions of art to class and discuss their merits. How does the theatre differ from other arts, such as painting or sculpture?

5. How does a play differ from such literary forms as: (a) a novel; (b) a book of history; (c) a poem?

6. Compare in detail the improvisational reality of an hour of class—the one being experienced at the moment—with what a playwright might do in dramatizing the same class hour for the stage. What is dramatic? What is peripherally dramatic? Why is the peripheral more interesting than the obvious that everyone sees?

The Overview of Play-Analysis

DEFINITION

There are seven major areas of play-analysis: (1) given circumstances; (2) dialogue; (3) dramatic action; (4) characters; (5) idea; (6) tempos; (7) moods. Although this breakdown is arbitrary for the purpose of explicit discussion, you should recognize at the outset that they overlap, and that some of these areas are so thoroughly dependent on others that they do not take shape until the force of the others has been determined. Other words might be used to define the same concepts, but this set, when fully delineated, answers the purpose very well. We know that basic communication in textbooks rests on clear definition of the terms used. Therefore, you must recognize at this point that the study of directing in this book is based on the meanings given to the terms here and in the following two chapters. For the purpose of discussion in logical steps that you can readily follow, the seven areas are treated under three major headings: (1) "The Framework of the Play: Given Circumstances and Dialogue," discussed in this chapter; (2) "The Hard Core of the Play: Dramatic Action and Character," discussed in Chapter 4; and (3) "The Derivatives of Dramatic Action: Idea, Tempos, and Moods," treated in Chapter 5.

You must also be alerted at this point to a matter of great importance: each of these words (e.g., dialogue) or two-word phrases (e.g., given circumstances) stands for a concept. Merely to define them is not to understand them. As in acting, *doing* in directing will lie not in defining terms or in debating concepts but in absorbing them so thoroughly that they are immediately recognizable in all contexts. You must discover for yourself the breadth and depth of these concepts so that they become an intuitive part of your thinking.

At first, you will be tempted to push aside the examination-in-depth of these concepts. After all, simple impression—how I feel about it!—is much easier. But if you do, you will soon discover that you really do not know much about the inside workings of a play and that you do not really know how to get through to actors. But once you have mastered the techniques outlined here, you will feel a security you have not known previously, since you will at least know something very specific about your primary tool—the playscript.

CONCEPT

Another problem usually confronting the student in his first contacts with play-analysis is the difference between the playscript as mere story and the structure of that story. Most students entering training programs in the theatre have only *felt* plays, that is, they haven't actually looked at how they are made because they have never taken any plays apart except in a superficial way. Structural analysis deals with taking a play apart and looking at its mechanics. The story of a play is made up of so many things so well blended together, that an unoriented reader merely experiences its final effect, its moods, its feelings. But through play-analysis, the director can get at what makes those moods and feelings and thus have greater assurance that he can call them up in actors and move audiences accordingly. In comparison with live theatre, the moving picture as a form is static, since once the image has been perfected through several takes and retakes, it is set forever; it is impervious to change. In the theatre, the same playscript is repeated by actors over and over, with a certain level of effectiveness that must be achieved in each playing. This life-living force gives the theatre its individuality and its rarity. Your awareness of play structure, then, will give you the seeds for all that can happen later, when you put a play into production.

In the discussions of the seven areas the terms are first defined and then developed as concepts. Some examples are given to illustrate each step in this technique, but your comprehension will come about only through application of the approach to specific plays. There is no skipping around in this procedure. Try to understand and apply the concept of one term before you go on to the next. The series of seven is developed in an intentional order to show how each draws on what precedes it.

PROCEDURE FOR CLASS DISCUSSION

A one-act play of high quality, such as J. M. Synge's *Riders to the Sea,* should be used as an example for structural analysis. By confining all the analytical problems to one play, the seven aspects of analysis are better understood both individually and in their interrelationships. (See note attached to Exercise 2, p. 65.)

EXERCISES

1. Tell the story of the latest play you have read. Did your narration interest your hearers? If it did not, why not? Did you miss the point? Did you try to convey your feelings about the play rather than the specific story line?

2. Compare the stories of a recent moving picture you have seen and a play you have either read or seen. What is different about each form? Try to avoid focusing your discussion on the differences in production, but place the emphasis on the different ways the story lines are developed.

3. What is meant by technique? Why are techniques necessary for people working with art forms?

The Foundation and Facade of a Playscript

After you have read the following pages you will better understand why "Foundation and Facade" has been chosen to head this section. All you need to understand at this point, however, is that both given circumstances and dialogue frame the play just as deeply rooted pilings and a covering of glass and steel frame a modern skyscraper. The given circumstances resembles the deeply rooted base of a building—the substructure upon which it is built, its foundations, and dialogue the outer shell, the transparent encasement covering the activities that will go on inside. If you keep these images in mind, you will be able to see why the real guts of the play, its hard core, resides in dramatic action and character, but that neither of the latter can be built into the structure without the foundation of given circumstances and the facade of dialogue.

GIVEN CIRCUMSTANCES (PLAYWRIGHT'S SETTING): THE FOUNDATION OF THE PLAYSCRIPT

Definition. The term *given circumstances* (playwright's setting) concerns all material in a playscript that delineates the environment—the special "world" of the play—in which the action takes place. This material includes: (1) environmental facts—the specific conditions, place, and time; (2) previous action—all that has happened before the action begins; (3) polar attitudes—points of view toward their environment held by the principal characters.

Given Circumstances versus Playwright's Setting. Although Stanislavski's phrase *given circumstances* will be used throughout this text after this initial explanation, the parenthetical phrase *playwright's setting* was used above because you are probably more familiar with it. However, as a term, it is so frequently confused with what a designer makes—the actual stage construction—that you should avoid using it altogether. Many readers of plays, including students of the theatre early in their training, commonly assume that the explicit setting directions usually appearing in the printed editions of modern plays have been set down by their authors, although such descriptions, more often than not, depict the settings used in their first productions and thus represent the conceptions of the designers, rather than of the authors. Therefore, what may actually be suggested in an opening addendum of this sort may be only how some designer met the design problem usually in the first production, or how a stage manager or an editor recorded that particular design. Even when such a description comes from an author's own manuscript, a further danger exists, because the author may try to play the role of stage designer—a role about which he may know little or nothing at all. If you, as a reader-director, are not aware of this pitfall, you may find it very difficult to free yourself from these initial suggestions, because print gives them the power to seduce. There is much less harm in reading these directions after you have studied the play thoroughly, for then you will have a strong conception of the inherent setting and you will not be nearly as open to influence as you certainly would have been earlier.

Dialogue is the only reliable source of given circumstances. When you study plays, you quickly become aware that all authors write their settings directly into their dialogue, either overtly or subconsciously. Setting is a matter of feeling about objects and places; it is about time and what has happened before the play begins; and it is about the feelings of the characters for the special world of the play. This totality is what a playwright must communicate to his audience as deftly and as accurately as possible, for what happens in a play will be based on these given circumstances.

You will note in the suggested analytical technique that follows that the first two sections—"Environmental Facts" and "Previous Action"—are far more factual than the third—"Polar Attitudes." Yet it is this last that will actually set up the beginning point, for it is the most important aspect of the given circumstances. Look for the facts, yes; but the attitudes of characters toward those facts are extremely important.

Environmental Facts. All plays establish some delineation of the exact place and time of the action as well as giving specific information about the environment. These elements are called the facts of the play, whether the playwright has been historically accurate or not, because they remain fixed throughout the play. The director should isolate them by systematically noting them under the following categories:

1. Geographical location—the exact place. This category should also include climate, since weather often defines specific location and can affect dramatic action.
2. Date—year, season, time of day. What is significant about the date?
3. Economic environment—class level, state of wealth or poverty. If two or more economic levels are used in a play, be certain to record the facts of each level.
4. Political environment—the specific relationships of the characters to the form of government under which they live. Many plays have definite political settings, which will strongly affect the behavior of the characters. Many other plays tacitly accept a form of

government that has established basic restrictions on the characters. Do not take what you may think is direct omission to mean that it is unimportant. Look carefully for clues throughout the script, for the author may be taking this given circumstance for granted on the assumption that those who read the play will understand the context. But you cannot make such an assumption. He will leave a trail of implications behind him, and these you must dig out.

5. Social environment—the mores and social institutions under which the characters live. These facts are extremely important because they may be manifested through their restrictions on the outward behavioral patterns of the characters and consequently may set up basic conflicts in the action of the play.
6. Religious environment—formal and informal psychological controls. Much that applies to (4) also applies here.

When you study the given circumstances of a play, you must strictly avoid reading anything into the play; all facts must be explicitly stated or implied as is suggested above in (4). Do not assume anything. Some plays will involve all of these categories; others only some of them. Above all, *do not try to reconstruct your own idea of historical fact* surrounding a play; *if it is not in the play, it does not exist.* A playwright is not writing a history but telling a story; and he may not know his history well at all, or he may be deliberately shifting the facts to suit his own purposes. Do not try to correct him but record his facts exactly as he prescribes them.

Previous Action. It is necessary to make a sharp distinction between *present action*—what an audience actually sees *happening* immediately in front of it—and *previous action*—what an audience is *told happened before the present action begins.* All plays begin somewhere in the middle of things; thus, *given circumstances* must include some *narration* of past action so that the present action has a base from which to move forward. Some plays depend very little on past action, whereas others—those of Ibsen, for instance—require much retelling of past events. Both kinds of action—previous and present,—are included in what is loosely defined as a story. But the director *always works specifically with present action* although one of his major problems is to decide how to make the necessary narrations about the past as active as possible. In modern plays based on psychological revelation, the past plays an enormous part in the explanation, as it does in a Freudian psychoanalysis; yet the vital play for audiences lies only in what is actively happening immediately before its eyes.

You must, therefore, learn to separate these two kinds of action. The previous action though it may take all of the first act and sometimes longer to narrate fully, sets the point where the present action actually begins. Once you learn how to make this distinction, you will know how to make narrating interesting on the stage, for narration in itself is very dull compared to present action. Yet, a good playwright will always make this narration exciting because he will give the character a present action in the process of recalling it; that is, he will arrange for the recounting to do something to a character we are watching. Thus, to the director, there is never any dull exposition but only a recalling of the past under the excitement and tension of active engagement with other characters in the present. A director who does not know this point of structure will lose control of his audience very quickly. He will lose the key to handling the plays of Ibsen and Chekhov as well as a great deal of twentieth-century drama.

A technique for separating these two areas of action is the simple one of underlining in a text all the lines that *recall* the past. A text by Ibsen contains many, particularly in the first act, and often there are important revelations later in the play, especially when new characters are introduced. If you list these previous actions on one half of a sheet of paper as they are introduced and put down the present actions on the other half as they occur in relation to the previous actions, you will see their direct relationship.

A director can obscure a production by careless inattention to previous action, for some playwrights handle the necessary recalling in such subtle ways that an audience will miss important points unless the director carefully sets them out. Plays do not talk themselves; they are talked by actors and directors who know what they are talking about. Congreve's *The Way of the World* is a great play—one of the greatest in the English language—but if an audience misses the point, made very briefly in one line, that Mirabell was once a lover of Mrs. Fainall, that he left her pregnant and that he arranged for her marriage to Fainall, the import of most of the action that follows involving Mirabell as well as Fainall will be misunderstood and its significance lost. This example is extreme, but in kind it is forever recurring.

Learn what previous action is and then you will know what to do with it in production.

Polar Attitudes. Every character in a play, as in real life, is conditioned by the special world he is caught in, and he will hold specific attitudes, or points of view, toward that world. These attitudes will consist of his prejudices, his tolerances, and his assumptions about his special world, where he is forced to have relationships with others and is forced to take actions affecting both himself and others.

What is meant by the *special world* of a character? It is conditioned, of course, by environmental facts and by previous action, but it is on a significantly higher level of meaning than the other two, for the special world comes into being when the character deals with other characters and is thus forced into conflict with them. The special world is the world of relationships between characters, with all its implications. This is the *inner* environment of a play, the environment that sets up the conflicts and the problems: the environment of love relationships in and out of marriage; the environment of family pressures that cause love and hate between mothers and sons, fathers and sons, mothers and daughters; the environment of political, religious, and social pressures that force people to behave in ways that may destroy their families and their relationships to these families; the environments of fear of power, disregard of others, indifference to wealth or love of wealth, indifference to religion or its opposite. A character always has a strong attitude toward his special world.

Here is an important fact about plays: In the course of a play a principal character *does not change* as a character, but *his attitudes toward the environmental world of the play change* under pressures from forces outside his control—the other characters who serve as instruments to his change. As he meets these forces, he must adjust to them, and, as he does so, certain capabilities dormant within him come to the surface and force him to act—capabilities that have been present all the time but have never been called upon and thus recognized as points of character. The development in a play's action is composed, therefore, of the changing attitudes in the principal characters towards their *inner* environment.

It is also important to point out here that all of the characters in a play do not change their polar attitudes, but only the principal characters do, a fact which makes them principal. Secondary characters act as instruments in these changes but usually do not change themselves. In a play-analysis, it is always the primary characters that concern us most, for then we can determine the exact force and function of the secondary characters.

Most plays show radical shifts in the attitudes of the principal characters from the positions they held at the beginnings to those they hold at the ends. A philosophical way of expressing this shift is to say that a character moves from ignorance to knowledge: he sees the world in which he lives more and more clearly, *after* the actions he has been forced to take, than he did before. Therefore, it is necessary to pin down the attitudes towards the inner environment held at the beginning of a play by each principal character so that a director can see clearly the ending pole of each character, and can later help the actors find these poles. What happens in between these poles is the dramatic action.

By setting out the polar attitudes of each principal character, the director can see the scope of what happens in between the poles—the stretch of the characters—and the explicit effects given circumstances have on the characters. Thus, the shape of the play is explicitly declared in the polarities of the characters.

What we mean by the beginning of a play, then, is the defined positions of the attitudes held by the principal characters of the play toward the special world they are caught in and within which they will take action. These positions declare explicitly where the *present action* begins. The characters in most plays (Ionesco's anti-hero is an exception) will have strong attitudes of either like or dislike for the present environment in which they find themselves. The plot that follows (present action) will either shake them loose from their liking or bring their dislike to liking (or, at least, to acceptance). If a character does not finally accept what he dislikes at the beginning of a play, he will probably die or exile himself in the process of resisting the forced change that others bring upon him and become what we call a *tragic hero*. If a character strongly resists being pried loose from what he already likes intensely at the beginning, he will survive, but he will be ridiculed and thus he will become what we call a *comic fool*. But whatever happens to him, the attitudes he has at the beginning will certainly be radically changed by the end (or if he is a certain kind of comic fool, he may go on blissfully, never realizing that anyone has tried to change him).

An attitude at the beginning of a play is usually more *general* than specific. It is something the character has taken for granted, and he is therefore not consciously aware of it, although it most certainly will be pointed out to the audience in one way or another. The action of the play will make him aware of his specific world, because it will subject him to a test of his attitudes through direct conflict with others. The initial present action in a play will usually make clear to him where he stands in contrast to others, although he may be very blind about why he stands where he does. The attitudes of characters, then, should be general statements and not tied specifically to the present action which will follow. Here are some examples of initial attitudes:

> Men are foolish and romantic and can be manipulated rather easily. (Hedda in *Hedda Gabler*. What is her final attitude?)
>
> The only thing that really matters is money. (Regina in *The Little Foxes*. What is her final attitude?)
>
> "Good" women are dull, embarrassing, and impossible to talk to. (Marlowe in *She Stoops to Conquer*. What is his final attitude?)
>
> A king is sacred and no one can challenge his God-given right to dictate. (Oedipus in *Oedipus Rex*. What is his final attitude?)
>
> Love of women is all romantic adoration and worship. (Marchbanks in *Candida*. What is his final attitude?)

When you have learned to pinpoint the special world of a play, you will understand the secret of its inner workings, because you will know what are the environmental forces that hold the principal characters in check at the beginning; and this knowledge will show you what they must fight against to overcome those forces in order to arrive at the final pole. In the actual practice of trying to determine polar attitudes, it is easier to find the initial pole for each character by noting what has happened to each character at the end. Remember that the interest of an audience will be focused on what happens between these poles, for it is the dramatic action.

EXERCISES

1. Using any modern Realistic play (*Riders to the Sea, Ghosts, Hedda Gabler, Desire Under the Elms*), list the *environmental facts* in the specific categories suggested in the text. What do these facts suggest about a possible stage setting? Can you see the setting? Can you visualize some possible costumes? What do they tell you about body movement? About decorum? Do they suggest what the characters think about and what they feel? What does physical circumstance have to do with human behavior? (See the note attached to Exercise 2, p. 65.)

2. Delineate the *previous action* in the same play you have studied in Exercise 1 by underlining all the parts of the speeches in the first act that literally refer to actions that have happened *before* the here-and-now of the act begins. If you are looking at *Hedda Gabler* or another play by Ibsen, how many lines by actual count contain references to previous actions? (Be very careful not to include those recountings of actions that the audience has already witnessed as present actions; those narrations are present actions because the playwright intends the audience to weigh and evaluate a character in terms of that character's judgments of what has happened.) In your own judgment, what is the effect of this accumulation of knowledge about the past? Does it have any effect on what is happening in the present? Does it tell us anything about the characters? Can you see why it is unimportant in itself, but only as it affects a character's present action?

3. As an alternate exercise, study several opening pages of a play by listing the previous action on one side of a sheet and the present action on the other. In this way, you have a ready comparison of what the playwright is actually doing.

4. In working with the same play used in Exercises 1 through 3 above, delineate the attitude of each major character towards the special world or the inner environment of the play. What does he think about life around him? Whether he likes it or not is unimportant; what he likes about it or does not like about it *is* important. Look for such hidden attitudes as: love for others, fear of power, disregard of others, indifference to wealth, indifference to religious feeling. Does he admire monarchy? Does he love

freedom? Let the total given circumstances tell you exactly how each major character reacts to the given world at the beginning of the play.

DIALOGUE: THE FACADE OF THE PLAYSCRIPT

Definition. While dialogue is obviously the conversation between *two or more* characters in a play, it is not so obvious that *its primary function is to contain the dramatic action.* Dialogue is the vehicle of dramatic action, the lifeblood of the play. In addition, although dialogue may appear as a written line on a printed page, its primary intention is to be *heard* rather than read. It is thus talk and not writing.

Dialogue Is Action. It is essential at the outset in the study of structure to understand the intricacy of theatrical dialogue. Dialogue is not merely a verbal interchange between characters but an artificial, highly economical, and symbolic intercommunication of *actions* between characters, in which they force their wants and needs on one another. *Dialogue always exists in the present tense,* because it comes out of the mouths of speakers who think, as in life, only in the present, and who talk to one another to get what they want.

Dialogue is a building process: A says something to B, and B replies; this talk causes A to reply to B and B to A in a continuing cycle. But no matter how refined a speech may be, no matter how elaborate the choice of words, the purpose is always the same: to seek response in another person as we do in real life.

Thus, the nature of dialogue is its built-in characteristic of *forcing.* The words used on the outside may try to conceal this forcing in a very elaborate way, or they may be very direct and not conceal it at all. Dialogue is the covering, the clothing of the dramatic action. From an outside view, it is the text of the play; but its basic function is to contain the heart and soul of the play—the subtext or dramatic action.

Dialogue Is in Verse or Prose. Plays vary greatly in the choice of language used by characters, a choice which the given circumstances will dictate, since they will specifically delineate the decorum or outward show, that is, how the characters behave—their manners or lack of manners. Most modern plays are written in prose because of its likeness to the reality of everyday life, but plays also use dialogue in verse, as did many plays of the past. Verse forms are obviously more artificial in their use of language than is prose, but the basic intent is always the same: the containment of the dramatic action. More will be said about verse later in Part IV in the discussion of period acting. It is sufficient to point out here that verse form is not merely a decorative exterior but a heightened, more compact language for conveying intense feelings and high actions. The effect of verse is often as potent as physical body movements simply because verse conveys intensive inner feelings in a compact and heightened way. It thus has the capability of direct contact with the audience. This is why many playwrights who write dialogue in prose try to find a language somewhat more elevated than what is used in everyday life.

Dialogue Is Inner Language. Dialogue should be analyzed in detail to discover its peculiar characteristics in addition to its function as a cover for dramatic action and its direct reflection of given circumstances. Even within the narrow range of the given circumstances for a particular play, an author has a large scope in his choice of words and their arrangement, and in the images he may devise. Dialogue is thus usually much more connotative than denotative, much more weighted with feeling-meaning than dictionary usage or definitive meaning. In the human context of plays, characters feel or sense one another, as people who live closely together do in everyday life, and who consequently do not talk at one another but with one another. Thus, the language of drama is highly subjective, inner language. Realism has used a wide variety of folk-speech patterns—dialects—in the interest of showing how people talk from their guts and not from their minds.

Dialogue Is Heard Language. Any study of a play written in dialect requires penetration beyond the choice of words and the modification of vowels, for an author who has really heard the speech he uses for a certain character will reproduce all sorts of cultural overtones buried in the outer form, a subtle delineation of given circumstances. Thus, Brooklyn or Dublin or London-Cockney speech reflect through sound the hardness of city life, just as southern American speech reflects the slower rhythm of the South. Most recent plays that intend reproduction of local idiom (Harold Pinter's plays, for instance), do not set down the modifications of sound in spelling as playwrights once did but rely on the specific choice of words or lack of them to convey the inarticulate aspects of the characters. The dialect (quality) is thus left to the actor to supply.

Directors must, therefore, learn to hear dialogue in their mind's ear: not only the literal reproductions of sound as they hear it in everyday life, but the reproduction of word-feeling as playwrights set them out in characters. You must learn the craft of matching speech decorum, as perceived in a play's text from the given circumstances, to character decorum. More will be said about this technique later in connection with acting and actors.

Dialogue Is Structured of Lines and Speeches. As has already been pointed out, dialogue is artificially contrived. A close examination of any good play text will show that the author has usually arranged his sentence structure to throw the important phrase—the actual point of each line—to the end of the line. This placement makes it climactic.

Speeches made up of several sentences are carefully constructed in the same way. When a director is aware of this technique, he can be more certain of getting good line readings from his actors, and he will be more able to accomplish the desirable emphases that he knows the play requires throughout.

The director's knowledge of line and speech structure can be aided greatly by the study of what is labeled *Interpretation* in university curricula. In that study, the attention is concentrated on word and line values. At its base is the study of grammar, for grammar is the basis of effective speech, though no one actually thinks of grammar in carrying on a conversation. No director can go very far with actors, however, without a full awareness of word forms and their distinctive uses in the interlocking arrangements that comprise sentence structure. Many directors and actors trained in Stanislavskian approaches assume that if the subtext of a line is fully comprehended, the technical delivery of that line is assured. This assumption is simply not true, for the subtext *and* the text must both be communicated. This double value will be discussed in detail at a later point, but the important thing to understand here is that the *basis* for all dramatic meaning is the subtext—the inner quality of the line. This will be discussed under "Characteristics of Dramatic Action" in the next chapter.

EXERCISES

1. Read aloud some dialogue from *Riders to the Sea,* or another study play and attempt to reproduce the lines according to the word order and other speech modifications. What does it sound like? Can you get the swing of it? Now play a phonograph recording of an actor speaking in a dialect (Dublin slum-Irish or London-Cockney will do). Why does it sound more genuine than your attempts? Can you pick out any national characteristics in the sound alone? Can you hear social and economic circumstances? Can you hear specific character traits in the sound?

2. Examine some prose dialogue from a play by O'Neill. Point out the specific characteristics in the choice of words, the length of sentences and speeches, and the climactic build in each speech (Is the important word or phrase at the end?), and each kind of word image. Does he seem to repeat over and over any particular group of sense words? What does O'Neill's dialogue sound like when spoken? Try it.

3. Have two actors read aloud a play by Harold Pinter. Examine in detail Pinter's development of a particular line, and then of a group of lines. Do you hear given circumstances in the lines? What do you sense about the articulation or inarticulation of the characters? What sort of dialect does Pinter intend?

4. Read aloud a passage from Maxwell Anderson's *Winterset*. Can you hear his regular beat, his verse form? What does the verse form do that prose would not do? Repeat the same experiment with T. S. Eliot's *Murder in the Cathedral*. Can you hear his different verse forms? Can you identify their beats (number of stresses in each line)? What does his word choice and verse form add that prose could not accomplish? For contrast, read aloud a passage from Eliot's *The Cocktail Party,* which he wrote in a verse form although he declared that it ought to sound like prose.

Note: Exercises in the dramatic-action characterisics of dialogue are intentionally delayed until after the explanation of *dramatic action* in the next section.

4

the hard core of the playscript: dramatic action and characters

Dramatic action is the clash of forces in a play—the continuous conflict between characters. Because *drama* means doing or acting, the hard core of all plays is (1) action and (2) characters—the instruments that effect the action or are effected by it (forced to take action), for dramatic action and the characters in a play are inextricably tied together, a fact of dramatic form that you will understand better as you work through the contents of this chapter. The word *plot* is used here in its common meaning to describe the sequential arrangement of the conflict-incidents that compose the action. For the purposes of detailed discussion in this chapter, dramatic action and characters are treated separately, so that you can see their individual characteristics more clearly in isolation.

Understanding the nature and mechanics of dramatic action is a primary study of the director because action is the life-force of a play, and because it is the living blood and viscera out of which all other forces grow. Unless the director comprehends its workings, he cannot possibly command the play in directing the actors or in effecting the physical production. He will always be guessing. What happens in a play is the action; it is what holds an audience—thrills them or makes them laugh.

Unless the student of directing understands the concept of action, unless he pursues it avidly to the core, he will not master the basic tool of his trade. Once he has discovered what action is and how it works in various plays, all the other worlds of play production will open up to him. As has already been pointed out, plays are not realities but artificial devices—contrivances, if you will—that may be likened, through analogy, to a human body. Just as the heart and other vital organs make possible living and breathing in the human being, so dramatic action provides the same life-giving force to the play.

Since a play is a work of art, it can be examined and taken apart. Thus, a student who fails to study a play's action is proceeding only on the tenuous grounds of his feelings. His job is to find out not what he feels about a play but what the author, the other improvisor, has put into his playscript. The hard-core study in play-analysis is understanding the action.

Characteristics of Dramatic Action

PRESENT TENSE

As has already been noted in the discussion on dialogue, dramatic action exists only in the present tense. Thus, the participants in the action—the characters—are always in a state of "I do" not of "I did." This is what gives the living quality to a play and what makes us aware that it is occurring here and now. Whenever two people meet in a play, as in real life, they start doing to each other, and this is what we watch through a time sequence. A play turns-on life, and we watch and hear it being lived in front of us. There is never any past tense during a play's life; everything that happens, even the ways the previous action is conveyed, must occur in the present.

ACTION VERSUS ACTIVITY

It is important at the outset of this discussion to understand the difference between dramatic action and an actor's activity. The latter is the *illustration* of the action: what one actor or one director may have decided best shows the action. Such illustrations or pieces of business—sitting in a chair, crossing the stage, gesturing with the hand, etc.—can be infinite, but the basic dramatic action is fixed within a narrow range. Acting is, therefore, the process of illustrating the dramatic action—through activity. Acting is the *how;* action is the *what.*

It is necessary to point out these distinctions, because the nineteenth-century common stage tradition, usually accepted by actors and stage managers, held that illustrations or pieces of business performed by actors were the actions themselves, a tradition still surviving in opera. This misconception of action has unfortunately been carried over into some theatre training with the result of placing a director's attention on superficialities rather than on basic drives and forces in a play. Understanding Realistic plays as well as knowing how to exploit the methods of the modern actor both require uncovering the dramatic action, for only then can the search for appropriate illustrations to externalize it take place. Activities are thus the externalizations of dramatic action.

ALL ACTION IS RECIPROCAL

As defined above, action is the clash of forces, the forces being the characters. All action, therefore, forces counter-action, or action in two directions with adjustments in between. The cycle goes this way: (1) A *does* to B; (2) B feels the force of A's action (adjustment) and decides what action to take; (3) B *does* to A; (4) A feels the force of B's action (adjustment) and decides what action to take. This cycle is then ready to begin again but this time on a new and different level. This reciprocal process is carried on until either (1) A or B is destroyed; or (2) some outside force interrupts the progression (another character enters); or (3) the playwright arbitrarily interrupts (with a curtain); or (4) the playwright arbitrarily concludes the action.

All dramatic action is therefore *reciprocal;* there is no one-way road but always a *returned* action. Forcing goes on in both directions. Note that a very important part of this cycle lies in the adjustment that each character must make before taking a new action. As a result, much of the acting an actor does lies in receiving the force of the other character's action and in deciding what action to take himself.

The forcing or the doing, however, can take place in so many gradations that it frequently *looks* as if one character were dominating the other so strongly that the scene gives the appearance of one-way action. But this appearance is all a matter of quiet, low-key adjustment, as is the timing of the adjustment; the action will shift in the other direction before long, and the dominated becomes the dominator. Scenes in plays are composed of A's dominance with B taking retreating actions; then B takes over and dominates A, who takes retreating actions. The climax of the scene is reached when either A or B successfully dominates the other completely. But there is always another possible encounter, for a play is made up of delayed adjustments and the new actions they foment. Sooner or later the dominated one will have another chance, with the possibility that he will emerge as the dominant force. A play moves forward, and the audience continues to be interested, just as long as A and B are in conflict over who will dominate. Once this question has been answered satisfactorily, a state of relative calm prevails, and the play is concluded.

But unless both characters (forces) are destroyed, the end of one play may only set up the given circumstances for the beginning of the next one. It is possible, then, if characters are of sufficient interest, for a playwright to write more than one play about their conflicts, as did the Greeks and a few modern playwrights, such as Eugene O'Neill in *Mourning Becomes Electra* or Lillian Hellman with the characters of *The Little Foxes*. All endings of plays are contrived, and some rather unsatisfactorily. Rather than to say the dramatic action ends, it would be better to say that it is in a state of relative quiet, a dormant state awaiting new forces and pressures.

THE DIVISIONS OF ACTION

The total action of a play is divided into major sections. Since they intended their plays to be staged without interruption, the Greeks punctuated their major sections of action with choral songs. Shakespeare ended his scenes with rhymed couplets and may have followed them with a brief musical interlude. Today we lower a curtain or the stage lights and give the audience a rest break, an intermission, with the audience actually leaving their seats and moving about for ten to fifteen minutes. But whether we play the action continuously or take intermissions, we know that all plays are artificially constructed, that they are broken—plotted—into parts. The plot of a play is, then, the arrangement of the action: what a playwright thinks, out of a total possible story, must be shown to an audience. Thus the play may be divided not only into acts but also into formal scenes—i.e., Act I, Scene 2—each with arbitrary limits.

Printed playscripts in the French theatre, though they follow divisions into acts, further separate the action in a way that tells us much about all play construction. Whenever a character enters or exits, a new scene is declared. These *French scenes* show us that the major sections of action (the acts) are also broken arbitrarily into smaller sections of action.

Close analysis of French scenes, though there is no printed symbol to mark them, shows further sectioning: whenever characters in concert shift the line of talk (action) in a new direction, or shift the dominant focus from one character to another, a new unit is declared. The word *unit* is Stanislavski's word for divisions in dramatic action, his word for delineating all the segments of the plotting, even the very smallest ones. This definition provides a far better way for a director to see a play's action than by using the traditional act-scene concept or the division into French scenes, for he can then visualize the total action as one major unit broken into dozens of sub-units, all interrelated and all pointing in one concerted direction. But although the large units are easily perceived, the small units are much more difficult to delineate, because they vary in size from two or three lines to a dozen or more, or sometimes they may consist of a single line followed by a significant pantomime (silent activity). Every experienced director knows that audiences can be aroused to excitement only by the clear and explicit acting of these small units, for a good play is packed with these detailed, revealing moments. The director's mastery of the unit concept is an absolute necessity if he is to understand at all the nature of dramatic action.

The smallest designation of dramatic action is, of course, the line. Every speech of every character throughout the play, as has already been pointed out in the section on dialogue, contains a dramatic action. If a speech is of more than three or four sentences in length, it may contain additional actions. Do not worry about long speeches until you have mastered the technique of extracting the action from short ones. Then you will be far more sensitive to the shifts in action in major speeches.

Thus, each speech contains a forcing—an action—and it is directed toward another character. To repeat the phrasing already used in the above discussion: A does to B (Speech 1); B receives the forcing and adjusts to it; and B does to A (Speech 2); A receives the forcing and adjusts to it; and A does to B (Speech 3), with the process repeated until that series is stopped suddenly by interruption, pushed aside to be taken up later, climaxed by a joining of the two characters on one side of the separation (love) or by further dividing of the characters (hate). Thus, the actions (speeches) lead to the climax of the unit, which then ends, and another unit begins, repeating the process all over again.

Each unit, therefore, has its own *objective*. It is the progressive (always moving ahead) building of these small unit objectives which accumulate into the larger unit-objectives, which, in turn, finally make the objective for the entire play.

The work of the director is primarily that of helping the actors find not only the speech-by-speech dramatic action in a play but also the objectives of the units throughout the play. At the base of this concept is the hypothesis that all actions are reciprocal (A does to B and B does to A), and that *the director's function is to see that the appropriate reciprocation actually takes place* with the actors. The process of acting is not just doing individual actions, but reciprocating all actions. Unless A does to B and B does to A, nothing will happen for the audience. Emotion can emerge and the audience be moved *only when the reciprocation takes place,* for emotion is a by-product of dramatic action. Emotion cannot be made directly in itself but is brought about by the forcing of one character by another. More will be said about this process later in the discussion on acting and the director's relationship to the actor. It is sufficient here to state that the actor who acts alone (without reciprocation), and is permitted to do so by the director, cannot possibly produce emotion, for he is not acting but only performing like an individual entertainer in a night club who plays directly to an audience without help from others.

A play is always a dialogue—action between two or more characters—and never a monologue. A soliloquy or interior speech used in some plays is *not* a monologue but an argument carried on between two warring sides within the same character, frequently between his outside self —what others force him to be—and his inside self—what he knows he must be.

FINDING AND LABELING THE ACTION

Since each speech in a play is intended to do, to force, each speech can be reduced to a verb in the present tense because verbs are the symbol-words for action. The subtext in several speeches, for example, could be recorded in this way:

A shames
B ignores
A pleads
B softens
A begs
B rejects
and so on

Notice how each of these actions is expressed in the present tense, and how each successive verb seems to grow out of the preceding verb, thus effecting reciprocation. And notice that *no other qualifying words are used.*

Your problems in using this method will not come from what you may think is a shortage of vocabulary, for the verbs of dramatic action must fall within the readily available vocabulary of actors and directors or they will not be useful at all. The real problem lies in discovering what is going on in a line and in a unit. Thus, the problem is one of perception: if you can sense the action, you can find the verb easily. Don't work too self-consciously, too intellectually, but let your feelings and responses tell you what is going on in a series of speeches. Once you catch on to this game, the technique of playing it is not difficult at all. But a very real problem will always be there: What is going on in the line? What is the subtext? This question can sometimes be quite baffling. No matter how many years of experience a director or actor may have, or how mature he may be, this problem will always exist. As we have pointed out previously, to directors and actors, playscripts should be thought of as the improvisations of others—the playwrights—and, as such, the inner recesses of their plays may be very difficult to rediscover simply because what goes on may lie outside of the personal experiences of both actors and directors.

But once you, as a director, have learned this technique of looking for the subtext and setting it down in verbal form, you will have at your command the most important key available to the director in communicating with actors, for they can both talk the same language: the verb-motivations that the actor can act. Anything less lies in the cloudy, fuzzy obscurity of "how I feel it should go," instead of in "what I (the character) am doing"—the only way a director can get through to an actor.

Look again at the examples of verb choice presented on page 37 for a sequence of speeches. These are the kind of verbs you should use because they can be acted. Some verbs simply cannot be acted. All verbs that are too general, that apply to the nature of dialogue itself, are practically useless in director-actor communication. In this category are such verbs as: ask, tell, say, question, interrogate, explain, show, see, perceive, illustrate, examine, reflect and all others like them. The question you must always ask is: "Can the verb be acted? Can it lead to illustration?" If you do ask it, you will discover that the search is for specific and not general verbs, for acting is a specific thing, never a general thing.

Another class of verbs to avoid are those that overtly and directly call up specific illustration: run, jump, walk, bounce, laugh, smile, etc. Occasionally these verbs can work for you, but most of the time you will use them as surface illustrations and not for the deep-lying, motivating actions you must look for. The clearest verbs are those full of direct, though not overtly stated, doing, for they contain the basic passions and emotions.

Again, if the verbs are too general—for example, I love, I fear, I hate—they will not stimulate the actor to specifics, and, therefore, they basically will not be actable, except in a general way. Each of these verbs stands for a whole category of gradations and as such they are too gross when they stand alone. Since the full intention of verbal delineation is to reach the actor, only a specific verb, a verb that delineates the exact gradation, can accomplish that end.

Finally, note that the word used is a verb. Let an initial stand for the character, and *do not use any other qualifying words.* If you know grammar, look only for transitive verbs, for in them you will find the action words.

RECORDING THE ACTION

During the training period, the student director should practice the verb technique by explicitly writing down his analysis of the action. The following procedure is suggested:

1. Divide a short segment of a play (ten minutes with two characters only) into units.
2. Write down in verbal form, as indicated in the example given on p. 37, all the actions in each of these units.
3. Now make a summary for each unit by finding a single verb that summarizes the action of each character in the unit. Use this form of expression:

> A does to B and B does to A. (A more specific example: Mary pleads and George softens.)

The statement above is now a summary for the whole unit; it is reciprocal because both forces are shown; it is reciprocal also because the use of the coordinating conjunction "and" ties the two characters inextricably together as if they were on either end of a tightly held rope.

4. Record the summaries of all the units that make up the segment of the play selected. These summaries are what you, as the director, can retain in your mind as the unit objectives to be accomplished. The actors may get lost in the details of the action and thus lose sight of the objectives. If the director also loses his way, all is lost. If the summary is well done—if the verbs are well chosen—the structure of the play can be seen readily. The total play will be only as good as the unit perception has made it, for the director will communicate only what he sees, and if he doesn't see very well, neither will the actors or the audience.
5. One further device is of specific use: the titling of units with a nominative phrase. It is another, though not very accurate way, of describing what goes on in a unit. The phrase must be a simple one: The Arrival; The Close Attachment; The Announcement of the New Plan; The Announcement of the Other Plan; The Head-on Struggle; Left Alone. Such phrases are a good supplement to the reciprocal summary sentences, and they can help the director find the verbal statements. They are also good phrases to use for conveying objectives of each unit when he is talking to actors. But though they are helpful devices for communication, they are not actable in themselves.

TYPES OF ACTION

The types or kinds of action—tragic, comic, melodramatic, farcical—are not treated at this point because they are so complex in theory that they tend to confuse the beginning director during the period when the techniques for play-analysis are being mastered. It is sufficient for the director to be aware that there is another level of analysis that he will learn later, when he has mastered the basic concepts of play-analysis. From a practical point of view, it is suggested that young directors in choosing plays for projects select serious ones because of their usual straightforward directness. Dramatic action in comedy is usually not only more difficult to perceive but it presents many more problems for young actors, and thus for the director.

EXERCISES

The best way to work with dramatic action is to study a one-act play, or, better, a ten-minute section of a long play. The instructor should select such an example for class use. Later, each student should work out an action-analysis from a play of his own choice. The following exercises should be done in the order indicated.

1. What are the major divisions of the action of the whole play?
2. Distinguish between an arbitrary division (Act II, Scene 2) and a French scene.
3. Pick out several French scenes.
4. Select a segment of a play (ten consecutive minutes) and do the following with it:
   a. Isolate the units in the text by drawing a line separating one unit from another in the text. Note their beginnings and endings; try to find specific lines where they occur. Now number the units.
   b. Write down noun-phrase titles for each unit.
   c. Being careful to follow the procedure for such recording, write down the dramatic action verbs for each speech.
   d. Write out the reciprocal-action, summary sentences for each unit.
   e. The class should discuss in detail each of the steps discussed above.
5. Illustrate dramatic action backwards by setting up an improvisation. (It will be backwards because the class will see an action happening, one that it has not had to analyze from a playscript in advance of the playing.) Use number dialogue so that the improvisors can concentrate on actions and will not have to think of specific words. They will also be much clearer in their intentions than if they had to improvise both actions and words. The director can help shape the improvisation through offstage suggestions (low-volume directions to the participants) while it is in progress. The participants then begin the improvisation. The instructor lets it run for a few units and then stops it. Immediately he opens up the following discussion:
   a. Designate the units.
   b. Why did the improvisors make units automatically?
   c. Why did some units (name one) not work well? (Did the improvisors know what they were "doing"?)
   d. Why is it very easy to delineate the actions behind each speech? (Relate illustration/activity to dramatic action.)

  e. Specifically designate some actions behind speeches.

  f. How would real dialogue have helped to delineate and intensify the actions behind speeches?

6. Repeat Exercise 5 two or three times until the class can answer all the questions with perception.

Characters: The Second Hard-Core Element in Play-Analysis

DEFINITION

A character is made up of all the dramatic actions taken by an individual in the course of a play. Therefore, we define *character* as a summary statement of his actions. (Note: The word character is used here to describe what a playwright makes, which reserves the word characterization for use in this book to define what an actor makes.)

CHARACTER IS ACTION

In the *Poetics*, Aristotle places dramatic action first and character second, with the second flowing out of the first. Although playwrights may not actually write plays in that order, since plays can be conceived and evolve from many stimulations, they must end this ordered association in the final draft, or the character will not have a life of his own. A character does not exist except in a superficial, external way, through what he says he is or through what others say about him, although these clues help us to see him more clearly; he exists in what his actions, particularly those under pressing circumstances, tell us he is. Consequently character is wrapped up in action, and it is for this reason that we can say a *character,* when we analyze his connection with a play, is *a summary statement.*

Mere impressions of a character—what one feels he is—are no substitutes for a director's close analysis of the action. An actor, on the other hand, can discover character piece-by-piece in the process of trying to put him together by *doing*, by *acting* the various incidents in which the character is involved. For this very important reason, in the rehearsal period, directors should encourage actors to play the scenes over and over, with new suggestions for each playing, rather than discuss the characters in an intellectual way.

CHARACTER IS REVELATION

From the discussion above, it follows that an actor cannot play the entire character at once. Certainly before a rehearsal period has ended, an actor must be fully aware of the complete body of the character he is acting, just as a playwright must be aware of his whole play, but if he tries to play the full character at the beginning, or even in the middle of a playscript, he will find himself confused and lost. A character takes shape and is revealed in the course of the action. Thus, characters do not change; they *unfold*. The stuff a character is made of has always been lying dormant there, and only under the impact of conflict—of the forcing of both himself and of others—will the buried qualities come to the surface and stand revealed. As we have already noted in the previous section, dramatic action is a progression of incidents, with one incident leading to another. Action is therefore self-revealing with a sort of inevitability guiding it: "This must be told, this must come out!" As a result, a play is made up of discoveries and surprises. Some are minor; a few are major; and one is exceptional. They are the climaxes. As a character meets each of these moments in a play, something in him comes forward to meet the circumstance—a character trait.

In this way, aspects of character are fully illustrated in a series of climactic moments. An audience can keep these traits in mind because, if the author is a good one, they will have a logical relationship and a close association with the traits still to be revealed in the following climaxes. Thus, the actual progression for the audience, what interests each spectator in the play, is the progressive unfolding of character traits that finally accumulate with clarity and force at the major climax, when all the previous character revelations come together in the *major action* and the *discovery* of the character. What will he be like when he stands fully revealed, when we can see what really makes him work? is the audience's anticipation. And they see him at that moment, and they are excited and moved. What follows this climax is usually very brief, for all we need to know now is what the character is like after his head-on collision with the forces he has tried to overcome.

For the director, analysis of the action is paramount if he is to comprehend a character, if he is to see him grow, and if he is to bring about that growing in the actor he will direct. Progressive unfolding is the concept he must understand. It will tell him where the climaxes of the play are, what they are about, how important each one is, and what to do with them in getting the play acted. This concept has the most personal significance to a director because he can work intelligently and perceptively with actors when he understands these points. Progressive unfolding is a core of director-actor communication.

SIMPLE AND COMPLEX CHARACTERS

The density of a character—how simple or complex he may be—is determined from how much he participates in the action of a play and from the quality of his participation and what kind it is. It is the density that separates the primary characters from the secondary or supporting characters who act as instruments for revealing the principals. We know these secondary characters much less than the principals—we know only a few traits—because they have little opportunity in the action to tell us who they are since most of the attention is focused on the principals. A third level—house servants, aides, etc.—we know scarcely at all, though good actors may seem to give them more body (personality) than they actually have. A fourth level is a group or a chorus—a collective body with a collective trait; we know nothing about the individuals who compose the group because we see only a group mind and a group feeling.

Although a play focuses on all the principal characters, one character usually dominates the action. Since conflicts cannot exist without two forces, a protagonist and an antagonist are specifically required, and the play's action revolves around these two, or possibly three, centers if there is more than one antagonist. The director must determine during his analysis who the principal character is (*whose play* it is), along with the primary antagonist. Thus, another polarity (other than the polarity already discussed in the section on polar attitudes in given circumstances) can be specified if the director understands the nature of character and how characters are used in plays.

A beginning director is sometimes confused by studies of plays (dramatic criticisms) that point out that certain principal characters are very poorly drawn, or that characters—in Greek plays for instance—are very *thin*. Greek plays have very few incidents to reveal character, so they incline to greater simplicity in this respect; but this simplicity does not mean that they will be any less effective. Simple characters in certain contexts can have great power over an audience. One of the characteristics of modern drama, one aspect that delineates the Realistic style beyond the minutiae that make up the given circumstances, is the complexity of character development, which is brought about through a large number of incidents in a play. Many character traits are thus demonstrated to an audience, and what we can say about a character is that we know the complexity of his psychological self. But we can often become confused because there is too much to assimilate. Good direction is the ordering of this complexity with such clarity and emphasis (which also includes de-emphasis) that an audience can readily assimilate the main points, with the secondary points relegated to their proper places.

When a director understands how action reveals character, he can understand more fully how to direct plays with simple characters as well as those with complex characters, and to recognize the different values developed in each. Without this comprehension, he may try to impose the values of the complex on the simple, or vice versa and may be confused about why a play does not work.

TECHNIQUES OF CHARACTER DESCRIPTION

Writing down the character is an excellent way to assure yourself that a character analysis is fully developed and nothing has been missed. But you must be absolutely certain that you determine what a character is *through an analysis of the action,* as has been emphasized above, for you will be strongly tempted to read the descriptions authors sometimes insert in their plays. If you do, you must keep in mind that the author is providing these suggestions for a casual reader and not for a director, a tip-off to the reader of what to expect. You must remember that a character is determined *only after* his actions, not before. Thus, a playwright's advance suggestions may certainly give you a hint about character, but such suggestions can be quite misleading in the overview and can cause you to miss the dominant traits. (See Exercise 8 below.) Consequently, you must treat author descriptions with great caution, and perhaps avoid them altogether.

The technique suggested here bases your analysis of a character on your own perception of the dramatic action. What follow are the categories you should consider and record in detail for each character:

Desire. Desire is a statement of what a character wants most. It can possibly be a material possession, but it is usually an intangible one, such as power or dominance over others. It may also be love for another; self-integrity; dominance over fear, etc.

Will. Will is a character's relative strength for attaining his desires. How strong or weak is his inner strength? Is it strong enough to push him the full limit, or will he compromise? We take actions in everyday life out of our will power; in plays we see will power clearly and dynamically illustrated.

Moral Stance. A character's moral stance—the stance that will strongly affect the attainment of his desires—consists of his values. How honest is he with others and with himself? Does he have any sense of moral responsibility to others? What is the moral code that governs his inner behavior? What is his sense of integrity? "Evil" characters are given low value ratings because in their view the end justifies the means. "Good" characters are given higher than average values, and these values we admire in heroes.

Decorum. Decorum describes a character's physical appearance—what he looks like, his manners, and his poise. Although such a projection of an image is only the outward appearance of a character, and is thus superficial—what a person looks like is no prediction of what he is—it can be of some value if only to help us project the character into the society in which he lives. It is also possible that his physical makeup may be closely related to his mental and emotional temperaments. It can be helpful to make an actual list of a character's physical characteristics seemingly required by the given circumstances, although you may go in the opposite direction when it comes to the point of casting the play. How does he behave in the varying contexts of the play: how does he walk; how does he stand; how does he speak, and what is the quality of his voice, and so forth. Is his outward manner affected by occupation, the social mores in which he lives, and others?

Summary Adjectives. Summarize all of the categories above by the use of adjectives only. *Do not set down a character's dramatic actions but only the traits of character they reveal.*

Character-Mood-Intensity. Character-mood-intensity is the physical or body state of the character—his nervosity—at the *beginning* of the play and at the beginning of each group of associated units. By describing a character's initial physical state, the director has a point of departure—a springboard—for all the ups and downs in the character that follow. The character-mood-intensity is the level of feeling in a character when he begins, for if an actor can start at the appropriate level of intensity, assuming good concentration and awareness of the action, he will continue to build from that level. This communication device is very important for the director, for with it he can directly help an actor find the appropriate level.

Character-mood-intensity thus means the actual physical state of the character: his heartbeat; his breathing; his state of perspiration; his muscular tension or lack of it; his stomach—queasy, jumpy, calm, etc. *Nervosity* means all of these—his total nerve vibration, his sensory awareness. Since these states are points of departure, the actual shape of the play can be understood and made evident in the acting.

You should also be aware that each character in a play begins *at a different* character-mood-intensity because each character is independent by definition and will feel differently from another character, who will be in a different state of nervosity about the same situation. A director's job is often to point out to the actors the difference in these points of departure —the different beats of the characters. Defining a character-mood-intensity for an actor is like backing him into a scene: he feels the level of physicality first; then, when he plays the dramatic action, he can sense its validity as a beginning point. Since all that follows will be based on this beginning point, he will become aware of the necessity for appropriate departures. The pitch of the action can thus be assured.

You must remember that when an actor initially faces a new character, that character will seem strange and odd to him because it is so different from the actor's self. Therefore, for an actor, approaching a new character is like trying on someone else's coat: it hangs too long, or pinches, or smells—it simply does not fit or feel right. In this sense, the character-mood-intensity is the new coat defined, for the actor will know why it does not fit and what he must do to make it fit. The director can directly assist the actor by helping him to delineate the feeling of the character he is trying to play through character-mood-intensity.

EXERCISES

1. Compare Sophocles' *Oedipus Rex* with Ibsen's *Hedda Gabler* in the density of character development. What do you note about each?

2. Compare character density in Shaw's *Candida,* or in another modern Realistic comedy, with Ionesco's *The Bald Soprano.* Try it again with Elmer Rice's *The Adding Machine.* Are the plays by Ionesco and Rice more nearly alike in their development of characters? Why?

3. Read a brief, early scene—one that concerns the principal character—from a class-study play. How does the action in the scene reveal a character trait? What trait is revealed? Study another, later scene and ask the same questions.

4. Continue Exercise 3 with the same character by selecting the climactic scene. What character trait is now revealed?

5. Study the first act of a long play (the same one used in Exercises 3 or 4) and note each incident. What are the character traits revealed in this act? Make a list of what you know by the end of this first act. Be very careful *not* to include any traits revealed in the *previous action.* Now study the last act of the same play. How much more do you know?

6. Analyze the principal characters in a study play by applying the technique that has been suggested: desire, will, moral stance, decorum, summary adjectives, character-mood-intensity.

7. Compare the character-mood-intensities of two characters, in the analysis made in Exercise 6, where they introduce a formal division of the play together or very close together. How different are these character-mood-intensities? A scene can mature only through this difference.

8. Using a study play, list any character traits an author may have inserted in his text as description. Now carefully assess these traits against the action in the play in the interest of discerning their relevance. Note carefully important traits the author *does not* mention, and whether those he does are relevant to the main line of the play. This exercise should convince you that it is necessary to use action instead of an author's description as the primary source of character traits.

5

the derivatives
of dramatic action
in a playscript:
idea, tempos, and moods

You will recall from Chapter 3 that the structure of a playscript was compared to the construction of a modern building: given circumstances were pictured as the deeply rooted foundation, and dialogue as the facade. This image was then developed further in Chapter 4 to show that dramatic action and characters formed the inside core of the building, the viscera that provides the life-force and the energy in a playscript. Now you are ready to complete the building by putting on the top—the *idea* in a playscript. You are also ready to put the building to work by turning on the dynamos of action and characters and to give it living vibrations and a nerve system—the *tempos* and *moods* in a playscript.

The word *derivatives* has been used here as the clearest term to describe where idea, tempos, and moods actually come from; but they are so much the living expressions of dramatic action and characters, so much an inherent part of them and so buried in them, that you will have to work hard at seeing their separateness and their individualities. As in the two previous chapters, idea, tempos, and moods are treated separately here, so that you can more readily distinguish their differences and know the force each exerts on the structure of the play.

Idea

DEFINITION

The *idea* of a play is the core meaning of what it has to say. Idea is both derived from an assessment of characters in action and is a summary statement of such action. Consequently the idea is the sum total of the playscript.

INTENTION OR CREATIVE ACCIDENT

Because all good plays appear to be well ordered, and because some plays seem to sell certain ideas, very specifically, the unoriented reader may well assume that a playwright begins with formal ideas and then develops them in incidents and characters as he might do in a formal essay. Such is seldom the case. A great deal of what we mean by creative playwriting is letting things happen. Consequently, a playwright may begin his improvisation in any way—for example, with an imaginary character involved with another character, at a particular moment in the action, with a given circumstance, or with a patch of dialogue—but as he works with his characters, letting them be themselves, they will determine the flow of the action and, eventually, the idea. Starting with an idea is more like writing this textbook: the definition is set out first and then it is explained with supporting evidence. But such an approach would be far too confining for the creative playwright, although some of the so-called thesis playwrights early in the century appear to have worked in this way.

But no matter how he goes about putting a play together, sooner or later a playwright must decide what his characters are doing fairly consistently and what they are trying to discover. In other words, he begins to make *unity in the action;* he will make the action all about one thing, one idea. He may never actually state his idea of the unity directly in words, because he believes that creative drama is subliminal. An audience must experience an idea through *feeling* the action in a play and must not be told overtly what the idea is. For this reason the idea of a play must be subtly buried, and finding it—pinpointing it—may be relatively difficult. But an idea is surely there and the director must find it, for it will declare his unity of the playscript and subsequently his unity in production.

MEANING IN PLAYS

In the moving-picture version of Jean-Paul Sartre's *The Condemned of Altona,* the actress, who plays a principal role, says that she clings to the theatre when all else is crumbling because "the theatre is the world compressed, and with meaning." This view may well be Sartre's own personal paradoxical attitude toward drama, because in the midst of the absurdist world he describes—where men have lost purpose and reason for being—he still seems to see meaning in writing plays. He may know that he cannot change the world, but that he can help describe it and perhaps explain some of it—with meaning.

"The world compressed and with meaning" may be the master paradox of drama: when all else is confusion, it is still possible for man arbitrarily to make an art form that tells him that life is meaningful, that all we need do is to compress it in order to see it positively. In this view, plays are artificial devices for reassuring man, for giving him strength, perception, even wisdom. This book is no place to pursue the philosophical aspects of drama, but it is essential to point out that all plays, no matter how poor, have inherent meanings. Pinpointing them is often the problem.

IDEA IS ACTION

To understand the relationship of *idea* to the other elements in play structure imagine that a play looks like a pyramid. *Given circumstances* provides the underground foundation. *Dramatic action* is at the ground level and moves upward, with each incident, to unfold *characters* until the summit—the idea—is reached. The whole structure is covered with a framework of *dialogue*. Thus, the idea is the result of characters acting out the incidents in the action. Not until the action, and consequently the characters, is complete, can we assess the meaning, for the major climax and the ending will tell us more explicitly than any other portions of the play what the play is about. On p. 50, is a graphic diagram of the play's structure that you have studied up to this point.

FINDING THE IDEA

Although there is no question but that the idea of a play will lie in the development of action and character, two other sources of information are sometimes useful guides: (1) a play's title; (2) a philosophical statement in the dialogue.

A play's title is frequently a symbolic or a metaphorical representation of the inner meaning—a playwright's image of the poetic statement he is trying to make. After reading the plays, few people would have difficulty in discerning the idea behind such titles as: *The Little Foxes, The Hairy Ape, Death of a Salesman, Cat on a Hot Tin Roof,* and *Riders to the Sea,* although it is true that the danger in taking them too literally would be oversimplification; the essence of each of these plays has been stated quite obviously in the titles given them. But other titles may only lead the director into confusion, for instance: *The Bald Soprano, The Birthday*

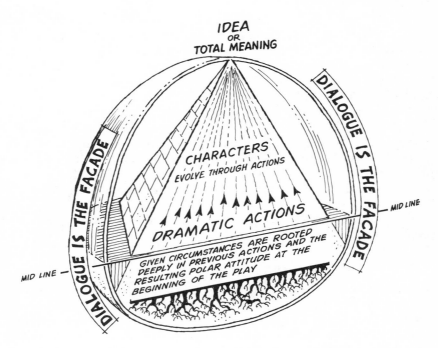

Party, Happy Days. Others tell us very little—*Hedda Gabler; The Lark; Luther; The Homecoming*—although each says something. But when a title is supported by an analysis of the action, the director has a guiding metaphor that will bring him close to a playwright's idea.

Philosophical statements, although they may occasionally be pinpointed in specific speeches, are not very common in plays and are frequently apt to be misleading, for most playwrights, in their desire to remain on the poetic level, shun obvious statements of meaning. They are poets, and the function of a play is to reach an audience on a poetic level rather than on a stated, didactic level. The experience of playgoing is the fun of uncovering meaning, not because an author intends to obscure or to baffle, but because his job is to reach an audience directly on the most primitive level of understanding: emotional understanding. Intellectual statement is therefore too obvious, too self-conscious.

The principal means of uncovering the idea, then, is to search within the dramatic action of the principal character, or characters. Where is the emphasis in the action leading? Why does the principal character take the climactic action that he does, and what is the result of that action? There must have been other courses of action he could have taken, so why did he take this one? At the high point of his agony, what seems most important to him? After the major climax, what is the effect of the discovery on him and on others? There are many questions a director can ask himself about the action that will lead to the idea. Once he thinks he grasps the idea, he should set it down in words as briefly as possible, and, then, again test his statement against the action.

One of the easier ways to see an idea is to place it in a simple sentence combining character and action. This sentence will be the idea *stated in action*. Thus: "This play is about a childlike woman who. . . ." By completing the statement of action, the director will still keep the idea submerged up to a point, but bringing it to the surface will be easier because of the emphasis thrown on one character and on the principal action.

You can often find the idea by recording the action in a play, taking great care in setting it down as accurately as you can in the order it occurs. A director should be able to record the action of each act in three or four sentences. This record is a précis or summary—the easiest way to find the focus in an action. You must learn to tell an action briefly and to the point.

More will be said about finding ideas in Part IV, which you can pursue only after you have a specific understanding of play-analysis as outlined in this part of the book. It is sufficient at this time for you to know that there are a few other ways of finding meaning, for sometimes it is derived from the values associated with sympathetic characters in contrast to those values associated with unsympathetic characters and sometimes from symbols and metaphors other than those used in the title. You will also find in Part IV a discussion of the work that you may need to do *outside* play-analysis in order to perceive a play's meaning, for it may escape you if you do not have sufficient background in either the historical or the modern world to see it. Part IV will also show you how a play that is not immediately topical in its idea is seldom successful; and that if it cannot be universally applied, it will not endure.

EXERCISES

1. Test the validity of the title of a study play by pinning it down in terms of consistency with the play's action. Do the title and the action say the same thing?

2. Compare the title of a serious play with the title of a comedy. Do you find the latter essentially different? Could it be taken seriously and could a serious action be construed from it?

3. What do you think might be the actions in the plays of the following titles? *Luv; You Can't Take It With You; The Importance of Being Earnest; Ah, Wilderness!; Barefoot in the Park.* Play this exercise as a game with people who do not know what is in each play, and do not let others participate until the first group has finished guessing.

4. Examine *Riders to the Sea* for a philosophical statement. Do you find one? If certain lines seem to be immediately obvious, are they completely verified in the action? Are they misleading? Remember that *Riders* is also about Nora and Cathleen and not just about Maurya.

5. Arrive at the idea of a play by analyzing the action, that is, by drawing the logical conclusion from the actions. Express the idea in one, short sentence. Each student should do this exercise separately and then the results should be compared. Is there any agreement on the idea? Why may there be differences of opinion? (*Note:* If there is wide divergence, the action of the play should be reexamined by the group in order to be certain that each member understands exactly what is going on and sees the significance of what is transpiring. Understanding the action in some plays may require more maturity than certain students have; but without understanding the action, finding the idea is impossible.)

Tempos

DEFINITION

Tempos are the changing rates or beats of the dramatic action in a play. When a sequential arrangement of tempos are combined, that is, when the varying beats of several consecutive units are strongly felt, you have identified the pulsations of a play—its rhythm.

UNIT-BEATS

Because all plays are made in units of action, which, though related, are different in content and purpose, each unit has its own particular tempo, or, to use a term employed in music, its own *beat*. A play is made up of varying tempos, or *unit-beats*. The director must become very much aware of this built-in musical characteristic, because it not only strongly determines a play's individuality, but it also declares a primary way the play holds an audience's attention.

A musical sense is one of the marks of talent in the director, one of his best natural tools. If this sense is poorly developed, if he cannot readily discern the difference in beats or have the exact sense of time that an orchestra conductor has, he will not be able to feel sensitively enough the up and down swings of a play. Unlike music scores, where tempos are marked—where the rates of speed of the various passages are indicated by a series of directions such as *largo, molto, allegro,* and often by exact metronomic markings—plays have no such textual warnings. The playwright may occasionally insert a word suggesting tempo, but this clue is exceptional. The director and the actors are expected to sense the beats. If the reader has *dramatic imagination,* he will also sense them automatically: he will feel the flow. But even the talented director must search each playscript for the unit-beats in order to verify and make conscious his perceptions of tempo. If your sense of tempo is poorly developed, you must set about improving it through the rhythm exercises provided by dance or music training.

SURGES

A play is like the waves on a seashore: as you watch them, you can see the small waves accumulate and finally climax in a major breaker that runs headlong toward the beach only to dash its force on the sand, then to disintegrate, to lose its force, and to draw back toward the sea again. When a storm (the major conflict in a play) is coming, the waves increase in size, and their pattern becomes less regular than before. A play is made up of such surges, retreats, and new surges, all with accumulating force that finally culminates in a climax (the storm). The director, then, must not only see small unit tempos but the cumulative, large ones as well. His primitive sense of the large surges will tell him, in one way, what the play is about, for a play has these surges built into it; its "music" will be hidden without delineation of these elements of tempo.

One problem with the ocean metaphor used above is the danger of assuming that plays have regular surges that only grow in size and intensity. This assumption is quite misleading. Although some plays have this regularity, many are as erratic in their structures of tempo as is modern music. One of the ways of sensing a play's tempos is to compare it to a piece of music—actually find some music that seems to match its beats. This paralleling of form has the distinct advantage of bringing the beats to your awareness without trying to make them so mind-conscious that it becomes more intellectual than emotional. "Beating a play" or parts of a play on a drum, that is, finding different beats for each unit, also helps bring about a partially conscious awareness of the inherent tempos.

RHYTHM

Rhythm refers, in part, to the accumulative effect of the unit-beats and is, perhaps, another way of describing surges. Webster's definition is useful as a starter: "The effect created by the elements in a play . . . that relate to the temporal development of the action." From this definition, we can see that rhythm is the *effect* of accumulating tempos, that it is a way of describing multiple tempos brought together. But this is only a partial definition of rhythm, for the moods in a play exercise an important effect on rhythm and must be considered in defining it. Because of the illusive nature of the word *rhythm,* and because of its double nature when being applied to the theatre, it is not used much in this discussion. The emphasis has been placed on tempos and moods as the keys to discovering rhythm. If you can master these concepts and put them to work for you, you will have a very good understanding of how to find rhythm in a play. A sense of rhythm is largely an inherent talent, but it can be developed to an extent through training in music and dance.

SOUND AND SILENCE

Do you remember the quotation from Jean-Louis Barrault in the second chapter: "A play is interrupted silence"? Note carefully the idea in that definition. Barrault did not say, "A play is sound interrupted by silence," the way we usually think of it, but he said it the other way around—silence interrupted by sound. It is an extreme view, to be sure, but it is a good way of understanding the concept of drama. In one sense, it can be said that a playwright starts with a silent void and then fills it with sound—the cover of his action. But if he is a good playwright, he will never completely fill the silence; he will only punctuate it.

What he leaves in the way of silence is the pause—an element of tempo. *Pause* is a silence gap that has theatrical effect on the stage because its tempo values can be very moving: what is not said is often just as important as what is said, and the duration of the pause tells us much. The director should study and mark the pauses in a playscript; again, he will have a half-buried device that will tell him much about a play's structure.

The silent moments are also the moments for the actor's pantomimes. Nineteenth-century acting was too often made up of an alternation of speaking, illustration, speaking, illustration, etc. Today, because of the prescriptions of Realism, we are much more motivated to do them simultaneously. But in this process, we too easily forget the extreme importance of the silent moments—the erratic gaps of tempo. The director's imagination should lead him to a careful examination of a playwright's suggested illustrations for the silent moments. Whether he follows them religiously or not is a matter of personal decision, but at least he knows that the gaps are there, that they form part of the tempo structure of the play, and that they cannot be ignored without causing much damage to the rhythm structure.

Ostensibly a play is very much like a dance-drama set to music. Without hearing the music—the sound and silence—you almost entirely lose the play's form. If the director has a musical ear, he will *hear* the written play.

EXERCISES

1. One student beats a drum at different, improvised speeds. The rest of the class imagines the following for the rhythms:
   a. Different character types, which each beat prescribes.
   b. Different character-mood-intensities for each beat.
   c. A unit improvisation (one unit only of reciprocal action).

2. One student beats a drum at three different speeds. Try to improvise a story for the three units indicated.

3. One student beats a drum at the speed which he *feels* expresses a unit from a specific play. The class describes what they feel about the tempo he has played on the drum. They compare their feelings by reading the unit from the playscript.

4. Play some music. What visual images are suggested by the beat of the music? Take care in this exercise not to confuse tempo with mood as you presently understand the latter term.

5. Play some recordings of spoken plays (the Mercury recordings of Shakespeare are excellent). Note the tempo of the music used in between scenes. Does the music contrast with the tempos of the spoken units?

6. Each student finds some music that expresses his feeling for the rhythm of a study play. Compare the findings.

7. Examine a study play for *sound and silence*. Pick out the silent moments. What will specifically punctuate them?

8. Suggest improvised business for the opening and closing of a certain section of a study play. How does the visual, as imagined, emphasize the action of this scetion? What is the tempo of such visual activity?

Moods

DEFINITION

Moods are the feelings or emotions generated from the clash of forces in the dramatic action. When taken together in their accumulative effect, moods declare the *tone* of a play. An appropriate tone for a play is the goal of the director. Moods are thus the *tonal feelings* of a play.

EFFECT ON THE AUDIENCE

This discussion is begun with *effect on the audience,* because the concept of mood can be understood better by going backwards from how an audience receives a play to the playscript itself as the generator of the reception. Of course, there is no question that a director must become consciously aware of the moods in a play as he studies it on the printed page, but, like tempo, mood is difficult to understand as a concept, and it is particularly illusive to put into words. However, once the student director understands the nature of mood values and their relationship to the other elements in play-analysis, he can see how to put mood values to work for him.

Moods are not mysterious; it is only explaining them that makes them seem illusive. Moods are basic feelings; they are the disturbances, the excitements we are moved by as we watch a play. When you are a member of an audience, you experience the play; that is, if the play is well acted, even you, who may be studying directing and are, therefore, more conscious of what is done on the stage, will lose your objectivity and become immersed in the play—you will *feel* it and be *moved* by it. You are moved by the mood values. This arousal of feelings in the audience can begin early in a performance, and accumulates in force throughout, rising to a peak at the major climax of the action and then gradually calming as the play closes.

We all know this arousal to be the fun of watching a play—the vicarious experience. Experiencing the shifts of mood not only holds our attention in a performance but at the end leaves us tired, or even exhausted, or happy, or ecstatic. We are so busy feeling the emotions generated by the characters in action—empathizing—that even though we know that a play is only an artificial thing, that it is not real life but only a semblance of it, we have expended almost as much physical energy on the play experience, so we think, as we might on a real-life happening. It has been a vicarious experience, to be sure, but it has involved our feelings—all our nervous system. For this reason, we go to plays: we like the sensation of being aroused, of feeling intensely without the traumas that real-life experiences hold for us.

There is always something akin to the sex life of the average human being in the theatre experience. Our minds and our body feelings are so played upon by a performance that we are titillated and aroused to peaks that resemble, in kind, those we experience in real life. These two experiences—one fake, the other real—are not the same by any means, of course, but they *appear* to be the same, and plays are once removed from us because they happen, not to ourselves, but to other people. We do not feel defrauded by this fake experience because we knew what it was when we went to the play, and we find something of value, something that makes life richer, by participating in the human behavior of others caught in situations and circumstances that may resemble those possible in our own worlds.

The moods of a play, then, are what move an audience beyond itself
into imagined experience.

DRAMATIC ACTION AND MOODS

Again, before discussing the director's work with the printed script,
we can get a clearer idea of mood by noting its relationship to dramatic
action.   Since we think of action in units, so must we also think of mood
in the same terms.   A play is thus composed of many mood shifts, with
every unit of action having its own specific mood.

As you have already noted in the section on characters, the phrase
character-mood-intensity means that a character enters a unit of the play
at a certain physical-nervous pitch—the nervosity of the character at that
point.   And you know that as he participates in the action of the unit, his
mood intensity will shift; if he begins at the right pitch, what he does to
another character and what that character does to him will modify his
mood intensity, either making it more relaxed or more tense.

As members of the audience, we experience these specific mood
changes, for in a play we always move forward in a cause-effect progression.   The goal of a unit of action, then, is a mood-goal.   Several of these
mood-goals put together cause the surge in a play, and, as audience, we
surge with it.   The dramatic action, then, is the source of mood, and the
characters with their changing mood intensities are the instruments.
Later on in this book, we will discuss how the actor *makes* mood through
his technique of acting.

TONE-GOAL

The *tone* of a production is, therefore, the achievement of the appropriate moods in a playscript.   Tone is what the director is striving for,
because it is what the playwright felt when he improvised his play.   Tone
is the maximal state of feeling, the actual purpose of the play.   Unless
the director achieves this state, he achieves nothing.   All of his prepara-
tions, all of his production designs are for naught unless he can move his
audience in the way the play demands.

The rediscovery of the tone of a play and the achievement of it in
production is thus the goal of the director.   Note that it is not *a* tone but
the tone, for the mood-goal will contain the ultimate *meaning* of a play
because the audience will receive the meaning subjectively and only a
few will ever consciously try to bring that meaning to the surface.   An
audience's experience with a play for the most part will depend on the
director's perception of the mood-goal and how well he is able to achieve
this without his actors.

But though the audience's perception may be subjective, it does not
follow that the director can achieve the mood-goal by being subjective

himself. He must not only keenly feel the tone of a play on the first reading or two, but he must be able to achieve this tone after weeks of involvement in the details of rehearsals and production.

THE DIRECTOR'S ANALYSIS OF MOOD VALUES

When most people read a play they *sense* the shifts in mood: they are impressed or get the impression. This response is expected and natural. But the director must be much more aware of, more consciously perceptive to, these mood shifts as well as to the overall tone. Many readings of a playscript together with the disassembling and detailing that goes on during a rehearsal and production period can often obliterate the first feelings a director may have had about a playscript. Since the director's major job is working with actors, if he knows the unit-mood-goals and the overall tone he wants to achieve, he will not only be able to help the actors find these goals but bring them into a unity within the play.

How to record your initial feelings about a play may at first seem illusive to you because it involves trying to record your personal and very subjective reactions. But once you have worked at this sort of conscious reproduction of your feelings, you will find it of enormous value in communicating with actors.

Moods can be recorded in words in two different ways: (a) through mood adjectives; (b) through mood metaphors.

Mood Adjectives. Since moods are emotions or feelings, they can be recorded in the way an actor works, because the result of acting is showing others through *visual* and *aural* means what a character is feeling. Though the actual process for the actor lies in the execution of the action, out of that execution flows the feeling—the goal. In real life a person can be undergoing a tremendous emotional response to some happening but show very little on the outside. On the stage, the actor must demonstrate what is happening. His language of transference is through the physical sense: touch, taste, smell, hearing, seeing—all feelings. Therefore the words that can best describe moods are the adjectives that fall into "feeling" categories. Here are some examples:

> *touch:* rough, smooth, hard, soft, sandy, cool, hot.
> *taste:* tart, sweet, puckering, cool, hot, smooth, rubbery.
> *smell:* pungent, perfumy, stinky, sweet, sharp.
> *hearing:* loud, soft, raucous, blaring, piercing.
> *seeing:* red, blue, all words of size and shape, all varying words of light-
> ness and darkness.

A number of these adjectives strung together will help you recall unit-moods and to talk about them directly.

Mood Metaphors. A *metaphor* is a figure of speech in which a word or phrase literally denoting one kind of object or idea is used in place of another to suggest a likeness, or analogy, between them. The mood adjectives are highly useful, but they are more limiting than metaphors, which allow your imagination to play freely and creatively on a play because you are trying to find images that resemble the feelings you have about the units. You therefore say to yourself, "The mood in this unit is like a _____," and you fill in an image. Do not try to think in the sense categories suggested for mood adjectives, but let yourself go free. Here are some examples.

The mood in this unit is like:

a *moth fluttering around a lamp* (the unit-mood-goal is nervous, fluttering, indecisive, trembling, etc.)

an *air compressor riveting machine* (the mood-goal of the unit is noisy, hammering, erratic, jolting, etc.)

lemon juice (the unit-mood-goal is sour, flows like liquid, smells fragrant but would pucker the mouth, etc.)

Learn to think in metaphors, because they are the way of bringing to the surface the subjective feelings of the director. And inherent in metaphors are ways of talking to actors and designers in order to convey something that really exists only in the doing.

RHYTHM IN MOODS

It should now be obvious that the mood structure of a play can declare its basic rhythm. *Rhythm* has a far wider meaning than restricting it alone to tempo, for tempo, like heartbeat, is tied inextricably to the shifts and changes in mood. Further discussion of rhythm at this point may only confuse you, but you must always think of a play as having a rhythm structure in its moods, which rise and fall with increasing intensity as the play progresses.

ATMOSPHERE

The *atmosphere* of a play is actually the mood-meaning of the given circumstances. If the latter are perceived well, the atmosphere will automatically be evident in the reader's mind and feeling. A director who is thoroughly aware of the atmosphere or aura in a playscript, and can state it in a particular way, will be able to exert a strong command over the design of his production. A director must thus be able both to see and to hear the given circumstances of a playscript and then be able to translate these feelings into the concrete terms of stage production.

EXERCISES

1. Discuss how you receive a play. Try not to let your self-conscious attitudes now developing in your training, interfere with an honest appraisal of your experience as a spectator. This exercise can be done best after your class has watched together the performance of a scene or a play.

2. Examine the nature of *empathy*. How does it work in the other arts? It means: Feeling out the lines of an object. Apply empathy specifically to a theatre experience.

3. Examine the difference between a real-life experience you have witnessed and what it would look like as a unit in a play. Be certain it is limited and specific enough for you to make the comparison.

4. Record some mood adjectives for a unit of a study play.

5. Record some mood metaphors for a unit of a study play.

6. Examine some units in their mood-goals.

6

the director's play-analysis:
the basis of communication

A director's preparation is a written analysis of: given circumstances; dialogue; dramatic action; characters; idea; tempos; moods. *It
must be written, because this method is the only way a learning director
can be certain that he has covered all the points.*

Homework

No matter how skilled a director may be, no matter if he has been
directing for many years, he will always have to do intensive homework
—the study of the playscript. Like him, after you have done several written analyses, you may not actually record in written detail all of the structural facts about a play, but you will record some of them in your head
and some of them on paper—always in the interest of clarifying your ideas
and of developing specific communication that will be necessary between
you and your actors and designers. *But beginning directors must work
hard at written analysis, if only to be certain that all its aspects have been
covered thoroughly.*

Therefore, the basic function of homework is not only to help you
ferret out and understand a playscript, but also to put you in a position

of extensive and sensitive communication. Homework will make you articulate in the right way. Good directing is not talk, talk, talk—a gab fest; it is a very economical and appropriate suggestion at the right moment. The job of the actor is to act, to physicalize; it is not the job of a student in a seminar, where talking prevails. The director who thoroughly comprehends his primary tool—the playscript—will have a dozen ways of communicating a difficult point to an actor, not just one or two ways that may emerge after the director has stumbled around in a maze of language. A director's suggestions must be simple, direct, honest, economical, pointed. At the same time, they are imaginative—imaginal (full of images) is a better word—not coolly denotative but existing in the half-sublimated language that director and actor both understand.

Directions are also personal because they are directed to a particular actor and not to a puppet, or to a robot, or to a bit of pasteboard. Actors are *not* modeling clay. The director who knows his business will be ever ready to make the appropriate suggestion. Plays in rehearsal are built in a ladder-like construction—ever upward—with the director building on what the actor contributes, and the actor building on what the director contributes, with this reciprocal process repeated over and over. The prepared director can make it work, but the unprepared director will be forever working out of his own subjectivity, and instead of being able to answer questions he will forever be posing them to his confused actors. The director's job is to lead the actors, not to be led.

The purpose of a director's homework is to place him in the best possible position for communication to actors. He will know not merely a play's skin but its guts, bones, muscles, and blood.

Why a Written Preparation?

There is something about writing down observations one notes about a playscript that particularizes and pinpoints them. At first, you may think that this procedure is a danger in an artistic process like production, that it could inhibit, or at least restrict, your flight as a director. This fear is nonsense. After you have done an analysis or two and have seen them work, you will know that analysis does just the opposite: preparation acts as a freeing device. By writing down your ideas, you see many more possibilities begin to open up. After all, the playwright had to record finally his improvisations in a written playscript. Why shouldn't the director pin down his own understanding of the playwright's work in the same way? If a scene designer went directly into a shop and began building with only an idea in his head and had not recorded this idea in detail on drawing paper, the operation of building a play would be like a recreation hour in a madhouse. Without adequate, formal preparation a young director's work with actors will not only be haphazard but will follow a line of general directing and not of specific directing. A general development is dull and boring, only the specific can hold the attention of an audience. Do not think of a written preparation as an albatross around your neck but as the best possible tool with which you can provide yourself.

A Sample Outline for Play-Analysis

Although you can plunge into an analysis at any point, a better technique is to approach it systematically in the way outlined below. Thus, you should begin with given circumstances, and then proceed to dialogue, dramatic action, characters, idea, and wind up with tempos and moods. This procedure works well, because the analysis of given circumstances tends to flow into dialogue, and dialogue into dramatic action, and so on. You can also, when a fresh idea comes, check it with what you have already recorded; if it is logical, it will tie in easily, and the freeing process can begin to work.

What follows is a suggested plan for a play-analysis. Although this plan is set down here in outline form, an analysis of a scene taken from a long play (ten minutes, with three to five units) or a short one-act play would easily fill several pages; in other words, you must not complete the outline in an abbreviated way as you do in answering a true-or-false question, but develop your answers in detailed exposition.

Work Sheet for Play-Analysis

I. *Given Circumstances*
  A. Environmental facts. Discuss under the following numbered headings:
    1. Geographical location, including climate
    2. Date: year, season, time of day
    3. Economic environment
    4. Political environment
    5. Social environment
    6. Religious environment
  B. Previous action
  C. Polar attitudes of the principal characters, both in the beginning and at the ending

II. *Dialogue*

    A. Choice of words

    B. Choice of phrases and sentence structures

    C. Choice of images

    D. Choice of peculiar characteristics, e.g., dialect

    E. The sound of the dialogue

    F. Structure of lines and speeches

III. *Dramatic Action*

    A. Titles of the units. Number the units in the scene or play and give a nominative phrase as a title for each unit.

    B. Detailed breakdown of the action. Arrange the elements in numbered units. Express the action in each line by using the initial of each character followed by a present-tense verb. Example: N fears.

    C. Summary of the action. Summarize the action of each unit by following the number of the unit with a compound sentence expressing reciprocal action. Example: A (present tense verb) to B and B (present-tense verb) to A.

IV. *Characters*

    Treat *each* character under the following headings:

    A. Desire

    B. Will

    C. Moral stance

    D. Decorum

    E. Summary list of adjectives

    F. Initial character-mood-intensity at the scene opening expressed as:

        1. Heartbeat

        2. Perspiration

        3. Stomach

        4. Muscle

        5. Breathing

V. *Idea*

    A. Meaning of the title

    B. Philosophical statements in the play. Cite actual quotations.

    C. Implications of the action

    D. For the scene in preparation: Cite its purpose and use in the play.

VI. *Tempos*

    After the number of each unit, designate the rate of speed for that unit by using a rate word. Examples: fast, medium slow; largo, molto. Also make a horizontal graph of the tempo relationships by inserting connecting perpendicular lines to a horizontal line in order to show the peaks and valleys of tempo changes.

Example:

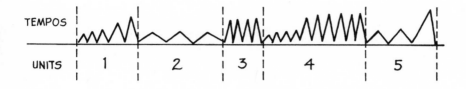

VII. *Moods*

After the number of each unit express the mood for that unit in two categories:

A. A list of mood adjectives with one for each of the senses

B. A mood image

EXERCISES

1. Review the outline in detail in class discussion. Be certain you understand all the parts before attempting a complete analysis. The instructor may wish to provide numbered forms for all sections.

2. Select for group study a one-act play or a five-to-ten minute scene from a long play. Each student does his own analysis. The group then examines the play or scene in detail by comparative reporting from the prepared analyses. (*Note:* This exercise can be an accumulative one for the entire chapter if the student writes an analysis of each part as it is studied. In this way, a full play-analysis is prepared during the course of the study of Chapters 3, 4, and 5, and the total analysis will be on hand for discussion at this point.)

3. Each student selects a ten-minute scene (4 to 6 units) from a long play and analyzes it.

II

COMMUNICATION I:
THE DIRECTOR-
ACTOR RELATIONSHIP

. . . let your own discretion be your tutor: suit the action to the word, the word to the action; with this special observance, that you o'erstep not the modesty of nature. . . .

HAMLET
in *Hamlet*

7

directing is communicating

Now that you have a sensitive understanding of play structure and can appreciate the very great importance of doing an exhaustive play-analysis in written form in order to pinpoint dramatic values, you are ready to study the difficult process of communicating a play to an audience. Communication is what Parts II and III of this book are about. You should notice, however, that this process is divided intentionally into two parts, with Part II devoted to the relationship between director and actor and Part III to the relationship between director and designer. Both relationships, of course, have the same goal of conveying in emotional terms a play to an audience; yet, the processes of communication are quite different. So that you can readily comprehend how each works in its own ways, these processes are discussed separately and then joined together in Chapter 19 with a major project—the production of a one-act play.

You may also have noticed that this part of the book seems to consist largely of techniques for visual illustration. Do not let that observation worry you at this point, for if you carefully read the contents of this chapter, you will understand why. But you should also note that Part II con-

COMMUNICATING: ARTISTIC LEADERSHIP

tains a chapter on "The Oral Tools in Director-Actor Communication," a very important section because most directors tend to be seduced by the visual and forget that the theatre experience is a carefully balanced composite of the visual *and* the oral. Finally, you should note that Chapter 13 will put you to work as a director, for as soon as you can understand the process of communication with the actor, you are ready to undertake your first level of directing. You will expand this understanding in the second level in Part III, and to the third in Part IV. But the contents of Part II must first be mastered.

Communicating: Artistic Leadership

As the first chapter of this book has pointed out, the director's field of action is communication. But about communication you must make a very important distinction. Although the director's ultimate responsibility is to touch and move audiences with a play, he cannot do so by himself but must tell audiences how he thinks and feels through actors and designers—his agents. Consequently, what the director manages to bring about will depend entirely on his talent for and his capabilities in communicating with these agents, for he will be successful only if he has a strong faith in their creative abilities and can see his own job as one of encouraging and stimulating them to their highest expression.

But here is the rub! Because he is so devoted to helping others, the director can easily be called a leech, a bloodsucker, a hanger-on; and also a pusher and a bully. Yet at his best, he is also a friend, a confidant, a lover. Once the learning director recognizes that communication is his corework, he will concentrate on using every device he knows to *get through.* But at that same time, because he expects people to pay attention to him, he must be very unselfish in paying the closest attention to them. Actors and designers are tender people, and the creative simply does not flourish in an aura of confusion and tension. A director communicates when he is a natural leader who knows how to work *with,* and not *at,* other human beings. Because he loves the artist in himself, he can love the artist in others.

How well you will be able to do this will depend on the sort of person you are, because touching other people with theatrical ideas is a vastly intricate process largely outside the purely intellectual. A director who thinks that all he need do is talk with actors on a logical, expositional level fails to understand the sort of creative person with whom he is working. Acting problems are not solved in discussion but in doing, and the director is the freewheeling agent who can find the images or the circumstances that will make doing more likely to succeed. Communication with actors is, therefore, a matter of a director's interest in and understanding of human beings, and not just of an interest in their acting capabilities. Getting through is not a mysterious process; it is based on a director's meticulous homework as well as on his recognition that there are no actors in the abstract but only individual "people" who must be reached on a level of personal feeling. If he understands something about how the creative imagination works, and if he understands the process of acting—the using of the human instrument to effect communication, he will be able to do his core job of energizing actors in the right way and of inspiring them beyond their usual capacities. Both actors and director are working for the same goal—communication of a play to an audience, but only the actors will carry it onstage and bring about the actual contact.

This description of the humanistic director does not at all imply weakness. Though the director must watch his manners at all times—politeness is akin to gentleness—he will find that an appropriate use of directness will not hurt or injure, not because it has more professional impersonality about it, but because it is not open to suspicion or worry on the part of the actor. A good director is a strong director because he does not leave actors, who have strong creative imaginations of their own, in doubt about what he means or intends; consequently, he takes great care to keep his directions clear so that the actors can easily accept and adjust. Appropriately used, strength is not dictatorship but an honest expression of opinion that can be supported and opened to discussion without generating fear and insecurity. The dictator-director is the director who is very unsure of his ground, which actors will quickly detect, and though as people they may try to be very cooperative, they will find his leadership hard to accept. There must always be a certain amount of the salesman in the director, because he must get across his ideas; yet, it is the soft sell, not the hard one, that will keep him on top of a situation.

The Director Is an Image-Maker

All the people who work on a play—the playwright, the actor, the designer, the director—are image-makers. Because a play is an artificial device, an imitation of life and not life itself, its poetic power resides in its capacity to arouse the imaginations of the watcher-hearers. We have already defined this penetration on the sublimated level as *empathy*—an automatic response, if conditions are right, to what is seen and heard. All aspects of the produced play are more symbolic, more typical than they would be in everyday life because they have been carefully selected and simplified, carefully arranged, and carefully unified. And because of this treatment, they possess the inherent capacity of arousing images in members of an audience, each of whom can then connect them with his own personal experiences and views of life. Thus, we can say that the produced play actually hovers in the air between the actors on the stage and the audience in the house; it is a froth of images waiting to be rescued and assimilated by the audience. Consequently, the playgoing experience does not stop with what is literally set out in these images from the stage but continues in a very personal way in the minds and feelings of the viewers. Everything a viewer sees and hears is converted automatically into his own images. This conversion is his work on the play. It becomes obvious that the process of play production cannot be completed without him. Consequently, the kind of image-making by the director through the actor is very important in the theatre.

As you can now readily see, if a director is to justify his place in the theatre as a theatrical artist, he will have to be someone who can not only help actors enhance their own capacities for image-making but also someone who can discover *appropriate* images for certain passages of a play and can see that they are set in motion. The young director must therefore become highly aware that the theatre experience is primarily a sensuous experience, and that image-making involves the visual and oral deployment of the senses—seeing, hearing, touching, smelling, tasting. That the theatre is sense-arousing we can see readily in a performance of a play when we respond warmly to the color and texture of a costume, to the line of a piece of scenery, or to the sound of something mechanical, such as a clock bell or an offstage airplane engine. What we are usually not so aware of is how actors continually assault all of our senses by making us constantly taste, smell, and touch, as well as see and hear, in very special ways. We are inclined to take them for granted because much of what a good actor does is usually so deftly and subtly done and is so right and truthful that we are rarely conscious of the process. Yet this is the process of acting, for *acting is reaching audience imagination through the direct transfer of sensuous imagery.* What an actor touches, we, as audience, touch in our imaginations; what he smells, we smell, and so on.

The young director, then, cannot be fully alive to his communication possibilities until he comprehends the sense-arousing aspects of acting. He will know that he can get through to an audience only when he can bring about in his actors the images with which he wants to assault the audience. The final goal is, of course, to bring about a high state of *involuntary* attention (unaware or unself-conscious attention) in the audience. How well a director can achieve this goal depends on the sensory inspiration he can bring about in his agents. A director must first be an image-maker to his actors if he is to be an image-maker for an audience.

Techniques of Communication

INTELLECTUAL TALK

You should now be aware that there is a good deal more to the communication process between director and actor than exchanging ideas about a playscript on an intellectual level. This fact does not imply that a certain amount of useful information cannot be conveyed to an actor in an objective, intellectual way, for it surely can, but when it comes to the hard core of dramatic action and character, such a self-conscious method usually fails. Young directors are often baffled about why they are not getting through to actors without being aware that they are trying to reach the actors largely through objective discussion. Consequently, you must learn to work in many different ways, realizing that your intention is to free, rather than to tie up, the imaginations of actors, for an actor who thinks too much cannot act. Actors must move spontaneously out of natural responses, as we do for the most part in everyday life, out of their senses, and not out of their minds.

You must, therefore, learn to restrict intellectual discussion to those matters that do not strongly affect the senses of the actor, and you must learn how you can free his imagination, can give him flight, in other ways. Objective talk will take your actors only a short way. Image-inducing direction will make him imagize, and that accomplishment will comprise your major communication with the actor. Talk little; do much.

IMPROVISATION: A TECHNIQUE
IN DIRECTOR-ACTOR COMMUNICATION

Improvisation has become a much used technique in director-actor communication in recent years because it has become a basic approach in actor training. As you know yourself in your experience as a student of acting, when you started doing improvisations, you began to see what acting is all about—that it is not a laid-on process of exterior development but that it starts from inside yourself and is all tied up with relating intensively to other actors. At first, your improvisations were probably arranged to show you how relaxation and concentration could let you show something with honesty and believability, through yourself and without self-consciousness. You probably did brief sense exercises, sometimes with imaginary objects, sometimes with real objects. Later you worked with dramatic actions, and eventually you tried complex exercises that involved other participants—improvisations that worked only when you learned to play *off* the other improvisor. You learned that improvising requires the utmost attention to what the other improvisor does to you because you have to adjust to him before you know what to do yourself. Do you remember how free you felt without a scenario or an established line of development such as a pantomime would prescribe? You could let the improvisation take form and develop out of that freedom. Did you feel the exaltation and power that freedom gave you?

This is the sort of feeling you must induce in your actors when you use improvisation as a technique of communication. The goal is discovery in the most personal way possible, for that is what moves from the inside of the actor outward. Improvisation becomes a device enabling an actor to discover his relationship to another actor on an intimate level (reciprocation); to establish a relationship to another character; to feel the sensation of the dramatic action being expressed; to discover dramatic action; to discover an illustration of dramatic action; to feel the special quality of a given place and its climate; to feel the decorum of a character in a given circumstance; to hear what the voice is like at high volumes and low volumes under forced conditions; to find the extent of movement and body behavior under specifically delineated circumstances. These are only a few of the enormous number of things that can be accomplished with improvisation, for it is literally imaginative game playing that can open up a play's mysterious moments. The director is, of course, the leader, and as such he can use improvisation for any purpose he wishes. Some directors use it extensively throughout the rehearsal period and do not shape a performance until the final rehearsals.

There are many problems, however, in using only the improvisational approach as the means of releasing actors. Beginners will have a particularly difficult time with it simply because improvisation requires experience. Advanced actors may do somewhat better, and some will be very good at it. Nevertheless, the primary problem with improvisation is that it has no performance status of its own; that is, although it can lead to very sensitive moments of discovery, they are still only moments, and a performance is made up of joining those moments together. What happens in between making improvisations and making a performance is of primary concern. Some directors try to show the improvisations they have made in rehearsal to audiences without any modification whatever, and then wonder why the improvisations do not work. You will keep out of trouble if you remember that improvisations are highly valuable as devices for discovery, but they are not intended for performance because they inherently lack the essential power of projection, and without projection (selection and emphasis) an audience cannot gather together the whole play.

If you can see improvisation primarily as a rehearsal technique, then, it can become a valuable tool for you. Used for its proper purposes, it can help you reach many actors on very primitive levels, with the result that your play can be that much more sensitive. But recognize at the outset that it is a rehearsal and not a performance technique, and that it requires experience and talent in the participants to accomplish success-fully.

There will be more comment on improvisational techniques along with some specific suggestions in Chapter 13. But after you study the inter-vening chapters on organic blocking, you will be in a better position to know what to do with improvisation. A good book to help you learn more about this approach to actor training is Viola Spolin's *Improvisa-tion for the Theater*. If you study her methods of handling actors, you will know a good deal more about what can be done in a specific way. At this time, you should rely on what you have learned about improvisation in your acting classes.

ORGANIC BLOCKING: A TECHNIQUE
OF COMMUNICATION

Organic Blocking refers to the stimulation of the actor's imagination through the use of six visual tools: (1) groundplan, (2) composition, (3) gesture, (4) improvisation with properties, (5) picturization, and (6) move-ment. Its function is to help actors uncover dramatic action and to illus-trate it. Inherently, it contains both rehearsal and discovery techniques and techniques of performance.

In line with the previous discussion of improvisation, you must first understand that these six tools for director-actor communication are used for the purpose of communicating directly with the actor, who will, in turn, communicate with the audience. You must, therefore, view these tools as *actor stimulators,* for by using these tools as external suggestions, a director can ignite all kinds of chain reactions within an actor. The word *organic* is used to denote that such blocking is in no way superim-posed on a play or forced on an actor, but it implies that such blocking suggestions derive from the play (the organism) itself and are therefore inherent in it. *Organic Blocking,* then, is not a pictorial process, is not a way of making a performance more beautiful through stage arrange-ments, but is an inherent activation of a playscript through a body of physical suggestions that can arouse imagination in actors.

At first, this technique may be difficult for you to comprehend espe-cially if your dramatic training has been dominantly improvisational with the emphasis always on the inside-to-outside process, but skillfully used, the outside-to-inside approach to actors can work very well indeed and will not be at all in conflict with the other approach. As a matter of fact, both can be used, and are used, simultaneously. Indeed, many actors like the assurance of the outside-to-inside approach because it is tangible and physical—they know in a physical way where they are going.

The question here is what seems to be, in the view of some directors, a strong conflict between using improvisation and blocking at the same time. These directors argue that blocking freezes the actor and that improvisation is the only avenue to his release. The answer to this argument is that there is no single way to release actors. Either or both of these approaches can be used effectively, and often in combination, paradoxical though that may seem, since blocking is self-conscious and objective, whereas improvisations are largely intuitive and subjective. However, if both are used with care, they do not battle with one another but tend to support and intensify one another. You will need to learn how to do both if you are to take full advantage of available director-actor techniques of communication, for shutting yourself off with improvisational techniques only is to limit greatly what you can do with actors. In addition, if you should decide to work in the professional theatre, you will find that actors use a wide range of techniques.

Actors frequently feel quite uncomfortable when they participate in first readings because a play—an ensemble effort—can be very confusing until it has been given some outward form. A director can be of great assistance in helping them get over this initial discomfort by placing them physically in specific relationships to one another in conformity with the dramatic action. This process will not only give an actor time to locate himself, but it will allow him to know who his adversaries in the play are, something he may already know intellectually but not in a physical sense. Anyone who has acted in a play knows the discomfort described here; yet directors who are busy looking elsewhere too easily forget the difficulties of first contacts.

When the refinement of illustration begins later in rehearsal, the concept of aiding the actor with visual suggestions can be stepped up in full force, always with the intention of *communicating* ideas to the actors— ideas about emphasis, about intentions, about shadings in the action. If you keep in mind that transfer to the audience is a transfer of sensory images, you will begin to appreciate the full value of this sort of direction. A good actor will, of course, provide much of this illustration on his own, but illustration is infinite, and the best selection must be made. The director's function is to assist with selection, by constantly working toward what he believes to be refinement and improvement. Where an actor stands on a stage in relation to other characters or other objects, how and why he moves and the nature of that movement, how he handles an object, are all of primary concern to a director, for all of these considerations will convey images. The important question is: Do they convey the appropriate images, the ones the director has decided he wants?

You will have more control over some of these visual tools than you have over others, but they are all tools that you can put to work. *Learn to tell the truth* with them by finding appropriate images, because the tools have great capacity for telling lies, because the actor can speak one thing and do another. Hamlet's advice to the Players quoted on the title page of Part II is the best instruction that can be given to a director: ". . . suit the action to the word, the word to the action." This principle is what the actor is learning to apply. If you can exploit his own training to the full, you will find yourself in ready communication with him.

Actors are also great experimenters. Always remember that the process of rehearsing a play is *not talking* about it *but doing* it. One thing you must learn is that you should not freeze actor illustrations until late in a rehearsal period when you must use consistently the best ones you have discovered. Some students think that by learning techniques their imaginations will be dried up, that they become more rigid, but just the opposite actually happens. You will certainly be self-conscious when you are learning how to see these tools and how to use them, but later they will be part of you, like the multiplication table, and you will know how to exploit them to the fullest possible advantage. Scene discovery or opening up the action will usually depend on experimentation with these visual tools. Gamble on shifting and changing their values as part of the process of discovery in rehearsals.

Organic blocking is developed rather extensively in the following chapters not only because, as a technique of director-actor communication, it must be understood in some detail to make it work, but also because it provides the process for the projection of a play in performance. As you work through these chapters, you will see how to use these tools to make clear and forceful statements of dramatic action and character—statements that may take shape in spontaneous ways during the rehearsal period but can be sharpened and focused during the polishing period. You will also notice that these six tools form the body of conventions employed on the proscenium stage. But while they have particular pertinence to that stage, it will also become clear that they can be used, with slight modifications, on any stage you can devise, for they are essentially ways of making actors effective before an audience.

But however these tools may be projected into use on other stages, it is important for you, as a student who is learning directing, first to master the techniques used on the proscenium stage. You are more familiar with this stage than any other, and you will more readily understand its prescriptions. Moreover, the proscenium stage is still the prevailing mode of stage production and may well continue to be for some years to come.

You should also keep in mind in working through the following chapters that the six basic tools have been isolated here as individual working tools, although we never actually see them in such an abstract way when we watch a performance because an actor uses several of these tools simultaneously and so quickly that our eyes cannot readily delineate their separate ways. Yet, without this detailed separation, student directors cannot possibly understand the individual force of each tool or know how to exploit each as a way of reaching actors and manipulating them. The discussion of the tools begins with the groundplan in the next chapter and continues in Chapters 9, 10, and 11. So that you will see how they work in concert, the second part of Chapter 11 will put them together again in a synthesis. Only by understanding the parts as separate tools can you grasp the whole.

EXERCISES

1. Discuss as a group the various approaches used in *your* acting training. When did you first think you were really acting, as distinct from merely using your exterior personality? What was the experience like?

2. What kinds of communication reach you as an actor? Examine the various approaches directors have used to bring you out as an actor? What worked best? What was least effective?

3. What is an image? Read some short poems and analyze each for its imagery. Look particularly at some five-line Japanese poems and their imagery. Why is poetry so compact?

4. Talk to another student in images, using as few words as possible. You will be surprised at how few words are actually needed to convey ideas and human feelings.

5. How does organic blocking differ from merely blocking a play? Can you see how the first is deeply rooted in both dramatic action and in actor training, and the second tends toward the pictorial only?

6. Discuss the good and bad points in using improvisation as a director's method of communication.

7. Define the proscenium stage. What is the use of the proscenium wall? How does the wall concept differ from the arch concept? Why does Realism as a style require the proscenium stage? (Note the capital on Realism because it is a distinct and specific way of writing a play.) What is the audience's relationship to the actor on a proscenium stage? What rules do you think should be observed by actors performing on the proscenium stage? In discussing the proscenium stage, the tendency is to think of it only in terms of set design. How is it a playwright's stage? An actor's stage? What are its merits? What are its limitations? (The proscenium stage will be discussed in detail in Part III, but it is important at this point that you understand it in a minimal way.)

8

the groundplan:
the basic tool in director-
actor communication

A *groundplan* is at once a representation of the given circumstances and a tension device for discovering and illustrating the dramatic action of a play in specific terms of space and of the necessary obstacles that break up that space. It is the basic tool in director-actor communication because all the other tools are dependent on it and flow naturally out of it. If you can master the concept of the groundplan as a device for communication, you will be able to see how the other tools can also work for you.

Although a groundplan is usually represented in a two-dimensional drawing like the architect's floor plan you see in magazines about building homes, it is actually three-dimensional in concept, for the drawing represents physical objects occupying vertical space (from the floor upward) as well as space on the plane of the stage floor. A director must, therefore, always think in three-dimensional terms: stage space is a cube and not a rectangle on the floor. Using this point of view, he can see the vertical, as well as the horizontal, aspects of the design, and he can better visualize how he can suggest to the actors the feelings and facts about the given circumstances.

For this reason, in devising groundplans for Realistic plays, a director should also include walls, platforms, steps, furniture, and anything else that has height.   Only by doing so, can he define the cube he and his actors will exploit and his audience will see and feel.   Always try to see a groundplan in your mind's eye just as you would if you were looking at a perspective sketch of it with your eye-line slightly above the stage floor.

A groundplan is only incidentally a visual design for an audience.   Its primary service is that of an organic instrument to bring out the dramatic action through director-actor communication.   In composing a play, a dramatist will choose a symbolic place for the dramatic action because he feels that it exerts some particular force on the action itself, that is, he feels the pressure of the place.   A director must, therefore, reconstruct this feeling from the dramatic action (not from a physical description the author may have inserted) as nearly as he can, for what he must find is the appropriate obstacle course for that action.   *Obstacle course* is used here because an actor, until he is much advanced, can sense actions much more quickly and keenly with a physical obstacle between him and the opposing force represented in another character than he can when there is no obstacle.   A table, sofa, or chair between two actors gives them both something to struggle over, something which prevents them from getting together.   This technique is based on the premise that plays are mostly about clashes and not about harmonies.   Differences in levels—steps, platforms, etc.—do much the same thing, because one character can feel from such juxtapositions his dominance or lack of dominance over other characters.   *The purpose of a groundplan is, therefore, to give actors strong sensations of tension by placing in their way physical obstacles that must be overcome if they are to reach other characters.*

From this discussion, it should be obvious that a director must search for the *appropriate space* for the play he is producing.   What he finds will be a specific place, not a general place.   The given circumstances will tell him whether that space is large or small; whether it is frequently interrupted by objects, or whether it is only occasionally so; whether it has strong vertical possibilities (everything from platforms to balconies) or must be largely horizontal (low ceilinged, hugging the floor).   Good designers also think in these terms, although they are not apt to think about a director's specific communication with actors.   (For this reason, it is imperative that directors work intensively at developing their own sense of design for the groundplan.   When they work with designers, they can then be certain that the major point of a groundplan—director-actor communication—is accomplished.)   The detailing of the space and of the objects can be done by a designer because he can greatly intensify the visual effect, but unless the architecture of a groundplan is well conceived in terms of the dramatic action, not only will the director have lost basic possibilities for communication with his actors, but he will also have reduced the effectiveness of all the other visual tools for director-actor communication that depend on it.

An Improvisational Approach
to the Concept of Groundplan

You may wish to begin this section on specifics by doing the improvisational approach to thinking and feeling about the groundplan, which is outlined in Exercise 1 at the end of this chapter. If you do begin this section with Exercise 1, you may be able to understand better the concepts that follow. Although the exercise is an excellent one for grasping the difference between a groundplan and a room used in everyday life, it has not been inserted at this point because it would interrupt the basic discussion. Nevertheless, you and your class are strongly urged to try this game approach now in the interest of discovering essential feeling about groundplan design through doing.

Acting Areas

Because Realistic plays are sit-down plays in a literal sense—that is, the characters actually sit on chairs, sofas, etc., instead of standing as they do in much historical drama—involving as they do dramatic actions in such domestic environments as living rooms, bedrooms, kitchens, porches, backyards, and offices, the groundplan's potential power to illustrate can be measured by strictly defining all the *acting areas.* A very handy technique for doing this sort of advance forecast is the sit-down rule. According to this rule an acting area consists of *two sit-down* positions at least *six feet or more apart,* that is, two chairs or a sofa and chair in different parts of a room. As you can see, this rule arbitrarily excludes not only all standing positions but also those sitting positions, such as on a sofa, where two people are placed very close together. Further—and here is the second important part of this rule—a groundplan must have a minimum of *five* acting areas defined in this fashion if it is to be really effective. As you can see, at the base of this rule is the concept of keeping characters apart while playing a scene.

Note in Fig. 1 how each area is delineated by circling two sitting positions at least six feet apart, and how the merits of the groundplan as a whole can be tested by showing all of the available areas in one drawing (Fig. 2). Six areas are delineated in Fig. 2, but there are at least two or three more not shown because the lines would overlap too much and thus would obscure the drawing as an example.

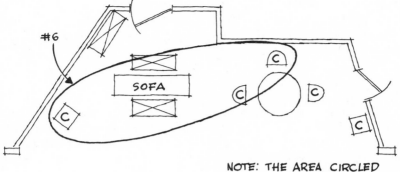

NOTE: THE AREA CIRCLED
IS #6 IN FIG. 2

FIGURE 1

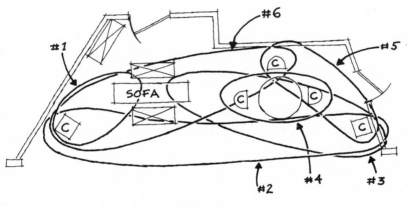

FIGURE 2

Now the use of this sit-down rule does not at all imply that standing positions are not frequently used in very effective ways, but quite the contrary, for standing positions will be all the more effective when enough obstacles have been placed in the room to keep the characters at some distance from one another. Each of the obstacles also acts as a physical support to any actor who stands near it because it will emphasize the weight and mass of the actor's body. *If any groundplan has less than five acting areas, then, it means that the number of obstacles has been substantially reduced, and this situation in turn reduces the possibilities for tension.*

Learn this sit-down rule because it is an effective safeguard in planning high-tension groundplans. A groundplan conceived on this principle of multiple acting areas will suggest all sorts of illustrative possibilities to actors because of its built-in tension, and you will find that it will become a quick and effective device for communication.

Tension Arrangements

A multiple-area groundplan always has high tension values because the possibilities for arranging furniture can be extensive. Your arrangements will need a certain amount of logic, of course, because rooms should more or less look like what they are intended for, but appearance is largely a secondary matter. Of much greater importance in a groundplan is its tension-creating possibilities, and if tensions are there, the appearance will probably be more than interesting, even exciting. Here are some specific suggestions for creating tension values:

1. Place your primary objects in space free of the walls, so that actors can move easily around them (Fig. 3). Objects placed against the walls merely create standing spaces with no obstacle course. They will provide a certain amount of verisimilitude (likeness to real life), but they will not normally provide possibilities for conflict.

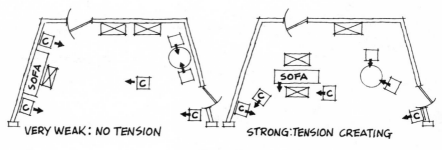

VERY WEAK: NO TENSION   STRONG: TENSION CREATING

FIGURE 3

2. Work on the diagonal principle wherever possible, because diagonals create more tension than objects parallel to the proscenium line. (Note the direction of the long arrows in Fig. 4.)
3. Place objects in contrasting positions that can create tension by their oppositional force. (Note the short arrows in Figs. 3 and 4 that show the directions the sitting positions face and, consequently, the oppositional forces they create.)
4. Note that walls create tension because they are broken up with jogs and diagonals (Fig. 4), which not only create architectural strength and interest but also cut into and pack more tightly the action

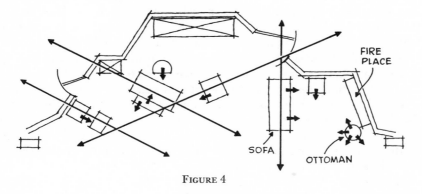

FIGURE 4

space. The placement of furniture definitely takes these lines into account. Good tension-creating arrangements will arouse strong feelings in actors, thus motivating them to work against tensions as well as with them. You will be amazed at the strength of the compositions automatically created by the actors when there are strong lines of tension in a groundplan.

Groundplan on the Proscenium Stage

Although creating strong tension values is absolutely essential, you must also arrange the groundplan in accordance with the primary convention of the proscenium stage—the convention that places the audience on one side within an arc of 60°–70° (Fig. 5). This arrangement implies

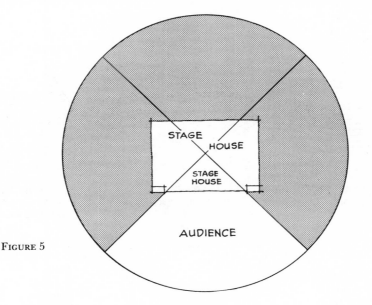

FIGURE 5

that some arbitrary rules are automatically put into force in order to help the audience both see and hear better.   Normally, we are supposed to be looking in at a reproduction of real life, but the placement of the audience makes the use of the proscenium stage quite artificial and not like real life at all.   The theory of the proscenium stage will be discussed in Part III, but it is essential at this point that you understand that you are trying to overcome the effects of a one-sided view and are compensating for the loss of a true three-dimensional quality.

Here are a few rules you must follow if you are to overcome the flat qualities of the proscenium stage.   They will also help your audience both see and hear best.

1. Open the side walls to the audience.   Side walls are usually raked to open up the upstage corners of a setting (Fig. 6A), although walls perpendicular to the proscenium line (Fig. 6C) can work if the audience's seating angle to the stage is less than 70° and if entrances are not placed in upstage corner positions.   You must never think of the upstage corners as dead areas, for you will need every possible square inch of space to keep your compositions interesting, especially in one-set plays where action is carried on for two to three hours. Always consider the sight lines in composing a groundplan (Fig. 6).

2. Open the set properties (furniture) to the audience.   Throughout the seventeenth, eighteenth, and much of the nineteenth centuries, actors faced the audience when they were speaking, just as opera singers still do today.   With the introduction of Realism at the end of the nineteenth century, however, turning away from the audience, even showing the back of the actor—a very shocking behavior to turn-of-the-century theatregoers—re-

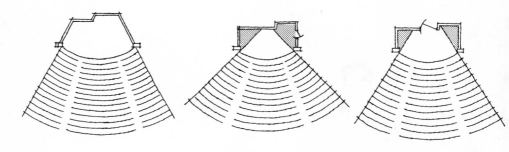

SATISFACTORY	VERY POOR	POSSIBLE
100% VISIBILITY	NOTE THE PLAYING	ONLY THE UPSTAGE
A	AREA LOST	CORNERS ARE LOST
	B	C

FIGURE 6

placed the old convention in the interest of creating a semblance of real life. But although a certain amount of pyschological truth was revealed in this way, turning away from the audience could only obscure both the actor's voice and face. Since there was much to be said for the old give-it-to-the-audience convention as opposed to the new concealment aesthetic, the new convention as it developed used both ideas, with the emphasis on playing to the house. The groundplan convention has developed in the same way, for the intention has been to help the actor deliver the play in every possible direction, but primarily to the audience. As the furniture placement took on more and more aspects of an obstacle course by occupying the spaces where the actors had always stood, it became general practice to compensate by opening individual furniture pieces to the house. The general rule thus requires that all much-used furniture pieces be placed prominently as far downstage and as near centerstage as possible. The *illusion* of reality is thus preserved, although the room is anything but real. Do not think, then, that you will help an actor by placing a chair on the curtain line facing upstage, for you will merely be blocking the audience's view of the stage and forcing the actor, if he sits in the chair, to talk upstage, thus cutting off the audience's hearing as well (Fig. 7). Such placement does not in any way create more reality but instead merely confuses an audience. Avoid such odd theatrics and, instead, comply with the conventions of the proscenium stage.

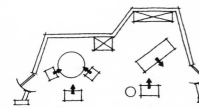
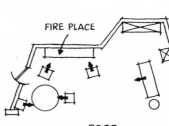

IMPOSSIBLE AND ILLOGICAL   POOR

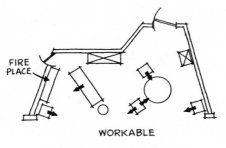

WORKABLE

FIGURE 7

3. Pin the downstage corners of the groundplan tightly to the rest of the plan. Because the illusion created should be of a walled room, you will not only help the effect of wall inclosure but also increase the illusion of depth to the room if you place pieces of furniture (chairs or other sitting pieces) at both of the downstage corners of the room *and encourage actors to use them.* This arrangement will provide a downstage foreground to contrast with midground and background, thus tying the groundplan together and intensifying the three-dimensional quality of the staging. This rule is very important because the furniture will help frame the actors in all the positions they take on the stage (Fig. 8). Moreover, without such sitting positions, actors will tend to avoid using the downstage corners, which will result in only a partial use of the total possible acting area.

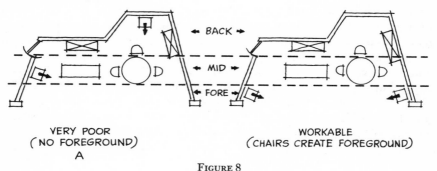

FIGURE 8

Ingenuity in Groundplan Design

You must learn to be ingenious in arranging groundplans. Always avoid the dull and trite—what we call the *no-room.* How dull it is: that bare, three-walled room without architectural jogs for relief; that room with a routine selection and placement of furniture; that room with doors placed'in balanced positions in the walls. New ideas about illustrating the actions will come to both you and the actors if you think and feel freshly about what makes up a groundplan.

Flexibility, Testing, and Improvisation

You don't make only one groundplan; you make several and then remake them. Since the groundplan is the base for all the other visual tools, it must be the best possible one you can devise. Therefore, your personal flexibility in this regard is absolutely essential; you must be ever ready to discard the groundplan that does not work and start over again, rebuilding on what you have discovered. Making a good groundplan always involves improvisation, for you are trying to project its uses through your own imagination.

One way to approach making a groundplan is to have some specific ideas in mind so that you can be a good leader, and then have the actors help you discover the best possible arrangement. They will enjoy this game of looking for fresh ways of illustrating, and such play will help them to a better understanding of the given circumstances. Remember: a groundplan is only as good as is its potential to arouse the imagination of the actors who will use it. They must learn to live in it and to exploit its every possibility. If you are to help them fly, you must help them find the flying machine that will get them off the ground.

Once again: make; test; remake; improvise; make; test; remake; improvise, etc.

EXERCISES

1. (See the first suggestion for creating tension values, under "Tension Arrangements," near the beginning of this chapter.) In order to understand thoroughly why the groundplan is an artistic device for presenting an illusion of reality and that it is not reality itself, do the following set of progressive exercises. Do it carefully step by step, and do not proceed to b before you have mastered a, or move to c before b is fully understood. Remember that the whole exercise is a game that must be played in pieces.
   a. Improvise a place with an inside measurement twenty feet wide and fourteen feet deep by lining up classroom chairs and having them face outward, on four sides. In setting up this place, you should practice the technique of rehearsal-room measurement by using the three methods for determining approximate footage: (1) if you know the length of your pace (the distance between your feet when extended in walking), as you should, you can make a fairly accurate measurement by counting your paces; (2) if you know the length of your shoe, you can mark out a desired measurement by placing one foot immediately in front of the other until you have covered the distance; (3) if the rehearsal room floor is made of square rubber tiles, you can find the exact measurement you want by counting the number of tiles (each tile will probably be nine or twelve inches wide).
   b. When the space is accurately determined, mark off two entrance doors to the room by removing chairs in appropriate places. Now arrange living room furniture (classroom materials) in a very similar fashion to that in a room you know in real life, your living room at home, for instance. Note that you will probably be making at least one conversational group with a sofa placed against one wall and chairs placed in relationship to it. It will probably look something like Fig 9.
   c. Improvise some dramatic action in this room. Here is a suggestion: A host receives three or four visitors, one at a time. Note where they sit down, for it will probably be in the easiest available spot, un-

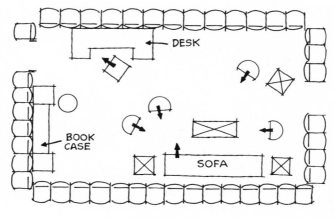

FIGURE 9

doubtedly in the conversation group. Also note that most living rooms this size probably have only one conversation group in order that everyone sitting in such a room can be easily included. Note how easy it is for people to carry on conversations in this physical relationship. Try some conversation, using numbers dialogue. Try two or three other improvisations before going on to *d*.

d. Now convert the room to a groundplan by:

(1) placing two chairs to represent a proscenium arch twenty-eight feet apart on one long side of the room and centering them on the middle of the room;

(2) removing the chairs on that side and raking the side walls of the room along with any furniture placed against them to meet the proscenium chairs—the chairs mentioned in (1). Note that the room will now look like Fig. 10.

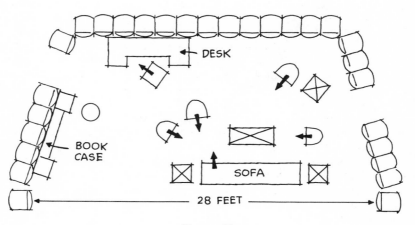

FIGURE 10

Note that the walls have been raked to allow good sight-lines. Thus, it should now be clear to you that a groundplan is an artificial device that is not reality but only an illusion of reality.

e. Increase the departure from reality further by reversing the sofa and coffee table so that they face the audience. It will now look like Fig. 11. But this groundplan is still not good because it is too simple to provide refreshing illustration for a two-hour play. Rearrange the furniture even further by placing pieces in the downstage corners of the room (pinning down the corners) and by making a second conversational group on stageright. It should now look like Fig. 12.

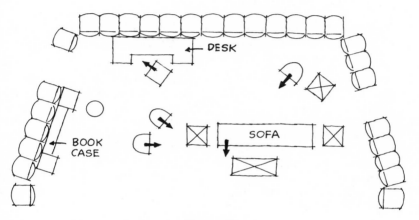

FIGURE 11

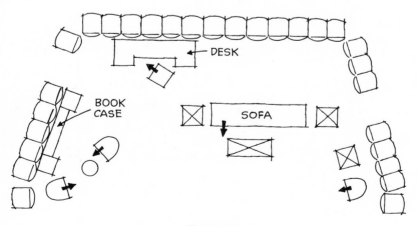

FIGURE 12

f. Now increase the architectural strength of the room by creating a jog in the upper left corner. Note that this modification makes the room more interesting architecturally because it reduces the obvious symmetry of the wall areas. Add chairs and furniture pieces to make it look something like Fig. 13.

g. Now note the following:

   (1) an obstacle course made of furniture has been established
   (2) two conversation groups allow more flexibility about where people can sit
   (3) the "acting" furniture for the most part occupies the middle planes of the stage—a clear departure from the real room we started with
   (4) multiple acting areas have been established, allowing very flexible use of the groundplan
   (5) the corners of the groundplan have been tied tightly to the rest of the plan, thus making the groundplan as a whole seem to hold the stage more solidly and to frame the actors.

2. On the basis of the given circumstances of a study play, each member of the class designs a groundplan. (Be absolutely certain to avoid any directions in the playscript that may prescribe a setting. Find all you need *in the given circumstances buried in the dialogue.*) Now answer the following questions about the groundplan: How many acting areas does it contain? What is tension creating in the plan? How ingenious is it? Now compare your groundplan with those groundplans done by other members of the class. Evaluate the differences carefully. Who has been trite and who original? How many different kinds of furniture has the whole class used?

3. Design groundplans for two or three other plays and measure their effectiveness with the same criteria as in Exercise 1.

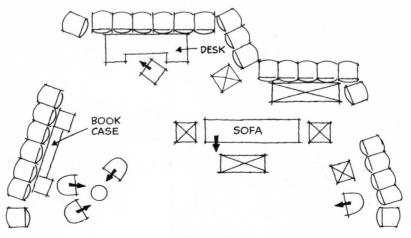

FIGURE 13

4. Set up a groundplan on the classroom floor by using whatever classroom furniture is available, and discuss its effectiveness. After suggestions have been offered, alter the plan to produce a maximum of interest. Repeat this exercise several times, with different students setting up plans and others criticizing their effectiveness and doing the alterations. Work for ingenuity and freshness.

5. Do a group improvisation in one of these plans, using three or four improvisors. What did the plan suggest to the improvisors? What can you as a director suggest to them to help their imaginations find different uses of the plan? Redo the improvisation after discussing the plan and after reviewing the possibilities of dramatic action in the improvisation.

9

composition: discovering and projecting basic relationships

Now that you understand the groundplan as a device for communicating with actors through appropriately occupied space, you are ready to undertake a second level of communication—the utilization of that space. *Composition* is the physical arrangement of actor-characters in a groundplan for the purposes of discovering dramatic action and of illustrating it in the simplest possible way through emphasis and contrast. If actors are made aware of basic physical relationships, they will perceive dramatic action in greater depth.

Because the proscenium wall (the wall that separates the house from the stage) has a frame and the audience sits out front and looks through it, all the basic requirements of perspective drawing apply; that is, we must be able to see depth as well as width and height. The director's job, then, is to help arrange the actors in this three-dimensional cube of the stage in a series of still shots—a full play would require several hundred such still shots—so that an audience can sense and feel basic forces in a play.

Strictly defined, composition does not involve movement (transit of the actor from one point on the stage to another) at all. Composition is static. It is a caught moment. It is a primitive form on which will be superimposed the other elements that make illustration and which we have yet to discuss—gesture, picturization, and movement. Without the primitive, architectural arrangement of composition, actors cannot convey their most basic meaning and feeling about a dramatic action.

Because a play is spoken—an enormously important fact of the theatre —an actor's body must be relatively, if not entirely, quiet during much of a play, or an audience simply cannot hear what the actor says. The animated illustrators—gestures and movement—are so alive and vigorous because of their living and breathing qualities that their meanings are conveyed first (the eye is quicker than the ear); so, they must not be allowed to dominate composition. But at the same time that you must keep the still shot concept of composition in mind, you should understand that a play in performance is made up of a very great many of these shots that are tied together by movements of the actors, which place them on one or another part of the stage. In this sense, a performed play is a continuous alternation of composition, movement, composition, movement.

Back in the nineteenth century when the laws of the proscenium stage were taking form, this rule of alternation was observed quite rigidly, and today we see its holdover in operatic acting, where the singer is directed to sing to the audience in set positions, with business interspersed when convenient. With the passing of nineteenth-century poetic drama and with increased emphasis on visual representation in the twentieth-century theatre, the rule of alternation was modified by allowing actors to move during their own speeches as well as during the speeches of other actors. The easier-to-hear prose dialogue not only made it more feasible to break down the old rule, but it also encouraged the desire for a more completely animated performance. However that modification may be, a large amount of movement is risky when significant speeches are being delivered. Consequently, experienced directors and actors learn to stand still and to *hold composition* at important moments. Movies always appear more animated to us than plays because they seem to be continuously moving, but when you watch the work of a good moving picture director you will see an enormous number of still shots (largely close-ups). We hear a film because we are forced to do so by the director's selection of shots, and by actors who learn *not to move their heads* because they want the greater effectiveness of moving their eyes and lips— a required moving-picture technique. An important principle in acting is learning to hold the body and head still, so that when they do move, they will say something specific.

A composition on the stage is thus a photographic still shot of great value. Once again here is the point: the director must learn the importance of encouraging actors to evolve good compositions because they form the basis of all good illustrations by containing primitive meanings and mood values.

Characteristics of Composition

COMPOSITIONS HAVE BASIC MEANINGS

From the above discussion, you can see that a composition involves *two or more* actors taking specific places on the stage. Try to see composition as made up of bodies without moving arms or legs—neutral forms like manikins—who stand on marked points on the stage floor but have the capability of facing the body in different directions or of bending it to kneeling or sitting positions. This neutrality of the body position is very important if you are to see the meanings that come from compositions alone and are not to confuse them with those that come from gestures and movements.

Now observe the relationships of the two bodies in Fig. 14. The arrows on the heads represent the directions which the bodies are facing. What does each composition mean? Try to guess their meanings before looking at the suggestions below.

Here are some suggestions for each of the five illustrations in Fig. 14:

1. A and B either like one another or are confronting one another in anger.
2. A is playing hard to get, with B the weaker.
3. The situation in (2) is reversed with B playing hard to get.
4. The relationship between A and B is disrupted completely with backs turned to one another.
5. Although A and B face each other, A is now much separated from B, indicating a coolness, though opposition is still present. If you try these same exercises with A *or* B seated, you will see that new meanings emerge. What are they?

Here is the point: All compositions are made of roughly these same juxtapositions. Characters in a play are either together, apart, or conform to some gradation of these two basic situations. Composition thus illustrates for us in the simplest possible way the dramatic action—the conflicts—between two or more characters. Without good composition there is no clear storytelling.

COMPOSITION AS DIRECTOR-ACTOR COMMUNICATION

The communication inherent in composition is now evident. A director can suggest to his actors their basic relationships with other char-

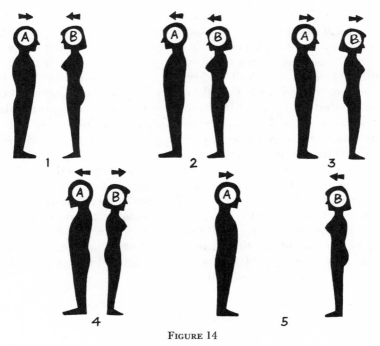

FIGURE 14

acters by merely placing them in stage arrangements: by keeping the actors apart they can sense some level of their separation; by placing them close together they can sense the intensity of their conflict (and love is also conflict). Actors usually accept these hints quickly and are eager to experiment with them.

However, when doing improvisations, young actors, in the interest of developing an action (maintaining improvised dialogue), will forget that composition is a device for illustration. Though the action may be intense in the minds of the improvisors, it will appear to a viewer to be completely internal because it is not illustrated. In other words, the improvisors may understand the action completely, but without employing strong compositional values, they fail to illustrate it (or else they illustrate it very poorly); frequently, they will use the same two or three compositions over and over again. On the other hand, a well-trained actor sees composition as one of his most valuable tools for illustrating his actions, and he will look for every possible variation to keep that illustration as fresh and as varied as possible.

Composition can be used most effectively as a device for communicating with actors when rehearsals are well advanced. It is then that a director can communicate his most subtle points about the action by helping the actors find fresh and meaningful compositions, particularly in accord with the set properties in the groundplan. These properties always play a part in compositions by becoming animated when they are employed by the actors. A director who is afraid to introduce new compositions late in a rehearsal period fails to recognize their values as communicative devices, for good illustration of dramatic action can only be found through constant experiment, and the director must learn to gamble with new compositions in the interest of stimulating in the actors new insights into dramatic action.

Composition is, therefore, not something arranged only for its pictorial value to an audience, but it is a basic device for communicating to actors perceptions about their relationships with other characters. If this arrangement is dynamically effected, even though a composition holds a set place on the stage floor, it will move an audience. There is certainly something pleasurable in the harmonic balance of a stage picture, but that matter is secondary. If the action is illustrated honestly and intensively, its beauty will emerge in all its truth.

Techniques of Composition

The actor, as well as the director, must learn all of the following basic techniques of composition in order to know as many ways as possible of bringing variety to stage illustration. Holding an audience for two to three hours requires much skill in finding variety, especially if only one setting is used.

THE INDIVIDUAL ACTOR

When we talk about composition, we mean the arrangement of two or more actors on the stage. But the director and actor must be fully aware of the compositional force of each individual on the stage before any arrangement of groups can take place. We seldom see actors on the stage alone, and the purpose here is not to discuss that special circumstance but to see the individual isolated in order to assess his potential force in a group arrangement.

Body Positions. Stageright and stageleft are the actor's right and left as he faces an audience. Now face the body to the major points of a circle, and you have the body positions (Fig. 15). Note the designations for these positions: full front; one quarter left, etc.

The force of body positions is very great in any composition, for turning your back on another actor has one meaning, and facing him another,

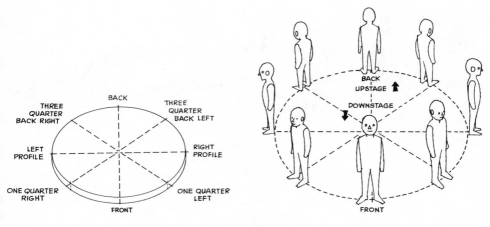

FIGURE 15

as we have already suggested in Fig. 14. Variations between these extremes give us the nuances. Beginning actors either want to face the audience because they don't understand the concept of reciprocation in acting, or they want to face other actors continuously, thus losing the freshness and new ideas brought about by varying the body's position.

EXERCISES

1. Six actors assume different body positions, with the members of the class identifying each. Be absolutely certain that each actor observes the neutral position, that is, arms at the side, head facing the same direction as the body, no facial expression.

2. At a signal from the instructor, each actor takes a different body position, and the class identifies all the different positions. Repeat this exercise many times until the positions are thoroughly learned and can easily be identified in the stage terminology indicated in **Fig. 15**.

3. What is the basic meaning of the full-back position? The full-front? Either profile?

4. Can one actor force another (dramatic action) through his use of body position?

Levels. By levels we mean the actual *head level* of the actor. He is at his highest level when he is standing, and any variation that takes his head toward the floor is a change in level (Fig. 16).

When he uses an artificial level introduced in a set design, such as platforms or steps, his level changes even more drastically (Fig. 17).

FIGURE 16

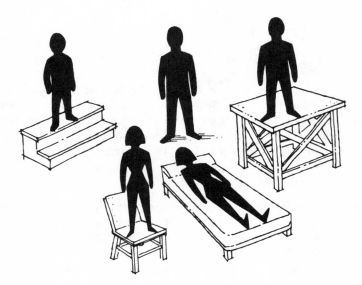

FIGURE 17

EXERCISES

1. Without using any artificial levels, have three actors, observing the rule for the neutral actor as far as possible, assume different body levels. Identify these levels. Now, at the instructor's signal, each actor assumes a new level. Identify and repeat.

2. Repeat Exercise 1 with artificial levels (platforms, chairs, etc.), beginning first with fully erect actors then progressing to variations in body level. Identify and repeat several times. Be sure to observe neutrality as far as possible.

3. What are the meanings of the various levels? Compare the meanings of a standing actor with those of a sitting actor, then with those of a reclining actor. Do you see how each position conveys a general meaning? Keep in mind that until Realism came to the stage in the nineteenth century, actors seldom sat on chairs or other objects but performed plays in standing positions. As was pointed out in Chapter 8, Realism is sometimes defined as sit-down drama in contrast to the stand-up drama before the middle of the nineteenth century.

4. Contrast the meanings conveyed by an actor when he first stands on a high platform and then reclines on the floor. You must suggest the most basic meaning, not the story-telling or pictured meaning, such as making a speech or sleeping, because the actor could be doing a dozen different things in each position. How dominant would he be in the elevated position? How weak would he be in the reclining position?

5. Can one actor force another (dramatic action) through the use of levels?

6. Combine body positions and levels by having three actors work with separate chairs. At the instructor's signal, each actor takes a different body position and different level. Note the variety and contrast that is possible.

Planes. As a concept, stage planes applies only to the proscenium stage, where the term is used as a way of pointing out that the proscenium stage has depth as well as width. When we talk about an actor *moving through the stage planes,* we mean that he moves upstage or downstage. *Up* and *down* are terms which have been used by theatre people for nearly three hundred years to indicate directions because stages were raked; that is, stage floors actually inclined upward toward the rear of the stage, some of them very steeply, as can still be seen in the famous Teatro Farnese, built in 1619 in Parma, Italy, where an actor quite literally walks *up*hill or *down*hill, depending on which way he uses the incline. Although in modern times stage floors are flat so that scenery can be erected with little difficulty at any place on the stage, the old stage terms are still used to specify depth, and therefore the concept of stage planes. To compensate for the loss of the incline, theatre architects have had to incline the audience, sometimes very steeply.

Although planes are purely imaginary in our talk about them, you could see them easily in a physical way if you were to hang several drops on stage battens located two feet apart, and then were to look at them either from overhead or from the side (Fig. 18). Each drop would represent a plane.

Now remove the drops but keep the idea of the positions they occupy by placing actors in each plane (Fig. 19).

A human being is about a foot thick, but we cannot actually see much difference in planes if they are too close together, so we think of each

PERSPECTIVE VIEW
FROM A CORNER OF
THE STAGE

PERSPECTIVE VIEW
FROM THE FRONT, SLIGHTLY
ABOVE THE THEATRE

FIGURES 18 AND 19

plane as being about two feet deep.   And more important, because the audience sits directly facing the stage in a proscenium theatre, objects close to them seem much larger than those farther upstage.   Thus, instead of the representation in Fig. 19 above, we actually see more nearly like this (Fig. 20).

Understanding the concept of planes is valuable to an actor, because then he can think in terms of moving from or toward an audience as well as crossing in front of it.   Most beginning actors and directors think only in terms of the latter and do not see the strong dramatic ideas that can be conveyed by the graduated upstage and downstage positions.

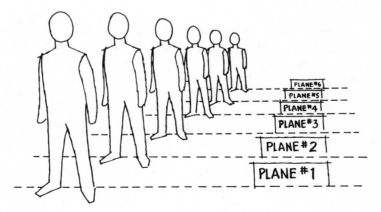

FIGURE 20

EXERCISES

1. If your class is working on a stage, lower some battens and try to see drops hanging on them. Count the number of lines on your stage and note the space between them.

2. Place six actors, all facing full front, in six *successive* planes (two feet apart) in a slanting row upstage. Observe neutrality. Can you see the different planes? Can you see the difference in size? Squinting will help you see better.

3. Now place six actors, all facing full front, in different planes but in various parts of the stage. Observe neutrality. Identify the planes.

4. Place one actor in an extreme upstage plane and another in an extreme downstage plane, both in full-front positions. What is the meaning of each position? Why is the one nearer to you stronger?

Horizontal Locations. Just as planes are the depth designations of stage space, so horizontal locations declare the position of an actor on the width of the stage. Thus, we say *stageright* (SR), *stageleft* (SL), or *centerstage* (CS). We often divide the width into even more precise locations, left center (LC) or right center (RC) as in Fig. 21.

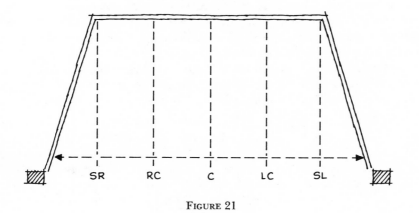

FIGURE 21

This concept of horizontal location implies that the stage has horizontal meaning as well as depth meaning. We also see differences in the actual location simply because in a proscenium theatre, where the audience sits in front, the center can be seen well by everyone. Thus we think the center location strongest, and the two side extremes less strong in the same way that we can see differences in the extremes of upstage and downstage.

EXERCISES

1. Place five actors, facing full front, in the five horizontal locations designated above. Observe neutrality. Identify each position.

2. What meaning does an actor have in the center location? What is the meaning at either the extreme right or extreme left locations?

THE GROUP: CREATING EMPHASIS

Since all compositions are made up of two or more actors, a problem immediately arises over which actor will have the emphasis. If a director looks at a composition purely as a member of an audience, he realizes that he must create that emphasis or the audience cannot follow the dramatic action simply and effortlessly; that is, it will not know easily who is talking or who is strongest in the action. But when he looks at his possibilities for director-actor communication, he knows that his best hope of finding the appropriate emphasis is to convey to his actors *what* he thinks is important in the action and how important it is. Only out of this sort of suggestion will a natural emphasis flow. He thus encourages specific groupings to suggest not only literal meanings to the actors but sublimated ones as well; he is again working on the principle that sensitive and varied compositions will arouse appropriate tensions in the actors, who will then communicate directly and much more sensitively to an audience. An actor who is given a dominant position will certainly exploit it fully in his forcing of other actor-characters.

Emphasis, then, is a basic necessity in good composition. You create it by contrasting the four variables of composition—body positions, levels, planes, and horizontal locations—in the following group arrangements:

Focuses. There are two kinds of focus: (a) *eye* focus, in which one actor looks directly at another actor (Fig. 22); (b) *line* focus, in which one actor turns his body directly toward another actor, and may emphasize it further by pointing with arms, legs, or torso, or all three simultaneously (Fig. 23). Both kinds of focus work on the principle of *imaginary* lines which run from one actor to another; the lines may be only partially suggested, but such is the nature of the imagination that it is able to complete the lines by seeing them in the mind's eye. (Note the dotted lines in Figs. 22, 23, 24.) We frequently use both eye and line focus at the same time (Fig. 24).

EXERCISES

1. Illustrate *eye focus* by placing two actors in contrasting one-quarter positions with eyes straight ahead. Without moving his head, have A turn his eyes on B. What is the effect? Now have A turn his head and look full

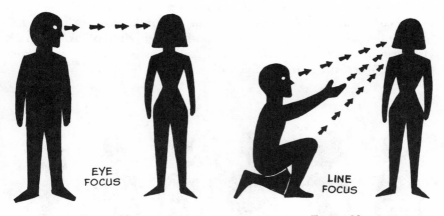

EYE
FOCUS

FIGURE 22

LINE
FOCUS

FIGURE 23

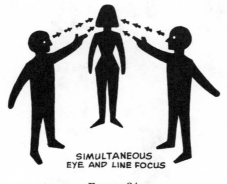

SIMULTANEOUS
EYE AND LINE FOCUS

FIGURE 24

face at B. Is the effect even stronger? Now have him turn his body as well. What is the effect? Repeat this exercise many times in all variations of A and B making contact through eye and head positions. What do the actors feel?

2. Illustrate *line focus* by setting up many compositions like the examples given in Figs. 22, 23, and 24. Place the class at a distance from the compositions so that they can actually see the lines. What do the actors feel? What do the compositions mean? You can actually see the lines in a literal way if you use a piece of cord attached to each actor. A large piece of rubberized material, such as an elastic band, works even better because the tension between the two actors can be literally illustrated.

Diagonals. A composition of two actors may be made with the actors in the same plane. This is a *shared* composition because each actor has equal emphasis (if the level and body positions are similar), as in Fig. 25. However, they will take on different meanings if the planes are contrasted, thus creating an imaginary diagonal line (Fig. 26).

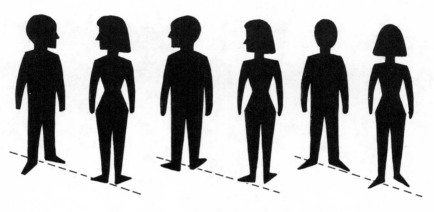

FIGURE 25

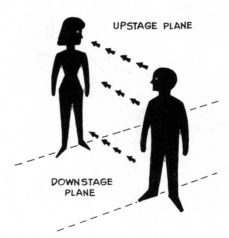

FIGURE 26

The diagonal is more emphatic than a line parallel to the front line of the stage because it moves both horizontally and vertically (upstage) in the imagination of the spectator. Directors learn to employ diagonal composition because of the tension which it readily creates.

EXERCISE

Illustrate the strength of diagonals by showing the contrast they make to those lines parallel to the front line of the stage. What do the actors feel?

Triangles. Compositions of three or more actors are arranged in triangles. It is obvious that if three actors stood in the same plane, they could not easily see one another, for the actor in the center would block the vision of the other two (Fig. 27).

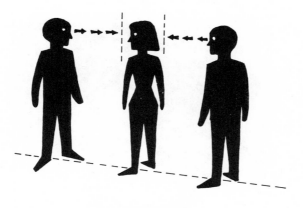

FIGURE 27

In addition, triangles employ diagonals, the dynamic lines on the stage. By varying the four basics of composition (body positions, levels, planes, horizontal locations) at the points of the triangle, a variety of meanings will emerge.

An endless variety of interesting compositions can also be made by varying the triangle in the following ways:

1. Shortening or lengthening of the legs of the triangle (Fig. 28).

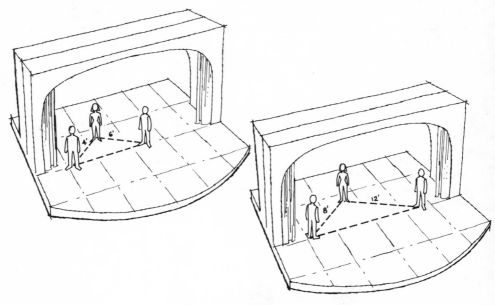

FIGURE 28

2. Increasing or decreasing the angles (Fig. 29).

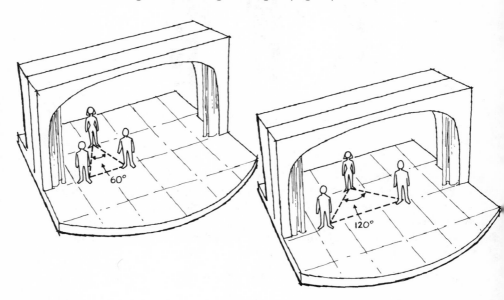

FIGURE 29

3. Changing the total area of the triangle (Fig. 30).

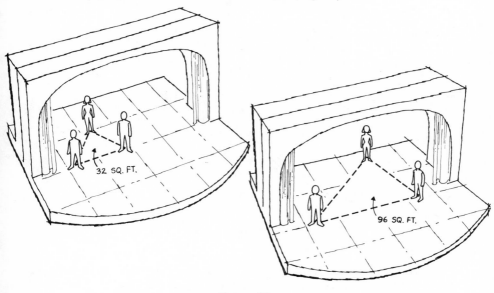

FIGURE 30

4. Changing the position of the base leg from a line horizontal to the front stage line (Fig. 31) to a line that runs diagonally to it (Fig. 32).

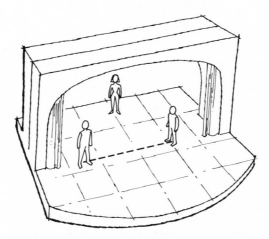

FIGURE 31

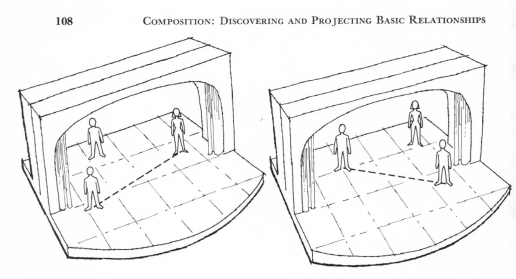

FIGURE 32, A AND B

5. Breaking the legs of triangles when there are more than three actors by inserting actors at points in the legs (Fig. 33).

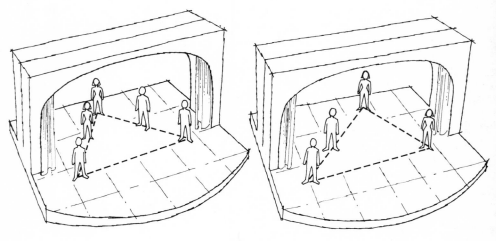

FIGURE 33

You must learn to avoid *flat* triangles (those having little depth), because they can neither be seen by an audience nor can they convey to

actors much sense of relationship character. Make a rule for yourself not to allow triangles less than two or three planes in depth (Fig. 34).

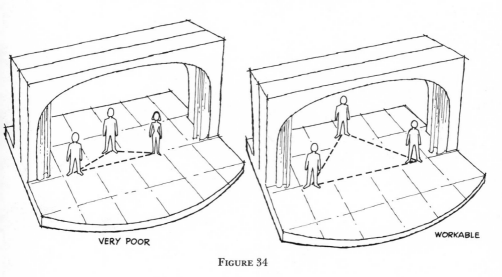

VERY POOR   WORKABLE

FIGURE 34

EXERCISE

Illustrate the use of triangles by setting up all the examples described in this section. Identify the location of the points of the triangles and the length of the lines. Make some flat triangles and illustrate their ineffectiveness in contrast to deep ones. What do the actors feel? Do you see differences in meaning as the triangles change?

Space and Mass. Effective compositions can be made by isolating one actor on one part of the stage and contrasting that isolation with a number of actors on the other side (Fig. 35). The single actor is thus surrounded by space, which gives him emphasis and individuality, and the others make a mass with only identification as a group.

EXERCISE

Do several illustrations of making emphasis through space and mass. Evaluate each of them.

Repetition or Support. When four or more actors are used, the dramatic action frequently places them on two opposing sides. The supporting actors who stand behind the principal actors are thus said to repeat or support the principles, thus giving them emphasis (Fig. 36).

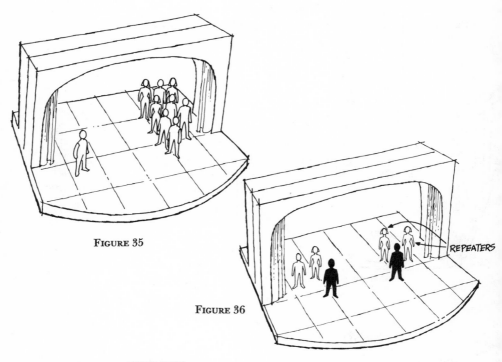

FIGURE 35

FIGURE 36

EXERCISE

Do several illustrations of making emphasis through repetition or support and evaluate each.

Climactic Compositions. As we have previously noted, old compositions give way to new compositions continuously throughout a play because they are the still shots that an audience can easily comprehend simply because it knows who has emphasis and thus who is speaking. These changes consist of variations on the actual distance of separation between actors, which depends on the illustration needed to show the forces between the actors. Thus, two actors may play at the extremes of the stage or very close together, with each composition having explicit meanings. *When they are close together (less than six feet) they are in a climactic composition.*

Climactic compositions should be used for only two actions, including all their variations: (1) extreme love, in which the actors are about to embrace; or (2) extreme hate, in which they are about to fight. Climactic compositions must therefore be saved for the climactic moments of a play. Young directors and actors incline to overuse climactic compositions on the stage as a matter of course because they see them so continuously used in moving pictures and television where bringing two people close together is necessary to get them on camera. But this technique does not work in the theatre where the medium and the long shots predominate. A climactic composition, therefore, has the force of a close-up and must be used sparingly for this purpose or it will have no meaning at all.

PLATE I *Rhinoceros* by Eugène Ionesco

Body positions: Note the different body positions from rightstage to leftstage—full front; full front seated figure; ¼ right; full front; right profile. Why does there seem to be tension in the composition despite the fact that three figures are facing front?

Levels: Three figures are seated; two are standing. Note how the figure at the lowest level attracts attention through his contrast in level with the others.

Planes: Three planes are represented, with the upstage figures occupying planes relatively close together. Note how the downstage figure attracts attention through the sharp contrast in stage planes.

Space: The important element of composition in this illustration is space—the space around the isolated figure. Thus, he has strong attention values because of the space that the others do not have.

PLATE II *Morning's at Seven* by Paul Osborn

Can you identify all the body positions in this composition? What are the different levels used? Four planes are employed. What are they? Can you see the use of foreground, midground, and background planes?

Area: First count the number of acting areas (related places to sit) as defined in the previous chapter on the groundplan. Do not forget the steps since they are formal sitting positions as well as the chair and stumps. How many acting areas of this kind are there? After you have done that, look at the composition from the point of view of the second definition of *area*. Do you see how this composition occupies a full-stage area, whereas Plate I illustrates only a partial area?

Focus: Two kinds of focus are employed in this composition: *eye* focus and *line* focus. Note the strength that the upstage figure adds to the composition simply by looking directly at the two figures near the tree, and though we cannot see the eyes of the rightstage figures, we know where their attention is directed. Should the leftstage figure have been looking at the figures at the tree instead of at the rightstage couple? Now note the line focus created by the two rightstage figures facing ¾ back and also by the woman pointing directly with extended arms to the figures at the tree. Note how the latter point toward each other with gestures and crouching body positions.

Triangulation: Two major triangles are created in this composition: one downstage with the two figures at the tree making the apex, and one upstage with the character at the gate as the apex. But where is the center of attention? Note how the regularity of the triangle is broken up by breaking the lines with additional figures.

It is, therefore, necessary, to think of compositions as a succession of shots that show actors in successive stages of either making contact or breaking it (Fig. 37).

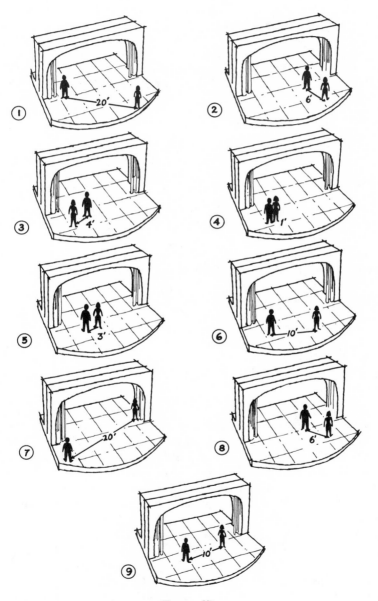

FIGURE 37

EXERCISE

Illustrate climactic compositions by first setting up one, and then by dispersing the actors to extreme positions. What do the actors feel?

Stage Areas. Compositions may occupy (1) the entire stage, (2) the left or right halves of the stage, or (3) a quarter of the stage (Fig. 38).

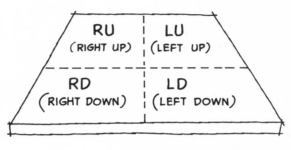

FIGURE 38

Compositions that occupy less space are usually climactic and can be placed in any location on the stage. But since climactic compositions must be used sparingly, the director must learn to use a wide variety of larger compositions placed contrastingly in all the areas (Fig. 39).

EXERCISE

Illustrate stage areas by setting up compositions on (a) the fullstage; (b) a halfstage; (c) a quarterstage. At an instructor's signal, shift the composition to different areas. Evaluate.

Compositions with Furniture. All the above illustrations have assumed a bare stage because the intention was to show the techniques of making good compositions, but the bare stage is, of course, a very exceptional circumstance in Realistic drama. The problem is to see compositions in the midst of furniture (properties) placement. If a workable groundplan has been devised, compositions will fall naturally into it, for actors will feel relationships on the basis of where they can sit or stand. Groundplan designing thus always gives prime consideration to how composition can be exploited by the actors and the director.

One important aspect is how furniture pieces *participate* with actors in compositions. Without actors, they are dead objects, but when actors move around them and use them, they take on an animation resembling that of silent actors. Triangles in all their variations can be made in this

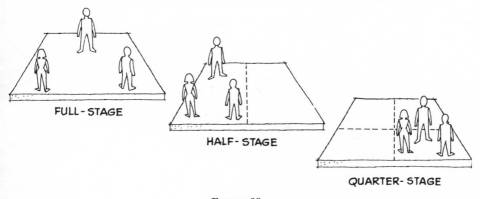

FULL-STAGE

HALF-STAGE

QUARTER-STAGE

FIGURE 39

way, with two actors and a piece of furniture as the third point. Again, if you and the actors think of a groundplan as an obstacle course, good compositions will mature of themselves, for using the stage composition-ally is *not* clearing the space for the actors to move in front of the furni-ture pieces, but is allowing the pieces to interrupt space (obstacle-course concept) and, thus, to interrupt an actor's goal to reach and touch another actor (Fig. 40).

An obstacle course will automatically defeat the desire of actors to make climactic compositions, which then can be saved for the appropriate mo-ments. An actor moves *in* a groundplan not in front of it, for the basic concept declares that the only space available is that space falling be-tween objects. Consequently, the more objects there are in a ground-plan, the more difficult it will be for one actor to reach another. There-fore, if your groundplan is skillfully devised, you can suggest to actors compositions that will impede them, that is, will keep them from reach-ing one another easily, with the result that they will unknowingly inten-sify the illustrations of their dramatic actions.

Composition as Actor Communication versus Pictorial Communication

You may be surprised if you compare the limited treatment of com-position in this book with the rather extensive development in other text-books on directing. This limitation is intentional because the concept of composition laid out here is director-actor communication and not pictorial design. This concept presupposes that the only aspect of thea-tre which really matters is to move an audience through dramatic action

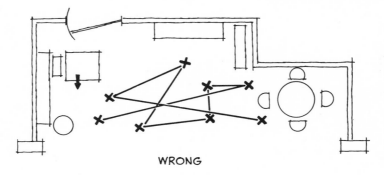

WRONG

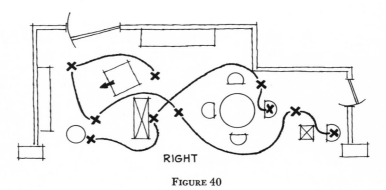

RIGHT

FIGURE 40

and characters, and therefore that the principal function of directing is to arouse actors to assume the positions that will be most effective in communicating appropriate imagery to an audience. Furthermore, although it would be possible to delineate more rules of pictorial design, it is assumed that the young director can neither absorb them nor can use them at this point.

However, as you grow more experienced, you will develop your own sense of the pictorial, or, like some recent directors, you may regard the pictorial as superficial and relatively nonessential in conveying the meanings of some plays. But you must not abandon the pictorial altogether, for you must recognize that you have failed in your job if a play does not finally communicate to an audience, and the pictorial can definitely help. The more you know about composition as the liaison between actor and audience, the better you will be able to communicate. Therefore, practice composition diligently from every point of view, for good direction is also good picture-making.

Summary Exercises for all Aspects of Composition

1. Coordinate all the exercises inserted throughout this chapter by setting up a groundplan (with furniture pieces) on the classroom floor and by arranging compositions within it. Use three actors who change locations, thus making new compositions, when the instructor gives the signal by clapping his hands. Other students should identify all the elements in each composition, and then evaluate the effectiveness of the elements in the groundplan.

2. Each student should compose at least three different groundplans, and then set up multiple compositions on each. Intensive practice in this problem will prepare the director for all that is to follow, for without a basic understanding of the techniques and the uses of composition, he will not be able to bring about truthful illustrations in a play.

PLATE III   *Outward Bound* by Sutton Vane

Try to identify all of the elements of composition in this picture that you have studied thus far: body positions; levels; planes; areas; eye focus; line focus. What do you note about the groundplan: How many acting areas are there? Is it a good obstacle course? How would the downstage corners of the setting be used?

Triangulation: What are the characteristics of the large triangle? Note the length of the legs, the size of the angle at the upstage apex, the relationship of the base line to the proscenium line. Note how each of the legs is interrupted by figures.

What are the possibilities for different uses of level in this ground-plan? How could the figure downstage right attract attention? If he were to cross to the center chair and sit, what would the other figures do to throw focus on him?

IO

helping the actors intensify: gesture, improvisation with properties, and picturization

Gesture, improvisation with properties, and picturization as tools of director-actor communication all perform similar functions in organic blocking because they help actors to discover the subtleties of dramatic action and to build character illustration with imagination and sensitivity. The two previous chapters have shown how the groundplan and composition can lead actors into discoveries about given circumstances and relationships in dramatic action, and thus to basic image making. This chapter will show how the director can lead actors into making highly detailed and refined visual illustrations.

Gesture

Here are two dictionary meanings for *gesture:*

> The use of motions of the limbs or body as a means of expression.
> A movement usually of the body or limbs that expresses or emphasizes an idea, sentiment, or attitude.

Note that these definitions suggest three things: (1) that the body is set in one location; in other words, that gesture is *not* movement, which takes the body from one point to another on the stage; (2) that gesture is the animation of all the moveable parts of the body; (3) that gesture is capable of expressing ideas, sentiments, or attitudes. Now go one step beyond these definitions by thinking of this activity as taking place in the body's sphere—the sphere that stretches from tiptoe to the fullest extension of the arms in all directions. Here are some illustrations of what we mean (Fig. 41).

FIGURE 41

From these drawings, you readily see that gesture is as extensive as an actor's imagination will make it. Think of gesture as moving outward from the center of the body's sphere and occupying whatever space an actor wishes to give it, frequently only part of the space as in the figure on the far right. Gesture can thus be as large or as small, as free or as restricted, as an actor desires in expressing character.

In contrast to composition, which is architectural and abstract and always expressed in terms of the neutral body, gesture is the living quality of the body—the body's animation. Although it may seem that certain ethnic groups, such as the Italians and the French, speak with more gestures than others, all human beings employ gestures in very great numbers. Shakespeare's line, "the hand is instrument to the mouth," is the very essence of gesture, for we always use the hand in the hope of amplifying the meanings of the language we use, or, in the words of one definition quoted above, "to emphasize an idea, sentiment, or attitude." Words are one kind of symbolic expression, and gestures are another, with each having specific uses in conveying ideas.

Gesture is, therefore, a prime means of actor communication. The suppression or the controlling of gesture is what we usually designate as poise, the body behavior we usually associate with refinement and cultivation; for we tend to designate levels of cultivation by the amount of gestures employed, with the inference that the more a man can suppress his gestures, the closer he is to being dominated by his mind. Thus, in plays and movies we are apt to see lower-class characters illustrated with many gestures and upper-class characters with relatively few, that is, until they lose control of themselves and revert to the animalism that hovers in all men.

Gesture can convey ideas simply and clearly, as is illustrated in its use by the deaf and dumb, who not only talk with their hands and fingers but also indicate attitudes with their whole bodies. Watch them closely and you will see how really animated they are in their own type of conversation, much more so than people with normal hearing. As an animated tool of illustration, gesture can thus rephrase and intensify the crude meanings of composition into highly refined and subtle ones. But the actor must learn some very important lessons early in his training, principally that indiscriminate use of gestures will convey very little meaning, that he must be highly selective, and that he must, above all, start from the neutral position of basic composition.

GESTURE IN DIRECTOR-ACTOR COMMUNICATION

So subjective is gesture that it is primarily an actor's, and not a director's, tool for communication. Yet the director who is unaware of its force does not know how to reduce or increase its use. An actor who does not stand still or hold his head still usually cannot be heard or is heard poorly. *The eye is quicker than the ear* very aptly applies. The director must also know how to strip an actor of gestures and to help him build new gestures that will reveal the character he is playing, not just himself as an actor (what we call actor mannerisms) or the gestures belonging to another character. Certain gestures, as well as their size or the state of their control, can also be suggested by the director and thus can become subtle ways of communicating dramatic action from the director to the actor. An actor, in learning to characterize, will discover that the appropriate use of gesture—always within the range of his character and always economically—is the subtle visual delineation of character states and feelings.

DECORUM

As was suggested above, an actor can declare some aspects of a character by the gestures he uses—gestures that can indicate not only a character's inner feeling but also his outer position in life—his position in society. *Decorum* means specifically the outward show of a character—an appropriate reflection of the given circumstances in a play. A king moves like a king because he leads a life of ceremony and is as much symbol as person. Likewise, a ditchdigger moves like a man who uses his body continuously in physical labor. Decorum is simple symbology for what we expect from these occupations, but they are nevertheless prototypes. In real life, we see such decorums often enough to expect them, but the rules of decorum do not always hold, a fact which encourages actors to look for the exceptions that can be carried over to the stage as fresh observations.

Because decorum is the outward show of a character, a director and an actor must search for the appropriate decorum for a character. Without this, the outward show will lie about his given circumstances, and the audience will be left in confusion about what to expect. Occasionally, directors exploit this confusion, with the full intention of misleading an audience into fresh thinking about a character.

So much pressure is placed in actor training on developing the inside core of character—that is, of insuring full comprehension of the dramatic action—that actors frequently give little attention to the force of the exterior look of a character. In contrast, fine professional actors always find the appropriate decorum of a character in order to convey given circumstances quickly to an audience, just as a designer does with his stage scenery. By imaginative suggestion to an actor about a character's decorum, a director can arouse fresh ideas about interior action, because the actor can see more clearly the contrast and conflict between the outer and inner selves of a character. He can also encourage an actor's sense of physical illustration and thus be able to convey many more specific and appropriate images to an audience.

EXERCISES

1. Have one actor demonstrate the sphere concept of gesture by assuming different positions that will occupy the full sphere. Compare and contrast formal dance (full use of the sphere) with acting by illustrating the use of gesture in both forms and showing how they differ.

2. Repeat Exercise 1 by using several actors who change positions at the instructor's signal. Try to keep the positions within the boundaries of everyday human behavior. These illustrations will show not only the full opportunity an actor has in occupying the limits of the sphere but also how his movements *stretch* outward from the center point of the body.

3. Do a series of huddled gestures to show how head, arms, and legs can also be drawn inward toward the body.

4. Have one actor sit on a chair in front of the class. At the instructor's signal, he changes his gestures to convey different inner feelings (dramatic action). Identify the meaning of each. How do the gestures help his face? Repeat with three actors, unrelated to each other.

5. Place two actors in a composition in a groundplan and encourage them to add gestures after telling them, out of the class's hearing, of their rela-

tionship to each other (dramatic action). Have the class describe the gestures and their meanings.

6. Have two actors illustrate decorum by sitting or standing in their spheres after you have suggested (only to the actors) different occupations (an aspect of given circumstances) to each one. Do not let them move from one place to another on the floor, but encourage them to take within their spheres any positions that they like. Have the class identify the occupations they suggest. Can other aspects of decorum be recognized?

7. Do Exercise 6 in the opposite direction by suggesting a decorum to an actor and letting him improvise dramatic action through that decorum. Repeat extensively with other actors.

Improvisation with Properties

HAND PROPERTIES

Definition. Hand properties—any objects that can be held in the hand and easily manipulated—are extensions of gesture because they increase the variety of possible illustrations with the arms and hands and, frequently, with the legs and head. Because the director can suggest the use of specific hand properties and how to use them, he can make them specific tools of director-actor communication.

Concept. Although a hand property has inherent meaning—that is, an umbrella is something to ward off rain or sun; a book is something to read; a cigar is something to smoke; or a cup is something to drink from —most of the hand properties used on the stage should be employed for reasons other than what their literal functions intend. Only occasionally do we draw an audience's attention to a hand property in its functional use, that is, cutting with a knife, shooting with a gun, or wielding a weapon of any sort, although many plays employ one or two such properties. Nor are hand properties merely used to provide the obvious exterior reality of everyday life in the interest of saying, "this is the environment," and "these are the things people use in it." Hand properties, however, do serve useful design functions by reminding us where we are; but, by and large, audiences should notice them only peripherally and should not be made to concentrate on them, except in unusual circumstances, when attention is obviously drawn to them. Hand properties have many more values than their functional qualities.

The principal use of hand properties is to help actors talk, for they can: (1) extend the length of the arm (with a pointer); (2) increase the size of the hand (with a book); (3) make·the hands and fingers active (with a cigarette); (4) produce sound (by closing a book); (5) show nervousness (with a handkerchief), etc. Everything an actor touches, if he uses it properly, can convey a sensory impression simply because an audience can actually feel the way the actor touches it and can empathize with him.

The primary purpose of a hand property, then, is not its functional use but its potential for pointing dramatic ideas—the subtle aspects of characterization. In one sense, properties provide an additional pair of eyes for the actor. Because an audience varies in its actual distance from the stage, with a large number who cannot actually see the detailed eye movements of the actors, the skillful use of hand properties by the actor can actually tell the audience farthest away what his eyes are doing, so closely is such amplified gesture allied with inner feeling. The moving picture with its close-ups has no such problem, but the stage must rely on other significant illustrative tools to augment the eyes, particularly with Realistic drama, and hand properties are one of the most important of these tools.

Characteristics of Hand Properties. Along with actors, directors should be highly aware of the qualities and characteristics of hand properties. It is *how* an actor uses a property that will convey idea, and the *how* can be exploited only if the property is completely understood. As a director, you must develop a keen imagination with properties if you are to learn how to exploit them fully. Make a habit of looking carefully at a property. What are its peculiar and individual characteristics? If it is smooth, can it be rubbed against the face? What are its "sound" characteristics (does it snap, pop, etc.?), and how can they be exploited? Will its weight cause it to do certain things in the hands of an actor? Can it be stretched or rubbed against other materials? Can it be torn or pulled apart? All questions of this sort open up the imaginative, fresh use of properties. The trite use of a property by an actor implies that he does not actually *see* and *feel* the property, does not actually know its nature and its possibilities.

As you can see, then, all of the questions above are pursuing the same point: How can a hand property be used effectively by an actor to illustrate dramatic action in a fresh, active, and sensitive way. *To reveal a character's state of mind is the purpose, not to show the property itself.* The audience's attention must be on the feelings of the character, and it must not even be conscious of the object as an object, except in those rare instances when an object becomes momentarily the dramatic action itself —for example, when a gun does the forcing when a character is no longer able to rely on his own weapons of speech or body.

For these reasons, you can see that such an action as eating is not intended to improve the health of the character in front of the audience or to give a reason for sitting at a dining table, but, instead, to give to the actor some hand and mouth tools for illustration. A book in an actor's hands might possibly be read to show the audience that the character is improving his mind, or that he is the intellectual sort, but usually it is used to illustrate nervousness, to emphasize a point by banging the book closed or by banging it on a table, or to show preoccupation and interior disturbance. Hand properties, when appropriately used, possess the inherent capability of revealing detailed psychological states in characters in line with the structural core of modern prose drama; they have distinctive capacities for revealing subtext.

Improvisations with Hand Properties. The word *improvisation* is used here to denote what the actor and director must do in order to find the best illustrations. Only through constant experimentation, can a property be fully exploited or another property substituted to make the necessary revelations. Actors should always work with real hand properties just as soon as their hands are free from carrying scripts, because properties will suggest buried dramatic action to the actor, as well as tell him how to show what he already understands. Only when the use of a property has been fully exploited in rehearsal does it become a set piece of business in the old sense. Even if a playwright requires specific use of a hand property, the actor must work with it improvisationally to exploit its highest potential. The old idea of set pieces of business, handed down through tradition—a procedure still prevalent in operatic acting—is irreconcilable with modern training in acting, in which each actor must first decide whether a property is needed to illustrate a dramatic action, and then must discover for himself how *he* can best make it meaningful.

EXERCISES

1. What is the difference between hand properties and set properties? Look ahead at the definition at the beginning of the following section if you do not know. This distinction is an important one.

2. Have the class look at one hand property placed on a table for five to ten seconds. Remove the property and have each student then write a complete description—exactly what it looks like: its size, shape, weight, color, etc. Compare results. Repeat several times.

3. Repeat Exercise 2, except for the description. In its place, define the characteristics of the property—what its special nature is; what its peculiar characteristics are.

4. Repeat Exercise 3, and add to it all your suggestions of how it could be employed to illustrate dramatic action.

5. Place a dozen chairs evenly distributed in a fifteen-foot circle facing away from the center. Now have a dozen students stand facing center on the

inner side of the chairs. At a signal, each student places a hand property (something personal) on the chair behind him, being careful not to look at objects placed by other students. At the instructor's signal, the students start revolving their circle, always facing center. At the instructor's signal, they all stop, and one student is designated to pick up the property behind him and to describe its characteristics to the group. Repeat several times.

6. Now repeat Exercise 5 in a spontaneous improvisation. The student who picks up the object examines it for a few seconds, then, employing the object as illustration, selects another student in the circle and does a dramatic action with the other student. The class then evaluates the use of the object. Was it used too literally or with imagination? Did the student really find the peculiar characteristics of the object? Repeat several times.

7. Have each member of the class do improvisations, each with a different hand property. The intention is *not to point the property* but to use it as a means of revealing dramatic action. (Example: The improvisor enters a store to buy a hat. A hat becomes a mere illustration for an intensive conflict with the saleswoman or manager.) This exercise is invaluable in pinning down the difference between pointing at objects and using their qualities for illustration. Therefore, it should be repeated several times to reinforce the concept.

SET PROPERTIES

Definition. Set properties are those large items, usually pieces of furniture, permanently placed in a groundplan. They are specific tools of director-actor communication because they can amplify and intensify the meanings of compositions and picturizations by participating directly in their design. On occasion, such as in moving a chair, they can become hand properties.

Concept. In Chapter 9 on composition, it was emphasized that pieces of furniture not only become animate when they are used by actors but they also participate directly in compositions because of their space-occupying characteristics. You will also remember that the groundplan has been referred to several times as an obstacle course that must be run by actors in illustrating a Realistic play. Again, you must be fully aware of the dramatic, storytelling strength of this use because, you must learn to exploit set properties in this way.

Tie into the furniture, which you may have heard experienced directors say to actors, merely tells them that their composition will be stronger if they stand near or touch a piece of furniture. It has significant validity as a director's suggestion, because furniture pieces not only give mass to the actor by extending his stage values, but they also help him discover subtleties in the dramatic action. Members of an audience will take for granted that an actor sits on a chair or sofa, but a great deal more is being done for them than they imagine. If the specific piece of furniture on which an actor sits is well selected, it will help tell the actor what to do and how to do it, just as hand properties do. Even more important is what a well-selected piece of furniture can do to encourage sensitive reciprocation between two actors. A suggestion given to one actor to use a chair in a certain way may immediately arouse ideas for adjustment in the other actor—adjustment that can set off a chain of physical illustrations around the set piece, which will communicate strong feelings to a watcher.

Variety in using pieces of furniture is a necessity if the illustrations are to be fresh and alive. Sitting on the backs of sofas or on tables is, of course, valid if the given circumstances permit characters such behavior, but chairs and sofas can be used in dozens of ways without employing exceptional uses. As with hand properties, the director must be fully aware of the characteristics of the set properties he introduces for actor use if he is to exploit them. Fresh uses of beds, desks, stools, cabinets, etc., all lie within an actor's imagination, and the director can set them free with perceptive suggestions.

EXERCISES

1. Have three class members "play" on and around chairs without moving them, each actor doing something different with his chair at the instructor's signals.

2. Try the same exercise with a table and a chair. Each actor should continue to work independently.

3. With one student as the leader, have the class improvise a usable groundplan. Criticize and revise the plan to get as much ingenuity into it as possible. Now have two actors use the groundplan, changing locations on signals from the instructor. Have the class judge the freshness of their uses of the set properties.

4. Repeat Exercise 3 several times, each time trying to find ingenious uses of furniture pieces. Have students, acting as directors, suggest specific uses to the actors.

5. Have two actors improvise a dramatic action around and on a chair. Warn them that they must not point the functional use of the chair but must employ it only in finding contact with one another. Let the chair tell them what to do. Repeat the exercise with a table, with a sofa, etc.

6. Combine the use of hand properties and set properties in the same improvisation as outlined in Exercise 5.

Picturization: Group Intensification

DEFINITION

Picturization is detailed storytelling brought about by the use of composition (the arrangement of the group) combined with gesture (the individual moving within his own sphere) and, very frequently, improvisation with properties (objects added to composition and gesture) for the specific purpose of animating the dramatic action. Note that although gesture pertains only to the individual, picturization concerns a group of actors in which each actor uses the gestures appropriate to his own character. Picturization, then, is a still picture containing detailed storytelling illustrations brought about by individualizing and personalizing composition through the use of gestures and properties.

CONCEPT

Picturizations are what we actually see in the performance of a play, as we see them in real life when two or more people are involved in a close physical relationship. Again, you must remember that a staged scene of a play is composed of a succession of still shots, with a new composition born every time the physical relationships of the basic elements are changed. We use the term *picturization* in order to say that we have added the storytelling details of gesture to composition; but remember that composition is an abstraction because we never actually see it in its clear form, except in exercises; nor do we see gesture stopped and held as in a tableau. In actual practice, when we set up compositions we wipe gestures from our eyes in order to see whether we have established a good composition, then we put them back in our eyes to see if we are making a good picturization. Can you see the logic of this reverse order?

Picturization means that each actor in a group is presenting the dramatic action of his character in the decorum of that character. The aim is to create the *appropriate psychological relationship* between characters, and out of this relationship emerges the strong feelings to which an audience reacts. Remember, only when a group of actors plays the action intensively, will feelings emerge. Picturizations are thus the projections of group feelings. So the actors must find the proper character-mood-intensities for the picture in order for it to project the desired emotional truth. And remember also that picturizations are *visual* illustrations—only part of the full illustration that involves speech as well as movement.

TECHNIQUES

Good picturizations involve expert use of a well-conceived ground-plan because the obstacles in such a plan will suggest all sorts of picturization ideas to actors. Thus, the groundplan is again a primitive means of communication. As understanding of the action grows, actors will physicalize much more intensively and in greater and greater detail. If the basic composition is right, fresh ideas about gesture—the individual

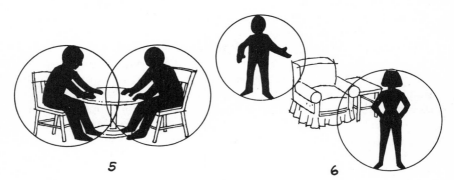

FIGURE 42

in the sphere—will emerge, and along with it, the improvisational use of properties, and thus picturization will grow.

Here are some specific suggestions:

1. Encourage picturization over and around obstacles (Fig. 42).
   Remember: *Obstacles prevent climactic compositions and thus intensify conflict.* They also help to emphasize actors by taking on animate qualities in compositions.
2. Encourage space separations between characters, and the use of different planes, levels, and body positions (Figs. 43 and 44).

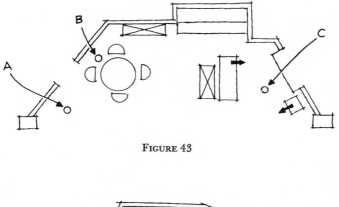

FIGURE 43

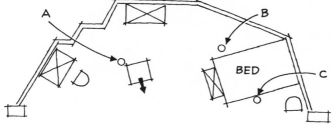

FIGURE 44

3. Look for intimate climactic picturizations (Fig. 45), and encourage actors to touch one another.
4. Look for the appropriate character-mood-intensities of the different characters. This procedure will declare the tension levels in the pictures by encouraging the actors to find illustrations at the levels of their nervosity in the scene. All pictures will contain character-mood-intensities of some sort, but the major problem is

FIGURE 45

finding the *appropriate* intensities so that the illustrations will tell the truth. Here gestures play an important part in picturization values.

5. Exploit gesture in every possible way by encouraging actors to vary their illustrations within their spheres by taking them, on occasion, to the full limits and withdrawing them to the opposite extreme.

6. Encourage the continuous use of triangles in setting up compositions, but vary them in as many interesting ways as possible. There is nothing so dull in picture-making as the repetitious use of triangles of the same size and shape. Remember that a good composition must be at the base of every good picture, so make your composition first; then add details.

7. Encourage the use of hand properties because they have high picture-making potential in forcing body positions, levels, etc.

8. When you have exhausted all the director-actor communication possibilities for making good pictures by insuring that the actors understand every detail of the action, you can turn to the secondary functions of picturization, which include:

   a. Balancing the stage. Remember that your picture on the proscenium stage is in a frame, and it is possible for you to make a visually beautiful picture if you follow some of the rules of good perspective painting. Picturizations thus have pictorial values that can give pleasure to an audience whether it is conscious of them or not. Study the groupings in Medieval and Renaissance paintings to see how the masters made exciting picturizations.

   b. Exploiting the stage cube. Remember that you are composing pictures in a cube and not on the floor of the stage. Thus you can find many unusual storytelling pictures through the use of high levels such as stairways, balconies, etc. Learn to exploit the contrasts in levels to the full.

PLATE IV   *The Shewing Up of Blanco Posnet* by Bernard Shaw

Identify the body positions and levels of the actors in this composition. Note specifically the different planes. What function do the actors in the background serve?

Furniture: Can you see how the table helps to tie this composition together? Do you feel its animate qualities from the way the actors are using it? The table is an obstacle that keeps the actors apart during a moment of high tension, thus preventing a climactic composition. Note how the Sheriff in the midground leans on his table. Does he increase the tension of the composition?

Triangulation: The three principal figures form a triangle. What is its size? Which is the base line? Who has the center of attention? What does eye focus have to do with forcing that attention? Do you see line focus in the triangle?

Properties: How would the properties in this illustration be used? What can the character with the Bible do with that property in addition to what he is presently doing?

Picturization: What story does this composition tell? Has "group intensification" really taken place? Pick out all the points that make this picturization effective.

PLATE V   *Fuente Ovejuna* by Lope de Vega

Who has the center of attention in this composition? Note the strength of eye focus. How is line focus employed?

Furniture: Note how the forms (set properties) help to shape the composition.

Repetition: Do the spear carriers repeat the central standing figure? How do they reinforce him?

Picturization: What story does the composition tell? Are the attitudes of the four principal standing figures the same, or does each have a slightly different variation of the principal action?

What can be done to strengthen the picturization? The rightstage character at the left is as important as the kneeling figure. How can you improve his strength and increase his dominance?

    c. Exploiting the extremes of the stage floor. This means using the full depth of your groundplan by encouraging actors to play the upstage and downstage extremes and by using the full horizontal width through an insistence on far-right and far-left positions. If you play the extremes, you will have the other places to go to; if you cannot, your pictures will seem cramped and underillustrated.

PLATE VI   *Saint Joan* by Bernard Shaw

Identify body positions, levels, planes, eye focus, line focus.

How does the furniture assist the actors?

Picturization: What is the psychological drama being played out in this picture? Is there tension in it? What function do the priests in the background serve? Do you see foreground, midground, and background in the composition? Does Joan have the center of attention? Why?

EXERCISES

1. Arrive at a picturization by (1) starting with composition, (2) adding gesture, (3) then adding picturization. Improvise the following:

   a. A group of three actors decides on a given circumstance and an action.

   b. It sets up a composition, being extremely careful to keep the neutrality of composition.

   c. It now moves the composition to a previously set-up groundplan and uses one of the furniture pieces as an obstacle.

   d. Each actor in turn adds gesture to his part of the composition by experimenting until he finds fresh gesture, and then holding it in tableau.

   e. At least one actor, possibly two, works with a hand property.

    f. When the actors have added gestures and hand properties, they adjust to one another (in terms of the dramatic action) and form the picturization.

    g. The class now identifies the picturization as accurately as possible. What story does it tell? What is its emotional level? The class also comments on the various stages of the exercise.

    h. Repeat this abstract exercise (abstract because it isolates the stages in forming a picturization in a mechanical way) several times, because it will make clear all the stages that lead to good picturization.

2. Improvise picturizations that involve furniture pieces and hand properties with two or three actors. Set up three teams of actors, using the same furniture piece and hand properties, and then change pictures at the instructor's signal. Note how each group will do something different. Have the actors work for as fresh an expression as possible.

3. Improvise picturizations with three or four actors in a preset ground-plan. Shift pictures at the instructor's signal, with the class closing its eyes so that it will not see the movement from one location on the stage to another. Repeat in other groundplans.

11

the dynamic tool
of movement and a synthesis
of all the visual tools

Up to this point in our discussion of the visual tools in director-actor communication, we have been concerned with how the director can help actors penetrate the subtext of a play through suggestions that have been, with the exception of gesture, primarily of a static nature. The intention in this chapter is, first, to reveal the dynamics of movement as the most powerful of all the tools in organic blocking, and then to wind up our discussion by showing how it combines with all the other tools to make a synthesis of stage illustration of given circumstances, dramatic action, characters, tempos, and moods.

Movement

DEFINITION

Movement is the actual transit of an actor from one point on the stage to another. It includes gesture in that the body sphere is always animate during the process of movement, but it is a separate tool from gesture in that the actual distance traveled, the route of travel, and the speed of travel all declare specific values, in themselves distinct from gesture.

CONCEPT

Think of movement as continuous lines on the floor of the stage between points (Fig. 46).

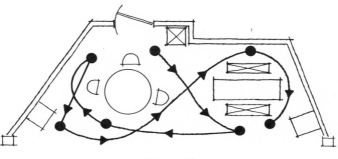

FIGURE 46

When a point is reached, an actor stands still and we have a composition. Movement thus takes place *between* compositions. In order to see movement on the stage, that is, in order to see its meaning, the distance *traveled must be five feet or more,* for anything less will look like gesture (the body in the sphere). Movement is, therefore, climactic in that all the other tools—groundplan, composition, gesture, picturization—must be operating before movement can take place, and since it is climactic, it is the most overtly powerful of all the tools of director-actor communication. Because it is large, because it is continuous, because gesture animates it, movement can convey illustrations to an audience quickly and with force. An actor walking conveys a very different idea from an actor running or sauntering; and walking toward an actor means something very different from walking away from him. Movement, therefore, has tempo values: it takes place in time.

THE DIRECTOR AS CHOREOGRAPHER

In a most restricted sense, a play performed on stage looks like a dance, for it is a dance that starts and stops, starts and stops—movement, composition, movement, composition, etc., with gesture working continuously. Thus, a director tries to find the appropriate dancelike movements to punctuate the *still shots.* If he and the actors find them, their production will have the appropriate animation—the rhythms—inherent in the playscript.

In the movies we see many close-ups that punctuate the long or medium shots—shots that usually contain movement, either that of actors in transit as we have defined movement here, or that of the camera moving. But on the stage, compositions act as close-ups and movement as the long and medium shots. Yet a playgoer always sees both at relatively the same distance from his eye, whereas movies can vary the size of images greatly. In this comparison, the stage is enormously limited—a limitation that can be overcome in part only by intensively articulate and highly selected movement—movement that is potent with meaning and idea. Because of its dynamics, then, all movement must be inherently motivated directly out of the dramatic action; *it cannot be laid on but must be generated from within.* For this reason, some directors prefer to have the actors improvise their own movement, because it can flow freely from their inherent comprehension of the action. But this approach also has limitations because actors often prefer gesture for illustration rather than movement for illustration. The director must, therefore, learn to communicate to actors with suggestions for movements.

KINDS OF MOVEMENT

Although all movement must be motivated by the dramatic action, it is convenient to note what seem to be different kinds of movement in order to see the full range of this valuable tool.

Playwright's Movement. This kind of movement is formally prescribed by the playwright, by what he considers the basic playscript requirements. They include all entrances and exits, as well as those movements to locations on the stage prescribed by the author as necessary for the completion of certain business absolutely requiring that location by the dramatic action. Thus, if an actor must climb a scaffold to man a machine gun mounted thereon because the playwright has located his action there, an actor is performing *playwright's movement.* If actors are required to dance, to play a game that requires movement, to participate in a military parade, to fight a duel, to crawl around on hands and knees looking for dropped jewels because a character has instructed them to do so, they are performing playwright's movement. As you may note, these movements are quite arbitrary in their demands. However, except for exits and entrances, most playwrights prescribe a minimum of this kind of movement.

Technical Requirements. The choreographing of a play is not entirely free improvisation but is partly mechanical, for two hours of staging a play, often in one location (one setting), creates an immense traffic problem. How to get actors on and off the stage quickly and efficiently, particularly if there are many characters, and how to bring about the performance of business in appropriate areas of the stage are of utmost importance to the director. Thus, parts of playscripts must be blocked by directors, either in their minds or on paper, to be certain that they are exploiting their groundplans in the most imaginative ways.

A director will, therefore, occasionally require an actor to move arbitrarily from one location to another, and only then look for the motivation to support it—motivation which can always be found if the actor is imaginative enough. The actual placement of a piece of business may be extremely important to the revelation of character, which of course requires detailed treatment; so, the director arbitrarily locates the scene for his actors as a beginning core for the later illustration. Actors may thus be required (1) to cross the stage at a certain time; (2) to uncover from behind other actors who may stand in front of them; (3) to close in or spread out as the business requires; etc. This manipulation is always essential when several actors are involved. The intention is arbitrary arrangement that can be made to look like spontaneous improvisation. In arranging group scenes, a director may want to distribute the actors in a particular way to show balance or imbalance, and the movements by which they reach their assigned points, though otherwise motivated, are probably technical movements. *Probably* is used here because actors can frequently reach assigned positions through primary dramatic action. The skillful director will use technical movement only as a last resort when the use of primary dramatic action simply will not solve the traffic problems.

Movement Derived from Dramatic Action. Ninety-five percent of all movement in staging a play is derived directly from the dramatic action —what the subtext tells the actors and the director to do. Actors who know their trade will move spontaneously out of their feeling for the moments in a play, and the director's job becomes that of suggesting more or less movement, in actual quantity, more selective movement, more or less speed on certain movements, and often the specific destination of these movements in order to indicate to the actors the next important composition. Beginning actors, on the other hand, are movement bound; that is, they will not move unless required by the director to do so, because they have not yet learned the illustrative values of movement. In handling such actors, directors often suggest much of the movement that will eventually be absorbed into the performance; but this procedure, because it is arbitrary, definitely impedes the actors' imaginations; though, if it is used skillfully, it can open up the subtext to the actors in a very real way—the outside-in approach.

What is difficult about all of this—whether the actors develop movement on their own or the director suggests it to them—is finding the *appropriate* movement directly inherent in the playscript. As we have said several times in this book, every line of dialogue is a word statement of a dramatic action, and a dramatic action is the forcing by a speaking character of another character. Thus, it is in the forcing or in the reception of the forcing (adjustment) that the movement inherently lies. For this reason, we use verbs to express dramatic action, for a verb is a statement implying activity. We note this point readily in such obviously active verbs as run, jump, tear apart, rip, cry, grab, pull, caress, kiss, etc., because these verbs are *verbs of visual activity*. But the verbs we use to express dramatic action are not nearly so obvious. Note that there is no obvious hint in such verbs as plead, command, seduce, love, hate, fear, and all modifications of such verbs; yet, they contain movement (and gesture) in exactly the same way as the others, though we do not associate typical body behavior with them as we do with run and jump. If you always think of verbs as possessing inherent movement, you easily will see how actors and directors can readily devise this sort of illustration.

Therefore, the director must study the dramatic action of a play intensively, for he must be certain that, whether an actor presents a movement or he suggests it to the actor himself, the truth is being told about an action. Movement can tell a bold-faced lie, can even tell the opposite of what is intended. Therefore, both director and actors must be certain that actions that go toward and actions that retreat actually do that in the visual movement unless opposite movements are consciously intended for very specific reasons.

There are only two directions of movement on the stage: the advance and the retreat. Whichever one is used depends on the meaning of the subtext. Movement is played like a Cat-and-Mouse cartoon with characters switching to play Cat or to play Mouse depending on the meanings of the actions. One character will always be the aggressor and one the pursued, and the change in roles will occur very frequently, perhaps as often as every minute or two.

MOOD VALUES IN MOVEMENT

Because they occupy space when actors move from one location to another, because they require time periods (duration), because they are large and dynamic, because they can vary greatly in their rates, movements have many mood values that need the most careful control if they are to be continuously expressive. Here are some of the values you must consider:

Length of a Movement. Long movements tend to be weaker than short ones, unless they are used with the greatest care; yet, they can have strong mood values when used in the appropriate places. Remember that all movements, if they are to be seen and recognized as movements, must traverse five feet or more. Continuous short movements, however, unless specifically intended, have a choppy effect, something like a series of simple sentences. Learn to vary the lengths of movements with the moods you want illustrated. On the whole, inexperienced actors tend toward short movements; so, when working with such actors, you will need to show them how relaxation and ease can be illustrated in generous movements.

Movement and Space. Although movement technically occupies space only when it is being made, it possesses the psychological value of tying areas of the stage together, thus making it seem as if movement occupies more space than it actually does. Learn to exploit this value by interrupting long patterns of movement with momentary compositions that will occur each time an actor stops. *Travel the diagonals of the stage,* because they will give the feeling of occupying the upstage areas and far corners of the downstage areas. If the movement zigzags with interrupted stops, it will appear to occupy space. The mood values of small-space occupation are quite different from those of large-space occupation. You must learn to use each appropriately.

Size and Dynamics. Movements vary in size according to the number of gestures employed while making them. If an actor plays his character-decorum and his character-mood-intensity appropriately, he will vary the size and dynamics of his movements. Encourage the use of the sphere (gesture) while moving if you would increase or decrease the size of a movement, and thus affect the mood values it reflects.

Rate or Tempo. The rate of speed of movements is most important in expressing mood values because audiences are so easily affected by rate. The major problem with actors lies not in just helping them discover when and where to move but in how to vary the tempos of the movements in line with the character-mood-intensities of the scenes. The tendency with inexperienced actors is to take all movements at the same rate of speed, so that movement as illustration becomes quite ineffective. You must therefore be certain that actors move at their appropriate character-mood-intensities, a condition which will come about only if they understand their dramatic action thoroughly, because two characters never have the same rate, but each moves according to his nervosity. Only by understanding this concept can actors learn to make moods through the use of movement.

Movements in Series. You must learn how to plan movements so that they are joined in a series, with each move proceeding from the logic of the previous one. Thus, movements are more interconnected than they would seem to be, and moods can evolve out of their accumulation. If you learn to play this chess game sensitively, you will find that you can control the moods of a play more through movement than through any of the other visual tools.

Movement in Relation to Speeches. Movement is so dynamic, so eye catching, that it exerts great power over line-reading illustration. Thus, the exact point at which a movement is to be made becomes extremely important, something that you and the actor must decide together. To point a line, the actor moves *before* he says the line. To point a movement, that is, to have the movement actually say more than the line, the actor moves *after* the line. It is for these reasons that actors tend to move *on* the lines, because by making such movements most of the time they can then save line or movement pointing for special moments. However, you can readily see that unless your actors are fully aware of the pointing values, many of them will not use movement as illustration at all, and thus you will lose the most valuable tool in your directing kit. Therefore, you must learn to mix up the speech-movement relationship and to exploit it in every possible way.

Quantity of Movement. At first you will not need to worry about putting too much movement into a scene because you will have difficulties in finding enough. But after you understand the values of movement and learn the knack of arousing such illustration in your actors, you will learn to select all movement with extreme care. Excessive movement, that is, movement on nearly every line, can kill the other tools of expression; but insufficient movement will mean underillustration. You will also learn that experienced actors do not need as much movement as the less experienced because they know how to exploit *all* the tools of illustration and not just one or two. But to help the inexperienced you must learn how to suggest movement to them, for this suggestion will build their confidence by giving them something specific to do and will lead them to the use of the other tools as well. The quantity of movement, then, must be determined not alone by the character of the play you are producing but just as much by the quality of the actors you are using. You must learn to judge both with care and objectivity.

Because young directors tend to ignore movement as a tool of illustration, you are encouraged at this point to work as much of it into a scene as you possibly can and then to remove what you consider excess movement at a later stage of rehearsal. Movement can be your most potent tool in helping actors discover the dramatic action, because when they move, they feel on the outside the way they should on the inside, and that feeling will give them a strong hint about what they should be doing as dramatic action.

EXERCISES

1. Examine a class study play, underlining all entrances and exits. How
   many are there? What other movement does the playwright formally
   prescribe? (Look for the use of objects that the playwright specifically
   placed and then incorporated in the required visual illustration.)

2. Select a play for study that requires a group (*Riders to the Sea* is a good
   one), and actually block the entrance of the group. Who will enter first?
   How many together? Where will they move to on the groundplan? How
   will the principal characters adjust to this entrance? Now arrange an
   exit. What problems does this arrangement involve?

3. Improvise a living room–dining room scene with six to eight characters
   (*Ah, Wilderness!* is a suggestion). Play an action in the living room, and
   then move the actors to seated positions around the dining table. Note
   the extra movements required to bring this change about effectively and
   efficiently. Improvise the same action, but use the whole groundplan for
   the first action before moving the group to the table. What problems does
   this procedure involve?

4. Assign verbs to several actors. Have each one improvise movement to
   illustrate his verb.

5. Improvise an action involving two actors. Using numbers dialogue, let
   them play the action. Did they use much movement? If so, was it meaningful? If not, why not? Now play the same action with the aid of the
   instructor, who urges movement when necessary from the side lines, and
   who also on a signal demands that the actor playing "Cat" start playing
   "Mouse," and vice versa.

A Synthesis of the Visual Tools
in Director-Actor Communication

COORDINATION

It was emphasized at the end of Chapter 7 that the treatment of each
tool separately would be necessary in order to see their values and
strengths in director-actor communication. To isolate them is, in a sense,
to view them as abstractions; however, the better you, as a director, learn
to see in great detail everything that happens in a physical way on the
stage, the easier it will be for you to see the simultaneous use of these
tools. So, while you are learning, you must run the film at quarter speed
if you are to isolate these tools at all. Yet, we know that the strengths of
a scene's moods depend greatly on highly selective uses of these visual
tools. The director who fully understands them will know how to exploit them.

Coordination, then, means using *all* tools with as much variety and freshness as possible—a technique that can come about only if the beginning director constantly reminds himself of the many tools at his command. The most frequently neglected tool is movement; the dullest is usually the groundplan; the tritest in its uses is hand properties; the least exploited is composition. And so it goes. Not until the director has all the tools working for him will he be of genuine help to actors in search of dramatic action and how best to illustrate it.

The director's job is to make a scene work, that is, to bring about appropriately *illustrated reciprocation* of dramatic action between two or more actors. And once the young director fully comprehends that dramatic action cannot be conveyed movingly without convincing and believable visual illustration employing *all* the tools, he can begin to consider himself on the way to becoming a director. Play production is the *articulation* of idea, not the invention of the idea itself, which is something the playwright has already done.

BLOCKING

Although a director in training should gradually move toward the goal of controlled improvisation, he must practice paper blocking as a necessary step in learning the values of all the tools of communication. Paper blocking is the homework preceding rehearsal periods when a learning director can improvise in the quiet of his study without all the confusion and speed of a rehearsal situation, where he will likely be more self-conscious and less able to concentrate than the actors he may be working with. Since his job is to help actors, he must be, in one sense, a big jump ahead of them in his knowledge of the playscript and what he wants done with it. His blocking homework, then, is a playing of the scene in his own imagination: what he thinks it might look like visually. And because he has quiet and time, he can experiment with several ways until he arrives at what he thinks *at that time* is the best.

Paper blocking, then, is in no sense an arbitrary director's decision that he will force on the actors but a pre-examination of possibilities for director-actor communication. Instead of leaving himself with only one way to illustrate a scene, a director has investigated the possibilities widely enough to enable him to move in several directions with actors, although he may personally think that one is superior to the others. Paper blocking opens up a director's imagination instead of closing it, for a dozen suggestions are far better than one. Moreover, the job of rehearsal is to keep the actors working. If they must wait around while the director makes up his mind about how he thinks a play should go, actors will be tense and will be low in concentration. Imagination in rehearsing is often released in the appropriate speed and rhythm of a scene; too much slow-motion playing may dry up the actors' imaginations.

The following should be prepared on paper as the minimum initial homework of the director:

Groundplan Design and Testing. A groundplan for a Realistic staging is the floorplan of a walled setting. Therefore, the plan should show the lines of the enclosing walls, the doors, windows, levels (platforms), and all furniture pieces. *Always make an accurate drawing to scale.* Free-hand improvisation will only get you into serious trouble because you will not be accurate with the space relationships and will be misled by what you think you have instead of by what you actually have. Fig. 47 is a sample drawing.

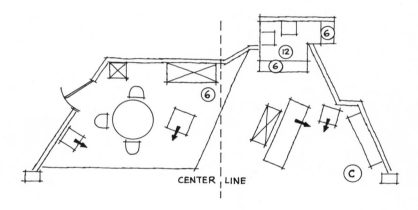

FIGURE 47

You must take the greatest care with the groundplan, for all the other director-actor communication tools will either depend directly on it or be strongly influenced by it. Remember: a dozen groundplans are better than one in trying to find the best because your imagination and improvisational force will be released. Select the furniture pieces with unusual care in the interest of projecting what they can do in stimulating actors to fresh illustration.

Test your groundplan by answering the following questions on the back of the sheet: (1) Does it have a minimum of five to seven acting areas? (2) Does it have strong upstage-downstage movement possibilities as well as stageright-stageleft possibilities? (3) Are strong diagonals possible? (4) Have you created tension in the placement of your furniture pieces? (5) Is it an obstacle course? (6) What is the potential for strong compositions and picturizations? (7) Is it ingenious? (8) Will it provoke actors to fresh and imaginative illustration? (9) Have you avoided the no-room?

Perspective Sketch. A perspective sketch of the groundplan will show the possible exploitation of levels as well as give ideas of proportion, balance, etc. It will tell you whether the room looks like a room and whether the areas have all been exploited. The mood of the *setting*— and it is now a setting with the walls added, except for color treatment and modifying details—will be declared largely on the basis of the distribution of furniture pieces, the sense of space created, and the size of the setting.

Making the Promptbook. In order to provide sufficient space for all the necessary notations, prepare a working promptbook by taking the playscript apart, if it is a printed text, and mounting each page on an $8\frac{1}{2}$ inch x 11 inch sheet of unruled paper. One procedure, if you are working with a printed script, is to cut windows in the paper so that both sides of the text are visible, thus requiring only one playscript. Now insert a blank page between the pages of the text so that each text page has its own work page. You should make a practice of binding the promptbook in either a hard-bound notebook cover or a strong folder-type cover with metal fasteners. A director, as with any craftsman, is known by the condition of his tools, in this case his promptbook. Therefore, don't be sloppy about making this primary work tool that will undergo a great deal of use.

Composition and Movement Notation. Now that you have the groundplan designed and the promptbook ready for use, you are in a position to record the compositions and movements in a detailed way. You will already have many ideas in mind from your work on the groundplan, but your intention now is to assess the groundplan in a specific way by seeing how well it will work continuously throughout the scene. If you have done a good job in design, you will find that this detailed working through will move rapidly and excitingly. Do not labor over making everything work, for if you move too slowly with this sort of notation you will lose the rhythm of the scene and what you intend doing with it, for blocking is a chess game that you always project five moves ahead. Remember that the blocking you "see" now will meet its crucial test only when you suggest it to the actors who will play the scene, and that the intention of advance planning is to put yourself in as flexible a position as possible.

Now enter on the upper half of each blocking page all the movements for that page of text (Fig. 48). Number each movement on this page consecutively and then place the same numbers in the text (Fig. 48). By setting down the movements you will automatically imply the compositions, and also, at least in your imagination, some projection of the picturizations.

Now prepare a small pasteboard cutout (a template) of your groundplan drawn to scale and reproduce it on the lower half of each blocking page (Fig. 48). Draw all the movements for each page on this reproduction of the groundplan, and indicate each character by a triangle with its initial inside (A). Show the direction of each movement by arrows on the lines and by the same number of the movement you have used in the written directions and in the text (Fig. 48).

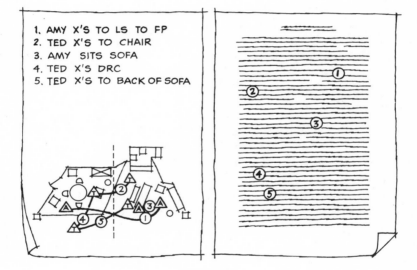

FIGURE 48

A different color for each character will aid in keeping them separate. Note also that the triangle is not equilateral but has sides longer than the base so that the point can show the direction in which the actor faces and thus the specifics of the composition.

Although gestures cannot be shown, as ideas come to the director they can be noted on the blocking page. Similar notes can also be made for improvisation with set and hand properties.

Master Movement Plan. When all the detailed blocking has been done for each page of text, the director should enter all movement on a single groundplan, this time by using enlarged dots to show compositional positions and colors to show movements (Fig. 49). When you finish doing this procedure, the drawing will look like a scribbled mess. Yet, it can reveal very quickly your exploitation of the groundplan— whether the movement, and thus the composition, has been concentrated in only one or two areas; whether the central planes have dominated, thus reducing the vertical use of the groundplan; whether the full groundplan has been exploited, etc. This check is quick and reliable to see how well the groundplan has been thought through. Here is an example:

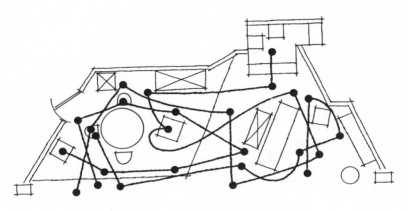

FIGURE 49

List of Properties. You have already made decisions on set properties when you designed your groundplan. At this point, you should review them carefully to be certain that you have selected the most idea-exciting furniture pieces you can think of that apply specifically to the given circumstances you are trying to reveal. Work for freshness and ingenuity, and regard the trite and dull as sure death as far as director-actor communication with the groundplan is concerned.

Now proceed to select with the greatest care the hand properties you think might stimulate actors. Verisimilitude to the given circumstances is again necessary, but remember that it is secondary, and that the primary value of a hand property is to aid an actor in his use of gestures. If too few properties are used, a scene will very likely be underillustrated, but too many can distract an audience by throwing emphasis on the properties themselves. So you must give your *appropriate* list your primary attention, with the accepted intention of adding other properties later as they are needed or withdrawing the ones you first selected if they prove inadequate.

EXERCISE

With the class using a common study play (a oné-act play is best), each student prepare a promptbook incorporating the following:

1. Full play-analysis as outlined at the end of Chapter 6.
2. Groundplan to scale.
3. Perspective sketch.
4. Playscript and blocking pages.
5. Blocking notations for the entire play if it is a short one.
6. Master movement plan.

I 2

the oral tools
in director-
actor communication

As you may have already noticed, this is the only chapter in *Play Directing* devoted to the oral tools of director-actor communication. It may seem inadequate to you in view of the extensive discussion of the visual tools in the preceding chapters, and especially after the strong point made in Chapter 7 that stressed that good directing means a visual-oral balance in production. This point of view is still primary in the total concept of directing set out here, despite what may seem like an unfair balance in the quantity of discussion.

In explaining this apparent shortage of material on the oral side, the learning director should appreciate the fact that highly developed seeing also means highly developed hearing, as it does in real life. Thus, part of the oral communication process has already been explained. In addition, to carry out his primary function of helping actors find their dramatic action, the director must use the visual tools as the strongest means of doing so. Explaining how is a complex matter and requires a good deal of space. The oral tools in director-actor communication, on the other hand, are not nearly as extensive in their uses. Furthermore, the development of the voice and technical capability in speaking are largely

problems of the individual actor, the essential tools he must provide himself with if he is to become effective on the stage. Since it is not the intention of this book to move extensively into individual actor training,
the only aspects of the acting process discussed here are those immediately concerning the director in his communication with actors. If actors
can bring to rehearsals an adequate voice and body instrument, the directing process can be what it should be: the development of an ensemble
of players who can, through appropriate imagery, transfer to an audience
the sort of play a director has in mind. If they do not, as is too often the
case, the director's problems will be greatly increased, for his job is to
shape the play, not to train the actors.

Thus, this chapter may be brief in its discussion of the oral tools in
the communication process, but it is very important because it deals with
those problems a director always faces in arousing actors to their best
aural image making. The "Oral Tools" of director-actor communication
treated in this chapter are therefore: (1) speaking the subtext; (2) speaking the text; (3) character decorum in speech; (4) projection.

Seeing versus Hearing as Director Emphasis

Because some directors think they can reach the audience directly,
they begin relying too heavily on the aspect of production that they can
more readily control—the visual design. They tend to concentrate on all
the visual elements from groundplan to movement, to settings and costumes, in the interest of obtaining a high degree of spectacle, but there
is no question that this sort of approach can greatly reduce the effectiveness of the spoken play. Unless a director is highly aware that a visual-
oral balance must exist in production, when he works with imaginative
designers his good fortune may well turn into misfortune because over-
laden visual design may well kill the play. Many actors and directors
could tell you that the best performance of their play took place in the
final rehearsal period before the physical staging elements were added.
What they mean is that the strong feelings in the spoken play, *the sound
of the dramatic action,* emerged in the rehearsal because the play was
about human behavior in conflict, and that without the trappings of production the actors were strong enough to make the play come through
with great force. Nevertheless, the visual designs can add greatly to a
play's total feeling if the *appropriate balance* is found. Although Aristotle placed spectacle at the bottom of his list of the six basic elements
required in a play, he nevertheless intended it to be a part, and ever since
the seventeenth century, when painted scenery was added to the staging
of plays, the theatre has had spectacle in great quantity.

The director's problem, then, is largely one of keeping the visual elements under control *because he understands the great significance of the*

oral elements. His problem is one of balance. In Shakespeare's day, people talked about going to *hear* a play, not to see one as we say today. This distinction is important because it tells us where the emphasis lies in our contemporary theatre. If a learning director does not appreciate this conflict in emphasis, he will fall into the trap of overemphasizing spectacle. He must therefore acquire early a strong prejudice toward the oral play, letting the visual take its natural course, for no one will safeguard the oral play unless he does. Consequently, the director must exert every effort to understand the oral elements in play production and how to give them emphasis. The moving picture is the art of the visual because the camera can see everything, from every position and every angle, and can make us feel with that seeing. In the theatre, however, where we cannot see in such a detailed way, it is the art of the human voice that finally moves us. We have lost too much of this art on our modern stage and we must learn how to get it back.

Good directing, then, provides an aural (hearing) as well as a visual experience for an audience, and a director's communication to actors must be poised to emphasize this point. He will constantly work at bringing about in them the power of a well-delivered play. Poetry in the theatre, though the actual language used may be lowly prose, is achieved in the aural experience, because then we hear humanity caught in dilemma, not just watch its pitiful suffering. A play is *not* a moving picture on a stage; it is an assault on the ear as well as the eye. Without this sensitivity to and delight in the musical aspects of the human voice in the theatre, a director will have great difficulty in communicating to an audience.

EXERCISES

What is the aural (hearing) experience of radio? Have you ever heard a radio play—a rare experience these days? Radio plays are scarce because of our demand for the visual experience which *we think* more dynamic. Play a side or two of a recorded performance of a drama or comedy. (A modern one like Murray Schisgal's *Luv* is an excellent example.) What is the aural experience? Can you also "see" the action? What would the visual add? How would it detract from the aural experience?

The Concept of Oral and Aural

We do not have a comparable word in English for the speaking-hearing process that is quite like visual, that is, a word that can denote the double process of making something visible and seeing it at the same time. In the case of theatre, *visual* means both the actor doing the illustration and the audience receiving it. The closest we can come when we talk about spoken dialogue is to use the two words that actually sound very much alike but have different meanings: *oral,* or the speaking of language or sound through the mouth, and *aural,* or the hearing of sound through the ears. In real life, we take this reciprocal process for granted, assuming that all anyone has to do is speak and we will hear. Yet we are constantly asking people to repeat what they say, and when they do, even then we may puzzle over the meaning of what they have said and may ask them to rephrase or explain further. But a play is an artificial contrivance in which an audience can do neither of these things. What is spoken usually must be *heard and understood the first time* it is said, although occasionally, if a playwright is particularly anxious to be certain a particular point is well heard, he may have characters ask for repetition, or he may have a character repeat the same material in different scenes to different characters. But this technique is more exceptional than typical, for usually 80 to 90 percent of a playscript is always new material to a hearer. For these reasons, most dialogue in plays must be heard the first time it is spoken or it will not be heard at all.

Bringing this about is much more difficult to achieve than it first appears because hearing what an actor says, if he is at all competent in his craft, frequently has little to do with the volume he uses or his actual capability in articulation (the precise production of individual sounds in speech). Playgoers frequently complain that they cannot hear young and inexperienced actors because they mumble and do not speak up. They say, "If they would talk louder, we could hear them." Low volume may possibly be the reason in some cases, but more than likely the fault lies elsewhere because there are so many things that prevent hearing besides the actor's actual volume-articulation capability. Chief among these is the actor's understanding of the subtext, and, running a very close second, is the distraction of the visual. Since we will treat the first in the next section of this chapter, a word will now be said about hearing versus the *distraction of the visual.*

The paradox of the visual is that its intention is to support the actor in his dramatic action (subtext) in every possible way; yet, the exact opposite frequently occurs. As we noted in the previous chapters, the visual tools can tell lies as well as truths; that is, actors and directors can unknowingly contradict themselves, contradictions that lead audiences into confusion because merely hearing the words is not understanding their contextual meaning. Physical production—the staging—when not performing its appropriate function, can also interfere with hearing by setting up irrelevant distractions between the actor and the audience. A playscript may have great clarity in its writing; yet, the production can cover up, smudge, or push aside that clarity, and, consequently, audiences will not hear the play very well. The director's job is to find a balance between the visual and the oral that will permit easy hearing. Again, hearing is *comprehension* of what is said, not merely receiving the words.

The oral-aural process, then, is given the best chance to work in the absence of distraction, for hearing a play well is a matter of intense concentration by both the actor and the audience. In one sense, a member of an audience has a right to blame an actor if he cannot hear, although the director and, through him, the designers often may actually be the guilty parties. The director's job is to keep a high concentration going in an audience by reducing distractions to an absolute minimum. The moving-picture director is able to control this by means of the close-up, which cuts out all other interference. In addition, through that control device we can watch both the mouth and eyes of the actor in great detail, and we can hear better because we are all stronger lip readers than we think we are.

But in another sense, a member of an audience can unfairly blame a production and those who have made it, totally unaware that he is incapable of receiving it, despite the fact that it may have been perfectly delivered. Plays are stories told to an audience—usually an adult audience—and to assume that they are going to reach everyone at all ages and with all backgrounds is assuming far too much. If you as a member of an audience cannot hear a play well, it may not at all be the fault of the actors, or because the dialogue is difficult as language, but because you are not mature enough or experienced enough to comprehend its content; you understand the elementals but not the complexities. We talk blithely about universals in drama, but by that term we do not mean simplemindedness. And often plays that may look utterly simple, *Oedipus Rex* or *The Bacchae* for instance, can be most complex at their cores. Hearing, then, involves audience capabilities as well as director-actor capabilities.

Yet, even if the audience is capable, there is no possible way of communicating a play through the speaking-hearing process unless the director is fully aware of his great responsibilities in this area of production. *The discussion that follows assumes that the oral-aural process is one of the director's primary responsibilities in production.*

Acting Is Speaking

We have become so accustomed in the twentieth century to the power of the visual that we have literally forgotten that great acting before our time was spoken acting. As was pointed out at the beginning of this chapter, in Shakespeare's day it could be said that people went to hear a play in contrast to our present-day common expression: going to see a play. There is no question that the twentieth century has discovered through the camera a more highly developed sense of seeing by more people than any other age has ever experienced. We look at everything, even such strange things as microorganisms enlarged thousands of times or such abstractions as sound waves and heart beats; we also look at scenery and faces of people in far-off places. On television, it is run-of-the-mill to see things at the exact time that they happen. Today we participate in wars in our living rooms by going directly to the absolute reality of the battlefield. In the moving pictures, so greatly have lenses and film quality been improved, that we are seeing close-ups of human beings in intimacies no age has ever witnessed. Actors often appear without makeup, and in a fifteen- to twenty-foot picture, sometimes even larger, we can see the hair on their skin, their natural perspiration, body blemishes, warts, and moles in the greatest detail. In real life, we all come to know a few persons in this way, but never have we been allowed to look so closely at so many as we are now permitted to do.

The theatre has an enormous task in competing with this sort of visual assault on our senses because we can never see acting on the stage this close. Stage makeup has always been used to enlarge and simplify features—to make masks with typical or symbolic meanings. Even if a member of an audience sits close to the stage, say within the first five rows, although he will certainly see the actors in much more personal detail, he may not actually receive any more of the play than those sitting several rows to the rear or in galleries above. There is certainly a limit to the size of a playhouse, but that limitation is not made on the basis of the visual but on the basis of the aural—what can be readily heard.

The art of the theatre, then, does not lie dominantly in the visual but in its balance with the oral-aural experience. Because the visual close-up is not possible in the theatre, the only thing that can take its place is the actor's voice because it comes from deep inside him; that voice is what moves us. And how very rare that experience is.

So much attention is placed today in actor training on the interior approach that young actors, as well as instructors who train them, literally do not realize that without a voice and the capability of using it, actors can get nowhere on the stage. In moving pictures and television, where small, realistic voices are possible, they may find a place, but certainly not in the cavern of the theatre. The voice is, therefore, an actor's prized possession because it is his principal tool of communication, and a director who does not comprehend this fact is simply bypassing his most potent means of reaching an audience. Reliance on the visual, though it may seemingly enhance a production with inexperienced beginners who have no voices, is certainly not the answer to mature performance. Acting is speaking in a very real sense. Instruction in acting cannot take the voice for granted but must make voice development a principal part of the training.

Oral capability is, perhaps, the one major difference between the amateur and the professional actor, and talent is often designated on this basis. The voice speaks from inside the nervous system of the human being; it "drags out the guts," so to speak, and forces hearing on the basis of its revealing intimacy. In this sense the voice has a greater capability than the visual close-up, for it can move more deeply simply because it becomes a heart-to-heart contact between actor and audience. A character literally lives in his human voice and not merely so much in what he looks like or illustrates visually.

The mature art of acting, then, *is* speaking.

Director-Actor Tools of Communication

SPEAKING THE SENSE OF THE SUBTEXT

As we have noted above, an actor may possess a fine voice and excellent articulation and yet be quite incapable of being well heard—well understood—by an audience. Much of the problem may lie in his failure to understand the subtext. If an actor speaks the way *he* thinks and feels, he may not speak at all in the way that the character he wants to portray thinks and feels. Finding the character means finding the subtext, and this is where the director plays an enormous role in the oral-aural process, for it is his job, as we have pointed out before, to help the actor find the subtext and to insist on its presentation.

Although prose dialogue in modern drama, because of its careful selection and intensification, is not an exact reproduction of everyday speech, it is very close to everyday speech. And because of this closeness, it is assumed that if an actor comprehends the dramatic action behind the actual words of a dialogue, he can make the words provided by the author his very own; that is, he can speak like the character. Although there are definite pitfalls the actor can fall into if he relies only on this one approach, there can be no question of its basic validity because dramatic action *is character*.

Here is precisely the core use of the director's intensive work on play-analysis, particularly his detailing of the dramatic action in verbal form as described in Chapter 4. In his communication with actors, he probably will not use the exact verbs he has set down in his play-analysis, for they may be too pure, too formal, for ready communication, but he will be able to imagize and stimulate in many different ways because he knows what must come out. The flexibility of his communication with specific actors is very great, and in working closely with them, in sensing and building on every contribution an actor may make, he can shape the action as he thinks necessary.

And again, to repeat the point of the discussion in Chapter 4, the director's most important job is to bring about reciprocation between actors, for each actor may understand his own forcings, but he may not be highly sensitive to what others are doing to him. Sensitive directing is insuring that each actor is hearing the forcings of others, perceptions that will lead to subtle adjustments before action is returned, for only in this way will emotion emerge from a scene. To repeat an important point again, acting can be described as primarily the process of subtle adjustment: actors play off one another with strong recognitions and discoveries. Thus, the adjustments may often be more important than the forcings in keeping an audience's attention.

"Hearing" the subtext, then, is at the very core of reciprocation, and the director is the outside person who can be certain that this part of the acting process is fully exploited. Communication to an audience cannot be made by each actor working separately but only when there is high communication between two or more who think and feel like the characters they are playing.

A practical example of how an audience reacts when it is deprived of the subtleties of subtext is in the experience with foreign movies where subtitles are printed at the bottom of the screen in English. We are afraid to look at the words for fear of losing the action illustrated in eyes and faces. In English-language movies we have no such problem because we can absorb the text and subtext simultaneously.

SPEAKING THE TEXT

As you can now see, speaking the text is first speaking the subtext. Nevertheless, the actor must do a very great deal directly with the text. Too often we take prose dialogue for granted because of its similarity to real life; only when directors are aware of its subtle complications and its artifice can they bring about the necessary hearing in an audience. Despite the theory of subtextual carry-over, actors can fully comprehend the subtext and yet throw away words and phrases. If an audience is to hear easily and well, actors must do a great deal of word and line pointing, and the director must be constantly on the alert to be certain they are doing it.

All that you have learned in a course in interpretative reading about emphasis, contrasts, and echos (repetitions of words or phrases) can be applied here. As a director, you will insist that all proper nouns (persons and places) be given special emphasis, with perhaps the slightest pause—a caesura—before the word, a technique you often hear good newscasters use. You will insist on accuracy in the text, which also means the employment of an author's punctuation (not a printer's, as in the case of Shakespearian texts) because his punctuation discloses what he thinks is the sense, as it does in all good writing. Good dialogue is highly economical, with every word selected and necessary; and you will therefore discourage corruption of the text by such means as substitution of or addition of words. "This is a very difficult line for me to say," says an actor. "Can I change the order or substitute these words . . . ?" More than likely he does not yet understand the subtext, or he is emphasizing the wrong words in the text. Since the author heard it, the actor can probably hear it if you help him find what is underneath the words. If you learn to spot the emphasis in a line—usually centered around the verb—you will be able to spot the subtext, and out of that subtext will emerge the meaning of the line, which can then be conveyed to an audience if the right words are stressed.

The pause is usually subtextual because it is tied closely to adjustment in the acting process. Its effect is very great, not because it gives lifelikeness to speech, but because it points and emphasizes what is spoken. Do you hear the silences in dialogue? They create the rhythm by punctuating the sound. If the audience is to "hear" the silences, you and the actors must hear them first. Help your actors find them, and you will discover new meanings. If properly placed, pauses can sustain attention in an audience more readily than sound because no one knows what will happen next.

As you learned in Chapter 3, dialogue is written with the emphasis toward the end of the line, which means that the line is constructed climactically by placing the emphasis near the end. Even though actors comprehend the subtext, they may fail to deliver the line with the strength of emphasis intended. *Pitch drop* occurs when an actor loses vocal force before the ending of a word or sentence and drops the pitch, thus destroying the hearing of this part of the line. Actors who are trained in subtextual acting become very self-conscious when a director points to such faults by correcting words or phrases. To correct this serious fault—if it is only an occasional dropping of a word or line—it is better first to look into the subtext for such failures because the actor may be missing the emphasis in the action; but if the failure is frequent, the actor is not fully aware of the climactic construction of dialogue and needs orienting on this point. A rehearsal technique used by some directors is to correct these failures through the use of written notes during the polishing period, when words, phrases, or line corrections can be absorbed readily by an actor because he understands the subtext; the written notes also communicate well because the actor can quietly be alerted to his problem.

The speaking of verse dialogue will be discussed in Part IV when the acting of historical drama is considered.

CHARACTER DECORUM IN SPEECH

In Chapter 4 and again in Chapter 10, we defined decorum as a character's outward show—what he literally looks like to others. This outward show also includes what he sounds like. Decorum is always a specific reflection of the given circumstances because environment defines social differences. We easily recognize poise or the lack of it in body movement; so do we also recognize it in speech, and perhaps with greater force, because characters, like people in real life, may refine their body movement but seldom change their strongly molded environmental speech patterns. A director must give primary attention to such physical verisimilitudes.

A common practice in playwriting up to a few years ago was for playwrights to record as accurately as they could in writing the actual sounds of speech they intended for certain characters. Good hearers like Bernard Shaw and John Millington Synge were very successful in this sort of sound transcription, but many writers who could not hear well could go no further than a generalized substandard language. More recently, writers have not attempted to transcribe at all but have left the sound in the hands of the director and actors, assuming that their awareness of given circumstances will lead them to the appropriate sound. But, unless a director is fully attuned to the dimension sound can add to production, he will lose one of his most important tools of communication. If he is attuned, he will know that significant meanings can often be conveyed through sound itself, aside from the words and the subtext.

We are therefore concerned not only with dialects (departures from the general American standard of speech) but with all speech we hear on the stage. Actors may have a full comprehension of the subtext in a Realistic play and yet not be able to convey the speech-decorum aspects of character at all. We simply cannot believe an actor playing a highly refined, urbane, and mannered gentleman who speaks with a distinctly country accent; and neither can we believe an actor playing a rough peasant with the cultured sounds of city refinement. Realistic drama forces this demand on actors and directors, and to sidestep it is to avoid the verisimilitude required of Realism. Nowadays, directors may cast actors on the basis of their speech characteristics alone and may prefer to work back into the subtext with the outward show in the sound already certain of adequate acceptance, for few actors can handle both refined speech and substandard speech effectively. In the commercial theatre and in the moving-picture industry, rigid casting lines are often observed, with native lower-class urban or country speakers usually employed to do dialect roles, and cultivated speakers for refined urban characters. How an actor sounds seems to be more important than how he looks.

Of more concern to the director than the special problems of dialects is the level of *good* speech, for it is the only requirement in a wide range of modern drama. The only determining factor in good speech, in the absence of any established American stage standard, would seem to be an absence of any readily recognized local dialect. The vowel structure in good speech would be close to what we recognize as the best urban speech of educated America—the speech we frequently hear from our best national network radio and television newscasters. To go further would rule out the wide range of acceptable American speech.

Speech decorum, in the sense we have been describing it, may actually be more of a casting problem than one that can be remedied during a rehearsal period. However, a director must be thoroughly aware that an actor cannot communicate to and be heard by an audience *without distraction* unless he can reflect the speech decorum of the character he is trying to represent. All a director can do is to hold an actor to the sound he had in mind during the casting period, although he may be able to improve it extensively by working with the actor on vowel modifications and technical approaches for producing better sounds. A director's best communication to an actor, however, may be in his expert conveyance of given circumstances that may stimulate an actor into adjusting his character's speech decorum on his own, but this decorum can be brought about only if an actor has a highly developed hearing capability, a relatively sophisticated talent that can make him sensitive to his own speech and how it can be adjusted. Speech is not changed by telling an actor what he is doing is wrong, simply because very likely he cannot hear his own speech unless he has been trained, as actors should be, in hearing. Good speech, and also good reproduction of dialects, then, can only result from an extraordinarily developed sense of hearing.

PROJECTION

Projection is a very real problem for directors working with young actors because they have not yet realized the level they must achieve in this technique before they can call themselves actors. The professional actor claims his rank as a professional on high performance capability in this aspect of acting, and he may very well continue working for years with voice instructors in an attempt to improve his capabilities. Unfortunately, far too much actor training in America does not insist on intensive work in projection, and too many educational theatre directors take a lax position regarding this aspect of play production. There can be no assumption that, because an actor understands the dramatic action, he will be readily heard, for much prose dialogue can be as difficult for an audience to hear as dialogue in verse.

Projection training is, of course, part of actor training, and we are treating it here only as it concerns production. However, since directors must constantly meet this problem head-on, even though they cannot teach projection in more than a nominal way during a rehearsal period, they must recognize its great importance to the effectiveness of a performance. Projection is a technical problem in communication, and the director provides the listening ear to monitor the actors.

The real problem for the director is bringing a performance to a high level of projection without making the actors so self-conscious of this technical aspect that they lose the high concentration needed in playing the subtext. One approach is to begin the rehearsal period with production techniques by using material other than the text, although it means delay in the work on the actual play in hand. But once the actors are aware of the director's ideas about projection, especially while everyone's ears are free of the text, problems can be met later on because a talking position has been established without fear of upsetting concentration on the subtext. As we have already pointed out in this chapter, an actor who understands the subtext has already greatly improved his projection position, but there is a great deal more to mastering the problem.

If you listen to first-rate actors in a stage performance or even in recordings of stage plays, you will be most respectful of their technical capabilities. Here are some of them:

Articulation. Speech is placed forward in the mouth cavity, where the articulators, teeth, tongue, lips, and gum ridges can be exploited fully. Good actors are remarkably energetic in the mechanical employment of their articulators by vigorously moving the jaw, lips, and tongue. Moreover, placing the speech forward overcomes the possibility of sound being buried in the back of the mouth, with a resulting loss of quality. English and German actors, and French classical actors, are among the very best in this respect; Americans, who by comparison, tend to slovenly articulation, are among the worst. As a director, you must insist on energetic articulation of sound. Also, avoid run-on or continuant sound, a very great failure since it obscures clear articulation.

Vowel Choice. Except in dialects and substandard speech, by *vowel choice* we mean the articulation of the vowels associated with what is considered to be the best American speech, that is, speech without marked regionalisms. These vowels are not nasalized, nor are they tense or flat. In the scale of the phonetic alphabet for American English, this means a soft [æ], occasionally used in certain words of the halfway vowels of New England speech [a] and [ɒ] but not the Italian [ɑ], except in those words employing that vowel in General American speech. Directors must insist that young actors eliminate characteristic regionalisms, such as the substitution of [ɪ] for [ɛ] in such words as those including *president;* [æ] for [ɔ] in *water;* a high, tense [æ] in *calf.*

Use of Regionalisms. In addition to the vowel problems in the word classes just mentioned, good actors will not employ regionalisms except in the use of dialects. The director should be ever watchful for such characteristics as the Southern dropped ending [n] instead of [ŋ]); the intrusive *r* of New England speech; the added vowels of Southern speech (Bill should not be [biIl] but [bIl]), and so forth.

Pronunciation. Good directors, when in doubt, use dictionaries.

Relaxation. A tense speaker is very hard to hear. Since body relaxation can improve projection tremendously, encourage your actors to relax and to use exercises to help them do so. A relaxed actor can speak at very low volumes and still be well heard if he has excellent articulation.

Quality. Relaxation and voice training will improve voice quality, although quality at its base is an inherent talent in an actor. In the Realistic theatre, however, the odd-toned voice can be exciting, especially in character roles; straight roles, on the other hand, require a better-than-average quality that an audience can tolerate through a full evening. This is a particular demand for actresses where low-pitched qualities have much to do with good audience hearing.

Volume. Actors do not reach audiences on the basis of high volumes but on the basis of line sense (subtext) and articulation. Only occasionally is volume actually used as a dramatic technique, and then, above all, the actor must exercise the greatest care to articulate the words, for it is easy to blast the hearability of a word with excessive volume. In general, good actors speak with fair volume, but it always appears easy and unforced, for forced volume is a great distraction to an audience because it can hear the actor pushing, as distinct from playing his character. Actors learn to vary volumes because they can convey subtle dramatic meanings by doing so, but they are very careful not to jump in and out of volumes in an erratic manner because such sharp contrasts can destroy hearing.

Pitch. An important factor in hearing an actor is his use of pitch. Good actors do most of their speaking within a surprisingly small range of pitch—perhaps even as narrow as plus and minus three notes on the musical scale from their median range of pitch. This might at first seem like a monotone to you when you think about it, but listen to a good actor and you will see that his steadiness and hearability in delivery lie in his narrow range of pitch, which leaves the rest of his range—perhaps as much as three octaves—available for special moments. Thus, he plays a scene primarily in his normal range, except for the climactic points when he will extend the range as much as the character-mood-intensity of the action requires. An actor who speaks lines with sharp variations in pitch in the interest of being dramatic is very hard to hear because a listener's ear cannot make pitch adjustments quickly enough to follow the speech. This fault is common in inexperienced actors and is one to which a director must constantly be on the alert.

Quiet Head. When he is speaking, a good actor always holds his head as still as possible. This rule is an absolute first in being heard. An actor who bobs his head will also bob the sound; he may also use erratic change in pitch because he wants to be very dramatic. *Let the speaking do the work in acting* is the expert advice of the good actor. *Use visual illustration, yes—when you are not speaking.* As a director, you must have faith in the dramatic action and in how well-spoken dialogue can transfer it. Overacting always destroys hearing because it creates distraction.

Energy. The mark of the professional actor is his ability to keep his energy behind his acting at a high level. *Acting is energy transferred to an audience;* this energy is really what the spectator has come to feel, what he wants to experience during an evening whether he knows it or not. Poor speaking betrays poor energy in the actor. As a director, you must try to get your actors to speak with the energy of their entire bodies and not just with voices from their heads alone. A performance is a tiring experience for a good actor because he works with his entire muscular, as well as his nervous, system. "Speaking from the guts" is no mere expression; it is the essence of projection. Also, keep in mind that rested actors will be much more capable of high energy levels than tired actors, for good voices depend on good health. When playing a series of performances with young actors, you will learn to insist that they have adequate rest.

Confidence. How well an actor is heard depends much on his stage confidence. If he loves to play, if he knows what he is playing (subtext), if he exerts his strong will as an actor, he will probably be heard. Communication is the desire to reach others; confidence is akin to command, and good actors command their audiences who hear them.

EXERCISES

The purpose of the few exercises that follow is not in any way to do more than what the chapter tries to do: to make the director fully aware of his responsibilities in the oral presentation of a play. Separate classes in interpreta-

tive reading, voice production, phonetics and regional speech are so widely offered in training programs that it is expected directors will pursue, perhaps extensively, the content of these areas so necessary to their work. Without a full comprehension of voice and speech, a director cannot hope to make an effective production.

The following exercises, then, are suggested in the interest of pointing out the ever recurring problems facing the director in any nonprofessional production. The instructor is urged to use his own range of examples and illustrations to augment an understanding of the often neglected content of this very important chapter. Remember, the most frequent complaint of the audience at amateur productions is: "I couldn't hear the actors." As a director, you must make sure the neglect is not your own fault.

A good collection of recordings is necessary for the following class exercises:

1. Listen to a recording of a Shakespearean play with Laurence Olivier or John Gielgud cast in a leading role. Criticize the articulation and range of pitch.

2. Listen to a recording of a modern play: Eva LeGallienne in *Hedda Gabler* or Michael Redgrave in *The Master Builder* are good ones for this exercise, but others made by first-line actors will do. Criticize the articulation and range of pitch.

3. Now listen again to Miss LeGallienne or Mr. Redgrave and note the perceptive use of subtext.

4. Have two actors who have no previous knowledge of the play read the opening scene of Murray Schisgal's *Luv* to the class. They should characterize the roles only as much as one hour of rehearsal will allow. After hearing them, play the recording made by the first New York cast (Eli Wallach, Anne Jackson, Alan Arkin). Was the sound a surprise? What does the sound mean to a production of this play? Are the actors illustrating the given circumstances of this play? What about the dramatic action?

5. Play the final scene of LeGallienne's *Hedda*. How do the actors play both the text and subtext?

6. Play a recording that employs either an American or an English dialect (Irish, Cockney, Bronx or Brooklyn speech are good choices). Pick out all the characteristics of the dialect: vowels; line of pitch; substandard English; rhythm structure; national character as expressed in optimistic or pessimistic sound. Repeat with other dialects. What basic elements are present in all the dialects?

7. Play a word-tossing game. One actor says a word with a certain vowel, and another replies with the same word and a different possible vowel. (*Possible* means that the word so pronounced must still be acceptable pronunciation for some group.) Can a third actor participate? A fourth? Now try varying the principal vowel in the following sentences: (1) I have to laugh to see the calf go down the path to take a bath in an hour and a half. (2) The rains in Spain fall mainly on the plains. Each actor

uses the same principal vowel sound in all the appropriate words. How many possible variations can be made on these lines. What would the use of each vowel mean in a set of given circumstances?

8. Play the dramatic action game with a common phrase, with each actor delivering the same phrase with a different action. Try: "I like you," or "I'm going downtown." Have the class identify the dramatic action behind each reading.

9. Devise a dozen word games for class participation. They are fun to play, and they will train your ears to hear sensitively.

I3

communication
put to work: scene practice
and diagnostic criticism

It should now be clear to you that a director's primary field of action is communication, first to his actors and designers (the latter relationship will be treated in Part III) and then, through the imagery they create and he helps to select, to his audience. Thus, the actors and designers are his media, for only through them will his ideas about a play take form and be able to reach others. Once again, here is the process: a playwright imagines an improvisation and gives it form through his use of given circumstances, dialogue, dramatic action, characters, idea, moods, tempos; a director then reimagines and recaptures the improvisation; he then helps the actors and designers to discover the improvisation he sees and feels in the way he sees and feels it, and to recreate it through themselves, thus giving it intensive personal life; if the images they create are strong enough and appropriate enough, the improvisation will be projected in such a way that viewers can receive it and act on it by reimprovising what they have seen and heard *in their own terms* (vicarious experience). Thus, a play is not an object transferred in a direct way but a series of improvisations capable of producing images and, consequently, strong feelings. In this sense, it can be said that a play hovers in space between the stage (playwright, director, actors, designers) and the audience, with the latter receiving it only if it has been released in terms the audience can understand.

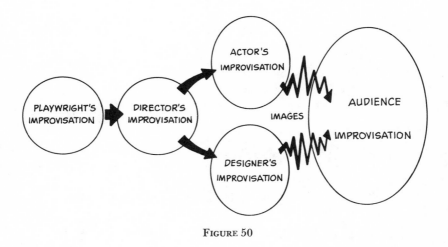

FIGURE 50

To comprehend further how this process works, we need first to summarize the relationship we have talked about in Chapters 7–12 and then to discuss the director's relationship to the audience in a more specific way than we have thus far treated it.

Director-Actor Communication Summarized

If you have read Chapters 7 through 12 with great care and have worked with many of the exercises or with similar ones you have devised yourself, you should understand a major approach in this book: application of the concept of organic communication, the kind of communication that works through the actor with the main purpose of arousing his improvisational sense, and thus the illustrations and activity that will flow from it. You should also be fully aware that the director uses two main areas of communication-stimulation—the visual and the oral—and that only when communication has been achieved through both means can it be said that the director has *gotten through*. Any director who concentrates on the visual alone or the oral alone is quite likely to make a poorly balanced presentation, for both approaches must be used if an actor's improvisational sense is to be aroused to the highest degree. The major exercises outlined later in this chapter—exercises that put together all the things talked about thus far in this book—will give you the opportunity of putting your skills in communication to work.

Getting through to actors, then, is the major problem facing a director. In working it out, you must learn to use *all the visual and oral tools of communication* at your command and not just some of them, and to use them in as many ways as possible, for the frustrations in the directing process result directly from the barrier wall that separates director and actor. You will also discover that student-directed scenes that do not come off usually fail, not because the actors cast in such scenes are weak and ineffectual, but because the directors have not broken through the director-actor barriers and reached them with such basic communications as detailed and delineated subtext, reciprocation and adjustment in acting, climactic illustrations of discoveries and adjustments, decorum, articulate conveyance of the text, exploitation of the groundplan, and the many other areas of communication so necessary to make a scene work. Not until you learn to take the blame yourself for your own failures in getting through, and do something about them, can you justly criticize actors for their shortcomings. Learn your own responsibilities first if you are to learn how to lead others.

Director-actor communication, then, will involve the organic use of groundplan, composition, gesture, improvisation with objects, picturization, and movement as the six visual tools for getting through, and speaking the text and projection as the oral tools. Improvisational techniques can be used at all stages, for once you have learned to work with this method of direct communication, you will see how intellectual approaches, such as director-actor discussion, are less effective ways of breaking barriers. And you will also learn that showing an actor how to do it, no matter how exaggerated your illustration may be, is a last resort and not a primary method. After all, your job is to bring out the creative in actors and not to tie them up in the restrictions of mimicry.

The Director as Audience

Although the director's primary job of communication is to get through to the actors (the previous chapters in Part II have been devoted to showing you how it can be done) you have now reached the point where you should be able to understand the director's second job: to be the eyes and ears for an audience. This second important function of the director has not been treated in *Play Directing*, not because it is less significant than the other, but for fear you would see this sort of work as the director's primary job and would, consequently, miss the all-important work of getting through to the actor, or of failing to understand that if you do not recognize the actors as media, you cannot get through to the audience at all. Arousing the appropriate dramatic action in a group of actors is a very difficult process, and you must know thoroughly how that process works before you can judge the quality of what is released to the audience's improvisational sense. Only now are you ready to consider this second major function of the director: judging the effectiveness of the transfer.

It is precisely at the point of transfer where the director performs a primary critical function, for now he is not concerned with just getting anything across the footlights but with the appropriateness and effectiveness of the thing being transferred: Is it the right statement? Is it intensive enough? Is it completely believable? Is the reciprocation between the characters of the desired sort? Is it moving? Or if the play is a comedy, is it laughable? What is the audience forced to do? Has it been put off balance? Will its curiosity and attention be maintained at a high level? Can it receive the ideas and images as presented? These are only a few of the dozens of critical questions that a director must ask himself, of which the sum total will be: Does it work? In other words, the director is so much the eyes and ears of an audience that if he does his job properly, as he responds, so will the audience.

What a terrifying responsibility it is to be the monitor of success for a group of creative people, each one hoping to show himself to his best possible advantage. After being immersed in the enormous detail of rehearsing a play day after day for several weeks, a director must set himself apart, must become objective about the subjective creation, in order to examine what he and the others have made. So begins the critical function of selection. Some professional directors would say that it is their primary work; that because professional actors know how to act and how to do their homework (bringing in something to look at), the director's job is mostly to select the best that can be provided or to suggest ways of playing scenes that will improve the selection. But such a procedure would not work at all with learning actors because so much more must be done to make the acting effective. It is also doubtful that even competent professional actors can find the *appropriate* action in a play without a good deal of director-actor communication regarding the contents of a playscript and the emphasis a director wants to give it. But no matter what level of actors a director may be working with, the final question is always the same for a failing scene: Why does it not work?

Here begins the diagnostic process that must be highly developed in every director: discerning why a scene fails, and then, like a doctor, prescribing a remedy. And, thus, the process goes on continuously throughout a rehearsal period, and particularly in the closing days—the process of judging the product and selecting what works from what does not, and all of this selection based on whether the director responds favorably or not. Somehow a director must be moved to laughter or to strong feelings in the spirit of whatever a play requires as he watches a run-through; if he does not react so, he will probably find that his potential audience will respond negatively as well.

How to be objective, then, about your own work—the total product you see and hear on the stage—is a state of mind and feeling, the critic in you that may take a long time to acquire, for many young directors cannot make the jump readily from the inner to the outer look. Yet jump you must if you are to evaluate what you are doing as a director. At best, you are the patient at the same time you are the doctor. The two major exercises that follow—"Scene Practice" and "Diagnostic Criticism"—should train you in working on both sides of the consulting desk.

Scene Practice

CONCEPT

Although you are not yet fully ready to stage a production, if you have conscientiously done all the work outlined in this book up to this point, you are ready to direct minimally staged scenes with live actors. The approach in this chapter, then, is to bring about a synthesis of all the techniques developed in previous chapters by discussing the director's job before rehearsals begin, during a rehearsal period, and after the first performance. Scene practice is the goal you have been preparing for all along, but there are also techniques involved in it that must be carefully followed if you are to accomplish your purpose even in a minimal way.

SCENE CHOICE

Scene *choice is designated here instead of* play *choice because it is assumed that young directors can profit most at this point by doing two or three ten-minute scenes from long plays before doing a one-act play.* The reasons are very simple. Although a one-act play provides a unity, that is, although it is all about one thing, it will not give you the opportunity to work on play-analysis in depth because the structural elements, particularly dramatic action and character, are considerably limited. In contrast, the structural elements of major plays, from given circumstances to moods, are fully developed even though a play as a whole may be of inferior quality. In addition, the study of a ten-minute scene from a long play is tantamount to studying the whole play because you cannot eat a piece of a pie without knowing what it all tastes like. By working with long plays, you will learn much about their complicated structures, the study of which should greatly increase your respect for the playwright as a craftsman of controlled improvisation. Finally, you will be able to direct one-act plays far better after you have wrestled with parts of long plays because you will know more about structure and will be able to handle the special problems they raise. It is commonly assumed that short plays are easier to do because they are short, but this assumption is a fallacy you will become aware of when you try one after working in depth on a major play, for a short play is a tour de force that requires the most experienced sort of handling to bring it to fruition.

Choose a climactic scene. Every play has a major climactic scene but each act will also have at least one—probably two or three—secondary climactic moments. What distinguishes the climactic from other scenes is *discovery:* an important character, usually the principal one, will discover something new in front of the audience; that is, an important fact will be disclosed to him through dramatic action that will decidedly alter his basic course of action. How important a climactic scene is to the play as a whole will depend on the importance of the discovery and the way in which the informant makes his information known to the character who receives it. Thus, the playwright excites the audience by the gradual process of building to the moment of discovery, but the actor caps it for us by the strength, duration, and quality of his *adjustment* on its reception, a high point in the acting process. The scene is climactic because the dramatic action has reached a peak in the discovery-adjustment cycle, leaving the recipient naked for seconds before the audience while he decides what to do; the audience feels the climax because it is suspended with excitement until it knows what course of action the recipient will take. Thus, a climactic scene is made up of (1) a slow build, sometimes very intricate, intensive suspense before the release of the discovery, (2) the discovery, (3) the adjustment, and (4) the new course of action taken by the recipient.

You must, therefore, exercise great care in choosing a climactic scene for a project. Other scenes may be effective after a fashion, but they will seem obscure to an audience, whereas the climactic scene will be received with comprehension and high interest because of the strong contrast among the units that compose it.

Do not choose a scene with the beginning and ending arbitrarily and formally established by a playwright. (Example: Act II, Scene 2 of a certain play where the curtain [or lights] is raised and lowered at both ends.) To all intents and purposes, this scene is a one-act play, and it does not provide the director the learning experience which the choice of a ten-minute piece selected from the beginning, middle, or end of a continuous act of a play can offer. When you choose a piece of an act, you will find out about the nature of climactic scenes because you will be forced to dig out what leads to a climax, what a climax is, and what leads away from it. Your awareness of unit division will also be intensified because you will learn that *a scene choice with only two units will not work,* whereas you will have a better chance with three, and an even better one with four or five, for we can see a unit well only when it is placed in contrast with other units.

Do not *choose a scene in which two characters discuss a third character who does not appear onstage during the course of the scene.* Such scenes are usually transitions in which a principal character uses a secondary character as a confidant. Although the action of the play as a whole is advanced, such scenes do not make interesting choices for beginning directors because they will usually lack the dramatic quality of direct confrontation and thus will become very difficult scenes to present successfully.

As a starter, choose a scene with only two characters, for with it you will still have all you can handle. You will also find that ten minutes with two people in a play will usually rise to a sharp, dramatic climax because the author has intentionally confined his dramatic action, probably to principal characters. This confinement will give you and your actors a tight unity around which to work, for you will need to lead into it (the beginning), bring about the climax itself with its usual big discovery (middle), and bring it to a state of suspension (the end).

The choice should, of course, be from a Realistic play because this is the style of play studied in Chapters 3 through 12. Other styles will be treated in Part IV, but you must learn how to do the dominant style of the last hundred years before you try to work with departures from that style. Further, it is suggested that you consider plays falling within the period from 1920 to 1960. You could, of course, go back to Ibsen or Chekhov and still fall within the category of Realism, but their plays are very complex, set as they are in the late nineteenth-century European environments, and it is suggested that you will do better in your first projects with plays of American authorship because they depict given circumstances closer to your own cultural background. Plays after 1960 are not suggested for the first projects in directing because their Realism is deceptive—they look like Ibsen or Chekhov at first glance, but they differ radically in many respects. In the 1920 to 1960 period, you must be certain to avoid all the Expressionistic or Symbolistic plays, as well as those of the Absurdists. Realism on the stage is *observed* reality—that is, the reality that can be easily seen and believed as the appearance of everyday life.

It is also suggested that you choose an interior *scene*—in a living room, bedroom, or kitchen—or a backyard scene where a groundplan can be arranged much like an interior setting although outdoor furniture is used. Avoid open beach scenes as well as those located in a woods or in any open space because you must first learn how to use occupied space— a groundplan obstacle course—before tackling the complexities of open space groundplans.

The choice should also be made from the standard repertoire of plays by well-known authors. Bernard Shaw's quip in the mouth of one of his critics in *Fanny's First Play,* "If it's by a good author, it's a good play," is certainly only the truism Shaw intended, but there is much to be said for the successful, regularly produced author because he has a command over play structure that lesser known or unknown playwrights usually do not have. Your intention in doing a scene project is to learn as much as you can about play structure; the best playwrights are the best teachers, so choose their plays.

Limit the length of the scene by the number of units. A ten-minute scene will usually contain four to six units, all you need if you have selected it properly. You may be in trouble if the scene runs less than ten minutes because the actions may not have developed quickly and intensively enough to make a satisfactorily unified statement.

Keep your audience in mind when you choose your scene. Although the primary function of scene practice is, of course, your own training in play-analysis and actor staging, you must recognize from the beginning that a play is not a complete form until an audience has received it on its own terms. Do not let audience consideration deter you in any way from choosing plays of high quality for you will discover that such plays can be acted more effectively because they are inventive and rich in dramatic action. Nor do you have to worry about losing your audience because it may think your scene is too obscure, too hidden in the play as a whole. If you have made a solid choice by observing the two basic rules for the number of units (four to six) and for climactic action, and if you have *expressed it imaginatively and with feeling,* any audience will be able to follow the scene. Remember: directing is not book work but communicating with audiences through actors and staging.

DO NOT EDIT THE SCENE CHOICE

Except possibly for the removal or alteration of a specific word or two that might be distasteful or distracting to your audience, *you must not alter the scene as written in any way.*

If you edit a scene by removing lines, or by removing a character because "he has only two lines, and I don't really need him," you have seriously changed the author's intentions. Young directors, thinking that they can make a better scene of the material, frequently want to edit. You must suppress all such urges! You really want to remove lines or characters because you do not understand them; that is, you simply do not comprehend why they are there. You can be sure that the author considered all such alternatives when he wrote his play. Have faith in him, because he is a far more experienced man at his trade than you are at yours. When you have had extensive experience as a director you may want to gamble on some editorial adjustments, but at this point you must stick exactly with the script. Further, do not select edited cuttings of plays for directing projects—cuttings made by editors who have deleted lines or characters within scenes, because in the interest of making plays quickly readable by a general public, they may have removed crucial dramatic action. Use only fully printed playscripts.

The only sort of editing you should consider is altering distasteful words such as profanity or words with strong sexual connotations. You are the judge of what your audience will shy away from, and you must make a decision accordingly about what to leave in and what to find a substitute for. You should not try editing a scene that is strongly marked by the continuous use of such language, for the playwright intended his language to exert great force; therefore do not choose that scene to do. But an occasional word can usually be readily replaced by a word of less strength. This substitution is done frequently in moving-picture writing because large amounts of money are concerned, and producers cannot take the chance of offending portions of the potential audience. Isolated words will not reduce dramatic action, nor will their alteration much reduce the strength of a text. The important thing is to remove the distraction these words might cause to your audience. You must not think of such editing as prudish but as good sense in many situations, for the world does not live on profanity. Furthermore, local audiences may be more conservative than those an author may have had in mind, and if they are shocked, they may fail to hear or see what is truly important in the scene; that is, they may vibrate over a word and become insensitive to the dramatic action.

PRODUCTION CIRCUMSTANCE

Scenes can be performed either in the classroom or on a proscenium stage. The latter will specifically confine the director to a set production form because of its architectural construction. And you must not violate the proscenium line by advancing in front of it, but always play behind it. That is essential. On the other hand, if you are using a classroom, set the proscenium positions by placing two chairs twenty-four to twenty-six feet apart or the maximum width your space allows (less than twenty feet will cause problems), and then observe rigidly all the laws of the proscenium stage as if you were playing on one. (A good substitute for chairs is to use a two-fold screen unit on either side of your stage.)

Use abstract forms for staging. As was suggested in Chapter 8 on the groundplan, you should learn to work with whatever rehearsal-room staging is available. It is far more important to learn how to occupy space with chairs or odd pieces and to learn the concept of the obstacle course as well as the nature of architectural mass and line, than it is to try to reproduce things exactly as they appear in everyday life. Use chairs as chairs, and tables as tables, of course, but if you and your actors use them properly, you can make them appear to be different sizes, different shapes, different textures, even different styles. You should let stacked chairs represent cabinets, or bars, or fireplaces, or even tables if necessary; and chairs side-by-side represent sofas, etc. Learn to get along on a few items, but never forget that you are delineating space, not leaving it empty.

The suggested items in the drawing Fig. 51 are explicitly designed for director's rehearsal use because of their wide range of deployment in proscenium staging as well as in other types. Note that they have a neutral quality and do not have to be used as literal representation. The four screen units are provided to give a variety of wall ideas because walls help directors and actors to know the limits of their groundplans. See Fig. 52 for sample illustrations of their simplest use.

Wall units (note the two-fold and three-fold units in the drawing) will also help to inclose all your other pieces, as well as to make your obstacle course specific. The stools, benches, and rocks provide a wide variety of sitting possibilities. A round table is included because it has different compositional possibilities than square tables. The practical pylons in three sizes open up all kinds of groundplan arrangements; note they can be used in front (closed) or back (open) positions with different meanings respectively. The platform and step units will encourage the use of levels.

A note about the color of these materials: all the items in this rehearsal set should be painted a neutral color, perhaps a pearl gray, so that no single item has any particular emphasis through color value. You may at first think gray is too somber, but you will soon discover that it lends itself equally well to serious plays and to comedies. The intention of using no-color is to reduce the materials to expressions of line and mass without the distractions of particularizing details.

But whether you use classroom furniture or the more elaborate rehearsal-room setup described above, you must try to be as ingenious as you can, remembering that a groundplan is a tool of communication to

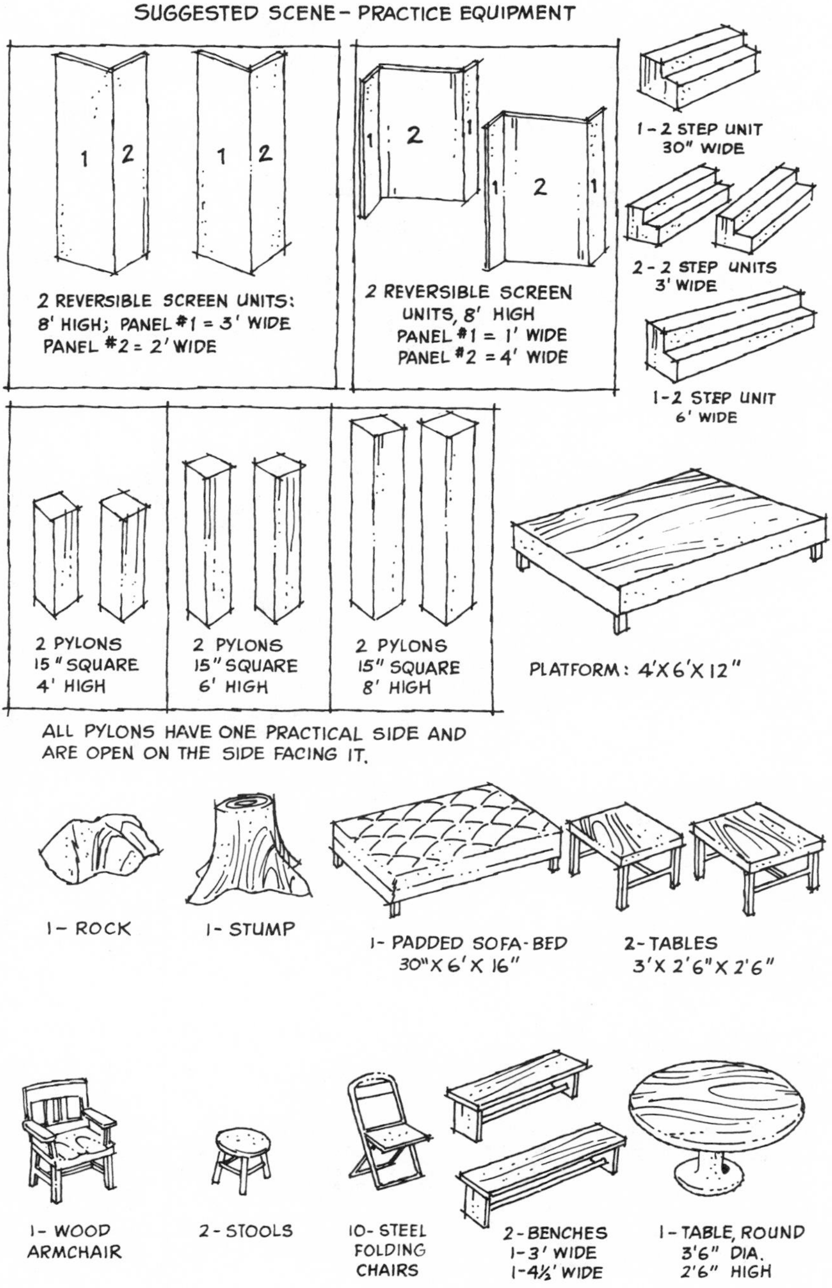

SUGGESTED SCENE- PRACTICE EQUIPMENT

2 REVERSIBLE SCREEN UNITS:
8' HIGH; PANEL #1 = 3' WIDE
PANEL #2 = 2' WIDE

2 REVERSIBLE SCREEN
UNITS, 8' HIGH
PANEL #1 = 1' WIDE
PANEL #2 = 4' WIDE

1 – 2 STEP UNIT
30" WIDE

2 – 2 STEP UNITS
3' WIDE

1 – 2 STEP UNIT
6' WIDE

2 PYLONS
15" SQUARE
4' HIGH

2 PYLONS
15" SQUARE
6' HIGH

2 PYLONS
15" SQUARE
8' HIGH

PLATFORM: 4'X 6'X 12"

ALL PYLONS HAVE ONE PRACTICAL SIDE AND
ARE OPEN ON THE SIDE FACING IT.

1 – ROCK

1 – STUMP

1 – PADDED SOFA - BED
30"X 6'X 16"

2 – TABLES
3'X 2'6"X 2'6"

1 – WOOD
ARMCHAIR

2 – STOOLS

10 – STEEL
FOLDING
CHAIRS

2 – BENCHES
1 – 3' WIDE
1 – 4½' WIDE

1 – TABLE, ROUND
3'6" DIA.
2'6" HIGH

FIGURE 51

SAMPLE GROUND PLANS USING SCENE-PRACTICE EQUIPMENT

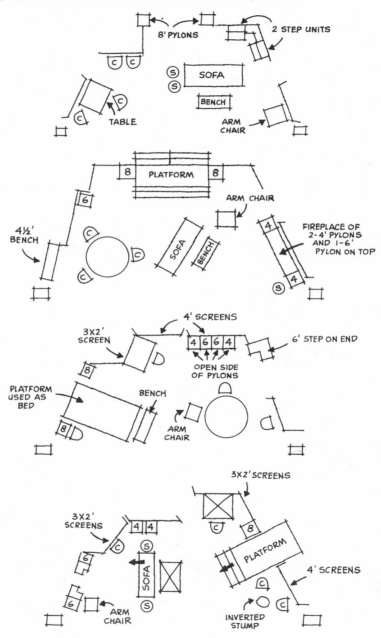

Figure 52

actors and that actors will be only as free as your imagination encourages them to be.

SCENE PREPARATION

Now that you have declared your choice of scene and know the circumstances under which you can produce it, you are ready to begin your scene preparation.

Do the play-analysis specifically as outlined in Chapter 6 (pp. 63–65). *You will need to analyze the play as a whole for most of the preparation.* This point is precisely the one on which many students fail: they think they can do a scene without knowing well the entire play. Such a view is absolute folly, for a scene is only part of a whole, and without an understanding of the whole, a director can only partially illuminate the parts. Be sure to study the dramatic action of the scene you have chosen to stage in great detail because out of your understanding of this action will flow all your other ideas.

Now make your promptbook as outlined in Chapter 11 (pp. 145–147). It will contain all your suggestions for the visual design from groundplan through composition, picturization, movement, and improvisation with objects.

CASTING

Acting instructors may possibly help you with the casting or arbitrarily provide you with a cast because they know more explicitly what they want their actors-in-training to gain from the experience you are providing. If you do not get such help, you will have to go through a minimum casting procedure with whatever actors are available. Although casting as a procedure will be discussed later in Part IV as an intrinsic part of play interpretation, at this point what you should be looking for are responsive and cooperative people because your first job is to find out how to get dramatic action adequately rendered and not how to arrive at a delicately poised interpretation. This job will be enough for you to handle. If you are lucky enough to find actors who are able to project some of the decorum and qualities your characters require, you will be ahead in the game. Above all, you should take care not to choose people who are much more advanced in acting than you are in directing, for you need to feel you are in command. You also need to feel free to experiment with all the devices and methods of communication, and actors who can too readily act the scene for you will deprive you of what you must learn about these approaches, and some may even take the scene away from you. You will also probably stand in the way of actors more advanced in their work than you are in yours by restricting them rather than freeing them. Consider yourself lucky if you have a cast of two people—whether they have the right qualities or not—who are also eager to learn, eager to experiment, and have strong wills of their own. Your job is to learn creative leadership—how to draw out actors and free them to their own imaginations—not the practice of arbitrary totalitarianism. You will also discover that the right qualities are not as important as you may think they are. Actors *act* action and in this way make characters. If you can get the action acted, you will be amazed at how much the particular actor is buried and how much character actually comes across.

REHEARSING

Rehearsing a play is putting to work all the concepts and techniques discussed in this book up to this point. The rehearsal is your field of action, and you must give it every bit of imagination and energy you possess, for the success of the performance will depend on what happens here, not in the extensive paperwork preparation you have done. Rehearsing a play is a technique in itself that you must be aware of and learn to do with the greatest care. Your detailed organization here will release both you and the actors to your creative selves, making the rehearsals fun as well as profitable. Putting on a play is like playing a game in which you are the leader and can call the signals. It is also very much like a party at which you are playing host. Here are a few suggestions that will make your work easier:

Scheduling. A ten-minute scene from a major play requires a minimum of eight hours of rehearsal. Calendar time is very important because an actor needs a good deal of actual time to make the strange garments of a character fit him, and it is therefore suggested that an hour a day over a two-week period is far better than two hours on one day, skipping the next, three on the third, etc. The time in between the one-hour periods will let both your own imagination and that of the actors work on the play, so that rehearsals actually become experimentation hours based on assessments of the previous day's work and imaginings of what can lie ahead. There is also time to make brief suggestions to actors during the interim period—suggestions that can stimulate new directions or new experiments in the rehearsal itself.

Rehearsal Plan. Each rehearsal should be designed to move your scene ahead as rapidly as possible. Here is a possible plan, with a discussion of the suggestions in the following pages:

1. Read through the scene. Discuss with your actors as simply as you can the structure of the scene and how you would like to stage it. Block the scene as traffic management so that the actors can feel their basic relationships.

2. Repeat the blocking of the first rehearsal. Now begin character development by helping the actors search out some of the dramatic action. Start improvisations now if your actors are capable in this technique. It is better to work on a unit or two than the whole scene.

3. Concentrate on the illustration of dramatic action in the interest of unfolding the dramatic action and thus the character relationships. Continue improvisations.

4. Lines learned. Improvisation with hand properties can be added to the other communicators, such as composition, picturization, and movement.

5. Run through the scene in order to assess the accomplishment of the dramatic action and thus the character development. Is actor reciprocation taking place? Is the groundplan working; if not, redo it, paying close attention to the number of acting areas, whether it is a good obstacle course, and whether it can excite the imagination of the actors. Are the principal discovery and adjustment in the scene being played with strength and careful pointing?

6. Reblock the scene as needed and work on dramatic action. Is the scene playing in units? Concentrate on actor reciprocation and on character development.

7. Make clear delineations in unit structure of the scene by working for tempo and mood goals. Concentrate on delivery of the text.

8. Do run-throughs, concentrating on rhythmic structure.

As you note, discussion is held to an absolute minimum. Actors must be kept busy acting, not talking about acting or analyzing the scene. They must discover the action and their characters by *doing* repeatedly, with stops for discussion only when your other communicators are not working.

Note also that in this rehearsal plan, the director blocks the scene in the first rehearsal in the interest of direct communication. This use of blocking does not in any way rule out improvisational techniques for the purpose of scene discovery (see pp. 181–182), but such techniques can be employed only if the actors and the director are already familiar with their use. If they are, improvisations become the method of direct communication. The purpose, however, is the same: the quick assimilation of the dramatic action by the actors while the scene content is still fresh. The sense of discovery is very important here, for the actors can see more clearly at this point the shape of the scene—the highs, the lows, the erratic points, the discoveries—than they will later when they have become too absorbed in the detail.

Do not go too slowly. If you are ready with some suggestions of compositions and movements, the actors will respond quickly to the demands of the scene. Your intention in the first rehearsal is to tell the actors *the shape* of the scene through the communicators—groundplan, composition, picturization, movement, and tempos; music played out of rhythm is no music at all.

The lines should be learned by the fourth rehearsal so that the actors can put down the scripts and begin experimenting with illustration at the same time that they begin listening carefully to each other. Scene discovery, remember, comes in hearing an action and in making an adjustment. Line learning from this view becomes sense-of-the-scene learning, and there is little to be gained by slowing down this process. Find the subtext first, and only then will you be able to start working at pointing the text.

The run-through suggested in the fifth rehearsal is very necessary so that you can see and hear what has been accomplished thus far and where to go next. Do not interrupt the actors in this first run-through, but insist that they play the scene fully as if they were playing it before an audience. Use all your set pieces and properties at this run-through. The assessment that follows is your most important decision-making moment in the rehearsal plan. Is the groundplan working for the actors? Is the shape of the scene fully established in their acting? Is character development (given circumstances plus dramatic action) well underway? Does the scene build climactically through sharp delineation of the units?

Now begin the final work on the scene. Do not hesitate to find new compositions or movements in the interest of stimulating new ideas; the actors will tell you instantly whether the new suggestions stimulate them. Shuffle up the groundplan on the same premise: the actors will now show *you* how to play the scene. Stretch out the scene limits by declaring the peaks and valleys much more dramatically. And if the mechanics are stimulating ideas in the action, concentrate on character decorum, character-mood-intensity, unit division, and, above all, on character reciprocation. This last, remember, is your reason for being: to help *two* actors find the characters in each other.

The final periods begin with cleaning up the text and in pointing the text in the interest of projection. *The first obligation of a director is to be certain that a scene is well heard.* Apply all the points discussed in Chapter 12. You can reach the actors easily by writing notes as they play the scene, underlining words or phrases in the dialogue that need pointing, and working continuously for the proper emphasis or for the flavoring of lines or entire speeches. Polish the scene in every way to eliminate distractions. Remember that the actors can now take directions easily and quickly, for they probably know more about the insides of the scene than you do. Insist on high energy and the proper starting points (character-mood-intensities).

Economy in Director's Suggestions: Do Not Talk Much. This rule is absolute. The purpose of rehearsal is to let the actors experiment with the acting. If you fill the rehearsal periods with your own chatter, the actors will want to talk too, and the whole thing will turn into a talk-fest shambles. Your directions must, therefore, be economical and explicit, quiet and assured, good-humored and alive. Remember, you are playing a game with the actors, and you, above all, must keep the rehearsal free and comfortable. But you must also insist on what must be done. Honesty is the best policy, because students working together will respect one another only on that basis.

Directions Are to Individual Persons. You must devise your directions always in terms of the individual actors who are playing the roles, never in abstract terms. You must therefore watch your actors carefully, especially if you do not know them well, until you see what kind of suggestions seem to get through. The better you know your actors as creative people, the better you will know how to communicate with them. Some actors will need greatly exaggerated suggestions or images to move them; others will need only the barest suggestions. If an actor is already playing in an oversized fashion, make your images small and delicate. Reverse your approach for the "small" actor. If you need to show an actor what you mean—a last resort—do so in very oversized terms so that he can get the *essence* of what you are suggesting, not the literal reality of that suggestion, for your intention is not to have him mimic you but to have him absorb your idea and turn it into his own feeling for illustration on his own terms.

Improvisation in Rehearsal. Improvisations are used in rehearsal for the purpose of (1) freeing actors' imaginations, (2) effecting concentration, (3) uncovering dramatic action and character relationships, (4) bringing about reciprocation between actors. The process is the usual game playing, this time with the material of the playscript before lines are learned or even well-established in the minds of the actors. The intention is to draw actors into the given circumstances and subtext of a play by developing in them a high degree of concentration by letting them feel their way into close association with each other. Two actors thus make a magic circle of their reciprocal involvement, for if such improvisations are done with seriousness and release, actors can literally feel the high-tension rubberband that always ties them together as characters.

How much improvisation is actually used in rehearsal will depend on both your knowledge and skill with this sort of communication device and on the needs of the actors: their abilities to concentrate and reciprocate, and how obscure the subtext of the play on which they are working may be to them. This is no place for a detailed discussion of improvisa-

tional techniques, but here is a suggestion of the sort of thing that might
be done:

> One of the main problems with beginning actors is that of re-
> leasing themselves to one another at the intimate level, where dra-
> matic actions take place in Realistic plays. You must, therefore,
> design your improvisations with the purpose of breaking down bar-
> riers between actors in order to gain intimacy. Remove their self-
> consciousness by working with them in private. Reducing the light
> level in the rehearsal room will also help, for actors will feel less
> self-conscious and be able to throw off their personal facades in semi-
> darkness. Now encourage your actors to sit close to one another on
> the floor and actually touch one another by holding both hands and
> looking into one another's eyes. After a communion concentration
> has been established (this may take several minutes), improvising on
> the material of the playscript can begin with "1-2-3" dialogue (See
> p. 13 Exercise 9) representing the dramatic action. Each partici-
> pant should feel the sensations of *forcing* the other, of *adjusting*
> when it is his turn to be forced, and of taking his new action on the
> basis *only* of his adjustment. As the subtext develops in intensity,
> the two participants should pull or be pulled, never disengaging, and
> always responding to the pressure (dramatic action) of the other.
>
> The improvisation above can be varied by having the actors sit
> back to back with arms interlinked. Or it can be played by hold-
> ing hands over a chair, with each actor in his forcing action pulling
> the other to the edge of his balance (where he is about to fall). Both
> variations have the same purpose: feeling the force of reciprocal
> action. Such game playing will induce concentration because the
> participants will become involved in a physical way with each other
> and feel the intimacy of bodily force.
>
> Once intimacy and the sense of reciprocal forcing has been estab-
> lished, the actors could try improvising the subtext without holding
> hands or arms. The obstacles in a groundplan can supply the same
> holding force if you encourage their use. You can also prompt such
> an improvisation from the sidelines if you want to push the actors
> into new areas of the subtext. The important thing is to have the
> actors hold the magic circle of their intimate relationship as long as
> possible; when it breaks, you will need to start them again.

Experiment. In a rehearsal period, nothing must be set in a final way
until it works. You must be ingenious, a constant innovator, ready to
shift and bend as the need arises. And you must instill this sense of creative adventure in your actors, for they will go beyond themselves if you do.
Your job is to make them creative, not to show your own virtuosity. Art
is made only in creative circumstances where the imagination can be released. The playscript already provides the springboard; you must provide the swimming pool, the sunshine, the just-right water, and a good
deal of the gaiety and laughter.

PERFORMANCE

The audience will tell you very quickly and emphatically whether you have succeeded or not. You must always watch your scenes *with* the audience, listening as closely to it as you do to the actors. Scene practice as outlined in this chapter should always be completed by playing for an audience, even if it is only the rest of the class. Introduce your scene quickly and effectively, telling them only what they must know to avoid basic confusions. Lengthy recounting of previous action, etc., will be meaningless to them, and will even put them off your scene. An audience wants to use its own imagination, its own capabilities, not depend on someone else's. Do not hurt an audience's pride in its own resources. It will feel insulted only if you tell it (often by overplaying, or overemphasizing, points) that, as individuals, it is incompetent or insensitive. Reaching an audience is a difficult process, but the actor can do it very quickly and easily if he plays the action intensively and with sensitivity. *An audience is not interested in actors per se, but only in the characters they create;* they love those actors who arouse character images and strong feelings in them.

Good actors will always listen carefully to audiences before whom they play. This is why the theatre experience is an intimate one: the audience senses the actor, and the actor senses the audience. The gulf of a wide apron or an orchestra pit, or too large a house reduces all of this reciprocal feeling proportionally—the greater the actual distance, the more difficult the reciprocation. An audience seated in the balcony simply does not experience the play at the same level of intensity as those sitting close to the stage. This fact is reflected in the various ticket prices for different parts of a playhouse: you get the kind of play you pay for. A theatre in a democracy, then, really ought to be a small playhouse, not a large one just for the purpose of getting everyone inside who wants to come. We will have more to say about this view later.

Diagnostic Criticism

DEFINITION

A *diagnostic criticism* is a written critical analysis of a scene directed by another director. In one sense, it is *scene study* in reverse—from final performance back to play-analysis and directing approach.

CONCEPT

Although diagnostic criticism is your own analysis of another director's work, it serves a very important function in your training as a director. Not only does it give you additional scenes to study, but it also can develop your capability in finding what went right or what went wrong, simply because you can look more objectively at somebody else's work than you can at your own. Such criticism is a detailed look backward from the finished product to its origins, with a retracing of the significant intervening steps. You are the doctor who examines patients who are well and determines why they are well, but you are also the doctor who looks at patients who are ill and tries to find out what has made them ill. Study of both patients is necessary because you need to recognize easily what works and what does not.

In this view diagnostic criticism is the most positive criticism you can write for other directors as well as receive yourself. Do not fear personal animosities if you are on the receiving end, for the diagnostic critic must prove his points, not merely make them as newspaper play reviewers too frequently do. Your capability at diagnostic criticism will greatly improve your capability as a practicing director because directing is *close seeing and hearing*. Being the eyes and ears for someone else also means looking back upon yourself as a director.

A PRODUCTION PLAN FOR DIAGNOSTIC CRITICISM

Diagnostic criticism cannot be put to work effectively unless it is incorporated into an organized production plan that allows critics time and opportunity to do their work. It is therefore suggested that the class set up a rehearsal and performance schedule that will give assigned critics (perhaps two or three) copies of a scene several days prior to a performance. Thus, the critics will have time not only to read the entire play but also to consider in detail the particular scene to be performed. In this way, the critics come to the performance with some ideas about the scene and what can be done with it. Although critics should begin their written criticism as soon after a performance as possible, a deadline should be set no later than three days after the performance in order to keep the criticism as fresh as possible and also to give the experience a few hours of objectivity.

SOME TECHNIQUES IN DIAGNOSTIC CRITICISM

Here is an outline of what to look for. Study it carefully.

An Outline for Diagnostic Criticism

Criticisms should follow explicitly the form outlined below. Please use the identical numbering system in writing your analysis.

I. *Action Summary.* Study carefully a copy of the scene, *before* you see the scene performed. Number the units of action, and give the action in each unit as *you analyze it in the playscript.* Be careful to show reciprocal action by stating it in abbreviated sentence form: A (verb) to B, and B (verb) to A. Your awareness and perception of the action, as stated here, is the basis of your criticism, and it will partially inform the director about how you arrived at your conclusions.

II. *Technical Analysis.* Discuss the produced scene under the following headings:

A. Groundplan
   1. Number of acting areas
   2. Usability
   3. Ingenuity
B. Composition. Discuss the use of areas, planes, levels, body positions, triangles, etc., detailing several examples explicitly.
C. Picturization. Detail successful ones particularly noticed.
D. Movement. Pick out specific movements, and comment.
E. Improvisation with objects. Detail objects used, and the effective illustration they have made possible. What objects might have been used to better advantage?

III. *Characterization.* In this section, discuss the acting of the scene by detailing what each actor has done and estimating the extent of the director-actor communication that has taken place.

A. Character A
   1. Against the ideal in the playscript.
      a) Delineate the character as *you* see it in the playscript;
      b) Compare how well the actor accomplished this ideal.
   2. Decorum
   3. Believability
B. Character B
   1. Against the ideal in the playscript.
      a) Delineate the character as *you* see it in the playscript;
      b) Compare how well the actor accomplished this ideal.
   2. Decorum
   3. Believability
C. Repeat A and B for any additional characters.
D. Synthesis. Discuss here the reciprocation: how well the actors played together—their intercommunication.

IV. *Overall Evaluation*

    A. Moods created. List here the specific moods created.
    B. Tone. Enter only yes or no; make no further comment.
    C. Qualifications. Qualify *B* here.

The reason for written criticism is that it forces you to put into words exactly what you have noticed about a scene, thus giving you specific practice in director communication. Merely "talking" your criticism—that is, doing it in a conversational way in the classroom without first writing it down—encourages looseness of expression as well as mushy thinking. If you write down your criticism in an organized way, you probably believe what you have to say and can support it. Type the criticism and proofread it carefully, for your colleagues will listen to you only if they know you have done your criticism with great care.

When the written work has been completed, the criticism should be discussed orally in the group. Oral discussion is the most important thing you do in this technique, because a director must be verbally articulate, and you can now speak your ideas because you are prepared to discuss them. You can also practice your verbal capability. The purpose is to *get through* to another director without so irritating and antagonizing him that you fail to communicate.

Note that the criticism begins with your own statement of the action. This sort of criticism is based both on your seeing the scene and on your study of a copy of the playscript itself. You should know the entire play, and you must be thoroughly familiar with the content of the scene performed. Put down the action carefully, as prescribed in the first section of the form for diagnostic criticism, because all that you have to say can be weighted explicitly against your concept of the action. If you see the scene before you record the action, you must be doubly careful not to let its *presentation* of the action sway your own opinion about what is going on. The secret of a good diagnostic criticism lies explicitly in your perception of a scene's action.

Also pay particular attention to the section on characterization. Again, you must set down what you think the playwright prescribes the character to be before you comment on what a particular actor did in making the characterization. A clear analysis here on your part will tell you something about the director-actor communication in the scene: Did the director get through to the actors? Other parts of the criticism will soon tell you whether he understood the dramatic action or not. The synthesis in Section III, D of the form is very important because the effectiveness of the scene will be declared specifically in the level of reciprocation with which the actors play.

Tone is used in Section IV, B as a word to indicate total accomplishment of the aims of the scene: Did the scene work? Did it accomplish its basic intention in the play? Was the audience moved to laughter or to the serious moods intended by the playwright? This sort of statement is, of course, pure opinion, but you know the strength of your own feelings, and you were also aware of how the rest of the audience seemed to respond. Take a sharp stand on tone, saying yes or no, and then modify your opinion in Section IV, C.

In writing this sort of criticism, always remember that you are writing to another human being—a director—who, like an actor, is very sensitive about his creative work. Practice your skill at honest, careful statement without being cruel and arrogant. Do not generalize! Generalities hurt and confuse. Be specific, and be direct, supporting all your points with carefully chosen evidence. The opinionated are those who speak out of their emotions, not out of their considered evaluation—a mixture of feeling and mind. Although a director is a person of very strong feelings, he is also a man with a mind, and a mind takes care how it talks. Remember that you are making a diagnosis, not writing a diatribe against a play like a professional reviewer with the intention of entertaining casual readers. You are a responsible person who respects the work of others, and your comment will be respected if it is offered with care and precision. But although you must always be honest and say what you think, there is no excuse whatever for cruelty and dishonesty. Look for the best in others to find the best in yourself.

III

COMMUNICATION 2:
THE DIRECTOR-
DESIGNER RELATIONSHIP AND
THE PRODUCTION PROCESS

O shows, shows, mighty shows!
The eloquence of masques!   What need of prose,
Or verse, or sense, t'express immortal you?
.   .   .   .
Or to make boards to speak!   there is a task!
Painting and carpentry are the soul of masque.

> BEN JONSON expressing his anger at designer
> Inigo Jones for subordinating the poet's
> words to scenery.

14

designing is directing

Nearly three-quarters of a century ago, English designer Gordon Craig, in a brief and very famous essay entitled "The Art of the Theatre," delineated the function of the director. It was a radical view when he set it down, but today it is the basis of our theatre. Although the director had been at work in one way or another for three or four decades before Craig wrote his essay, no one had defined his individuality so explicitly and so imaginatively. Predominately a scene designer, Craig began his stage career as an actor, a position from which he could readily see the enormous importance of a coordinating head if the theatre was to have any pretension as an art form. It was this sort of thinking that brought about the New Movement in Theatre Art early in this century, the movement that declared the director the twentieth-century's theatrical artist.

In his essay, Craig delineated two kinds of directors: the *artist*-director who creates everything, including the playscript, and the *master crafts-man*-director who is a designer-coordinator. Craig's artist-director has appeared occasionally in moving-picture making where diverse directors —for example, Charlie Chaplin and Ingmar Bergman—have shown us that such a creative individual is quite possible, but in the theatre, despite the directing efforts of several playwrights from Bernard Shaw to

Arthur Miller, he did not materialize until the improvisational productions of "The Living Theatre" in the 1960s, and even that may be a significant modification of the Craigian idea—a point that will be discussed in Chapter 26. It is Craig's master craftsman, however, that is the prototype of today's practicing director. The important thing to note is that Craig intended this sort of director to keep a very tight hand on all that happens on the stage from the development of the playscript to the final performance, for one person in charge of manipulating actors and coordinating staging designs obviously has many advantages.

Though he actually may not be acknowledged on a program as a designer is, today's director, nevertheless, is the principal designer of a production. As "the theatrical artist," he is responsible for both what is seen and what is heard. Thus, it is through his eyes and ears that an audience actually experiences a produced play. The last major section of the book (Part IV) deals with interpretation—a very personal way of thinking about a play and expressing it in production, but before we can talk about individual expression we must comprehend fully the mechanics of the stage: *how* it can be used as an instrument of communication.

Design is the physicalization of poetic idea. Consequently, unless a director can control the visual and aural (hearing) elements that constitute design, he is powerless in making an individual statement—a situation that would put us back in the dark ages of the nineteenth century when the "stage-manager" merely gave an order to the Stage Carpenter to have the Dark Fancy set, or the Kitchen set, or the Light Fancy set, or the Wood set placed on stage at a given time. That sort of stock scenery, as you can readily see, had no individuality at all in terms of a specific play, for it was intended to serve general purposes and not specific ones, as we use scenery today. Our present process may seem terribly expensive and wasteful, but it is part of our theatre aesthetic, which demands *individualization*. Therefore, as the principal designer, a director must take the responsibility for the individualized statement. If he is an artist he will speak freshly, for art is always a fresh, personal view.

Directing, then, is not a mere manipulation of the actor and the physical stage; it is *considered* and *appropriate* manipulation, what Eric Bentley calls "the correct presentation of a poem." The concept at its base is simply this: the playscript provides the dramatic action, and the director uses the many tools at his command to illustrate that action—he uses his visual and oral tools with actors, which you have already studied in Part II, and his scenic production tools usually with designers, which you will study in Part III. Each group of tools has its techniques and its values. What the director must learn is how to use well all of these tools and not just a few. The variety and complexity of his production effort will reflect what he knows about these tools and how well he can use them.

Learn the concept underlying each technique, and you will then know how to put it to work for you.

The next few chapters in this book will greatly expand the functions of the director as they have been so far presented, for you are going to look at the director's relationship to *the stage machine:* the stage itself, scenery, properties, lighting, makeup, costumes, and sound effects. The problems connected with using this machine are as complex as those in the director-actor relationship because the stage machine requires a diversity of talents to bring out its highest potentials. When a director does the whole job himself, as he might in a small educational theatre setup or in a one-man, community-theatre operation, all he has to do is argue out the designs with himself and then carry out what his own imagination and his physical resources allow him to do. But though there are definite advantages to such a setup, a director in this situation is bound by his own limitations—the same sort of limitations he would meet if he tried to act every role in a play himself. Consequently, a director should know how to work with a number of designers, each of whom has a capability for illuminating a play in his own particular way. *He will thus discover that his job is not only to synthesize a cast of actors but is also to synthesize a cast of designers who must be led into achieving unity in a production.* Only when a director can bring about a harmony of statement from both of his casts does a true synthesis in production occur.

The content of Part III is, therefore, devoted to *how* a director leads his designers toward the synthesis he desires. As you can readily see, if each designer is allowed to do as he pleases, a multiheaded, haphazard production can be the only result. Each man for himself, as it would in an acting situation, can produce nothing but bedlam. Only when a director "controls" his designers in the same way that he "controls" his actors, is it possible for a director's idea to emerge.

Yet, despite this problem of control, a director would be very foolish indeed not to give his designers the same sort of freedom he gives his actors, for designers are artists in their own right—the descendants of a much older breed of theatre craftsmen than the director. Their particular capability lies in their high degree of visual imagination. They see things. And it can be through their seeing that a normal audience can be aroused to many kinds of empathic response. A good designer is as rare as a good actor, and he is just as sensitive about what he makes and shows to others. Any director who imagines that he can see better is probably only fooling himself. The director's job, then, is not that of a specialist seer but that of a coordinating seer who recognizes designing talent and exploits it to the full. The director does not suppress designers in the interests of tight control but inspires and arouses ideas along the lines of his own vision. In this process he may find, as he does with actors, a new and better vision of the play than the one he held previously on his own.

The Historical Relationship of Direction and Design

It was this problem of synthesis that brought the director into the theatre. As has been pointed out frequently elsewhere, the contribution of the twentieth century to the history of the theatre has been artistic play interpretation, an integration process of production in which the director has figured prominently. In this century, we have looked at theatre history not only as a thing in itself but as a highly useful background for production, and it has led us to revivals of both earlier plays and ideas of production on a scale no previous age ever knew. We have tried to make our stage machine adaptable to every period and style—an effort that has led us recently into the trap of multipurpose theatre-building design. Whether such a multipurpose machine can really work is still an open question.

Previous to the nineteenth century, stage design for plays was more general than specific, more an appropriate background (and frequently an inappropriate one) for dramatic action than a participant in it. This approach directly reflected the concept of a play as a *presentation* in bold, broad lines. The development of science and technology in the nineteenth century found its way directly into the theatre in forms that not only required that scenery appear to be like nature but that it create specific environments for specific plays. This scientific naturalism required much greater control of the stage machine as well as of acting, and it was at this point that the director was brought into the theatre as a much-needed craftsman. The general use of the stage soon became the particular use of the stage, and out of this was born twentieth-century stage production.

Nevertheless, even though the actor did not actually perform within the stage setting during the seventeenth and most of the eighteenth centuries, we know that some coordination took place, that someone placed the scenery and told the actors where to stand. We usually assume that this coordinator, where there was one, was either the "stage-manager" or an "actor-manager," but it could just as well have been the stage designer. It is not stretching historical projection out of focus to imagine that when Inigo Jones made his elaborate painted settings for his spectacular masques at the English Court in Shakespeare's day, he also directed the

performers to certain positions in relation to the scenery, which he probably designed with their positioning in mind. Perhaps this "direction" is
what may have so irritated Ben Jonson and what provoked him to write
the lines condemning Jones that appear on the title page of Part III.
The designer as stage director has much support when we speculate about
the theatre of the past.

But whatever total function designers may have served in past ages, in
the late nineteenth century they were brought under the control of directors who could then harmonize their creativity with that of the actors in
the interest of making a total theatre experience. And so it remains
today.

The Purpose of This Book Regarding Design

It should now be obvious that the purpose of treating design in this
book is not to train you as a designer but to focus a hard and direct look
at the problems of coordination facing the director in today's theatre.
Design training is as difficult and involved a process as actor training, and
this book is no place for such complex discussions. What is of great importance here is that the director see his functions as designer clearly and
in depth. Such an intention cannot be carried out, however, without a
thorough study of the functions of stage design, for the many options
open to a director in stage production can be brought into focus only if
he understands what is going on at the base.

Furthermore, it is generally assumed, largely because of the Stanislavskian wave in actor training, that director training should be largely in
the area of acting, with its subareas of voice, body, and movement.
There can be no question that such specialization has its intrinsic values,
for who will teach acting if not the director. But this point of view also
assumes, unfortunately, that designers will take care of the other aspects
of production, that somehow visual design in the theatre is considerably
less important than acting design. This assumption is very shortsighted
because it overlooks the concept of total theatre, in which the director as
theatrical artist—the point of view of this book—coordinates both the
acting and the visual presentation of a play's ideas.

The training of a director in all the areas of design is, therefore, essential—not haphazard but full-scale, intensive training, for stage designing requires first an artist and second someone who can work within the
limitations of the theatre. Stage designing is not the making of an arty
background for actors nor the operation of a technical machine, but an
organic expression of a high order. Stringent comment on the background and training of prominent stage designers in our century is re-

flected in the fact that when it comes to writing theatre histories, it is not directors who have made the major contributions but designers. The program of studies suggested below is therefore set out with the intention of alerting the directing student to possibilities in design training. A well-conceived program would contain much of the following:

A cultural history of specific civilizations (Chinese, Egyptian, Greek, etc.) in order to comprehend the meaning of culture in its social and intellectual aspects.

A survey of painting and sculpture; a course in life drawing; an elementary course in painting; an advanced course in art history.

Theatre history: theatre buildings, stages, scenery, etc.

Costume history: a history of clothes as well as what was worn on the stage.

Elementary drawing for the stage: mechanical, perspective, and free rendition.

Scene design and staging materials.

Costume design.

Lighting design and engineering.

Such training may seem extensive to the beginner, but as he becomes more familiar with the complex, diverse problems facing the director, he will soon see the need for such a careful step-by-step building of his design capabilities.

Exercises in Part III

Since it is assumed that the student is simultaneously pursuing some sort of training in design, and, consequently, is actively engaged in regularly assigned projects, no exercises in design of the usual sort are suggested here or in the following chapters. Instead, two procedures are used: the first involves working through Chapters 14 through 18 with a full-length, classroom play for study as the principal device for emphasizing the director's options in design; and the second involves designing and directing a live production of a one-act play, outlined in Chapter 19, as a summarizing project for all of Part III. These two projects taken together will place you on the second level of directing—coordination and synthesis in play production. The third level—style—will be presented in Part IV.

Finding a good study play at this point is essential because investigating a director's options in the area of design requires a play with multiple possibilities if you are to see the full range of the problem. Furthermore, a long play is suggested because you not only need to study this form as a contrast to the one-act play, but you will also be able to see the concepts of coordination and synthesis much more clearly because of the scope it allows. Thus, you can make progress on two fronts. Although the class or its instructor can certainly make an independent choice, and may prefer to do so, for purposes of discussion here all the exercises in Part III are focused on Arthur Miller's *The Crucible*. This play offers many advantages because of its undated content, despite its writing date of the early 1950s; its multi-act structure with different locations; its style of Realism that allows a fairly wide scope in staging; and the many problems in coordination and synthesis in design that it presents. Exercises with this play begin immediately at the end of this chapter. They do not attempt to be exhaustive in any way but merely guide you and your class to the sort of questions a director must ask himself.

The main intention of Part III, then, is to insure that you comprehend the relationship of the director to visual design and to designers by understanding thoroughly the concepts of symbolization, synthesis, and the communication process in design. You will not only need to discuss extensively in the classroom all of the points in Part III, but you are also encouraged to pursue these concepts in talk outside with both directing and design students. Here is one place where directors can do a good deal of talking without getting into trouble.

In addition, you should be certain that you understand one concept before going on to the next. The material is laid out here in a logical progression, and you can advance only with step-by-step comprehension. Some of the points may seem obvious to you, but dealing with them is just where the difficulties begin, because your theatre-going experiences up to this point have probably been quite unoriented toward design and this lack of orientation may have led you to take a very great deal for granted. You will need fresh eyes at this point in order to tear apart the obvious and to discover that the obvious is not obvious at all, for someone has designed what you see and that means that decisions have been made about it. Always remember that a design is a conceived plan, not an accident.

You will learn to see well only if you remove your own blindness; no one else can do that for you.

EXERCISES

1. You should begin your study of *The Crucible* by doing an analysis of the play in a special way that will enable you to study its structure for design purposes without having to do the exhaustive study necessary for directing actors. This sort of study is what directors frequently do in making a choice of a play for production, that is, it precedes a major play-analysis but it still enables a director to get a firm grasp of the play in order to make preliminary decisions about it. But you should in no sense accept it

as a substitute for a full play-analysis, for you simply cannot direct actors without such study.

Your first job is to read the play by recording the action in two ways:

a. Record the story of the play by writing down both previous action and dramatic action on sheets of paper with lines drawn vertically to separate the two kinds of action. Record the previous action in red on one side and the dramatic action in black on the other. As you may remember, this exercise was the first one you did in doing a play-analysis. You can do this exercise easily if, when you read the play (each student should have his own copy), you make a note about what happens on each page of the playscript, and then carry this note over to your summarizing sheets.

b. When (a) has been completed, you are ready to do a director's scene-analysis. This analysis you do by making a list of all the scenes in the play that are performed by the two or three most important characters. These are the major scenes in the dramatic action because the playwright deliberately has centered the forces of the play around them. These scenes are also climactic, thus containing the principal discoveries and consequent adjustments. Thus, analyzing them will give you a quick grasp of the play's structure. (If you choose a study play with only two to five characters, be sure that you select the *principal* climactic scenes, since the play will be made up of two- or three-character scenes.) In *The Crucible,* you will find eight to ten of these scenes. Now write a comment about each scene with attention on two points: the scene's requirements in terms of acting; the scene's requirements in terms of staging.

2. When you have completed the two parts of Exercise 1, you are ready for a class discussion of the play. Proceed in the usual fashion for discussion of play-analysis, but instead of pursuing the seven major elements in detail, concentrate your discussions around specific points, such as:

a. Why is *The Crucible* not a historical play? Why is it not a costume drama? How is it very contemporary?

b. Who are the protagonist and the antagonist? Be sure you see Danforth's function in the play. Do you see Abigail's function as an instrument to effect the action? How do Proctor and Danforth clash head-on?

c. Characterize Danforth. Can you see him as a politician rather than as a stern judge representing the church?

d. What is the real witchcraft in the play? Should an audience believe in the witchcraft shown in Act I? What should an audience reaction be to this act? Could it possibly be laughter at certain lines? Should an audience hold the same view as John Proctor? Why?

e. What role does Reverend Hales play in the action? What are his polar attitudes? What are John Proctor's? What are Danforth's?

3. If you have done Exercises 1 and 2 carefully, you should be able to delineate the differences in structure between a long play and a short one.

What does the long play allow in the way of character development? How many major characters are developed in *The Crucible?* How complex is the action? How many plots are there in *The Crucible?* (*Plot* here means the separate lines of action: Abigail and the girls, Abigail and Proctor, etc.)

4. Read Gordon Craig's essay, "The Art of the Theatre." Discuss its contents in class.

15

the director
and the stage machine:
symbolization and synthesis

You have become so accustomed in this day of science and machines to see things around you only in external ways, to see your physical environment as merely useful and functional, that it is very difficult indeed to recapture the other kind of seeing you knew as a small child but somehow lost as you were subjected to the controls and conformities of adult life. Yet, it must be done if you, as a student in the arts, are to discover what art is all about. Wordsworth's verse "The child is father of the man" has very particular meaning from an artistic point of view because it epitomizes the very nature of the artist who must relearn, or have somehow retained, the freedom and simplicity of his childhood vision. Today's emphasis in actor training on improvisation and games has as its goal to free the individual from his rigid behavioral pattern and to release his imagination as an active, living force. The same thing must be done for the learning designer or director. In the art world, to see things eccentrically is to see them normally and freshly. Without this free imagination, one is forever tied to accepted and prosaic realities.

The moving picture previous to the 1960s and most television, from its beginnings to the present time, have had an enormous influence on this restriction in seeing. We have been drugged into the insensibility of *observable* reality: we assume that what we see literally and see quickly is all that there is. Consequently, we tend to disregard the other kind of seeing: that seeing which exists on the imaginative level. If the moving picture of the 1960s accomplished anything new, it might be said that it began to open up our vision again to the mainstream of the history of art forms, including the theatre, because many new films penetrated the surface realities and took some hard looks underneath. Such films, with their appeal made largely to an adult audience, had a greater sophistication than did their predecessors, but they found favor not because of their sexual content but because of their mature themes and complex perceptions. These films have had an effect on the theatre by helping to force the theatre back into the mainstream of dramatic literature, where revelation and poetic insights are possible.

The problem of seeing revolves around symbolization. Theatre is *not* reality; it is contrivance.

Symbolization means that we actually see life more clearly, more perceptively, by sensing it through the recognizable essences of things. This definition does not in any way rule out the use on the stage of what we regard as real objects. What it does force us to do as director-designers is to use objects in *appropriate* and *contextual* ways so that their full values can be exploited artistically and our vision amplified. When used in these ways, the stage machine becomes organic: not only do we show scenery, properties, light, or costumes for what they are in themselves, but we extend greatly their life and vitality, their image-making powers, through actors who reveal their essences.

As a director, then, you must learn the fine art of symbolization if you are to use the stage machine with any degree of sophistication. And you will learn that you can reach audiences excitingly and with direct contact through symbolization where you have failed with the mere use of surface realities.

Design is not decoration but organic symbolization.

Symbolization Is Theatre

CONVENTION

A stage convention is a contrivance with symbolic values.

Continuous use of a contrivance so firmly establishes it in the feelings of audiences that they accept it as part of familiar stage form without any effort whatsoever. They perceive its symbolic meanings and take it for granted. Conventions thus become deeply rooted, so much so, in fact, that artistic revolts are often needed to overthrow them. The raised platform is just such a form. So are the proscenium arch, the painted scenery, the architectural stone wall of the Greek theatre, and the stage projecting into the house in Shakespeare's day. The late nineteenth century went through a revolt in its attack on Romantic staging, replacing it with illusionistic conventions, and the twentieth century is going through a similar revolt against the illusory theatre in its attempt to break away from the conventions of Realism.

A director must grasp the concept of stage convention and the force it exerts on popular audience feelings and comprehension. This perception is also a basis of design understanding.

THEATRE HISTORY AND DESIGN

A look at theatre history tells us a very great deal about stage form, but directors do not study history with the intention of merely turning back to the past in order to copy it, for that procedure would not only be impossible in view of the scarcity of facts about such stages, but such a return would simply result in noncommunication with modern audiences, a point of view that will be discussed in detail in Part IV. What directors do is pursue theatre history intensely because it leads to a much greater comprehension of theatre theory and the function of design, for theatre history, apart from the study of dramatic literature—you must always keep *theatre* and *drama* separate as concepts—is largely the study of the use of the stage machine, including the buildings where the machines are housed, throughout two thousand five hundred years of Western culture. What directors want to know is how other ages handled the problems of stage form—the same form we are still using today, though our materials and methods of handling it are different. For example, how did other ages handle the problems of: the stage as a manipulative *place* for playing; the kinds of scenic materials that could be used to make that *place* more effective; the building or place of containment for the audience and the stage; what the actor should wear on his body and on his face to enhance his meaning in that place; how the *seeing place* could be lighted; what mechanical sounds could be used to intensify meaning? That is all there is to theatre production, and in one way or another it was all in use at the first performances Thespis devised in 534 B.C. just as they are today. The form of theatre does not change but only the conventions and styles within the form.

The study of theatre history, then, as distinct from the study of dramatic literature, is the study of variations in the use of staging concepts—variations that have been extensive. Thus, a director who is not also a student of theatre history can have only a superficial understanding of the major tools through which he makes his creative statements. There can be no question that this knowledge is necessary for the staging of historical drama, but you must also be highly aware that it is also of enormous value in the staging of modern drama simply because your knowledge of *what is possible* in making theatre can be greatly extended.

This book cannot possibly examine, except in a summarizing way, all you must know about theatre architecture, the stage place, scenery, costuming, makeup, lighting, and sound. Each is a specialized study in itself and should be pursued with specialized intentions in these areas. What needs to be pointed out here is the nature of change in the design function in theatre history and the necessity for a director's understanding of it.

Changes are clearly marked by shifts in conventions, but the constant factor behind all the changes is symbolism: each age found a characteristic symbolism for projecting its ideas through its stage machine. Imaginative theatre historians such as George Kernodle and Richard Southern have pursued these changes in great detail, and you should study their books for specific illumination of the subject.

Consequently, what follows is a brief résumé of the interrelationships of the staging tools. They are set out at this point in the interest of showing what the director must study in theatre history if he is to comprehend the theatre machine. These are the areas you must understand conceptually.

Theatre Architecture. The study of theatre architecture deals with the relationship between the playing space and the audience. Such study leads to: a comprehension of the "size" of plays and what this has to do with the arrangement of audiences; an awareness of the effects of physical distance on the relationship of actors and audience; an understanding of how see-ability and hear-ability of actors depend not only on this distance but the height levels of audience positions in relation to the playing space; a comprehension of the problems of acoustics and of an actor's projection arc (the maximum arc—from side-to-side—that a speaking actor can use and still be heard); an understanding of stage lighting through daylight or through artificial devices.

Playing Space. This area is concerned with what is commonly referred to as "the stage," but since that term is so often confused with a raised platform, the broader, more conceptual, term is used here. Any historical study of playing space would certainly reveal that actors have played on the ground level with the audience on the same level; on the ground level with the audience raised in graduated steps; on both ground level and raised platforms simultaneously; on raised platforms of varying levels, with the audience below or on various levels; in circular or square or rectangular or triangular arrangements.

Scenery. This term is used here in the broadest sense to delineate the backing of the playing space or the occupation of the space itself. Thus, it includes permanent architectural facades, moveable backing pieces, permanent or moveable objects, platforms, and other devices within the playing space. Study of theatre history shows a wide variety of uses, from the architectural facades of the fifth-century Greek theatre (perhaps also with some moveable pieces) to the painted scenery on cloth mounted freely or attached to frames, which we commonly refer to as Baroque scenery, to the architectural facades with moveable pieces in the playing space that we know today, to the latest devices of projected scenery, both stationary or moving behind the actor.

Costuming and Makeup. The actor has always worn something to declare his difference from members of the audience, although, as in the case of modern Realism, this difference is so subtle that it seems at first glance like no difference at all. Yet difference there surely is, because costume, like all the other tools in the stage machine, must symbolize. What we notice through a study of theatre history is that a costume can make an actor look larger than a human being by raising him on stilts or increasing the height of his head with extended headdress; that it can make him look wider, and thus more imposing, by extensions of shoulders and arm garments; that the actor's face and head can be changed into all sorts of shapes and meanings through the use of masks, wigs, and false hair, or through its pale descendant—painted makeup; that some ages have used what it regarded as the best of court dress; that some have used archeological and historical reproduction; and that some have worn practically no costume at all in an effort to find a *neutral body.*

Lighting. The history of lighting in the theatre is not as extensive a study as is, for instance, scenery and costuming, but the director must be fully aware of what *was* done in order to more fully comprehend dramatic literature and historical stage production. The fact that the Greek theatre, the Roman theatre of Plautus and Terence, the Medieval street theatre, and the Elizabethan public playhouse all saw plays in daylight tells us much about the workings of the plays and their productions. Likewise, to see the Renaissance drama in candlelight as did Shakespeare's audience at Blackfriars theatre, one of the first indoor playhouses in England, or at the Teatro Olímpico, or at Drury Lane in Garrick's day is to help us understand intimacy, confinement, and how soft light can create a rare beauty of its own. And to understand the gas lighting of the nineteenth century is also to comprehend the enormous revolution in lighting when it was shifted to electrical power and control. To see lighting only in its twentieth-century aspects is to miss its historical significance as a theatrical device and how it can act on our own ideas in lighting maneuverability. Why burn large torches in midday as was done in street theatre in the fifteenth and sixteenth centuries? A director should "get the feel."

Sound. The reed and stringed instruments of the Greeks; Shakespeare's live musicians above the stage and on the stage as actors; the Drottningholm's canonball track above the stage to make thunder; the nineteenth-century's orchestral background to the melo (music)-drama— all these are design ideas, some so thoroughly embedded that they became conventions that plays could not do without. We are so accustomed to hearing music as part of a moving-picture sound track that we take it for granted as a convention and are startled to hear a film deliberately designed without such a score. Can you hear the sound of an actor's voice in a huge Greek amphitheatre? From a Roman platform in the context of a fair? From a scaffold erected on a street for the commedia dell' arte? From the intimate forestage of a six-hundred–seat Georgian theatre? From the stage of an enormous three-thousand–seat, nineteenth-century theatre? The moving picture is largely a visual experience: we watch the face and eyes of a character through close-ups, and in this way, we come to know him intimately. In contrast, the stage is both a visual and an aural experience: we can be moved as intensively by the live human voice as by what we see.

It should be clear, then, that the study of theatre history is imperative for the director if he is to have any comprehension of stage design and the options open to him in producing a play. And even more important, only through this study can he truly understand the concept of symbolization.

Synthesis Is a Necessity

GENERAL DESIGN VERSUS SPECIFIC DESIGN

Stage design means making something for the stage by intention rather than leaving the effect to accident. This definition implies that stage design is an art form, a minor one though it may be. Consequently, stage design will have all the elements of artistic form: unity, coherence, proportion, arrangement, selection, economy, grace, and rhythm. A director's visual sense, like a costumer's or a scenic artist's, must be highly refined in order to be capable of perceiving these essences that contribute to the making of symbolic representations.

Design is, therefore, always a *specific thing* though a particular design may be stated so simply that it appears to have a general quality. But if what is placed on a stage is too loose, too free, if it lacks an interesting arrangement of line and mass, we cannot, as audience, perceive it at all. Thus, if a director-designer places only materials on the stage without conceiving their effect, he will not make a statement we can call design, for they will have no relationship to other aspects of the context.

The director has been needed in the theatre in the twentieth century, as you already know from previous discussions in this book, in order to bring about a synthesis in design: to place actors in relationship not just to each other but to the materials on the stage. In the nineteenth century, the whole process was much more haphazard, much more left to chance, although a self-conscious awareness began to grow when it was discovered that coordinated design could make the meanings of a play not only much clearer but more exciting. Actors had their own wardrobes which they either designed themselves or, if they were stars, had designed for them from the suggestions they provided. The scenery was usually designed for spectacular productions, but the intention was to create a pictorial background representing a place and a time; it was neither organically conceived nor was it symbolic. In the latter part of the nineteenth century, new designers like Appia and Craig developed the concept of synthesis, and with it the director became a necessity. At its most idealistic, this concept suggested that one person could do all the physical designs of scenery, costuming, and lighting as had occasionally been done by some designers since the nineteenth century, but what now became clear was that if he was to control the physical production he would also have to control the actor. Although the one-man autocrat has been rare in practice, the concept of synthesis has been well established, for it is the only way specific design can be controlled.

BALANCE AND IMBALANCE IN SYNTHESIS

Balance is at the heart of the concept of synthesis. Without balance in the media brought together, without the most careful joining of playscript, actors, and designs, there can be no synthesis. This statement does not imply that a production must have all these in equal parts and must turn out to be like a product of a vegetable juice blender—an undefined reddish mixture—but it is more like a well-conducted symphony in which the conductor brings out at appropriate times, and with appropriate strengths, the various components of his orchestra—now the violins, now the horns, now the cellos, now the woodwinds—while he is blending the whole into a sensitive, harmonic, and absorbing complex.

It is easier to see the nature of balance by looking at imbalance in production. Among the factors that contribute to imbalance, the following occur so frequently that they are worth pointing out as production traps: (1) self-conscious directing; (2) underdesign; (3) overdesign.

Self-conscious Directing. When we watch a production, if we are too aware of the mechanics, too aware of a striving for effect, we are watching self-conscious directing. Instead of being drawn into the inner story line and receiving the production with unbroken empathy on the level of our imaginations, we are disconcerted and distracted by a director who lays a production onto a playscript rather than pulls it out of the playscript. Thus, his blocking may be mechanically contrived rather than organically embedded in dramatic action, or the designs may be too self-conscious, drawing audience attention away from the actors. It can be said that directing is the art of *reducing distraction* in the imaginations of viewers in order to leave those imaginations free to do their own work. By pushing too hard for effect in the wrong way, the effect is lost. The focus of an audience must always be placed on the human values deriving from the playscript and not on the mechanics of projecting those values.

Underdesign. When a director is not thoroughly aware of what part visual design plays in play production, he may settle for a much less effective statement than a play needs for its best fulfillment. When this happens, such a production will lack vitality or enough symbolization to project the play into the imaginations of an audience. Theatre as distinct from drama means the actual live presentation of a play before an audience through *theatrical* means; it is not merely a play read for an audience. The values are very different. Some critics of modern Shakespearian productions maintain that far too many are overproduced, that they cannot "hear" the play because there is too much scenic enhancement. What they are probably saying is that they do not like theatre very much as a production art but are enamored of the text as a piece of literature. If we, as audience, get hung up over Shakespearian wordage, it may not be at all because of the elaborateness of the production but only because of the difficulty with an archaic language. Underdesign may perhaps make a Shakespearian production more easily heard, but it may lose the very essence of what is most Shakespearian about it which only the "vulgarity" of the theatre can reproduce. Underdesign and simplicity of design are not the same thing. Simple design can be highly organic and intensively arouse imagination. The director's goal is to release imagination in an audience, and he must find the necessary symbols for doing that with each play he produces.

Overdesign. The greatest danger that occurs when a director can work with skilled designers is doing too much. Each designer, as a matter of course, wants to make his own design as effective as possible, and when costumer, scene designer, and lighting designer are separate people, the whole problem of balance is intensified. The principal danger is that of overwhelming the actors who have difficulty enough in holding their own against the dynamics of visual effects. It is in controlling this situation, like controlling the balance in acting, that the director exerts a primary force on production. But the great problem is that, as with actors, he must work through the imaginations of others (the designers), and it is in guiding these imaginations, not in dictating their direction, where his primary work as a director-designer is done. Overdesign can be ruinous because it stultifies audience imagination by depriving it of focus on the interior values of a play. An audience can all too easily be swept away by spectacle, with the consequent loss of the play as a total theatrical experience.

COUNTERPOINT IN SYNTHESIS OF DESIGN

At first glance, it would seem possible for a director to achieve synthesis in the areas of visual design—set, costume, and light—by bringing the designers to the same point of view regarding the emphases to be made in a production; that all a director would need to do would be to declare the emphatic points as he sees them, and then have the designers emphasize those points. Such a procedure, however, not only does not exploit the design possibilities, but it may actually stultify audience imagination and cause distraction by too obvious overloading at the points of emphasis.

Although a director and his designers must have a mutual understanding of a basic common direction, full exploitation of visual effects lies *not in the likeness* of the designs but *in their difference.* You will understand this idea better after the discussion of the design process in Chapter 19, but at this point you should appreciate the fact that arousal of imagination frequently depends on clash and conflict in the visual effects, not on repetitive or seemingly harmonious statements. As characters clash in a play, so must the various elements of visual design.

A simple example of how counterpoint can work is a production of a historical play that uses an abstract setting, realistic costumes based on clothing of the period, and lights with strongly contrasted highlights and shadows—all to the accompaniment of modern jazz as musical background. As you can see, an audience will be disconcerted by the lack of expected harmony, with the consequent awakening of fresh imagery of all sorts. If the acting is strong and very much alive, this theatrical experience can be a truly exciting one.

The theatre is an attack on the senses as well as on the mind, and without sense-awakening approaches to design, the basic nature of theatre is lost.

Counterpoint as a design approach does not in any way imply that all production must be highly melodramatic and theatrical; it merely suggests that different areas of design can do different things, and that it is the total effect the director must work for—an effect that is disconcerting rather than restful.

Counterpoint is, therefore, an important principle in design. The director who does his own designing must give intensive consideration to this point, for he is a ready victim to the obvious in design. When he may think he is moving his audience with intensive design emphasis, he may merely be hitting an idea on the head with a sledgehammer and thus driving it away from imaginative audience reception. Do not wallow in design emphasis; counterpoint it.

EXERCISES

1. If you have not already done so, read Richard Southern's *The Seven Ages of Theatre*. This reading will give you an excellent idea of the concepts of symbolization and convention in various historical periods and in cultures very different from our own.

2. Apply these two concepts to *The Crucible* in a class discussion:
    a. Why is *The Crucible* not an everyday reality but a symbol in play form?
    b. List as many symbols from the play as you can find.
    c. How is the title of *The Crucible* symbolic?
    d. What are the conventions in staging that can be used for this play? How would *The Crucible* have been staged in Shakespeare's day? Is that sort of production still valid?

3. How can *The Crucible* be overdesigned? If you read the review of the first production in New York, you will know something about why Arthur Miller restaged it in a much simpler way. What do you think he accomplished by doing so? Is underdesign of this play quite possible?

4. What counterpoints would you propose in staging *The Crucible?*

5. Discuss symbolization as a concept.

16

director's options I:
choice of the stage

Although the goal of Part III is the mastering of the coordination-synthesis process in designing a production, you must, before you can approach the designer—either the designer in yourself or persons other than yourself—be keenly aware of the full range of possibilities and options open to you as a director. Many students study the areas of design through specialty courses without actually seeing how these courses overlap and how they may be similar in approach and arrive at similar concepts. But since the concept advocated here is counterpoint in design, the director must penetrate as deeply as he can into the differences in options available to him. The range is great, and when to use which ones is an important part of a director's decision making.

What follows in this chapter is a detailed examination of options in the choice of the stage. As you will note, this option, as well as those in the following chapters, is developed here in close relationship to the historical backgrounds outlined in the last chapter. The intention now is to show you not only how you can apply theatre history to the designing process, but also to give you an active idea of how your imagination must work if you are to preside as the leader in the process of coordination.

One rule is necessary in approaching this and the following two chapters: Do not take anything for granted, but argue it with yourself and with others until you have declared solid positions of your own on each of the many options open to the director.

The Twentieth-Century Stage Machine

No age has ever had such a highly developed stage machine as our own. Many of our recently built theatre plants, both for professional purposes as well as for educational training, not only have flexible stages where the architectural form of the stage can actually be changed, but they also have two or three theatres of different shapes and sizes where different sets of aesthetic values prevail. Similar changes in form and values also took place since the latter part of the nineteenth century in the development and use of scenery, properties, lighting, sound, and costume. The forty or more stage hands employed by Inigo Jones to move his seventeenth-century scenic wonders can now be done by one or two people with the use of electronic controls, and such spectacles that would have taken him months to build for one presentation at court have now become a regular production effort everywhere, for the concept that every production must have its own specific staging is so thoroughly implanted that we can scarcely see any other way.

Today's problem does not lie in the flexibility of the machine but in the same old indecipherable: How can audience imagination be excited? The machine-theatre may, perhaps, be a root cause of the failure of the theatre as an artistic force in our century, for it may have made the creative life in this medium too easy, with a consequent loss of ideas and imagination. Moreover, as the century has moved ahead, the theatre has had to change course simply because the electronic media of television and moving pictures no longer make staging miracles seem out of the ordinary. Where can we go from here? Can we find new impetus in fresh recapturings of past theatres? Can we endow the old theatres with new meanings? At the rate, we are working at it we would appear to think so. But wherever our projections of the future may lead us, we always return to the same point: the new theatre will be built out of the basic tools of the old, for it is only by knowing their successes and failures that we can discover new paths.

Our Present-Day Use of the Stage as a Tool of Production

The stage as a tool of production has probably undergone the greatest shift in concept of all the areas of design. Whereas past ages have had fixed stages on which to mount productions, our age is characterized by its concept of flexibility; that is, it is now assumed that no one stage form can do the work for all the historical and modern drama being produced. Consequently, a major set of options open to a director lies in his choice of a specific stage form for a particular play. This fact does not imply that the theatre in which he works does not have a permanent stage form built into the structure, for it probably does (usually proscenium in style), but if a director is to follow recent methods of production, he will find himself altering the stage form to meet the requirements of the other options, or finding a place to play outside his established theatre.

Four distinctive architectural stages merit discussion here: proscenium, arena, open-thrust, and forestage-proscenium. The order of discussion does not indicate any preference but has been determined by logical progression. The term *found space* might have been added to this list because it is much in use these days to describe whatever audience-actor relationship a director decides to use, whether it is in a theatre, a church, a hall, a garage, etc. It is not discussed here, however, because the use of such spaces, no matter what labels may be attached to them, probably falls into one of the four major categories. Further mention of found space will be made in Chapter 26 in the discussion of nonverbal theatricals.

PROSCENIUM STAGE

Although the dominant hold of the proscenium stage as the principal convention for presenting plays in our time has weakened a good deal since the mid-fifties, it is still very much with us and probably will be for some time to come. As a matter of record, new theatres, even some of the professional sort, are still being built with this stage as the architectural form. It is being discussed first here because you are already familiar with many of its workings from your study of Part II. In addition, if you comprehend the theory behind this stage, you will be better able to see the workings of the other stages discussed later in the chapter. Be sure not to take the proscenium stage for granted because it is familiar to you, but read the following material carefully, checking it against your present knowledge of this stage.

The proscenium stage as a convention is basically *illusory;* that is, it has the inherent capacity of creating the illusion of the real world we see every day about us. We sit *in front of it* and are expected to believe that what we see taking place through that rectangular hole cut in the stage wall is so close to an imitation of life that we can forget we are in a theatre. This illusion is heightened because we cannot see any changes of scenery made since the wall intentionally hides all the machinery, and either a curtain is closed or the lights are extinguished so that we will not be distracted. Furthermore, to reinforce the sense of illusion, the lights in the auditorium are turned off while a performance is in progress, so that we cannot see other members of the audience except for the backs of their heads as we sit behind them. In this sense, the experience is something like reading a novel, something we do alone; but by hearing responses from other members of the audience, we still feel part of a group.

This experience of the darkened, picture-frame theatre has been confiscated by moving pictures, which in many ways do a much better job because they can use unlimited scenic backgrounds, can employ the close-up, thus bringing the actor far closer visually to an audience, and can amplify sound so that hearing, even in delicate nuance, is never a problem. Movies can also maintain audience attention at a very high level through the techniques of moving the camera and making instantaneous changes of scene. As an illusory device, the proscenium stage is now a poor cousin to the moving picture.

Because of this competition with the movies, the history of the proscenium stage in the twentieth century has been such a rocky one that we have seen a gradual movement away from the convention. The first attack came in the development of new scenic approaches that since midcentury have all but removed the nineteenth-century box-setting convention and have replaced it with fragmentary walls, set pieces, and even projected scenery. Thus, this trend has altered an aesthetic that requires actual reproduction of places and has moved us towards a new art based on *suggestion* of those places, all in the interest of exciting audience imagination by forcing it to complete what has been left out. Architectural units—platforms, steps, etc.—have come into wide use in an attempt to create verticality on the stage, and, in this way, to overcome its flatness—flatness because everyone in the audience sees the same dimensions from its frontal position. There have been in recent decades so many alterations in the use of scenic materials on the proscenium stage that we must accept the fact that the proscenium stage has outlived its day and that designers have been doing everything they can to overcome this stage convention while still using it in the absence of other theatre forms.

However, because the proscenium stage is a highly developed machine that took over three hundred years to perfect, it will not be moved aside easily. It still has all the advantages of changeable scenery—in other words, scenery that can be moved while a curtain is down or that can be moved mysteriously before the eyes of an audience. If the pure proscenium as a convention is to pass, so, it seems, must the Baroque tradition in scenery. But, because painted cloth on frames can still excite audiences, it is hard to believe that other forms can completely replace such a device, even though we know that other theatres, such as the Elizabethan public theatre, did without it. At any rate, the movement to new stages is well under way.

Perhaps one manifestation of this movement away from the proscenium is the building of small playhouses—a university theatre, for example, which seats only four hundred to six hundred spectators. Even though such houses may be built in the proscenium style, there is a real question of how conscious of the proscenium most of the audience actually is. The opening, though it may be of standard dimensions, is so large in this small theatre when we compare it to the audience area that the arch effect literally does not exist for most of the audience. Critics of the Broadway theatre, a group that has not pushed the new concepts, have probably seldom truly experienced the closed, framed effect of the proscenium stage, and have thus not felt its aesthetic because they have sat so close to the stage that they have literally been within the frame. It might be said that in the twentieth century only the back-of-the-house or the balcony viewer has had much of a proscenium-arch experience.

Blocking Suggestions. Both composition and movement on the proscenium stage have been discussed extensively in Part II, where it was assumed that if the learning director understood the concept of the proscenium, he could move readily to other forms. In brief, the concept of composition and movement on the proscenium stage is illusory; that is, it must *appear* to be lifelike, although some very definite conventions must be observed.

Thus, as you remember, compositions are largely open to the audience, with the apex usually placed upstage. Actors can, of course, turn their backs to an audience, but such positions must be momentary simply because an audience wants to watch the frontal actor in order to follow his reactions and because it cannot hear well the lines that may be thrown upstage. Just as furniture pieces are placed in open positions, so must the actor place himself in positions of that sort as often as possible. But this opening front also necessitates de-emphasis, which can be brought about by back positions, using the weak upstage corners, standing behind furniture, etc.

One rule, however, seems to dominate the use of this stage: no actor must appear to violate the proscenium plane by walking through it toward the audience or must appear to be outside the prescribed lifelike lines of the setting. This rule does not mean that actors cannot look directly toward an audience or face that way, but it does suggest that compositions should be arranged (with downstage placement of secondary actors, for instance) so that they will not appear to be in violation of proscenium logic. It does suggest that an actor who takes a position at either corner of the stage gazing out into space makes a poor composition because it implies that the actor is facing a wall (the imaginary proscenium wall) and is thus doing an eccentric rather than a lifelike thing.

The convention of the proscenium stage is, therefore, an appearance of reality, not reality itself. No matter how lifelike a play may seem on this stage, it is never life itself.

ARENA STAGE

Although theatre-in-the-round or the arena stage, in which the audience tightly surrounds the acting area, has never been established as a major stage, it is certainly a workable one, especially in the community and educational theatres. It is discussed at this point because, like the pure proscenium stage, it was first seen as an illusionistic stage in its conventions, but recent users have greatly extended its possibilities, perhaps associating it more closely with the night club or cafe presentational stage to which it is definitely related.

This stage came into use in the 1930s, possibly growing out of both experimentation in theatre forms and out of a desire to produce plays on low budgets during the years of economic depression. The immediate advantage of such a form is, of course, that it requires no scenery, although pieces of furniture, hand properties, and costumes need the most careful selection and finishing. In this sense, when the acting is included, it can appear to be even more lifelike than the proscenium stage—like a play in someone's living room.

But another convention operates in arena staging that tends to break down its illusory elements: members of an audience can fully see and watch many other members of an audience. This panavision creates the paradox of an audience watching lifelikeness of a very subtle sort take place in front of them at the same time it is participating in an obvious *communal* experience, for when an audience surrounds a play, it is performing one of the oldest rituals of mankind: the tribe standing or sitting in a circle around its ritual dancers, its medicine man, its heroes who move around the fire in the center. Thus, the intimacy of arena staging is its prime convention, for the audience can sense the actor in a very personal way: his breathing, his perspiration, his body sounds, even the shower of his spittle when he speaks vigorously. The experience actually goes beyond that of the moving picture because, although both are capable of extreme close-ups, arena staging has no such barrier as the lifeless projection screen and can exhibit the flesh-and-blood actor to the voyeurism of an audience. The participatory-theatre experimentation of the 1960s greatly depended on this touching possibility of actors and members of an audience.

But how real is it all? Again, arena staging gives only the appearance of reality. The room created in the acting area may look like a real room, the food consumed by the actors may be real food, the costumes worn may be genuine clothes, the speeches the audience hears spoken in low tones and even whispered may seem realistic in the extreme; yet all this is not life itself, for a play is always an artificial thing that involves selection and exaggeration (less than life as well as more). One of the techniques in playing arena-style is to begin acting at a low level—as close to reality as possible—in order to draw the audience into the illusion, and then to raise it gradually in size and proportion until the acting resembles what is seen on the proscenium stage. Theatre-in-the-round is not for the inexperienced amateur but for the capable and trained actor.

Another convention that the director must be aware of in using this form is the specific location of the acting area. Should the actors stand on the same level as the first row of the audience? Should they be at least six inches or more below? Should they be a foot or more above the first row? Such a decision is crucial because the separation of the stage from the audience, which lowering or raising can accomplish, will subtly modify the convention. The raised stage may so set him apart from the audience that the result is a *platform stage* which may no longer be considered intimate or illusory. In this instance, the actor will loom over the members of the audience, part of whom will now look up at him. From this view, he may no longer appear to be just another member of the audience going through a dramatic experience but a superbeing—an actor. By raising the stage, the theatre-in-the-round may be converted away from an illusory aesthetic to a nonillusory one in which an audience's experience can be very different. Thus the circular location of the audience is the first convention of the arena stage, but the second is surely the level of the stage. The director must be aware of the changing aesthetics when he manipulates the playing area.

Moreover, because an audience sits on four sides is no reason to limit scenic design to furniture alone. You should think of this stage as having all the potentials of a circus arena, with vertical exploitation one of its important extension possibilities. Thus, this stage, just as with the proscenium, becomes a cube, which can be occupied dramatically and theatrically not only by actors but also by look-through scenery. Anything goes as long as it stays within the logic of its aesthetics. Placing covered scenery on this stage would certainly obscure audience vision, but when skeletal frames are introduced you have both good vision and the suggestion of Baroque scenery. Looking through such frames is no problem at all for audiences, for we actually see much in real life through interrupted views. You must learn to exploit this stage in every possible way, for the communal theatre has great potential for our times because it is quite different from moving pictures or television.

Blocking Suggestions. It should now be apparent to you why we emphasized the organic approach (using the tools of illustration for purposes of communication from director to actor) over the pictorial in our discussions on composition, movement, etc., in Part II. If you understand the organic concept, you will have little difficulty in arranging on the arena stage everything from the groundplan to composition and movement. The basic principle is still the same: By arousing the imagination of the actor through insuring his understanding of and sensitivity to given circumstances and dramatic action, the imagination of the audience can be stimulated to strong empathic action.

The pictorial requirements in arena staging are fairly obvious. The four-sided audience demands a four-sided look by the director, or better still: *forget* the one-sided view of the proscenium stage and direct the actors into intense character-action relationships and the compositions will largely take care of themselves. Two principles of all good composition should be kept in mind: (1) play the limits of the stage on an obstacle course, avoiding climactic compositions as much as possible; (2) play the Cat-and-Mouse game in composition, now one character pursues and the other retreats, and vice versa, for actors will frequently turn outward toward the audience as the most natural thing to do in getting away.

If the center point of the stage is thought of as the center of a clock, variety in composition is infinite (Fig. 53). A groundplan can readily be designed that will fan out from the center (Fig. 54). The use of a center object approachable from all sides will avoid the deadliness of a cleared space and will provide the obstacle course so necessary in a dynamic groundplan.

Note that Fig. 54 has four major stage areas. By using the areas in combinations with only occasional use of one area, a dynamic interlocking of the stage will result, and all four audiences will see the play equally well. An actor's back facing one part of the audience is an ac-

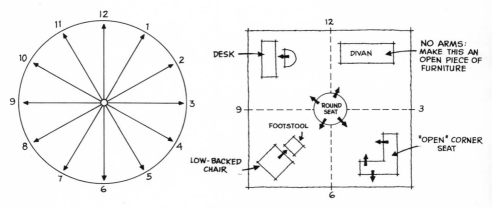

FIGURES 53 AND 54

cepted convention of this stage, but this rather extreme body position can be kept at a minimum by frequent shiftings to other body positions. When back positions must be used as the best illustration of a dramatic action, the neutral corners (entrances to the stage—where no audience is seated) can be employed effectively. The problem of quick entrances and exits on the arena stage is always difficult because of the distance through the audience that must be traversed, but this problem can often be solved by occasional use of entrance-walkways as acting areas: an actor starts speaking on the way in, or stops halfway out to give an exit line; or through the use of *vomitoria*—entranceways underneath audience seating—where actors can enter the acting area directly without being seen.

Again it must be emphasized that the purposes of organic blocking, as stressed in Part II, is to *free the dramatic action*. If the actors understand their intense relationships to one another, good blocking cannot help but materialize. This blocking can then be modified to meet the demands of pictorial necessity and variety.

OPEN-THRUST STAGE

Open-thrust is used here to describe a theatre setup in which audiences are seated on three sides of a raised stage, with the stage backed by a wall on the fourth. It is open because no portion of the stage is concealed from the audience (in this sense the arena is also open); that is, everything must take place before the audience; it is thrust because it juts out from a concealing wall *into* the audience area so that the audience sits around three sides of the stage in contrast to the one-sided frontal position in the proscenium theatre.

This is the classical stage, the oldest form we know, for a version of it (not a raised stage) was used by the Greeks in the fifth century B.C.; it is also the stage of Shakespeare and of classical Chinese opera. Its revival in the twentieth century has probably come about largely because of the emphasis on the production of historical drama as an active part of our theatre, but there is good reason to believe that it has won acceptance not only in reaction against proscenium staging but also because it presents a sharp contrast to the two-dimensional aspects of the moving-picture and television screens.

The dynamics of the open-thrust convention lie in its plastic, sculpturelike capabilities, for the actor is three-dimensional in every way. The theatre experience is thus greatly heightened in contrast to the proscenium style, for it puts the live actor back on the stage in full force where his energy and radiance are dynamic realities and are not withdrawn or are merely behavioristic experiences. The open-thrust stage might have the same illusory aesthetic as is possible in arena staging when the actors and audience are arranged on the same floor level, but its basic concept is that of a *raised* stage which precludes the same level; thus the intention is not representational but presentational.

Presentational is a term commonly used to describe the nonillusory theatre experience. This aesthetic—the oldest in the history of the theatre—makes no attempt to fool audiences into believing that they are looking at the real thing. "This is the theatre," it says, "and here is a stage, here are actors, and here is an audience, and what you see and hear takes place *only* in this theatre; it resembles life, yes, but it is definitely *not* life." Consequently, this stage is in sharp contrast to the concept of the proscenium stage where life and what happens in the theatre have

PLATE VII   *Doctor Faustus* by Christopher Marlowe

The intention in this staging of Marlowe's classic was to suggest a stage that would approach that of an Elizabethan public theatre as it might have appeared in 1590 when Marlowe was writing his plays. An open-thrust stage was used, therefore, with a shallow inner-below behind a draw curtain (the arras), an above position, also concealed by a draw curtain, doorways on either side of the slightly protruding structure, and a trap in the stage floor. Because it was desirable to keep the acting area as small as possible, two levels of steps were placed around the raised acting area. The stage floor was located approximately thirty inches above the floor level of the first row of the audience, thus placing the heads of that audience slightly above the stage floor.

been confused. Theatre as a pure art form distinct from life and stated in obvious theatre conventions is at the basis of the concept. The audience may become involved in a play, but it can never forget it is in a theatre—a place for play-making and not a peep show at a slice of life.

The treatment of the back wall of the stage is an important aspect of the open-thrust stage because it provides the background against which the play is seen. This wall may be designed as permanent architecture when the theatre is built, as the Greeks and Elizabethans treated it, or it may be partly architectural and partly painted, as in Chinese classical opera or in Japanese Noh staging; or it may be even a curtained wall, as in the extant drawings of early Renaissance playings of Seneca and Plautus. But whatever form it may take, it provides a more or less permanent facade against which the play is performed. Whatever alterations may be made from play to play are made in the acting area with the use of temporary materials either carried on by actors or placed before the play begins.

The open-thrust convention places full responsibility on the playscript and on the actors, and, in a sense, frees both from the confines of the visual statement of exact place. Thus, the stageplace can be anything the actors, with their costumes and properties, declare it to be. The now discarded suggestion by some early twentieth-century scholars that signs were needed on Shakespeare's stage to tell audiences where scenes were taking place can easily be seen as nonsense because we now know through the use of this stage that audiences can move quickly from imagined place to imagined place with only the slightest suggestion, either in an opening line, in a property such as a military banner, or in an explicit costume such as armor. Modern plays present no more difficulties about place than do historical dramas, and, as a result, we have begun to question the validity of exact place: Does it confine, more than release, an audience's imagination?

Lighting has become an important convention in the use of this stage, particularly with modern plays, because in the proscenium theatre we have not yet given up the convention of the rising and falling stage curtain to mark interruptions in the stage action. Consequently, plays are still being written with this dramatic cutoff in mind. On the open-thrust stage, as well as on the arena, light control is presently used to function as the curtain, with actors entering and taking places in the dark and departing in the same way. When plays are written for it—and the experiments of the 1960s turned up a few—characters will probably be given reasons for entering the scene and leaving at its end, as in historical drama, and with this technique the lighting conventions could change radically.

Another modern convention that has developed with this stage is the vomitoria—a very quick entrance directly onto this stage, usually from be-

neath the audience. Before the introduction of this convention, actors
either entered at the rear of the stage or approached the stage through
the audience as in arena staging. The vomitoria solved the problem of
quick entrances because a large number of actors would be "vomited"
onto the stage area very quickly and disappear at the end of a scene
within a few seconds. The entrance and exit tempos of the proscenium
stage were thus preserved almost intact.

The old convention of scenes above, as in Shakespeare's theatre, has
been retained with only minor modifications through the use of back-

PLATE VIII   *The New Tenant* by Eugène Ionesco

Here is the identical open-thrust stage that is shown in Plate VII.
It has been given a different appearance by placing a wall of flats at
the rear of the stage. The acting area thus becomes all of the space
forward of that wall in the usual definition of the open-thrust. Note
the ceiling to the Tenant's room has been suggested by the use of
a rectangular section of metal pipe and by a lighting fixture dropped
in from above. The metal frame at the front suggests a window. In
this instance the open-thrust stage is used to suggest a room "anywhere" that can be stacked with endless pieces of furniture to carry
out the idea of this macabre play.

wall structures that permit actors to appear above the stage on scaffolding or through windows in the stage wall. Vertical playing space thus becomes an inherent convention in this stage form. Even modern plays with their simultaneous use of upstairs and downstairs can be satisfactorily accommodated through skeletal look-through structures placed in the acting area.

Blocking Suggestions. Composition and movement on this stage follow the same usage as in arena staging, with one major exception: the neutral rear wall permits positions similar to those used on the proscenium stage—a pitfall for the inexperienced director because he too readily assumes he is working on a proscenium stage and encourages his actors to take much too frequent frontal positions. "Spin the wheel" and "face out from the center" are the major suggestions here. You must learn to see the acting from all three sides and to encourage actors to open up their illustrations to all three audiences and not just to one. If you follow the principles of organic blocking, as outlined in Part II, you will have little difficulty in showing a play to a multiple audience.

The placing of steps around the perimeter of this stage will aid greatly in achieving variety in stage levels, particularly if two or three steps are employed. Lower steps can be used to de-emphasize secondary characters and higher steps to focus strong emphasis on the principals. The center of the stage becomes the strongest position since it is equidistant from all parts of an audience. And you must learn to play the full limits of the stage space in order to enhance the climactic compositions when characters are finally brought together.

FORESTAGE-PROSCENIUM

Although other terms might be used to describe this stage, *forestage-proscenium* is used here because it tells us the way in which it has come about in recent years through joining proscenium conventions with those of the open-thrust stage. Nominally, it is the proscenium stage with a forestage erected in front of it, the same stage that was used in the seventeenth-, eighteenth-, and nineteenth-century theatres when the pure proscenium stage was in its making. For this reason forestage-proscenium might be regarded as a return to the past because it again moves the playing area forward of the proscenium line after nearly three hundred years of watching the play gradually retreat behind the line; however, it is closer to the fact to see it as a natural evolution from the pure proscenium stage.

As a modified proscenium stage, then, audiences still sit in the frontal position, although the side areas of ovular proscenium auditoriums now are given better sight lines than they ever enjoyed with the pure proscenium stage. The forestage-proscenium is an adapted form because it is neither fish nor fowl but tries to be both. It has undoubtedly come back into use in an attempt to modernize the proscenium theatre.

The conventions on this stage are therefore obvious: the proscenium wall conceals the use of stage rigging for the spectacle of painted scenery

PLATE IX   *The Good Woman of Setzuan* by Bertolt Brecht

This production was staged on the forestage-proscenium. At the top of the photograph, you can see the proscenium arch and the wall of the conventional theatre that housed it, and at the bottom the scaffolding used to support the forestage added to the main stage, in this case a depth of seventeen feet in addition to a four-foot apron attached to the main stage. An act curtain was hung on the lines that traverse the front of the forestage at the top. Both the rightstage and the leftstage front areas were manipulative; that is, could be opened out and extended toward the center. As a result, the acting area was largely on the forestage although many moments were played on the full stage space. Note the bridge effect in the foreground made by eliminating some sections of the forestage, thus allowing actors to descend below the bridge and move under it on occasion. The central stage at the back could be opened for the playing of interior scenes as needed. This highly flexible stage moved the playing into the audience area, thus making it more dynamic and audience involving.

while at the same time actors, who in this convention play largely on the forestage, appear to be more plastic, more three-dimensional to audiences. The proscenium arch itself is much reduced in value and may, by the judicious use of masking scenic pieces, appear to be blocked off entirely. A stage that seems to be very deep can thus be achieved, similar in kind although not in dimension to those of the late eighteenth and early nineteenth centuries when such theatres as New York's Bowery had a phenomenal depth of 128 feet. The Baroque scenic tradition can thus continue in full force on this stage, and the acting can be done both behind the arch and in front of it, allowing a director to greatly expand or contract his stage as he may see fit.

If the forestage is deep enough, this stage can also be brought close to the open-thrust aesthetic, for architectural backwalls and curtained walls

PLATE X   *The Judge of the Divorce Court* by Miguel de Cervantes

This forestage-proscenium production was acted entirely on the forestage, but note the effect provided by the screens at the back, which were hung in the usual manner from the regular proscenium rigging. The acting was brought out under the dome of the auditorium, increasing its presentational qualities and giving it more opportunity for audience involvement, while at the same time, the machinery on the proscenium stage could be employed. The choice of stage, therefore, partially supported the *commedia dell'arte* quality of Cervantes' interlude. Note how the very edge of the stage can be used to increase the vitality of this vaudeville.

can shut off the upstage area. The only problem is the largely frontal audience. The use of additional projections from the forestage, which places the actor farther out in the audience, can help to remedy this situation, but such a stage can never achieve the same feeling provided by the pure open-thrust form.

Blocking Suggestions. Proscenium and open-thrust blocking procedures must both be employed on this stage because of its combination of frontal and circular presentation depending on which areas of the stage are in use. Proscenium blocking tends to work better in upstage portions because of the hearability factor which must enter into any consideration of such a large stage space. Low volumes can be employed in extreme downstage positions but may not work at all when a scene is placed upstage. Rather than create disturbed hearing by raising volumes in the upstage positions and lowering them in downstage positions, the director can adjust the upstage or downstage blocking to meet the needs for volume, thus allowing the actor to concentrate on the dramatic action without worrying about oral projection.

As has been suggested above, the spectacle and dramatic value of a full use of the stage space can be very great. The director must, therefore, learn to use the extremes of the stage from far upstage to far downstage, from far right to far left. The actual physical distance between actors can take on significant meaning when used judiciously. In contrast, the director will also learn to exploit the intimacy of far-downstage positions, which can be collected and tightened by selected lighting, for effective presentation of intense dramatic ideas.

EXERCISES

1. *The Crucible* has been played in various productions on several different stages, possibly all four delineated in this chapter. Discuss the following:
   a. Why does the play seem to be open to flexible staging? Do you think Miller conceived of it as a proscenium-style play, or did he deliberately open the structure to other staging possibilities?
   b. What are the advantages and disadvantages of playing *The Crucible* on (1) an arena stage; (2) an open-thrust stage; (3) a forestage-proscenium?
   c. How would you approach the blocking of *The Crucible* on any of the stages mentioned in (b) above?
   d. Which of the four stages would you choose? Why?

2. How can you vary the arrangement of the open-thrust stage? What would happen if you thrust the stage too far into the audience, by making it much deeper than it is wide? If the stage were made twenty by twenty feet and you could vary the height of each of four ten-by-ten-foot sections, what would happen in projecting a play? Can you think of a play that would conform to such a stage?

3. Discuss the differences in the effect the following arena stages would have:
   a. One that is six inches below the first audience row.
   b. One that is two feet below the first audience row.
   c. One that is on the level of the first audience row.

4. Can you identify the stages represented in the following drawing? Note that each one is part of a circle with the degree markings representing the size of the audience areas.

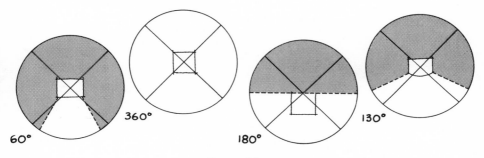

FIGURE 55

17

director's options 2: scenery, properties, and lighting

Now that you can see that the director's design function requires some very important decisions about what sort of stage to use in presenting certain plays, you are ready to look at the options open to a director in deciding what kind of scenic materials to put on the stage he chooses, and how to light those materials. This chapter is, therefore, concerned with scenic investiture or decor, and the stage lighting used in conjunction with it, for the coordination process is well underway when you make these decisions. It should now be obvious to you that the director exerts important leadership in shaping the direction a play will go in a physical way, and how very much he needs to know if he is to encourage designers to follow him.

Again, you must keep in mind that the content in these chapters is not intended to substitute for extensive training in design but only to point out to the director the many paths open to him in staging a play. The more you know about what can be done, the more inventive and adventurous you will be in producing plays, for reaching audiences with fresh imagery depends on knowing thoroughly the tools with which you work.

Options in Stage Scenery

As can readily be seen from the previous discussion on stages, if we think of scenery only as painted flats and drops, we can apply the term only to the pure proscenium stage and the forestage-proscenium. But nowadays this meaning is too narrow because the open-thrust and the arena can both use staging pieces that modify acting areas, and though these modifications may be simple, they are nevertheless scenic in concept. The word *scenery* actually derives from the Greek *skene* and Roman *scaena,* both of which stages had permanent architectural facades before which the actors performed. We must define scenery, then, as any device which makes a change in a stage, starting with the stage floor.

From this point of view, it is obvious that the director and the designer will approach each stage form in terms of its own concept and conventions. Scenic design is thus both architecture and painting, and may be both at the same time. Therefore, five distinct types of scenery are delineated in the following pages: (1) painted; (2) architectural; (3) painted-architectural; (4) projected; (5) fractionated.

PAINTED SCENERY

You are, of course, most familiar with this type which dates in its continuous use from the sixteenth century. It consists of painted cloth mounted on frames, the sort we still see in wing-and-drop settings, in box settings, and in set pieces (flats, ground rows, etc.) placed at any point on the stage. The convention in its commonest usage is illusory in concept, for the intention is to make such scenery appear to represent what we see in real life. Thus, it is largely either *painted* architecture (interiors and exteriors) or *painted* nature (wood scenes, etc.), or combinations of such content. In this sense, painted scenery is two-dimensional like easel painting, but it is cut into many pieces and so placed on the stage that it gives an audience an illusion of three dimensions, with depth as well as height and width. To heighten this three-dimensional effect, in its early usage the stage floor was raked upwards from front to rear, a tradition in stage construction that survived into the twentieth century, and pieces were hung from above and raked downwards from front to rear, thus forcing the perspective. As you can obviously see, such scenery required stage machinery (lines, pulleys, etc.) both for hanging it and moving it. Consequently, we have the changeable scenery associated with the proscenium stage, where the proscenium wall is used to conceal all the machinery necessary to make quick and effective shifts from one represented reality to another.

That such a convention would have such a long life in the theatre—a life unbroken until the twentieth century—is not difficult to understand.

The development of drama from the sixteenth to the twentieth centuries was a gradual approach toward photographic reproduction—an approach which reached its peak in the last part of the nineteenth century—and in this development, the statement of more and more exact places became part of the stage aesthetic.   The new staging—that is, the staging as it has evolved in the last half century—has been a revolt against photographic reproduction of exact place—a revolt that has led to new stages and new scenic concepts.

The nineteenth- and twentieth-century box setting is thus painted scenery carried to the extreme of representation: the photographic reproduction of an interior.   The painted walls and ceiling are made to look like the real thing in both color and texture, and the actual placement of

PLATE XI   *The Beaux' Stratagem* by George Farquhar

Painted scenery can do much to support historical plays although it is only occasionally used for modern drama in the way illustrated above. Note that properties can be painted on the scenery. In this production, the back wall of each setting was composed of four triangular prisms, with each prism made by joining three flats together. Each set of faces was then painted with a different scene so that when each set was revolved before the audience and joined together, the back wall appeared to be one piece. In the above photograph, you can see three of the prisms.

the flats with jogs, slanted walls, slanted ceilings, exterior views placed outside windows and doors, etc., are all intended to increase the architectural illusion to a point where it is difficult to believe that one is not looking into a real room. Yet, of course, it is all make-believe, with the intention that of fooling an audience. The adding to these painted flats of architectural pieces, such as real window frames, door frames and doors, wood molding, and wood-beam ceilings, increases the illusion of reality.

If the director is thoroughly aware of the history of this tradition, and of its full exploitative possibilities, he can understand much more readily the departures from this convention. And he will also know much more clearly how and when to use such scenery in designing productions.

ARCHITECTURAL SCENERY

Architectural scenery, as defined here, includes not only permanently built structures, such as the rear wall of an open-thrust stage, but also all structures that move upward from the flat stage floor and create a three-dimensional mass on the stage.

As we pointed out above in the discussion on open-thrust stages, the rear wall of such stages *may be* part of the permanent architecture, like the altars in many churches, and may be arranged in such a way that it can serve a large body of plays as did the Elizabethan rear wall; and it does not need to be a flat surface but can be projected onto the stage, as in Tanya Moiseiwitsch's design for the stage of the Stratford (Ontario) Festival Theatre. Thus, the wall may contain not only doors for entrances but also raised portions and approaching steps. But the wall is, nevertheless, a permanent facade. Although a few theatres have been built in this manner, it is unlikely that it will become the common stage device in this century. Nevertheless, the learning director must become fully aware of its concept and exploitative possibilities if he is to understand the nature of flexible stages.

But equally important as a concept is creating architecture through the use of platforms and steps. The Baroque scenic tradition developed the concept of moveable wings and drops, and, later, walls and ceilings; the "new" staging of the twentieth century added the development of the stage floor, not as a painted or raked plane which had been a convention for three hundred years, but as an architectural mass. Platforms and steps are always fabricated with hollow interiors, but the fact remains that they occupy real space, which makes them architectural in every sense of the word. The new concept, then, is of a three-dimensional stage with the capability of showing the actor *at any level* within the rectangular prism or cube that composes the stage area visible to an audience. To

know the values of such dramatic capabilities is to extend tremendously
the director's use of the stage.

PAINTED-ARCHITECTURAL SCENERY

Much of today's staging is a combination of both painted and architectural scenery.˙ This combination is so because we are a transitional
theatre with no single established form.   Thus, we use what is effective in
both types of scenery, with the pure forms relatively rare.   But only
through understanding the pure forms can the director decide on how
to best exploit a particular play.   A spectator's imagination usually is
easily aroused by fresh, dynamic impulses, but it can also be stultified by

PLATE XII   *The Lark* by Jean Anouilh

Architectural scenery was used for this production in order to provide multiple locations for the many scenes in Anouilh's play and to
give the historical material in the play a modern feeling.   The two
figures in this photograph are sitting on the very front of the stage,
with the lowest step at the same level as the tops of the auditorium
seats.   The depth of the platformed areas is approximately twenty-
three feet, a depth that allows the use of the flying system for some
changes of scene. The dominant playing areas are thus thrust into
the forward locations, with the platforms giving positions for emphasis and for varied compositions, particularly those throughout the
trial scene. Architectural scenery of this sort greatly enhances compositional values and can provide surprising intimacy with the use
of directional lighting.   At first, you may not regard such platform
arrangements as scenery, but when you see what can be done with
composition and picturization, how the stage can be made into a cube
in very simple ways, you will understand that architectural scenery is
as scenic as anything that can be provided to enhance the actor.

a too self-conscious use of scenic materials. The process is, as it always is in art, one of selection.

PROJECTED SCENERY

A completely new style of scenery has evolved out of the twentieth century's development of electric light and how to project it. Although we are still finding new ways of making statements after many years of experimentation—a fact which indicates that we still do not know its full range of uses—we are very much aware of the high theatrical values and the powerful statements of projected scenery.

Among other things, we have learned:

1. That projected scenery can take the place of both architectural and moveable scenery as a backing for a scene.
2. That it can be used simultaneously in direct coordination with moveable or architectural scenery when projected on a screen either built into other scenery or mounted in front of it.
3. That moving-picture projection as scenery with actors moving in front of it can provide unusual theatrical effects. Recent uses have

PLATE XIII   *The Lark* by Jean Anouilh

Here is another scene in the same production of *The Lark* as that shown in Plate XII. Note the use of carry-on pieces such as banners and the rood screen, and the use of additional banners lowered from above. This ostensibly bare stage was thus made to appear fully clothed in scenery in a matter of seconds, and all happened before the eyes of the audience.

PLATE XIV   *Six Characters in Search of an Author*
by Luigi Pirandello

Here is architectural scenery on a forestage-proscenium (note the
proscenium arch).   But like the Pirandello characters you can see
in this double exposure (Who is real: Pirandello's imaginary Characters or The Actors who spend their lives making illusory characters
on the stage?), this setting is not real but fabricated.   To give the
appearance of a bare stage, the back wall of the theatre in which this
production was staged was redeveloped with a few painted flats and
a stairway.   The doorway at the rightcenter rear is a real doorway,
but the stage wall was jogged forward, and with the addition of the
stairway, a very real architectural effect was brought about.   The
total depth from the edge of the forestage to the rear wall was thirty-
five feet, a normal depth for a stagehouse.   This permitted setting
up flats for the rehearsal of the play composed by the Stage Manager
and the Characters.   This production is used as an illustration of
architectural scenery because the effect is so good that an audience
will not take it for anything but the real thing; thus, whether it is
fabricated or not makes little difference.   The real flat stacked
against the back wall and the cut border tend to enhance the reality
of the back wall.

coordinated the actor and such moving scenery, producing the effect of the actor walking into and out of the projected, moving scene.

4. That projected scenery can be changed instantly and that multiple quick changes of location, as in moving pictures, are possible, as they never have been previously.

5. That projected scenery lends itself readily to abstractions, increasing the symbolic uses of backgrounds. When multiple, simultaneous projections are used, a montage effect is possible. Thus, it can be idea-building.

6. That projected scenery is very inexpensive to use by comparison to other types of scenery.

From the above, it would seem that projected scenery has an active future ahead. But one of the drawbacks is that it too readily imitates the moving picture, and this imitation takes the theatre closer to a form it is trying to escape. Yet in trying too hard to escape, the theatre may be only bypassing its own destiny, for the future may depend on an even closer liaison between these two forms.

Whatever its future may be, a director must be fully aware of the freshness of this scenic option and must learn how and where it can be appropriately employed.

FRACTIONATED SCENERY

This term is used here for want of a better one to describe a popular form of staging that deploys several types of scenic pieces, some connected, some unconnected, with the intention of suggesting a room or other place with a minimum of scenic materials. Thus, such staging may use flats, cut flats (a piece of a wall), screens, platforms, step units, curtains, hanging drapes, suspended flat pieces or window frames, ground rows, selected rear backings, skeletal framings, or any other scenic devices. A procedure used fairly frequently is to place whatever is used against a skycloth in order to convey a sense of greater space, or to give the impression of seeing inside and outside simultaneously. Fractionated scenery is, therefore, a direct move away from the representational effect of the box setting and a move toward simplified and extracted staging.

There is no question about the advantages of this sort of scenic statement, for it possesses the power of releasing audience imagination by forcing it to complete necessary but omitted lines or to interpret and put to use any inherent symbolism that may reside in such fractionations. Therefore, the justification for such staging goes far beyond the practical limits of low-cost production or easy moveability of such settings in a multiscene play. Simplified Realism of this sort can release the poetry in a play by giving the audience a free-flight experience instead of tying it down to prosaic realities.

Fractionated staging can thus employ all of the previous scenic options: painted, architectural, painted-architectural, and projected. Its free form may well account for its frequent use in contemporary scenic design.

SCENERY AND STAGE CHOICE

This section should not be concluded without brief mention of the random options in scenery available to a director on the various stages. Thus, arena and open-thrust stages can use look-through scenery set upon the stage floor, as well as architectural steps and platforms. Painted cloths (drops) can also be stretched above these stages to achieve effects similar to the "heavens" in the Elizabethan public theatres, actually the painted underside of the penthouse structure. Drapes or structural materials can not only be suspended from above but pulled up from the

PLATE XV   *The Shewing Up of Blanco Posnet* by Bernard Shaw

Fractionated scenery was used in this production to give Shaw's Western fable a semblance of reality while still giving it an imaginative flight. Only the outline of the barnlike structure has been given form, with some of these lines distorted. Real clothes and some set pieces, along with other set pieces that repeated the distorted lines of the scenery, made the play seem both real and a piece of fantasy through which Shaw's lecture on religion and morality could readily reach an audience.

stage floor, thus employing Baroque scenery but placing it in a different context than the proscenium stage. Trap doors can be employed advantageously on these stages as well as on the proscenium and forestage-proscenium arrangements to lend a further dimension by implying other "places" beneath the stage. Moving scenery on turntables or on tracks parallel to the curtain line can also be employed on the proscenium and forestage-proscenium setups to give the illusion of the actor moving great distances, or of changing places in transit.

The intention here is by no means to make an exhaustive list of possibilities in the use of scenic ideas on these stages but to suggest the scope of designing activity in which a director must become involved. Part IV will again consider these options in the discussion on individualization in

PLATE XVI *The Flowering Peach* by Clifford Odets

Here is another use of fractionated scenery to create a very real moment in Odets' play. Note that the unbalanced frame with its cloth drape serves the function of containing the fractionated semblance of a house. An architectural incline placed on the flat floor of the stage serves as the base of the inner setting, which has been given greater depth by the use of an arched window frame repeating the main arch of the room. This fractionated scenery thus gives a strong feeling of reality while it is, of course, a purely theatrical device. Note also how the very real rustic furniture gives reality to what is otherwise quite unreal.

stage production, but you should keep in mind that the stage as a machine can do anything you want it to do as long as you know its limitations thoroughly. Scenic design, as a fresh statement, can grow only out of your imaginative use of the broad range of materials available to you. You must study set design in depth if you are to become a director in the real sense of the word.

Options in Stage Properties

DEFINITION

As Chapters 8, 9, and 10 have already pointed out in some detail, there are two kinds of properties used on the stage: (1) set properties, as-

PLATE XVII *Idiot's Delight* by Robert Sherwood

The setting in this photograph is a combination of painted, architectural, and fractionated scenery. Painted scenery can be seen in the backdrop of mountain peaks at the rear of the stage, in the coat of arms that appears on several flats, and in the doorway and window frames that are painted on the flats composing the walls. Architectural scenery is used for the platform entranceway on stageleft, for the bandstand, and for the rear balcony. Fractionated scenery is used in the framework hanging above, which suggests the actual gablelike structure of this Swiss hotel. With real furniture and real clothing, the total effect is a close resemblance to life whereas it is quite artificial in its components.

sociated closely with the definition of acting space and scenic idea; and (2) hand properties, actually held in the hand by actors or capable of being held in the hand. Both kinds are extremely important tools for the director because they can determine in a primary way how actors will find their illustrations of dramatic action. To repeat again the premise: Imaginative use of properties, both set and hand, permits the actors to project *sense* imagery directly to an audience, which then puts that imagery to work in its imagination. Because properties are used in such personal and individual ways, the director, even more than the designer, must give the most careful attention to their selection.

PLATE XVIII *Rhinoceros* by Eugène Ionesco

Here is a use of projected scenery to overlay painted scenery. As you can see, the back wall of this setting has been painted with a minimal use of distortion. When the three heads resembling rhinoceri are, through lighting instruments, faded onto the wall a very startling scenic effect can be obtained. The actors can play in front of this projected scenery just as they would in front of painted scenery, since the projected light can be introduced either above the heads of the actors or, in more recent techniques, from the rear of the setting if the wall is made of translucent material. Note the use of fractionated scenery for the open-thrust staging of Ionesco's play. Real furniture and real clothing tend to tie the actors to reality whereas the scenic effect is that of nonreality.

SET PROPERTIES

If you have studied this book from the beginning, you will remember that in the chapter on the groundplan it was emphasized that set properties occupy space and therefore determine a very great deal of what happens in the visible acting areas. The actual selection of a specific set property may be the designer's decision but not before the director and designer have decided *together* how much space such a property will occupy and what its nature, and thus its usability, will be. Carefully selected set properties will delineate the specifics of an obstacle course, which will, in turn, declare emphases in compositions and the nature and kinds of movements. Set properties are often handled by actors because they sit on them, lean over them or against them, walk around them, sometimes actually move them. They also become animate in certain compositions, and their mass and shape are always factors in this animation. Reread the groundplan section and you will appreciate even more,

PLATE XIX   *The Good Woman of Setzuan* by Bertolt Brecht

In this production of Brecht's famous play, projections were used sporadically throughout the play to emphasize the theme of poverty and man's failure to do anything about it. At this moment in the play, projected scenery (a photograph) was used in front of architectural scenery to show the audience a reality against the stage fabrication. Although this play could be staged with projections alone, something is lost without the three-dimensional reality of real objects, particularly when Brecht places such emphasis on life as we know it in a physical way—as we see it, touch it, and smell it.

at this point, why the director must make set properties a primary part of his designing vision.

In brief, what can set properties do? The obvious functions are to delineate given circumstances and to provide common uses. In Realistic plays, they are invaluable in showing subtle gradations in environments,

PLATE **XX**   *Mother Courage* by Bertolt Brecht

Properties, both set and hand, played an important part in this staging of Brecht's classic. Note that the wagon is a moveable set property and actually serves the function of scenery in many stage arrangements for this multiscene play, as does the canvas piece hung on the clothesline. Carefully contrived detail in "sitting" properties and other items, such as boxes and baskets, along with hand properties, such as the chess set, tended to give this production a sort of superrealism. Although the play is nominally set in the historical period of the Thirty Years War, Brecht intends very modern meanings, that the War is actually taking place in our time. Real properties help this point of view.

240

PLATE XXI *Desire Under The Elms* by Eugene O'Neill

The set property of the rocking chair in this production was used symbolically to represent Eben's tie to his Mother, who does not appear in the play but exerts a very powerful influence on it. Note the use of the bed quilt against the fractionated scenery of beams. Because this open-thrust staging of O'Neill's play was very close to the audience, much attention was paid to the accurate detail of the properties.

and in most other plays they provide similar information, though not on such a refined scale. Set properties are functional in their common uses as chairs, tables, beds, desks, benches, stools, cabinets, etc., but above all, as has already been suggested, they serve as obstacles in a groundplan to keep characters apart and to make it more difficult for them to reach one another, thus creating activity and illustration. Well selected properties can greatly stimulate an actor's ideas about illustration.

The options open to a director, then, would consist of quantity (how many set properties can actually be used effectively?), size, shape, mobility (can they be moved on the stage by an actor, or do they contain inherent movement?). A director also has a choice of real (archaeologically accurate) objects or abstract objects such as geometric forms. Whatever a director decides to do, he will probably select set properties in coordination with the scenery chosen for a particular play, for the design of one will tend to enhance the other.

HAND PROPERTIES

Hand properties as an element in design has also been treated extensively in the section on improvisation with objects, and little that is new can be added here. To reiterate: hand properties are the extension of the actor's arms and hands; they are thus subtle tools of illustration because they possess capabilities of sensory illustration that the hands alone cannot provide. Any director who does not give primary attention to the selection of hand properties is merely ignoring one of the actor's principal tools of illustration.

For this reason, the final selection is not a designer's decision but a director's, oftentimes in consultation with his actors. Hand properties can be modified and even changed as actors use them during a rehearsal period, and they should therefore not be set permanently before rehearsals begin. Furthermore, they should be selected in terms of the particular actor who is to use them. Remember: there are no *general* properties, only *specific* ones. A designer cannot possibly be as aware of this fact as can the director, who should regard the choice of such properties as his own particular province and look to their actual selection with the greatest care. Be meticulous! No one else can be except the actor.

In summary, hand properties are occasionally functional in their common uses, provide specific reflections of the given circumstances of a play, enhance the individual actor as an instrument by giving opportunities for fresh illustration other than through the use of the hands, are capable of making light (candles, flashlights) and sound (snapping a book shut) and have inherent mobility (visible liquids, eye glasses, telephones, automatic weapons, books, flags, fans, etc.). The options open to a director concern type (size, weight, and shape), mobility, archeological accuracy, and abstraction (use of a stick for a gun, a cane for a sword, etc.).

Options in Stage Lighting

DIRECTOR-DESIGNER RELATIONSHIP

As with the design of properties, a director has a *primary* and personal concern for what happens with stage lighting. Light has the great capability of giving an edge to the final statement of mood of a scene, and if what is designed differs markedly from a director's intention with that mood, both the statement by the actor and the statement in the lighting will fight strongly against each other. Stage lighting is not mere illumination but specific illustration of a very subtle sort—the sort that can reach an audience's imagination more quickly and more subliminally than an actor often can. In everyday life, we know that light can stimulate delicate psychological feelings that affect us strongly; consequently, light in the theatre can affect us even more intensely because we intentionally select it. The director-designer relationship must, therefore, be a very close one, for lighting design is the actual extension of the director's most sensitive and most personal vision.

The director's training in stage lighting should be extensive because he should not only be able to visualize the scope of lighting, but he should also have a firm technical knowledge of how to achieve what he wants. Lighting designers can, of course, add greatly to the possibilities in any one situation, but unless a director knows this tool firsthand, he will not be able to communicate to a designer what he feels and sees in a play.

THE VARIABLES IN THE PROBLEM OF DESIGN

However a director goes about acquiring his training in stage lighting, he will most certainly learn a great deal about the following aspects of lighting design:

Illumination. The basic function of stage lighting is, of course, to make the actor visible to an audience. At first, this remark may seem to you a simpleminded statement—one that anyone could take for granted —but such is not the case, for good illumination on the stage today means not only a large quantity of lighting equipment but also expert use of that equipment to heighten the effects of the actors *in movement*. The problem is historical. When the English theatre moved indoors at the beginning of the seventeenth century, both actors and audiences were illuminated with the same light which came from overhead and sidewall candelabra. Subsequent developments in the use of the stage, along with the increased emphasis on illusion in the stage picture, brought about not only a gradual separation of the stage from the house, with separate lighting provided for each, but also eventually the convention of the darkened house. The control of light became increasingly important as candlelight was superseded by oil lamps, which in turn were pushed aside in the nineteenth century in favor of gas, which finally gave way to the incandescent lamp. The unusually minute possibilities for control afforded by electricity revolutionized stage lighting practice and provided us with the theories under which we are presently working. But the basic intention has always been the same: to make the actor readily visible to the audience.

Greater control of light on the stage, however, has not necessarily meant a better theatre experience. Hearability (an audience's capability of hearing actors), for instance, has a great deal to do with visibility. We have learned that when low lighting is used to achieve certain effects of mood, the capability of hearing is reduced. It is not that an audience lip-reads what actors are saying but more probably that feelings created by such light tend to cloud the hearing—a psychological problem. From another point of view, we know that too much light—now entirely possible because of improved lighting instruments and quantitative control —can reduce visibility: we lose contour in the faces of actors, and thus we not only reduce hearing but facial projection. We have introduced color into lighting as a technical convention, but we have discovered that it can be very tiring on the eyes, thus reducing both hearing and seeing. From the above, it should be clear that good illumination is not just a matter of turning on lights; it is the result of careful design for the appropriate circumstances of a play. *Selective visibility* is a good phrase for it.

Source Considered. One of the remarkable coincidences in the development of the theatre is the invention of the incandescent lamp at approximately the same date as the shift in the theatre to the new style of Naturalism. Naturalism, of course, means strict verisimilitude to nature, and in the theatre it means photographic reproduction. Electric light made this goal possible, as other lighting control could not possibly have done. Lifelike sunsets and dawns were now realizable on the stage; and interior rooms could be lighted with accurate window effects, shadowed corners and ceilings, lamp effects, and lighted entranceways. When wall switches were turned on, rooms were immediately flooded with light. Chandeliers, wall brackets, lamps, fires flickering in fireplaces, and sunlight and moonlight were the motivating sources of the light. The audience looked at an appearance of reality, and accepted all the logic of the sources within its own sight. Any violations of the logic could be quickly detected, and could therefore become distractions. If the lighting design was logical, the audience accepted the *source considered* and took it for granted. In the representational theatre, then, lighting has to have all the appearances of accepted motivation because we are familiar with what we see, and we believe in its reality.

Source Not Considered. The wave of Naturalism temporarily side-tracked the oldest theory of lighting: light from a nonconsidered source. Again, at first you may think this theory means merely turning on the lights without specific motivation from lamps, sunlight, etc., but it can mean much more than that. In contrast to representational light from a source considered, this kind is *presentational* light, or light as it exists only in the theatre; a spotlight that comes obviously from a projection booth at the rear of the house and is thrown on an actor is the most obvious example, but in general use it means that a motivating source for light is unimportant and, thus, is not considered.

Such light can come from above the actor, with the instrument concealed from the audience, and with the intention of providing an illusory effect, but since the light is not motivated from any logical source it becomes purely conventional. The actors are merely gathered in the light. As an audience, we do not worry about where the light comes from—it just comes, and we find other values to concern us. *Source not considered* is the lighting used on open-thrust and arena stages, and frequently on the forestage proscenium convention. Parts of the stage picture can thus be selected from the total possible picture for certain scenes, with the light areas changing from one location to another as various parts of a stage are used. Large stage areas can thus be cut into small stage areas; and grand scenes and intimate scenes can be played in sequence. The audience accepts the convention and focuses its attention on the dramatic action and not on the appearances of reality.

Composition in Lighting. Since stage lighting, in modern theory, must come from specific instruments and is not a general illumination from massive sources, the director-designer must be fully aware of the three-dimensional capability of lighting control. Actors and objects can be made highly plastic, with their depth emphasized. You will remember from the experiments in your lighting class that light thrown from the front tends to flatten faces, and that side light and back light, especially if unbalanced in quantity and color, will reveal their three-dimensional qualities. By manipulating intensity, direction, and color, the masses on the stage can be made more dynamic, more alive, simply by emphasizing their lines.

Good lighting, therefore, has enormous architectural values.

Color or Noncolor. Although there is always a certain amount of color in the pure electric light emitted from an incandescent lamp or from other light sources, what is being considered here is whether light should be projected through color media (gelatin or other filtering material) or left in its original state. The American theatre, in contrast to

PLATE XXII   *The Lady From The Sea* by Henrik Ibsen

Here is another instance of selective visibility through the use of directional lighting. Although the primary speaker is the figure on the left, he has been placed in relative darkness so that the emphasis will be thrown on "The Lady" in the downstage position who is undergoing intensive adjustment. Thus, the viewer is encouraged to watch the adjustment while listening to the story the upstage figure is recounting. The third figure (in the center) is lighted in a transitional way so that the total effect is that of three levels in the lighting. Note also how the form of the architectural scenery is enhanced through the use of directional lighting, with the background elements providing mostly outline for the major downstage happenings.

the European theatre, has tended to use color media much more extensively, but the growing development in repertory programming in the United States, as opposed to the fixed staging for one particular production, has introduced, perhaps out of necessity as it certainly has in European repertory theatres, the nonmedia approach. Since the intention in this chapter is only to show the range of possible exploitation, which direction you go is immaterial as long as you understand the values of both methods of lighting the stage, so that either can be used in designing productions.

First, the color-media approach. As you have already learned in your lighting classes, white light is composed of red, green, and blue light, so that it is possible to give an appearance of natural light by throwing a combination of these colors, usually highly modified, on the actor. The usual procedure is to create a living quality by producing highlights and shadows: warm gelatins from one side, cool ones from the other. And as you may know, blending light made of the same color components is often used, usually from the front by means of striplights or soft-light instruments, to soften the mechanical lines of the angular light but not in any way to destroy its effect.

But the range of possible warm and cool colors can vary greatly, and now the director-designer enters directly into the decision making because the light can strongly affect the pigmentary colors in costumes and in painted settings. A good lighting designer will, of course, consider what will happen when he sets up such a design, but unless the director is thoroughly aware of his coordinating function in this respect, he may lose the values of the other designs he has carefully nurtured. The worst that can happen is the graying out of pigmentation. Color media create many problems, which necessitate an extensive knowledge of light on the part of the director if they are to be met head-on.

Color in light is also a matter of taste, as it is in scene design and costuming, because it possesses highly sensuous values. We can see this obviously in moving pictures and in television when we contrast the effect produced on us by color film with that of the black-and-white convention. Color can greatly excite the audience, for it works on us much as any sensual excitation—we vibrate in psychological response. Perhaps light has played a larger part in declaring the style of Broadway theatre than any other element of design, for much of it has been erotic and sensual in its usage of gold, brown, orange, and amber light, sharply contrasted with heavy blues and purples. Whatever may have brought this usage about, it is apparent that heavy mood effects can be created entirely by the use of light alone, and that the mood is in the color. A director must be thoroughly aware of the potential of color media if he is to control not only the values in lighting but also the values in pigmentation of scenery and costumes.

In contrast, the noncolor approach seems to provide more ready control over design as a whole than does the use of color. But although it allows close-to-true colors of costumes and painted scenery to emerge, there is a certain brightness, a certain coolness about unfiltered light that can reduce somewhat the psychological grip of actor-audience contact. Much can be said for the days of candlelight on the stage, or even of gaslight, because those media were soft-light sources, and they tended to soften actors' faces and bodies. Unfiltered electric light, even with the use of properly adjusted makeup, tends to make for flatness and an unrelieved quality.

A possible compromise lies in the careful joining of both approaches: the use of softening filters—frosts, or filters with a light tinge of pink or amber, or noncolor light softened with border striplights. If instruments are properly placed to produce excellent compositions, the light can be increased or decreased through these softening filters, and the whole color design can be brought into harmony.

Light-color is a director's tool that must not be used carelessly but with the greatest skill.

Movement. We talk about *changeable scenery* and mean by it the creating of new places through the shifting of flats, drapes, borders, wings, wagons, and other elements, sometimes directly before the eyes of an audience. We can also talk in the same sense about *changeable lighting,* for lighting is the most flexible of all the elements of design in production, with the same capability for instantaneous change we find in the moving picture. Lighting can therefore be said to have movement— movement akin to music in its inherent rhythm and sequence.

The obvious examples are in those lighting designs that incorporate sunsets or dawns: we actually see the light move in changing patterns, and we realize that what we are watching is not simply a verisimilitude to nature but an artistic representation of natural phenomena. But what is less obvious is our acceptance of changeable light to open up or close down scenes. Controlled light has spatial properties that permit the declaration of infinite spatial relationships. Thus, within the same scene, we can, through the use of light, create different emphases, moving from one point on the stage to another, from one intensity to another, from one dominant color to another.

The fade-out and the fade-in of lighting provide the same function as the act curtain, although the speed of such changes can be adjusted dramatically with much more diversity than can be arranged with a curtain.

We can also cross-fade, moving from one light pattern to another, a convention similar to the wipe of the moving picture. We can follow the actor with a follow spot, thus seeming to move his scenery with him; and we can isolate him completely from others around him, and then have him seem to join the group again.

This inherent characteristic of movement in light can provide many theatrical moments, but when improperly used, it can be both self-conscious and distracting. Good stage lighting must seem to happen, to be exactly right for any given moment.

Moods. It is obvious from the above discussions that light has a very great capability of arousing moods—strong feelings. Moods in lighting are consequences of light, the goals of the director-designer. Light can create the bright, happy moods of comedy, or the cool, shadowed, dislocated light of the serious and troubled. It can draw us into the illusory world of representation; it can arouse images of the world of fantasy; or it can make us accept explicitly that we are only in a theatre and that what we see can only take place there. We can be plunged into strange feelings of darkness or inebriated with great quantities of light. We can feel the enormous shock of symbolic color—red is blood, yellow is sunshine, blue is night, brown-orange is heat, etc. And through the use of projections, we are allowed to sense much more strongly the idea of place without seeing its actual, three-dimensional reality. Light is not just seeing; it is feeling. And as the light goes, so go our feelings.

A director is a maker of moods, and light is one of his strongest allies in the making.

EXERCISES

1. *The Crucible* has been played on the proscenium stage with (1) highly developed, illusionistic box settings, and (2) fractionated scenery made of curtains and screen units. Discuss the effect of each production. Which would you prefer? Why?

2. What colors and textures would you use on painted scenery for *The Crucible?*

3. If you were to stage *The Crucible* with projected scenery, what would you choose for the projections? What would be the effect of such a production?

4. If you were to stage *The Crucible* in an illusionistic manner, what sort of research would be needed to locate the appropriate set properties?

5. Would you use look-through scenery for staging *The Crucible* in arena style?

6. Could you stage *The Crucible* on either the open-thrust or arena stages with set properties made of plain, boxlike cubes two feet on each dimen-

sion? What would be the effect? What other geometric forms could be used and what would be their dimensions?

7. Make a list of hand properties for use in Act II. What items did you add to the list beyond those specifically called for, such as the doll, the chains to tie Proctor, the whip, etc.? What can be done with hand properties associated with the fireplace?

8. What would be the effects if *The Crucible* were staged with each of the two approaches to lighting: (1) color and (2) noncolor?

9. Is *source considered* a necessary concept in staging *The Crucible?* What sort of instrumentation would you use for an open-thrust staging of this play? What would happen to the flow of the play if you used area lighting, raising and lowering it in various areas as they became dominant acting areas?

18

director's options 3: costume, makeup, and sound effects

Although it is always possible to build the other production designs around costume, the more usual approach is to make choices among those outlined in Chapters 16 and 17, and then to decide how costume, the most dynamic of all the visual designs because of its association with the moving actor, can fit into the whole plan. With this approach, the director can be much more certain about how he can bring counterpoint into the total design. In addition, he will know how close the costumes will be to the audience, what kind of scenery will be used, what the color plan can be for the settings, and what the lighting potential may be. With these considerations in mind, the director can then make the major decision about how far to stretch or contract any or all of the designs, and costume in particular. The makeup design will, of course, have to wait on costume decisions, for it is inherently part of costume and should be designed in close coordination with it. The following discussion of the director's options in these two areas will follow that order.

The final decision that must be made in design coordination is what to do about sound effects, including the use of music. Because of its very important mood-inducing characteristics, sound effects must wait until the director knows what can be achieved through visual effects. Consequently, the last section of this chapter will be devoted to the director's options in the use of sound.

Options in Costume

DEFINITION

We are so accustomed to thinking loosely of costume as historical dress—actors dressing up in clothing much removed from our own times —that we are apt to misinterpret the basic concept of costume. Although it may be defined in several ways, one of the best is to see costume as live scenery worn by an actor in a particular role in a particular play. Acting is impersonation, not reality; so is costume, for it is the *exterior* reflection of the actor's impersonation, which assumes that the person portrayed is someone other than the actor himself. Just as the playscript is an artificial device because it involves specific selection and arrangement, so also is costume, for someone—the actor in other ages, the designer in our own —has to choose the particular and appropriate dress for a particular circumstance. Costume is therefore an integral part of production design, and the director must pay the most careful attention to it.

How strange you feel as a person when you try on someone else's clothing—a jacket, a coat; and you feel even more self-conscious the more personal the item of clothing actually is, because it may actually bear the scent of the owner. What you are feeling is the strength and individuality of the person to whom the clothing belongs. In this sense, costumes *belong* to other people, and the actor's job in his process of impersonation is to make the dress belong to the character he creates.

As with the other tools of production, the intention here is to discuss costume, not as training in depth but only as one of the director's possibilities in production—how does the director look at costume and what are his options in using it to stage plays? It must be assumed that your overall training will involve an intensive study of costume design and construction, for only in such a study can you really comprehend the range of this complex craft. Because costumes are so close to actors, a director must have a thorough knowledge of their potentials and how to control them. Without this knowledge, he must rely entirely on the work of others—an approach that can be disastrous as far as production idea and unity are concerned.

CAPABILITIES OF COSTUME

A director should not only be fully aware of the nature of costume but also of its capabilities as a tool of production. What follows is a summary of the main ways in which costume can directly affect production:

Given Circumstances. Because costume has the capability of locating the time and place of a play with some accuracy, all the aspects of a play's given circumstances must be considered before any decision can be made. Costume is much more specific than scene design because it can locate the characters of a play in a very individual way simply by being scenery on the move. Thus, it is possible to reflect economic circumstance as well as social, political, religious, and climatic aspects of a given environment. In particular, it can bring onto the stage all the rituals in a given circumstance: the synagogue or the church, the evening dress of the military or the diplomatic corps, the pomp and circumstance of court ritual, or the decorations of a country wedding. Dress can tell us immediately where we are and can provide much of the detail affecting a particular environment.

Character and Dramatic Action. Costume particularizes and individualizes because dress moves with the characterization being made by an actor. Since the personal choice of clothing is a suitable reflection of the individual who wears it—he feels like his dress—the director-designer must always look for the specific, rather than the general, idea. Costume design is not ordering dress from a rental agency where the materials are assembled as general items with very little regard paid to individuality because they are to be used over and over again in different ways, but it is the result of the particularization of character, usually with a specific actor, who is to play the role, in mind. Using the general design of a costume house may be a quick way out in a tight circumstance, but the loss of individuality—of character as it is perceived by the director and designer—is the usual result. Such an approach is not design but merely dressing, for a rental agency's view of a play can be no more than general since it cannot possibly know what a director has specifically in mind about a play and its production. The same failure in design is also possible when dress is pulled from a stock wardrobe if the director and costumer skip the crucial and time-consuming problem of design—the search for fresh and individual statements.

What does the clothing say? Does it say it in the specific terms of the dramatic action embedded in the playscript? What do the appearances of a character have to do with the actions he takes at the strongest moments of forcing? Does he look different on the outside from what he really is on the inside? These are the questions about the dramatic action that must concern the director. In real life, we find much concealment, much covering up; so, it is logical that we find the same types of concealment in plays. A brutal king might be an elegant dresser, but he also might be a careless one. The convention of dark clothing on a nineteenth-century villain might become light and colorful dress on a twentieth-century character. Since dramatic action frequently deals with the opposites of appearances, the intention of design may often be simply to surprise an audience into unexpected revelation. To find that in Edward Albee's *Everything in the Garden,* the suburbanites, who dress casually in disarming sports wear that reflects excellent taste, are also capable of murder when the secrecy of their lives is endangered, is to shock audiences with *where lies the monster?*

Costume is character.

Color, Texture, and Form. By *form* in costume we mean silhouette or shape. It is the sum total of the lines in a costume, and it is thus the most basic aspect of a design. The lines may follow the contours of the body, or they may create artificial lines related to the body but nevertheless distinct from body lines, and they may do both at the same time. Thus, we have the changing aspects of fashion—the relationship of the physical contour of the body to materials in order to alter the exterior line. Because form is basic, it is more *general* than either color or texture, but without the basic architecture there would be nothing on which to build specifics. Costume begins with form.

As we have already pointed out in the discussion on scenery and lighting, color has strong sensuous, even sensual, values: we find it exciting, often erotic, and frequently theatrical. As we move in color in real life, so also we move on the stage where there has been no possibility of passing through a black-and-white convention as in the moving picture and in television. The director who misses the option of using color in costuming is simply missing an important emphasis in design.

The same can be said of the texture of materials, for without texture and color we cannot see contrasts or find emphasis. Texture gives boldness and clear statement by providing the necessary exaggeration that makes possible the projection of ideas from the stage. Cloth can vibrate: it can seem to stretch or hold rigid positions; it can lie in soft folds or be pressed in such a way as to seem firm and unyielding; it can have great bulk or be nothing at all. We see and feel texture, just as we see and feel color.

Movement. As has already been pointed out, costumes are not static but, by their nature as coverings for human beings, they are dynamic and moveable. Only the few items that seem to be arbitrarily fixed—tights, corsets, metal armor—violate this characteristic. And because costumes move, they convey to viewers the many images inherent in flexibility—images that range from stiffness to complete freedom and flow. In this sense a costume lives *if* the actor inside it is fully aware of how the costume ought to move.

For this reason, matching footwear to the style of a costume is so important. A body moves as its feet move since the whole body structure depends on what happens from the ground up. An actor cannot make a costume move in its inherent logic unless he can "walk" the costume properly. A director must have a full awareness of the capabilities of costumes (and this awareness includes wigs and hats), if he is to exploit them, that is, to create them as logical and living clothing on his actors. Part of his job is to show actors how to wear their dress in the appropriate way.

Composition. Since costumes are seldom seen alone on the stage, the art of costume design is to foresee all the possible compositions (actor groupings) that might turn up in the staging of a play. The problem is much more complex than arranging scenery because costume is always dynamic—it can move with the actor to any position on the stage—and, yet, it must always do its most effective work no matter where it is. To the costume designer, the effect of the ensemble is as important as the individual costume; it should also be of prime consideration to the director because his compositions which reveal the basic action of a play can literally be destroyed, or at least, greatly weakened, if the costume ensemble is not properly designed. This is why the director and costumer must work very closely together.

Composition in its simplest form means placing the strong costumes —those striking in color, mass, line, texture—on the dominant characters and designing the dress of the secondary characters to recede away from the primaries, with those of third and fourth importance definitely placed on the fringe of the design. Since color is so powerful as a centering force in composition, it is usually made the springboard in design, with the other design elements following closely on its heels. The color palette —the arrangement of the entire ensemble in gradations of color—thus becomes a significant principle in the technique of costume design.

It is for these reasons that the director must be absolutely certain that his costume designer sees the play as closely to his own vision as possible, for, like the lighting designer, the costume designer is an alter ego of the director. Without this parallel viewing the director has no control over the subtle physicalization of the moves a character makes, because an audience will actually see most gesture and all movement *through* a costume, and it cannot be a barrier but must be a helpful illuminator. Yet, the relationship of the director to the costumer must be a free one—a fully creative one for the costumer. The best way of communicating lies in the common ground of the playscript, which can be discussed, or even read together, without treading on the sensitive ground of the actual design itself. In this way the director can make his points clear, can even give *gross* examples of possible directions, without inhibiting the work of the costumer as a visual artist.

Mood. Because costume is worn by the moving actor, it is a more intensive and continuous conveyor of mood than either setting or lighting. Our feelings as members of an audience are definitely aroused by costume, even though we are not conscious of how the effect is made, as

PLATE XXIII *Fuente Ovejuna* by Lope de Vega

In this production of Lope's famous Golden Age drama, costume played a very important part in conveying ideas in the play. Each level of society was given its line-mass values and symbolic color scheme: gold (sunburst), white, and black (symbolic of power) dress for the Court; long black tabards over chain mail, with the blood-red cross of Calatrava mounted on breast, sleeve, or cape for the Master and his officers: earth colors of brown-tan-yellow for the peasant homespuns. Vertical lines showed dignity at all levels but particularly in the Court, where the vertical motif combined with large masses to become conical. Against the starkness of the setting and the enormous heraldic banners carried onstage by soldiers, the bold sweep of line and mass displayed by the Court costumes spoke with Spanish grandeur, authority, richness, and ceremonial form. The dignified fifteenth-century military silhouette captured meanings of Christian knighthood and emphasized the irony of corruption. The monochromatic earth colors on the peasants held them rigidly apart from the formal decorum of the upper orders, although through the gold-browns they were positively related to the Court in the final scene.

we should not be. In this sense, costume *is* character, for we are led away from the actor and toward character through the particularizing aspects of good costume design, and it is character that moves us. If a costume is stronger than an actor, however, it can readily seem self-conscious and be distracting, a condition that definitely reduces mood possibilities. Costume must be an aid to feeling and not an inhibitor. Every aspect of costume design can evoke mood: color, line, mass, texture, movement.

SOME SUGGESTED OPTIONS IN COSTUME SELECTION

Overdressing versus Underdressing. It should now be clear that the line between overdressing and underdressing is a subtle and delicate one. If a costume is "right," it can do an enormous job in helping an actor, but if it varies too far on either side of the scale, an actor must work *against* his clothes. Finding the right balance depends on successful communication between director and designer.

Neutral Dress. This term means literally *no seeming costume effect at all*—a very difficult possibility in design since any clothing an actor wears takes on some meaning. Perhaps the dress that would be closest to neutral is the leotard—the thinnest sort of cover for the actor's body. It can be said to be neutral because it has no movement or mass in itself —what moves is the actor alone; and if all actors in an ensemble wear the same color of leotards, color will not be an individualizing factor in composition. The actor is thus left free to express his body idea without assistance from the amplifying and illusionary effects of costume.

Archeological Clothing. This term refers to stage dress that comes very close to the reproduction of the real clothing of any period. At its poorest and least communicative, such dress is actual reproduction; at its best it is modified and artistically conceived, though it is still closely related to the basic historical design.

Clothing worn in modern Realistic plays is usually archeological, since reproduction or the use of real clothing is one way of gaining verisimilitude. Yet, a director and a designer quickly learn that photographic reproduction will not stimulate imagination in an audience unless such clothing is most carefully selected in terms of its overtones—its symbolic values. Modern dress, because it is more subtle than that of other periods, is therefore among the most difficult designs in costume to achieve. When the clothing is well selected and arranged, thus becoming costume, it can perform the same function for a modern character as historical costume can for a character in a play of another era. In this sense, Realism is an enemy of costume design because the tendency is for directors to accept reproduction rather than design.

Ritual and Rite. Many plays contain actions that revolve around formal ceremonies or deal with characters closely associated with such ceremonies—gods, priests, hangmen, lawyers, warriors, etc. Since such characters are symbols in everyday life, they must be treated as such on the stage. Just as a director would be extremely careful in reproducing a religious ritual, so he must also exercise expert judgement and care in the design of the dress that illustrates such rituals. In the imaginations of a general audience, the dress becomes the ritual itself.

Abstract. In one meaning of the word, all costume is abstract because it is not reality, but here *abstract* refers to that class of plays in which dress must be invented. What do the devils look like in *Doctor Faustus?* What will man wear in the twenty-first century? What do the fairies wear in *Midsummer Night's Dream?* What does the Man from Mars look like? What do stage animals look like? What does a witch look like? Children's plays are full of this sort of costume requirement, and many adult plays include abstractions. Without a lively imagination about such costuming, a director cannot make the points he sees in a play. Can he help a designer without doing the design? This question is a real problem.

Summary of Costume Options. From the above, it should now be clear that the director can move in multiple directions in making decisions about design. But, instead of searching for historical accuracy, he will probably follow the usual route of adapting historical clothing by finding and reproducing its essence, or he may dress his play in contemporary modern—another way of saying modern dress, or he may use the fashions of a period quite different from the one associated with the play. But, if none of these options seem to fit the bill, he may turn to neutral dress or abstract form. The intention will always be the same, however: to reveal the interior meanings of a play through the outward show.

REHEARSAL TECHNIQUES

Approaching Costume. The rehearsal period is a time of experimentation when an actor searches for and hopefully discovers the character he is trying to play. One of the best aids to his imagination is the "feeling" of a character's dress, because it can show him how the character moves, how he gesticulates, and often, in a detailed way, how he feels. An actor can discover these things because the restrictions of a character's dress may differ sharply from what the actor normally wears in everyday life. Clothing is the shell of a character, and the actor must discover the qualities and the nature of that shell.

Rehearsing in portions of the final costume that an actor is to wear can, therefore, be very helpful; it is director-actor communication in a very real sense. If you, as director, do not know explicitly how a costume should move, enlist the aid of the costume designer to help you instruct the actors.

Shoes. Since a character's body movement is declared by his feet—how he stands and moves, appropriate foot gear worn in rehearsal is of specific help to an actor in devising his characterization. Thus, an actor in a Wycherley or Molière comedy should wear the high-heeled shoes he will wear in performance; or, if he is to wear boots or heavy shoes, he should work in them as early as possible. Women should wear high heels if the costume will eventually require them or sandals if they are the requirement. The actor who feels the effect of the footwear, who lets it work on his imagination, is telling himself much about the person he is trying to play. At first, the footwear will seem awkward and unfamiliar, but this is precisely why it is the very best moment for an actor to discover the new things the footwear does to him and to his characterization. If he makes imaginative discoveries, an actor will forget the difference from his everyday wear because he will have incorporated ideas about how his feet move into his moving character. "As go the shoes, so goes the body."

Other Dress. Period plays should be rehearsed as soon as possible in the basic costume, which may amount to no more than long skirts, coats, flowing shirts, or head wear. Underpinnings are very important because costumes move on the basis of what is worn beneath them. Restrictions of any kind—an amplified stomach, armor, corsets, tight vests, stiffened garments, etc.—will tell the actor much about how his character will move. Directors who do not insist on this kind of help early in rehearsals will face at dress rehearsals and performance actors who have not absorbed ideas about the clothing—a situation meaning that the actors move, but the clothing does not, or vice versa. Communication is a subtle process, and the director must use every device to help his actors find their characters. Costume is a way.

Options in Stage Makeup

In today's stage practice, makeup has two significant functions: (1) to make an assisting statement of an actor's chaacterization and (2) to counterbalance the effects of stage lighting. Both of these functions fall into the director's hands because the first is closely tied to how he thinks an actor can best illustrate a character, and the second is closely related to the lighting problem. The costume designer is also interested in makeup because of the good and bad effects that hair styles, both head and face, as well as facial coloration have on a costume as a whole; and the lighting designer is interested because the colors and textures of makeup can complement or seriously hamper his design. Thus, it is up to the director to satisfy all three specific interests as well as those of the actors who will not only be wearing the makeup but will be executing the actual agreed-upon design.

The usual process is for the director to talk about the problems with both costumer and lighting designers and then to set up a specific makeup design which both can study and approve. In this sense makeup is a welder of costume and light. A primary knowledge of this area, both of its materials and its procedures, is therefore necessary if a director is to carry out this work satisfactorily. Again, the intention in this section is not to explore the techniques of stage makeup in detail but to point out its options as a staging tool.

Stage makeup means the appropriate application of color—pigmentary color, the same as is used in scene painting and costuming—on an actor's skin with the intention of exaggerating the facial features in order to make them appear specific and emphatic. The actual design of a makeup depends on how the directional light is used in a particular setup—where it comes from, its color, its intensity. Good makeup is never noticeable to an audience except in those plays where it is used as an obviously stylized device, for it is part of the actor's face and is therefore part of his reality. Consequently, makeup cannot be a laid-on stage tool but must be organic in that it expresses the actor's characterization in the context of the stage lighting. Since it is the director's job to harmonize makeup on a technical level with costume and lighting, the usual procedure is for the director, in consultation with the costume and lighting designers, to design for each character a facial mask—what he looks like —so that this problem is considered systematically. Actors can then execute their own makeup and can be confident of their adjustment in a specific design.

Good makeup exploits given circumstances as a matter of course— time, place, social level, etc., because they are the outward visual show of a character. "What do I look like?" is the question the actor asks himself, and it is also the director's question because makeup can tell an audience—especially through the use of hair—about the degree of character conformity or nonconformity, about his vanity and his awareness of others, about his sense of personal style. Makeup provides an audience with its primitive visual idea of a character, the frame of reference from which the dramatic action can emerge. In this sense, makeup bridges the gap between a character's costume and the physical character in the body of an actor.

A director's options in makeup design, then, rest primarily on what happens in the lighting and costume designs. The more he understands about lighting, particularly about the specific effects of light-colors on pigmentation-colors, the easier it will be for him to effect the appropriate coordination. Exercises in a laboratory lighting situation where makeup can be introduced should be of great benefit. Likewise, the more he knows about hair styles and styling, the better he will be able to coordinate costume effect with character expression. You will, therefore,

PLATE XXIV   *The Good Woman of Setzuan* by Bertolt Brecht

What do gods look like? Masks are used in this production to provide a "reality"—a paradox—for abstract characters. The intention was to show the gods as weak men hiding behind "fixed" faces, immobile and conventional, to emphasize the point made in the play that the gods can do nothing to help man pull out of the terrible state of poverty and suffering he has inflicted upon himself through his own selfishness and greed, that they are relatively meaningless in a society in which man must help himself out of the quagmire. The character rightstage wears a conventional mask to represent one of the two roles he plays throughout the drama—a mask to indicate a coverup of his sensitive and out-reaching self. The impersonality of the mask, therefore, shows the audience the dead quality in the character. The other figures in the photograph all wear conventional makeup with no attempt to make them look oriental since they must represent Westerners and thus identify directly with the audience.

need to study hair in its relationship to costume, including basic knowledge of how wigs are constructed and worn effectively.

Good stage makeup is the result of a director's specific seeing, for many possible effects are lost by young directors who look at makeup as a general tool instead of a specific one. Learn to plan designs with the greatest care and with an eye toward theatrical possibilities. We have lost the art of makeup in the modern theatre, not only out of disuse but also out of negligence. With no one usually assigned to design this area of expression, it has been left in the hands of actors who simply cannot see themselves, or with a director who does not assume it is one of his primary coordinating responsibilities.

In brief, makeup expresses character, complements lighting, exaggerates, emphasizes, or distorts facial structure (through the use of putty or other structural additives). Through using his options, the director can call for historical accuracy in terms of hair fashions, for abstractions such as the use of symbolic colors or designs, for no makeup at all, or for the use of masks. The latter are as much employed in our theatre today as they have been in any theatre of the past with the exception of the Classical Greek, for we have found them extremely useful in expressing symbolic ideas.

Options in Sound Effects

The point has been made several times in this book that the theatre may be more of an experience in sound than in sight, for it is the actor's voice that finally moves us, wrenched as it is from the heart and the body. We are, of course, easily excited by the visual, particularly because of its sensual, erotic capabilities, but we are not apt to be so deeply moved by what we see except in an actor's spontaneous use of gesture and movement in support of his vocal sound.

It is not at all surprising, therefore, to find that supplementary sound has been used throughout the history of the theatre. Music has always played a part, sometimes accompanying the actor's voice either directly when he sings or indirectly as background to his speaking, a convention that had been employed on the stage for twenty-five hundred years before it was adopted by the moving pictures as one of its primary conventions. The other use of sound—sound effects—has been developed extensively in the Realistic theatre, although certain effects such as thunder have been in use since Elizabethan times or before. The director who is thoroughly aware of how to exploit sound is well on the way to making total theatre.

MUSIC

The director is usually his own sound designer because most educational theatre setups do not include a musician as part of the permanent staff of designers and even if they did, the coordination would have to be as close as that of the director and lighting designer because music is as personal and as delicately sensitive in its capacities for imagination arousal as is stage light. Music can often be a distraction and not an intensification as it ought to be. A most meticulous approach is therefore necessary if it is to be used as a helping tool.

Music in the play. Many plays are written with a specific musical requirement—a song, a dance, an instrument—which necessitates its performance on the stage in front of the audience. The problem is a double one: to find the music itself, if none is specifically provided, and to locate a performer who can do it. Finding appropriate music is often very difficult, a problem that can frequently be solved only by having the music composed especially for the production in hand. The latter approach has the merits of free flight on the part of the director because he can work closely in a stimulative way with the composer, accepting or rejecting what seems right or inappropriate as he would do with a lighting designer. But this approach also has its own inherent problems if it is not to be a distraction. Music within a play must somehow catch the beat of the particular moment of its use, for the playwright, if he is a good one and not just a maker of entertainments, has included it, not as a decorative device but as organic material that is intended to heighten, to intensify, to fill a gap where spoken words cannot do the work. Often the words of a song will be the key to the musical line the playwright hears; or, he may have suggested titles of specific songs, in which case the director must search them down in order to hear their ideas and rhythms, although he may decide for a number of reasons, including the capability of his actors who are to perform them, to have *similar* music written. But whether he uses something from the music library or has it composed, the director must be constantly alert to the fact that such insertions in a play are dramatic actions in themselves and must produce the same effect as actions in the dialogue of the play. Music has subtext as well as text.

The performer is often the key to what can be done, for his talents will determine how far the music can go and still be effective. Actors frequently have musical talents, but whereas an individual's acting capability may be particularly suited to a particular casting, his musical talents may lie far afield from the necessary requirements. To work around this situation, it has been frequent practice to place a live piano or other instrument offstage with the actor dubbing onstage; or to have an actor speak the words of a song, or half speak or half sing them. But these substitutions are poor seconds, for a live musician onstage can provide fine moments if he is truly an actor; however, he can be a genuine distraction if he is not. Insertions of music into a play are difficult to perform successfully unless the director has solved all the attendant problems.

Background Music. This is the mood music used as background to acting with which you are so familiar in moving pictures and television. In those media it is firmly established as a convention, but it has not been so used in the theatre since the passing of nineteenth-century melodrama—drama with music—early in the century. Perhaps it lost force as the moving picture took over as the popular entertainment, but more likely it served its purpose in the theatre of another age and was abandoned as other conventions for obtaining mood effects were developed—lighting, for instance. Nowadays it is occasionally used, and then usually with a logical offstage source of motivation. Thus, music does not seem to emanate from nowhere but may come from an offstage band or orchestra, or a single instrument played by one of the characters in the play. Good dialogue, because it is also good sound, does not need musical support to enhance its mood qualities, whereas in moving-picture writing, where dialogue is often secondary to visual effect, the work is done partly by spoken words, partly by the music, and mostly by visual storytelling. The theatre is a place for sound, but the legitimate play is not musical theatre; its own inherent sound values must be carefully discovered and preserved.

Music Between Scenes. This convention has continued in the theatre since Shakespeare's day because it can provide the mood-bridge from one major action to another. Such bridges can tie diverse sections of plays together, especially when changes of location are involved. A few seconds' wait while the scene is changed is a very long time in the theatre, and music can help to pass this time by bridging, in the imagination of an audience, the closing mood of one scene and the opening mood of another. One technique used is the overlap: beginning the bridge music a few seconds before the end of one scene and continuing it for a few seconds after the start of the next. Used in this way, the music not only helps the work of transition, but it also acts as a relief from the spoken play—a resting moment for the audience—and it gives a sense of quick passage of time. The theatres of the seventeenth and eighteenth centuries, and even of much of the nineteenth, used these bridges to cover the changing of the scenery before the eyes of the audience, but with the use of the act curtain and the darkened theatre as devices for separation between scenes, the convention was continued in the interest of occupying the audience. The use of this convention, is, however, a matter of the director's interest and taste, for some directors prefer a "clear" play—one that stands alone on its own organic sound. The strongest argument in favor of bridge music is that the theatre is a sound experience, and the assault on the human ear can be more complex, more arresting, than it can be with only the actor's voice.

The problem of finding appropriate bridge music is as difficult as finding appropriate musical settings for songs in a play, for the bridges must reflect the beat of the play. This requirement does not mean that the bridge must be the same beat, for effective bridges are often counterpoints to a completed scene or even to the play as a whole. It is the search for counterpoints that encourages the use of modern jazz or other modern music as bridge music in productions of classical drama. The counterpoint is what the director is after, for he wants to shift the audience's mood quickly from one emphasis to another; he may even want his audience to think and feel modern though the material of the play may belong to another age and time. By using classical jazz in Christopher Marlowe's *Doctor Faustus* or a Bach Chorale in jazz style in Shaw's *Saint Joan,* an audience can partially sense the modern quality and meaning of each play and be divorced from any preconceptions about it, for the music has been used to jolt it out of its expected responses and to give it a sense of present context.

The possibility of distraction with bridge music can be great. The director must therefore exert every care to be certain he has found the appropriate bridges in terms of the meaning of the production as a whole. Sound is as subtle as light and can easily throw an audience in a wrong direction.

SOUND EFFECTS

The use of offstage sound effects, with the exception of thunder and fire arms, is largely a convention of the modern Realistic stage. Such effects are an extension of onstage illusion because they give weight and quality to offstage places, even though such places can exist only in the imaginations of an audience. The development in the 1920s and 1930s of radio broadcasting as a total assault on the ear undoubtedly had a good deal to do with the recent development of sound effects on the stage because the theory was the same: excite the imagination through the use of familiar sounds. Thus, productions of Realistic plays often require the arrival or the departure of wagons, horses, cars; rain and thunder effects; crickets and night sounds; sirens, airplane engines, bombs, guns, blasting, cock crowing, clocks, bells, etc. Closely tied to this use of offstage sound is the use of onstage radios and television sets with their voices and sounds from elsewhere, and the use of onstage telephones which allow audiences to imagine nonsound replies at the other end while the visible actor speaks his part of the communication.

These conventions are still effectively in use, as recent productions of such plays as Ionesco's *Rhinoceros*, with its terror-arousing sounds of off-stage rhinoceri, can attest. The imagination of an audience knows no limits in the hands of a director alert to sound possibilities in the theatre.

Though not nearly as sensitive as music in the effect it will have on an audience, sound effects must be carefully selected in order to evoke clear and precise imagery. Bells of different pitch and volume have different symbolic meanings; the age and style of automobiles can be pictured by the proper selection of sounds; the mood effects of a storm in contrast to a rain can be very different. Thus the problem is one of appropriate selection. The careful director will enhance a production, but the careless one will merely add distraction.

Again, a play production is an experience in *sound* as well as in sight.

ELECTRONIC EQUIPMENT

The director must be thoroughly familiar with the use of all sorts of sound equipment. He may actually "cut" his own tape, that is, make a cue tape for a production. He should know how to copy, how to cut and splice, how to set up a cue tape with leader insertions, how to set up instantaneous cues on the tape deck. He should also be familiar with the capabilities of speakers and their offstage or onstage placement to achieve the best effects. Finally, he must always supervise the setting of the volumes himself in order to bring the electronic sound into balance with actors' voices. The fidelity of sound reproduction is an essential in the theatre of our time when excellent equipment is readily available.

EXERCISES

1. If you were to stage *The Crucible* in authentic period dress, what would be the symbolic meaning of the play? What would it be if you used highly simplified dress, that is, if you followed the lines of historical dress but reduced all decoration to a minimum? What sort of dress would you choose for arena staging? For open-thrust? Would nearness to an audience make a difference?

2. Why would a low-key color palette be a design idea for *The Crucible?* Would you decide to go in that direction? Would there be any difference in this choice when considering proscenium style or arena style productions?

3. How would you dress Danforth? How would he differ from the other clergy? Would he be more urbane, more sophisticated, more vain? What could you tell us specifically about him through the dress that he wears?

4. How would you dress Proctor in Act IV? What would Elizabeth wear in the same act? What about Tituba? What could you show beyond the specific images of physical torture and deprivation?

5. If you dressed *The Crucible* in dress approaching the authentic, would your men need wigs? If you decided on a much simpler dress, would Danforth still wear one?. What would be the minimum treatment in hair styles?

6. What would you suggest for makeup on a proscenium stage for Act IV to assist the costumes you devised in Exercise 4? On an arena stage?

7. What would the girls wear as hairdos in Act I?

8. One of the ways to set the different locations (time and place) of *The Crucible* and to tie the four acts tightly together in idea is by using a narrator. The usual approach is to record the narration on tape because the resulting sound would be distinctly different from the live voices of the actors on the stage. How would you go about making such a tape on a portable recording machine? Discuss how to cut, splice, and set up cues.

9. Would the use of bridge music increase the effect of the play? If so, what would you choose as music?

10. What sound effects are needed for *The Crucible*? Would you use live or recorded sound?

19

the design process and
practicing play production

You are now ready to undertake the difficult process of coordination in a live production. In working out this project, you will do all the designs completely by yourself, for every learning director must discover first-hand the complex problems facing designers in the various areas. In addition, as you do this project, you will be arguing out the procedures set out in this chapter with yourself, and in that way you will learn how to handle designers, because later on you will probably follow the usual route of working with a cast of designers as you would work with a cast of actors.

What follows in the first two sections of this chapter is a suggested procedure for working with designers (in the first few instances, with yourself). You should be aware from the beginning that your intention is to gain the full value of talented contributions by others and not to dominate them with your own stubborn demands of how designs should be done. Therefore, to insure that this freeing process takes place with a minimum of friction, a suggested procedure for the director-designer communication process is set up in four discussion steps. You should look at this number, however, as only a general way of approaching the problems with designers; for the actual process may require more or fewer contact periods, depending on particular production problems in the various areas of design, and on the communication capabilities of both director and designers.

The final section of this chapter outlines a sequence of six major exercises intended to bring you step-by-step to a live production of a one-act play. All directors in training want to produce as soon as possible a play with all the trappings of theatre, but there is much to learn by proceeding through these exercises in an orderly manner. Live productions require not only materials and production crews but also actors who are willing to give to a director their valuable time and creative energies. Young directors, therefore, cannot afford to waste such opportunities by undertaking production without a full knowledge of what they are doing and without sufficient experience to see them through the whole process. Stage-managing is no substitute whatever for directing. Know your job first before you attempt to lead others.

Play-Analysis as the Source of Director-Designer Communication

Just as directors read playscripts visually—that is, with active imagery of what it might look like on the stage—so do designers. In fact, many designers, like many impressionist would-be directors, firmly believe that their first impressions are the strongest ones and that their early images, because of their strength and intensity, are the ones an audience will respond to imaginatively. Thus, they feel that pursuing a play further in an analytical way will reduce their capacity for design. There is much to support this approach to designing, because designing can be largely subjective in nature—how one feels about a play—but the danger lies in the fact that the images a designer sees, like those seen by an actor assigned to a specific role, may not only be confined to his own area of design but they may also stem from the reading of a play that is quite different from what a director has in mind.

Since the main problem in synthesis is to find a total visual statement that will also coordinate with the statement the actors are making, a director's readings must be multidirectional, truly comprehensive; and because they are comprehensive, he is able to move and to adjust as needed to the visual images of his co-workers. In this sense, a director does a total design of a production in his imagination—how he sees it in its entirety. But as we will point out in the next section on director-designer communication, if a director tries to inflict his own specific images on the minds and feelings of his designers, he may directly inhibit their creative capabilities.

The best approach to director-designer communication is play-analysis because it can be more objective, more idea including in a basic way, than any stated imagery that a director may try to convey to a designer. It is also the long way around. But short cuts can be destructive, and the purpose is to free the designer—just as the director frees the actor—not to bind him. There are, however, problems in this approach depending on what a designer is capable of in the way of play-analysis. If he understands and works from this approach, as some designers do, communication between director and designer may be relatively easy. If he does not, a director may have to work with him on a subjective level which can be a more difficult road for a director to travel and, at the same time, leave the designer free. But whatever the method, the intention is always the same: to find *neutral* ground that both director and designer can till together.

Working with Designers: The Process of Design

UNDERSTANDING THE PLAYSCRIPT:
THE FIRST DISCUSSION

Since the director's intention is to convey his vision of a play, a certain amount of controlled discussion with his *group* of designers is absolutely necessary. This means bringing the play to a conscious surface, which is something of a risk with designers, but it must be done if a multiheaded production is to be avoided and only one idea is to prevail—the director's. Again, the best route to follow is play-analysis, even though it may have to be on a very simple level.

The problem is how to bring about this mutual understanding without reducing a play to a mere mass of intellectuality that could stultify designers. Yet, the risk must be taken if the neutral-ground approach is to work at all. Intellectualizing in too much depth can be prevented if the director keeps the discussion moving along the story line with concentration on the dramatic action and on the human elements of character. He can thus work similarly to the way he handles actors—revealing the action as simply as possible in the interest of arousing spontaneous and inspired illustration. By carefully pointing the emphases in his storytelling, a director can plant unit ideas, and finally the main idea itself.

A certain amount of challenging by the designers of the director's perception of the action at this point is useful for sharpening the emphases and for clarifying their necessity, but the detailed refinement of idea should be carried on in the next major step—separate discussion with each designer—in the interest of preventing overdesign as delineated in Chapter 15.

Although *style* (individualization) is the subject of Part IV of this book, it is necessary to emphasize here that the director's procedure in the first group discussion with designers should be focused on conveying his own perception of the style of the playscript—*not that of the production he may want to bring about.* Therefore, his discussion should be pointed toward conveying to the designers the points of style *in the playscript* he thinks can be developed and emphasized. When you, as a learning director, understand more about the nature of style after studying Part IV, you will be better able to understand why style is crucial in the first discussion between director and designers. It is sufficient to state here, however, that your discussion of the play will involve not only dramatic action, characters, and ideas, but also characteristics of the dialogue, the mood values, the tempos, and the given circumstances, for only when designers comprehend fully what a director sees as individual and different in a playscript, can they begin to move along the lines of that vision. But again, it must be emphasized that overdiscussion of these points can stultify, and that the primary emphasis must be on the skillful handling of the story line and of the human values in a playscript.

INDIVIDUALIZING DESIGN: THE SECOND DISCUSSION

As has already been suggested in Chapter 15, the director should work separately with each designer, if he has more than one, in order to prevent duplication of emphasis and to bring about desirable counterpoints in design. In addition, he must recognize the individuality of each designer, as he does in the case of each actor, and that each has his own way of approaching design idea and an individuality of expression. The second discussion (or discussions) must, therefore, take the direction each designer leads it in.

In this meeting, he may want more play-analysis, more explanation of the *whys* of the emphases declared in the first discussion. Therefore, the intention of the director should be the same: to leave the designer as free as possible in forming his visual images while he makes certain that the designer understands the playscript as he does. Once this understanding is assured, it is quite possible for the director and designer to discuss the latter's actual images, or at least to discuss directions those images may take. The director can also present certain images of his own, if he exercises extreme care about intruding on the designer—images that are perhaps highly exaggerated or generalized with the intention of conveying a broad idea of his conception without pinning the designer down to a specific, and thus confusing, image.

Some designers have been trained to approach the design of a particular play by looking for an overall metaphor—a total visual image—as a way of finding production unity. Now is the time to discuss the meta-

phor that the designer may have in mind and for the director to understand thoroughly all of its implications. This understanding can become
a basic position of discussion, another neutral ground, because it is a
broad imaginative statement of a play and is thus nonconfining. The
metaphor provides the unusual opportunity of visual projection, and in
this approach, both designer and director can come much closer to seeing
together.

Other designers do not work from this sort of unity-making device but
see design directly in terms of mass, line, color, and physical materials.
It is not that they are working from limitations, but that they want to
imagine the range of expression possible with the ideas of the play in
mind. Again, the director, with great care, can discuss expression of the
play through this approach, but he must now be careful not to commit
himself on specifics but to help the designer find the *general* range of
illustration.

IDEAS ABOUT DESIGN: THE THIRD DISCUSSION

With a mutual understanding of the play as the director sees it now
in hand, the designer presents some specific design ideas to the director.
The third discussion is much like the director meeting the actor in a
rehearsal, and the actor acting out his own understanding of a play while
the director looks on and then responds, thus becoming a critic of the
actor's efforts. It works likewise with designers, with the director's criticism pointed toward whether the design ideas reflect accurately and imaginatively his own perception of the play. If they do, agreement is easy;
if they do not, or do so only in part, further discussion is necessary, even
to the acting out of a portion of the play for the designer. The director
is now working closely with the designer, and the result is a collaboration
on the designer's visual images.

This is a crucial point in discussion, because both director and designer must be tolerant of the other's creative capabilities. If a director
does not thoroughly project within his own imagination the designs of
the designer, if he does not perceive how they differ from his own visual
conception, he may be discarding quite adequate statements, even exciting ones, because of his own prejudice. On the other hand, if a designer
does not give his work freely for inspection with some expectation of
modification, no meeting of the two is possible. All is based on mutual
trust and on the give-and-take of responsible, creative people. Without
this mutual effort the creative process in the theatre is impossible.

It is at this point that the director tests the proposed designs in terms
of what could happen. In the case of scene design, he would test the
compositions and patterns of movement as they could be projected out of
the obstacle course proposed by the designer. Some designers work di-

rectly from inherent movement principles; that is, in their view good design proceeds from strong compositions and effective ideas about movement. In this sense, a design is organic. If a director works with such a designer, he must analyze a design very carefully to be certain he understands the principles of movement and can readily see their exploitation possibilities. If a designer is not oriented in this approach, the director must work out in his own imagination how he can build the inevitable compositions and movements directly into the designs.

Similar *testing* of costume and lighting designs must also be made, with the most careful attention given to their exploitative possibilities. Discussion with the costume and lighting designers about imagined compositions at the principal climaxes in a play will insure the kinds of emphases needed from each medium at those points, with the result that designs can be "raised" or "lowered" to coincide with those emphases.

It is at this point that the director can exercise his strongest control over the counterpoint principle discussed in Chapter 15, for he can strengthen or weaken designs as he sees fit, whereas later when they are constructed, changes would be impossible. Only lighting design, as compared to scenic and costume design, has ready flexibility and can be shifted even in the final rehearsal periods. But the discussion period is the time for planning the number and location of instruments, for later shifts are difficult and time consuming.

THE DECISION: THE FOURTH DISCUSSION

Unlike the director's work with actors, transpiring as it does over many hours of regular daily meetings, often some twenty-five to thirty-five, and because of this becoming a gradual process of mutual understanding, work with designers must be concluded early in a production period and may involve only a few hours of actual director-designer contact. Furthermore, decisions must be made that usually become irrevocable because design deals with costly materials and hours of labor, the results of which cannot actually be seen until they are built into their final forms. Modifications in acting can take place through the final rehearsals, but not so with most designs that cannot be altered except in very minor details after decisions are once made. The director must, therefore, be able to project fully in his imagination the effect of the designs he may see only on paper or, at best, in scale models. Like all designers, he must be capable of full visualization in his imagination and the strength of his production will be reflected in the degree to which he can exercise this capability.

The *final testing* now takes place. Will the designs work? Does the director thoroughly understand their exploitative possibilities? Has a synthesis *in counterpoint* actually occurred as far as the director can now project it in his imagination? Will the dramatic action in the playscript actually be enhanced by the designs so that the moods will be clear and strong? Will the actors be able to dominate the designs?

Once the commitments to designs are made, the director must believe in his commitments with full knowledge that he cannot change them except in minor details. Fully aware of how he can best make the designs organic in the production, he can then move forward in his rehearsals.

KEEPING THE DESIGNER FREE

As you can now see, the most important aspect in design approach is for the director to free his designers, not to entrap them within his own specifically imagined designs. This capability takes a *strong* director, for a clash in design ideas is as likely as a clash with strong actors over dramatic action and its illustration. The approach to both designers and actors is identical, for the director's intention is to carry them, through inspiration, beyond themselves. Any director who fails to see that design exploitation is a major part of his work does not understand the nature of theatre at all. It is true that a play can live with actors alone, but a life of that sort will be anemic without the trappings of theatre. The major problem is the appropriate control of those trappings, and only with that control can an artistic whole emerge.

Practicing Play Production

If you have had sufficient formal training in all the design areas, as you should have had by now if that training has accompanied your instruction in directing, and if you have done many of the exercises in Part III on *The Crucible* or another study play, you should be in a good position to undertake a directing-design project on your own. As was suggested at the beginning of this chapter, although you may sooner or later work with designers, a director in training must go through the full process of design a few times by himself; that is, he must do all the designs in order to understand the concepts of coordination and synthesis. The content of this brief section, then, is devoted to exercises for the practice of play production.

EXERCISE 1

Before you begin work on a live production of a one-act play, however, you should practice coordination and synthesis in visual design and in sound design by doing a project specifically with that focus. A one-act study play (the same one studied in Parts I and II would be an excellent choice) should, therefore, be used by the entire class so that comparisons are possible in the completed work. You and your fellow students should observe the following rules for this production game:

1. You must do all of your work alone and without advice or consultation of any kind. Remember that this project is a test of your imagination and skills.
2. Follow the procedures outlined in the previous sections concerning co-ordination.
3. Prepare your designs with a specific proscenium stage in mind, for it is the type of stage you understand best through your work in Part II.
4. Do only Realistic designs—that is, designs extracted directly from what you see about you in everyday life, although you may use fractionated scenery rather than a box setting if you prefer to do so.
5. Make design plots for all six areas: (1) setting, including groundplan and an elevation sketch in color; (2) properties, both set and hand; (3) lighting; (4) makeup; (5) costume; (6) sound. Make all set drawings to scale and do renderings of costumes, makeups, etc., in color. Make complete lists of all materials required.
6. Be accurate; be neat; be comprehensive.

EXERCISE 2

When Exercise 1 has been completed, you are ready to make a class evaluation of what has been accomplished. Compare the projects and note specific differences. Each area of design should at first be treated separately but always with an eye to how it relates to other areas. The focus of the discussion should be placed on (1) freshness of the ideas presented in the designs; and (2) the problems of coordination. Group designing of the same play has the definite advantage of showing you where you stand in the development of your capabilities in designing. Therefore, each member of the class should evaluate the following:

1. What is my present capability as a designer in each design area?
2. How can I develop my skills in each of the weak areas?
3. What is my comprehension of the principles of coordination and synthesis?

EXERCISE 3

The class should now review the entire process of production in as detailed a way as possible, including all of the concepts and approaches outlined in this book up to now. You should give particular emphasis to the functions of play-analysis and to the relationship between the director and actors. Intensive discussions of acting are most valuable at this point, particularly if the emphasis is placed on methods of communication. The problem of design can also be given emphasis by encouraging students in the class who are specializing in design to discuss the ways in which they work and the kinds of communication that get through to them.

EXERCISE 4

You are now ready to do the major project. If time and facilities allow, you should design and stage (with the help of your cast) a one-act play of your own choice, using minimum laboratory materials, that is, the same materials as are suggested for scene practice on pp. 174–176. The choice should still be confined to the Realistic category and the designs to the Realistic style on a proscenium stage. *Minimum staging* provides the full opportunity of handling actors in the unity of a complete play without introducing the complications of full settings and costumes. If possible for this project, lighting and sound equipment should be employed, thus giving you the opportunity of putting to work your lighting, sound, and makeup designs. If hand-property substitutes can be found, this design can also be fully used. Costumes should be whatever the actors can provide after close consultation with you. Minimum staging permits a good basic production experience without the complications of set and costume building.

A detailed preparation, including the play-analysis and all the designs, together with the list of materials needed, should be submitted for approval in advance of the rehearsals. You should then cast your own play, if possible, and proceed with production.

EXERCISE 5

After the completion of Exercise 4, a thorough evaluation of your work should be made, considering the following points:

1. The Playscript
   a. Comprehension of the dramatic action
   b. Understanding of unit divisions as illustrated in the playing
   c. Sensitivity to moods and tempos
2. Design Areas
   a. Validity of design ideas, with each design examined separately
   b. Ingenuity in the designs
   c. Skill in execution (shop experience in technical skills)
   d. Leadership ability in handling a work crew
3. Acting Area
   a. Achievement of an exciting choreographic pattern (composition, picturization, movement)
   b. Skill in communication (achievement in reciprocation)
   c. Characterization development
   d. "Violence level" and climaxes
4. Tone Achievement
   Accomplishment of mood goal

EXERCISE 6

It is suggested that the staging of a one-act play with full sets and costumes wait until you have completed study of Part IV. Although it could be undertaken at this time, only when you understand the concept of style, will you be able to make a full statement in production with authority and individuality. Therefore, you should not waste your opportunities in production but should undertake them only when you are ready for them.

IV

INTERPRETATION:
A MATTER OF STYLE

*I told you my belief in the Renaissance of the Art of
the Theatre was based in my belief in the Renaissance
of the stage-director, and that when he had understood
the right use of actors, scene, costume, lighting, and
dance, and by means of these had mastered the crafts
of interpretation, he would then gradually acquire the
mastery of the action, line, colour, rhythm, and words,
this last strength developing out of all the rest. . . .
Then I said the Art of the Theatre would have won
back its right, and its work would stand self-reliant as
a creative art, and no longer as an interpretative craft.*

GORDON CRAIG
in "The Art of the Theatre"

2 0

the director as critic

Up to this point, the discussions of play-analysis (Part I: Perception) and of staging (Parts II and III: Communication) have been concentrated on the two basic elements of all the arts—form and content. *Form* is the shape and structure of something while *content* is the material being shaped. These terms were not used in previous discussions, however, because we preferred to define *structure* and *material* in a more intertwined way without drawing hard lines of distinction or attaching labels. Moreover, it was assumed that the learning director would only be baffled by this labeling and could best discover their meanings in the process of doing. You now have enough background to differentiate the meanings of these words and to see how they apply to directing. Understanding them is very important for defining the concept of style.

What we were doing, then, by studying play structure in Part I was studying the *form* of a playscript. To do so, we broke the play-analysis into seven pieces: given circumstances, dialogue, dramatic action, character, idea, tempos, and moods. In this way, we could be certain that we were examining the entire *content* of the play and that nothing would be overlooked—a situation that would very likely occur in a more haphazard approach. The content was thus revealed through an analysis of form. As you can see, form and content are inextricably bound together in play structure but can be separated in a mechanical way for purposes of discussion.

Likewise, when we studied the process of stage production in Parts II and III—the process that can bring alive the form and content of the playscript in stage terms—it was necessary to delineate a whole new group of structural devices, what we can now call "staging form," in the interest of giving the form and content of the playscript new dimension, the dimension of live performance in a theatre. *Form in staging* was thus delineated in the six visual tools: groundplan, composition, gesture, picturization, improvisation with objects, and movement; in the oral tools: speaking the subtext, speaking the text, decorum in speech, and projection; and in the stage tools: the stage, scenery, properties, lighting, costume, makeup, and sound. When all of these elements of form in staging are employed appropriately, it can be said that we also have a theatrical content. Thus, we have form and content in staging as well as in the written play.

The major point about form is that although content cannot be revealed without it, form is still a *general* statement of the content and not a specific one.

Style is what makes form individual and specific.

The approach up to this point, then, has been to show you how you can make the general object—a produced play—through a perceptive awareness of form and its relationship to content in both playscript and staging. The focus of this chapter and those that follow is on *how you must individualize production* if you are to hold the attention of theatregoers for an evening. A perceptive director at any level of his training, can, of course, suffuse a play with style, but in the case of the relatively untrained director such individualization is apt to be more accident than plan, because although style is not self-conscious, it is still the subjective self explaining itself.

The purpose of Part IV is to help you to pin down style in your awareness so specifically that you can see the possibilities in play production on an entirely new and different level. You probably remember high school performances that were dull and boring although you may have responded favorably, as did the parents present, out of loyalty and a sense of belonging. But occasionally something clicked and held your attention. That something was probably brought about through style. The college productions you see are apt to hold your attention more continuously because many directors and designers working at that level know how to present plays with style and have the actors and the staging resources to make it possible. Successful professional productions are marked by their individuality—their style—and it is the style that is discussed by everyone when he talks about such productions whether he knows what style is or not. Audiences always respond to individualization, for subtleties move them whereas general statements do not.

The main problem, then, is how to elevate the generality of form into the individuality of style. Part IV undertakes answering this problem by first showing you how to recognize style in playscripts and then how to make a *style-analysis* that will lead you to a second and very important level in the comprehension of a playscript. The discussion then turns to production with the intention of showing you how the director is a stylist and how he makes style in play production. Exercises are included in some of the chapters, many of them based on historical drama, with all of them leading to the third level of directing and the final project in this book: the designing and directing of a full-length play, which is set out at the end of Chapter 25.

As you will note, many of the examples in Part IV are drawn from significant historical and modern plays on the assumption that at this point you have a fairly good command of dramatic literature. You should view Part IV, therefore, as advanced study in directing, although you will be able to comprehend the contents if you have worked through Parts I, II, and III with attention and care, and if you have accumulated some experience from the live directing projects suggested at the ends of Parts II and III.

Here the hard work begins. Many young directors do not progress much beyond the directing level of Part III because they are too eager to get into play production and do not realize that there is still much preparatory work to be done. You will note that Part IV ranges much more widely than the previous parts of this book, and you will thus need to do a great deal of thinking and talking about it. If you want to be a really good director instead of a merely adequate one, you will have to give close attention to the many special studies outlined in the following chapters, for successful directors are stylists who make things of their own.

Part IV finally concludes with a discussion about the future of the director in the theatre. The intention is to show the change that has come about in the making of theatre, specifically the relationship of "non-verbal theatricals" to the historical tradition of verbal theatre. The director and his present function will be contrasted with the artist-leader as a means of looking at future possibilities for anyone undertaking training in this area of theatre work.

But first you must understand the nature of style.

What Is Style?

It is easy to recognize form, but style is much more difficult to delineate because we perceive it on the emotional level without being conscious of what we are really seeing, that is, until we make it conscious. In addition, oftentimes our recognition of a style depends on comparison—experience with many different objects in the same category. We all know what an automobile is when we see one, and we can easily tell the obvious differences among motor vehicles, trains, airplanes, and boats because we know the differences in their forms and functions. Even a young child with several of these objects as playthings can categorize them as modes of transportation, even to pointing out their obvious differences in form. Moreover, when the field is narrowed to motor vehicles, for instance, there is still little problem for most people in noting differences among passenger cars, pick-up trucks, trailer-trucks, and motorcycles. Now, when we reduce the field once more, most people begin to encounter difficulties in recognition. Because you in particular may be interested in cars and have looked closely, when you discount the differences in engineering performance, can you delineate the differences in sedan models among (1) Fords and Chevrolets or among (2) Buicks, Oldsmobiles, Dodges, and Pontiacs? Note that there are two groups mentioned. Can you separate the differences in the models in each group? If you can, you are involved in differences in style or styling, as the automobile manufacturers say.

Yet this example will not do for objects of art. Commercial design, whether it is a toothpaste carton or a package of cigarettes, involves a certain amount of style because manufacturers want you to recognize an individual item on a crowded shelf, but the style is intended for reproduction in thousands, sometimes in millions, of the same item. Yet, despite the quantity of reproduction, such items have an individual look and can be delineated readily from other items in the same form.

In art, we are concerned with extremely narrow categories, usually only a handful of items with the same individualized look. Thus we can talk about Cézanne's style as differing from Van Gogh's; about Brahms' symphonies differing from Tchaikovsky's; about Ibsen's plays differing from Strindberg's; about Arthur Miller's plays differing from Tennessee Williams'. We also see differences in stage productions by directors Tyrone Guthrie and Peter Brook; and in movie productions by Bergman and Antonioni.

Four points can be made about the above pairs of artists.

First, notice in these comparisons that we have delineated several pairs, with each pair in the same art form. This fact is important to our understanding of style because, although it is possible to make comparisons of one art form with another, and critics often do, we can much better understand style if we stay within restricted categories. Second, notice that the pairs (two people in each category) are contemporaries—they did their work or are doing it in approximately the same period. The important thing about dating art is that each age—and an age can vary from twenty to fifty years—establishes its own variations and refinements of form by setting up something that can be recognized as the style of the period, the individualization of that age. Thus, we can speak of Elizabethan style, French Classical style, Romantic style, Realistic style, etc. When we look at drama, we note that each age has made general modifications that all dramatists in the age use; and by noting these characteristics, we can delineate the style of a period. We can also do the same for production by labeling the styles Elizabethan platform staging, seventeenth-century Italianate, nineteenth-century Romantic, or twentieth-century Realistic, and by these designations mean a different look in each one, no matter whose individual work we may be examining.

Third, notice in the pairs listed that *names* of *people* have been used because this is the only way we can delineate the most subtle aspects of style. "Style is the man," goes the old adage. By this saying is meant that every creative artist will make individual alterations within the general style of his age, individualizations that people who look closely at art will recognize as unique in the artist—truly his signature to the work. Style, then, may have broad meanings referring to historical periods, but it can also have very narrow meanings referring to the unique work of individuals. In its most refined sense, style is the significant aspect in the definition of art itself: something unique and highly individualized.

Finally, notice that each pair of artists differs in how it makes contact with spectators or audiences. Cézanne and Van Gogh make direct contact through direct showings of their works in museum galleries. But Brahms and Tchaikovsky, as well as Ibsen and Strindberg and Miller and Williams, must depend on interpreters to present their works because the forms in which their works appear are incomplete *without audience performances.* Guthrie and Brook are interpreters of Ibsen and Strindberg through the medium of theatre, but they can overlay these plays with their own individual styles. Bergman and Antonioni are part creative writers and part interpreters because they usually create both the form and the content of their movie scripts and then interpret them through the form of cinematic staging. Although their work is in moving pictures, both Bergman and Antonioni are examples of Gordon Craig's artist-director, while stage directors Guthrie and Brook are what Craig labeled master craftsman directors, that is, directors who act as interpreters of the works of others. But no matter what the relationship may be between the creative and the interpretive, all the people mentioned in the pairs cited above have developed a recognizable style all their own. To be certain of making this point clear to you, we have represented various art forms along with categorical differences in style for each pair of artists, with the implication that each artist will make his own personal and individual statement.

Style is at once the individualization of art form and the way of moving spectators (those who only look) and audiences (those who both hear and look).

Interpretation Is Criticism

Interpretation is the director's goal because he *interprets* the work of the playwright rather than creates the playscript himself. Gordon Craig's artist-director—the director who creates the entire work including the playscript and the production—is very rare in the theatre although, as we pointed out earlier, he has appeared in a diluted form in close association with actors in the improvisational theatre experiments of the 1960s, and in the film work of Bergman and Antonioni, who have exercised complete control over camera and cutting in order to make possible the telling of their filmed stories with a minimum of the verbal form so closely associated with traditional drama. But our discussion here, as elsewhere in this book except for the last chapter, concerns the master-craftsman director who works with playscripts created by others.

In the interest of revealing the director as the primary critic of the theatre, it is most useful to isolate his differences from those of the other interpreters who work in and around the theatre—the newspaper reviewer and the dramatic critic. All three are essential to a vigorous and active theatre, but each has a distinct and difficult job to do. First, let us describe and define the newspaper reviewer and the dramatic critic.

THE NEWSPAPER REVIEWER

Most of the comment about the theatre we read in newspapers and periodicals is not criticism at all in the strict sense of that word. Rather, it is better labeled "reviewing" because its primary function is to look at a produced play in its natural habitat—the theatre—and then judge its merits and failures. Consequently, the five hundred to eight hundred words we read in a newspaper shortly after a first performance of a play is the opinion of a trained and experienced *viewer* who is reporting his reactions to a waiting public that, in turn, enjoys him as an entertaining writer and often listens closely to his advice about whether it should spend its money and time on a particular play.

Such persistent and personal news reporting serves the theatre by spreading an informed word about a produced play, but such reporting harms the theatre when the "critic" misinterprets what he sees and hears, or fails to see and hear very well. A mortal like the rest of us, despite his protestations that he is always objective, the newspaper reviewer can be highly prejudiced, opinionated, and bad tempered, as well as overly kind, generous, and blind to what he sees. Whatever he reports—and his report is usually very hastily written within minutes after leaving a performance, while his feelings are still hot about it—such reviews are always trained opinion and are always concerned with the final product on the stage. Writing such reviews in present practice is a tour-de-force. Although such a procedure fulfills the requirements of reporting events as soon as possible after they have transpired, it has many shortcomings as criticism. Thus, a reviewer's five hundred to eight hundred words will allow him to tell the story briefly, comment on the idea, judge the playscript's worth in a few sentences, mention visual aspects of the production, compliment the actors (in most American reviewing, actors are seldom blamed for what has happened), occasionally credit a designer, and either castigate or praise the director in one line or ignore him altogether. The situation is somewhat better because of the time delay, for the reporter writing for a weekly news magazine or for the Sunday columnist elaborating on a weekday review, but reviewing in general has many shortcomings and is still of questionable value to the people who work in the theatre, although through its controversial stance, it may entertain and even stimulate potential playgoers.

Reviews tell us little about the structure of a play or production, and only the most perceptive of their group—a genuine critic like Englishman Kenneth Tynan or perhaps the *New York Times*' Walter Kerr—can penetrate much beyond the surface. Because the theatre is a popular entertainment, so is play reviewing, for the reviewer's job is to report what he sees and hears in an entertaining way. But much too often, the reviewer substitutes his own opinions about what he thinks a production should have been for the one he is seeing. Instead of holding the eye of his reader on what is there, he focuses it on what he thinks should have been there. When the reviewer does this he moves into the director's realm of interpretation, and he thus becomes an armchair director.

What the theatre would be like without reviewers is hard to say. But at the same time that these journalists recognize the theatre as a living, breathing, immediate thing, and therefore newsworthy, theatregoers have given reviewers, as their public representatives in the theatre, a power of life or death—and they know how to murder more competently than how to grant life—over a playscript and over a director's interpretation of it. If they turn in a negative report on a production, its fate is sealed, for few can attract an audience sufficiently large to keep running, and the only future for such a playscript is to wait until another director or a dramatic critic rediscovers it.

THE DRAMATIC CRITIC

There is another level of criticism that is much closer to what the director does. Although dramatic criticism has appeared more or less regularly throughout the history of the theatre, it has never been so much in vogue as it is today. Simply described, it is essay-length interpretation —usually of one play although comparisons are often made with others— based on inherent, internal structure. Dramatic criticism is similar to the process outlined in Part I of this book, for the intention is the same: to illuminate the content of a play and what ties it together through close examination of the form and content in the work itself. When this sort of criticism becomes too literary (pursuit of the structure of dialogue alone), its uses to the director are limited, but when it adheres to those basic elements of structure that have clear theatrical values, it can be most helpful.

A dramatic critic is not a director-in-the-armchair because he is not concerned with a play's production but only with its inner, often hidden, workings. What a play is about, then, is the primary attack in a dramatic criticism, and the proof must lie entirely in the play's structure itself. This approach recognizes that plays are poetry and that playwrights are poets who communicate to others through metaphors, symbols, and other types of direct communication, and not merely through exterior dialogue.

A learning director should cultivate the habit of reading dramatic criticism as a way of developing his own sense of what to look for and how to find it. However, when he does so, he will also find that dramatic criticism has its shortcomings because its primary intention is to illuminate the mysteries of drama, but in doing so, it frequently turns out to be just another interpretation. The critic has looked intensively at the play to support his own ideas about the structure, and thus about the meanings, and has shown textual proof to validate his views, but he can easily be led astray by placing too much emphasis on what he has taken for proof. Unveiling the mysteries of poetic experience requires exceptional vision indeed, and such vision is rare.

THE DIRECTOR AS CRITIC

Despite the presence of the reviewer and of the dramatic critic, the director is the primary critic in the theatre. The function of criticism is to interpret and illuminate a work—a perfect description of the director's job. In comparison, the dramatic critic works only with the playscript, which in itself cannot be complete since by its nature it requires actors and production to give it full life; and the reviewer works with the finished production and provides a criticism of the director's interpretation, while, at the same time, he tries to fulfill the nominal responsibilities of a dramatic critic by examining the playscript. Only the director works in a firsthand way with both the playscript and the production.

The fact of the matter is that without seeking the job, the director has become the twentieth century's most important stage critic. The direct effect of the reviewer on the crafts of the stage, in comparison to the director's contribution, has been relatively slight, although there can be no question that as a watchdog over the director-producer, he has exercised a continuing pressure on taste in the theatre. More to the point, he has certainly been effective in keeping audiences away from the theatre where they might have been able to judge a director's interpretation on their own. Who will buy a quart of milk if he has been told that it is slightly sour? The business world has protected itself legally against such libel and slander through courtroom indemnity suits; only the arts, like the political world, are open targets for unsuppressed and often irresponsible attacks.

This vulnerability is all the more reason for the director to appreciate fully his responsibilities as a critic in play production. The relationship of the director to the literary critic is nowhere better illustrated than in T. S. Eliot's essay on "The Function of Criticism." This celebrated poet-playwright-critic discusses literary criticism, but without forcing the context, his point of view has explicit meaning when applied to the work of the director.

Eliot draws a sharp line between two major approaches to criticism. The first, the intuitive approach, he labels *whiggery*—what proceeds without principles from the *inner voice*. "If I like a thing, that is all I want," so the argument goes; "and if enough of us, shouting all together, like it, that should be all that you (who don't like it) ought to want. The law of art . . . is all case law. And we can not only like whatever we like to like but we can like it for any reason we choose." Such practitioners, Eliot maintains, are not concerned with literary perfection but only with momentary and personal values. The second approach—and to Eliot the only valid one—depends on "tradition and the accumulated wisdom of time." It is more analytical, more conscious criticism. It is the sort of criticism that a superior writer must apply to his own work, for the critical activity finds its highest, its true fulfillment, in a kind of "union with creation in the labour of the artist." This approach does not imply that criticism in itself is creative, but that the creative artist is able to approach his work in two ways: creatively and critically; and some creative writers are superior to others "solely because their critical faculty is superior."

At one time, Eliot took the position that the only critics worth reading were the critics who "practised, and practised well, the art of which they wrote." Later, he modified this view in the interest of finding a more inclusive frame, and he then concluded that the most important qualification for a critic was "a highly developed sense of fact." This allowed him to permit inclusion of critics who *write about* the works of others. In consideration of this view, Eliot points out the rarity of good practitioners: "For every success in this type of writing," he maintains, "there are thousands of impostures. Instead of insight you get a fiction." The best critic is one who sees a work of art steadily and sees it as a whole.

Now, in applying this distinction to the director, whiggery would seem to be as unacceptable an approach to directing as it is to criticism. How a director feels about a play will certainly affect his treatment of it because he is dealing with art and not science, with intuition and not scientific fact, which must be explicitly and fully explained; with the behavior of human beings as set out by the playwright and not with maneuverable puppets. Nevertheless, a predominantly subjective approach to directing is incompatible with the director's function of finding unity and order in the playscript, in acting, and in design, for he must constantly exercise his objective, analytical, critical view in order to control his media, which are subject to constant variations. As a stimulator of ideas, the director is involved in getting from the playwright the strongest play, if it is a new one and he can control its development, and in arousing the actor to his best performance and the designer to his highest creativity. The director's success is also tempered by his mastery of the physical materials of the stage. Among artists, he might be compared in some respects to the architect, who is also concerned with the limitation of materials and the ability of the craftsman on whom he must depend for the execution of his ideas.

Since the craftsman-director is the subject of this discussion, and not Gordon Craig's artist-director who composes his own play from start to finish, you must assume that the director's function, then, is largely one of interpretation, that his primary concern is *about* something that someone else has already created (the playscript), or, as in the case of the actor and designer, something that someone else is about to create. In this respect, the director is fulfilling the identical function of Eliot's critic, although he differs from the latter in that he can activate and test his interpretation rather than merely discuss it.

Something to Say

If the primary job of the director, then, is interpreting what has already been set out for him in a playscript, how can he make an individual statement that can be classified as style without violating the integrity of that playscript? The temptation of not telling the truth is always there.

The answer is relatively simple although the achievement of style is not. The assumption is, first, that a director will be in command of a production—both of the actors and of the designers—and, second, that he fully comprehends the *form* of the playscript and its *style*. *A director's style will be stated in the individual qualities and emphases he gives to the form, content, and style of a playscript through the production ele-*

ments at his command. The director's statement of style grows into being as he makes decision after decision about which direction he will take with a play. Here are a few of the basic questions he will have to find answers for and out of those answers will come his style:

> What is the dominant idea in the play?
>
> Whose (that is, which character's) play is it? (A very important decision about character emphasis.)
>
> What *actions* should be given the most telling emphasis?
>
> Is the production to emphasize text or subtext, and in what balance?
>
> How can the *given circumstances* be individualized?
>
> What dominant *moods* can emerge?
>
> Who shall be cast? (Texture and balance.)
>
> How shall the designs be stated? (Realistically or in departures from Realism?)

These are only a few of the many questions that will affect a director's statement. It is, therefore, obvious that a director must not only have something to say, but that he must have a very great deal to say. The playscript will work on him as an individual, for no matter how intent he is on maintaining the integrity of a playscript, he cannot prevent the forces in his own background, both his intellectual and emotional experience, from working on the playscript—the improvised poem, half-clear, half-mystical, devised by the playwright. W. H. Auden's remark that "a real book reads us" has significant meaning to the director, for the same thing can be said about a produced play: What appears on the stage is there because the dramatic imagination in the director puts it there by comprehending it out of his own personal experience. When you encounter difficulties in reading a play that age, time, and the critics have told you is great—difficulties such as boredom, inattention, problems in following the text, vagueness as to what it is all about—or when you have some personal reactions in seeing a play on the stage, do not blame the play but blame yourself. You may discard such plays now, but someday *they will find you* and then you will wonder why you had so much difficulty when you tried them earlier, and the only answer will be that you were not experienced enough to receive them.

When it comes down to the fine points in a play, then, there is no absolute interpretation. Its ideas will fall within a narrow range, but it is just that narrow range that is left open to the director and out of which will come his individual statement—his style.

Style is beyond form. Style is something personal to say.

Style Is Today's Statement

To reproduce an historical play exactly as it was first presented is impossible. Although we might be able to recreate a historical theatre building from existing architectural drawings or other exact delineations, there are so many significant gaps in our knowledge about stage properties, costuming, scenic materials, and, most important, about what the acting was like, that we would be completely at sea if we tried duplicating historical productions.   But even if all the information were available, we would not want to do such stagings because audiences simply would not understand them.   When we read a Shakespearian play, we are immediately conscious of all the odd words and phrases because we see them in print.   If we were to see a historical reproduction of a Globe theatre performance, it might very well look and sound much the same way, just as odd and peculiar to our eyes and ears.   More than likely, since the pronunciation of English has undergone extensive changes in the four hundred years since Shakespeare's day, the play would probably sound very foreign to our ears, something like an odd English dialect.   If you have seen moving picture revivals of fifty to sixty years ago—Sarah Bernhardt as Queen Elizabeth, for instance—you will remember how the audience you were with probably laughed at what looked like very odd, very elaborate behavior on the part of the actors, and at the overly exotic qualities of the settings and costuming.   You were watching acting and design styles of another age, and the audience was not able to reconcile it with its own prejudiced, highly indoctrinated, well-conditioned conception of style.

Style is the primary means of immediate communication.

No age has ever been more aware of the necessity for making today's statement than our own, a fact that we can blame on the pressure of our highly developed communications media, for photography has made it possible for us to see more clearly than ever before how quickly styles can change. From the seventies we look back at photographs of the styles of the sixties and find them old-fashioned, just as people looked from the sixties at the fifties, and so on.   Style says something to us quickly and easily.   This characteristic is readily illustrated in dress where new styles quickly become old styles in a continuously changing, arbitrarily-forced world of industrial design.   A designer makes a new-look dress; other designers more or less copy the creation to set the fashion; and when others follow in numbers a *fad* is declared.   A style remains in fashion only as long as it is not replaced by a newer style with more ready communication.

Avant-gardists are the makers of new styles, for they are always in search of a fresh means of communication, for a new way of saying something.   Again, the speed of present-day electronic communications—radio, television (photography), moving pictures (photography)—has reduced the length of time a style can stay in fashion.   Not so long ago, style seemed to last for several years, perhaps as much as one to two decades; now the "new" is given such quick circulation that a style's lifetime seems to be markedly reduced. Last year's avant-garde in the popular music field—the latest strange sounds, rhythms, and words—will be superseded this year by another style that will soon become the craze or the rage, words that to you may sound quite out of style.

An awareness of the immediacy of style, its quality of being contemporary, is most important to the director. His job is to get through to an audience no matter what may be the date of the play he is producing. The problem, then, is always one of communication through style. The director not only has something to say because he sees it vividly in the context of his own time, but if he is to communicate to an audience, he must also say it in the immediate terms most understandable to his audience.

It is the living, breathing immediacy of style that makes it one of the director's primary tools of communication. Although the *adaptation* of historical styles will be treated in a later chapter, it is necessary to note here that no matter how an adaptation is made, if the style is too unfamiliar to an audience, it will not be very effective, for the theatre demands group recognition. There is no harder demand on any artist than this one because the tendency is to play it safe, to be conventional and not to strive for the new. Thus, the range of style for the director is an extremely narrow one for he must constantly fight the paradox of reaching an audience on the level at which it can understand him at the same time that he is trying to find new and exciting ways of playing the game of communication. As a popular art form, theatre in the past usually lagged as much as a generation behind the other forms while it was waiting for the general audience to catch up. Today this is no longer the case, or so it seems, because with urban culture and its mirror, television, constantly before us, the new becomes old in a very brief time.

2 1

recognizing style
in playscripts

It is so easy to distinguish the form of theatre from the forms of painting and music because of their very great and obvious differences that we begin to take easy separation for granted when we make finer comparisons. We pointed out early in this book that (1) theatre *includes* drama as one of its basic media, and that (2) drama should not be grouped with literature as an art form but as something with a literary look that is distinct in itself. This last point causes some confusion to the beginning theatre student because he is accustomed to studying drama in literature courses where he may well be left with the impression that although such literary study is considered eminently respectable, theatre is often treated as a vulgar craft undeserving of a high place in academic curricula. To head off this negative point of view toward theatre study we should emphasize again that although plays have been printed for reading purposes since the invention of printing in the fifteenth century, only the twentieth century has thrown them into the literary pot, where they are all too often studied as complete forms in themselves without the recognition that they are only part of a whole. Serious study of this sort can lead to critical nonsense because literary scholars often do not hear and see what a dramatist intends an audience to hear and see through the use of acting and staging.

Although drama, then, is not a complete art form in itself, it can be studied as a contributing form to theatre if one always regards it in this part-of-a-whole sense. It is so treated here.

The *form* of drama in Western civilization, as distinct from theatre, has always contained the same basic elements since its beginnings in the fifth century B.C.: given circumstances, dramatic action, characters, idea, dialogue, tempos, and moods. What has made drama seem different over its twenty-five-hundred-year history is the rearrangement in value and emphasis of these basic structural elements. The intention in this book has been to set up an approach to directing that can be used in directing plays from the past as well as plays of today. Thus, although Parts I and II concentrated on working with modern Realistic plays—a particular style—with the intention of introducing the student intensively to theatre (and drama) as form, the intention now is to broaden the scope of theatre and its drama by including plays from various historical periods. Once a director has mastered some techniques in approaching play production, his work in the broad areas of theatre can be unlimited.

One of the facts about drama that makes it seem different from age to age lies in the emphasis given to each of the basic elements. Some ages, our own for instance, give great prominence to given circumstances, with detailed emphasis thrown on previous action, whereas others, such as the Elizabethan Age, ignore this aspect almost completely. Dramatic action is relatively simple in some periods (Greek) but extensive in others (Jacobean). Characters are largely primal types in some periods (Greek) but intricate and highly detailed in others (Ibsenite-Chekhovian-Strindbergian Realism). Dialogue is in verse form in some, with emphasis on variety in meters (Spanish Classical), and in prose, sometimes quite elaborate, in others (English Restoration Comedy).

It is just these variations in the basic elements of dramatic form, of course, which give us ways of distinguishing the drama of one period from the drama of another. The student should remember, however, that categorizing is only a general sorting of the thousands of plays we wish to know better. The only way he can be sure of what he has in hand is to take a particular look at a specific play through play-analysis. Playwrights, we like to think, are free improvisers like other artists, and only at certain times have they been expected to conform to established rules prescribed through one sort of pressure or another (Neo-Classical). We are so accustomed in modern times to think of playwrights as free spirits that we seldom realize how many restrictions on form and "community style" actually bind them. Like entrenched governments, revolutions by playwrights or theatre people, sometimes physical ones, are necessary to overthrow overused forms.   Victor Hugo's revolt with *Hernani,* J. M. Synge's and the Abbey Theatre's with *Playboy of the Western World,* and Ibsen's and Strindberg's with their shocking sex dramas are obvious examples.

Composite Types: Tragedy, Comedy, and Others— Emphasis in Form

One of the oldest ways of specifying differences in the form of drama is type designation.   Ever since Greek Classical times, drama has been divided into categories as a way of grouping plays of like intent and similar structures.   Although tragedy and comedy, the two major forms, had different origins in the ancient Greek world, with separate heritages of rituals and mythology, by the fifth century B.C. they were brought together within the same *general* form with both employing dramatic action, characters, idea, dialogue, choral groups, music, and spectacle, and both were performed in the same religious-theatrical temple—the Dionysian theatre.

The difference between these two major designations lay in how the basic elements of dramatic form were used and the kinds of emphasis given to each element.   This method of play description has been so useful that present-day dramatic critics wrestle with the same basic problems that faced Aristotle: What makes each type work?   What kind of emphasis must be given to each element in each of the two structures to achieve the total effect required by each structure?   Consequently, an extensive literature has developed around the theory of drama in the attempt of each age to define these composite types.   Critics know that the types work in the theatre, and the theoretical discussion is directed toward penetrating their poetic mysteries.

A learning director cannot advance very far into the realm of style unless he comprehends a good deal about these composite types.   What makes an audience laugh? or What can move it deeply? are most important questions a director must answer for himself.   An extensive knowledge of the composite types may not only unlock historical drama for him in a very direct way but give him the key to modern drama as well. With a strong awareness of types, the director can then proceed to unfold for himself how each individual playwright attacks his problems—what the playwright's style is all about.

The intention here is not to provide a theoretical study of the composite types but merely to describe these types in a general way in order to alert you to basic differences.   *Your course work in dramatic literature will help you develop your understanding in depth,* and you will add greatly to this understanding through regular practice in play-analysis.

Again, you must remember that each age has made its own description and sometimes *pre*scription, of these composite forms. It is therefore impossible to treat them briefly without including points that some ages would take strong exception to. Nevertheless, here are some general statements.

TRAGEDY

"Tragedy is . . ." and there you are caught in the necessity of defining what each age has thought it to be, for it has had the most intensive treatment of all the composite types. But, in general, all have seemed to agree that it is serious throughout; that it deals with man's relationship to forces outside his petty, domestic world; that it is about a better than average man, frequently highly placed in his society, who makes a discovery that brings about a great change in his life, usually resulting in his death; that he *usually,* but not always, comes to a knowledge about himself in relation to the outside forces; that what happens as a result of the discovery affects all that he holds most dear in his life, but he has the great courage and strength to face his destiny; that a member of an audience may be greatly moved to pity him for his suffering and, at the same time, may fear that the same thing could happen to him; that the language in which the play is written is heightened beyond that of everyday speech and frequently is set down in verse form.

Tragedy is about violence and suffering. These aspects are what make it so compelling in the theatre, for they can take us to the periphery, to the very brink of life's experience. During a lifetime, we all go through a certain amount of suffering and may even have an experience approaching violence, but few of us ever experience life even near the level of the tragic hero. Yet, we recognize that it could happen, that it is possible, and it is just this possibility that makes tragedy so utterly believable.

Isolating the violence is a key to understanding such plays, for it allows working backward from the climactic peaks in order to discover more readily what led to them. As a director, you will want to give violence great prominence, because through the very force of its presentation, an audience can experience the intense emotions of the aftermath. Great drama is always about the great passions in life where the desire to maintain integrity supersedes all other desires. Consequently, producing tragic feeling on the stage is a very difficult matter even when you understand what violence is and what precedes and follows it.

Today we have many problems in defining our drama as tragedy because emphases differ from those of the Classical forms. "Serious drama" or "a play" seem to be more apt descriptions because they exhibit no pretentions about the contents, which may include some humor, which may show the principal character in conflict only with other men or with groups in the society and not with forces beyond earthbound human contacts, which may not end in the hero's coming to know his own weaknesses. Yet, at the same time, serious plays contain the basic elements of all tragedy: fierce integrity on the part of the hero, which leads him to a do-or-die position, and the violence he undergoes when he makes his principal discovery.   Only when you make an exhaustive play-analysis of a serious play can you see why it is truly serious and what the consequences will be to an audience that views it.   Your directing skill will be marked by your perception of tragedy and the intensity with which you show it on the stage, for tragedy is mighty, and it greatly challenges the intellectual and emotional depth of any director who undertakes it.

EXERCISES

1. Apply the basic description of tragedy given above to the following plays:
   a. *Oedipus the King* (Sophocles)
   b. *Macbeth* or *King Lear* (Shakespeare)
   c. *Doctor Faustus* (Marlowe)
   d. *Phaedra* (Racine)
   e. *The Master Builder* (Ibsen)
   f. *The Crucible* (Miller)
   g. *Riders to the Sea* (Synge)
   How do these plays differ in structure and how are they alike?   Examine and compare their endings specifically.

2. Is Ibsen's *Ghosts* a tragedy?

3. What is a tragic hero?

4. Since discussions of tragedy can be most profitable, the class should devote as much time to thrashing out its complexities as students' backgrounds and time allow.   If possible, each student should do an analysis of a tragedy of his own choosing, with the focus on what makes it tragic.

5. If the students in the class are prepared with background for advanced study, and time is available, Aristotle's *Poetics* should be read and discussed at this point, with emphasis given to separating Aristotle's delineation of general play form from his specific delineation of tragic form.   The advanced student can also benefit greatly from reading Maxwell Anderson's "The Essence of Tragedy" and Joseph Wood Krutch's "The Tragic Fallacy."   Additional readings can be added as background and time permit.   But no readings can be a substitute for the analysis suggested in Exercise 4.

MELODRAMA

This word has been used for nearly two centuries to describe those plays in which highly theatrical *activities* dominate the dramatic action.

These activities tend to make the action superficial, which, in turn, reduces the development of character. Such plays live in large part on their external excitements, resulting in the capabilities of holding audiences in firm grip because their danger levels are both high and obvious. The word *melodrama,* since its earliest usage, has meant "drama supported and enhanced by exciting music," a perfect description of today's television spy, or detective, thrillers. Classical tragedy also had music, but it was used in support of choral songs and not merely to excite the emotions behind stage activities.

To see melodrama only in the light of those travesties of nineteenth-century *mellers,* where the villain operates the buzz saw while the heroine advances toward it on the log rollers, or in terms of twentieth-century TV spy films, with delicately turned bank robberies behind the Iron Curtain, is seriously to malign it as a composite form of drama. We frequently use the term *character-melodrama* not only to denote the stature of such plays but also to describe an entire range of dramas that cannot fall into the category of serious play or tragedy even though the moods of such dramas are indeed serious. They do not qualify as tragedies because their actions are always man versus man largely in his external dealings in everyday life: the protagonist must overcome his antagonist as in tragedy but for superficial gains—money, property, the law, and others. Though such plays deal with psychological aspects of character, they do not penetrate deeply enough to be intensive perceptions of life. Instead, they play on our sense of personal security, on our prejudices (we tend to destroy those things we do not understand), on our morbid curiosity, on our moral codes, and on our personal search for excitement to relieve ourselves from the boredom of everyday life.

A director must learn the sensitive skills of staging melodrama if he is to learn how to direct the intensive activity, often melodramatic, in the serious drama. In one sense, all directing is finding the best external means of communicating dramatic action, and a director should therefore get into the habit of looking at all plays as melodramas, if only to see how the excitements in them are created and what levels they reach. Without this skill of expressing external dangers, a director will never know how to project the quiet, interior dangers more deeply and subtly embedded in serious drama. The rhythms and tonal pitches of melodrama are the best possible avenues to learning what the term *theatrical* means in the theatre—a high sense of personal (audience) danger. You should direct melodramas, then, before you try to direct highly serious plays.

We tend to laugh at the melodrama of the nineteenth century without recognizing that no age has produced more melodrama than our own, especially in the popular form of movies and television. Melodrama is the stuff of popular theatre because it provides theatrical thrills without requiring serious work on the part of an audience. Melodrama is thus a popular form of entertainment that shifts its specific external look as prevailing activities become too obvious because of their overuse. But the basic emphases in this composite form always remain the same: intensive action, highly dramatic characters, moral tone, strong moods and tempos, and emphasis on external, and thus on theatrical, illustration.

EXERCISES

1. What is the difference in structure between *Oedipus the King* and *Night Must Fall* or *Dial M for Murder?* Why can the latter be called character-melodramas?

2. *Hedda Gabler* is sometimes labeled a melodrama? Why? Be very careful not to belittle characterizations in that play.

3. Why can *Macbeth* be labeled, as it sometimes is, a tragedy with melodramatic overtones?

4. What is melodramatic in the folowing plays:
   a. *The Dutchess of Malfi* (Webster)
   b. *Woyzeck* (Büchner)
   c. *Camille* (Dumas)
   d. *An Enemy of the People* (Ibsen)
   e. *The Little Foxes* (Hellman)
   f. *The Homecoming* or *The Birthday Party* (Pinter)
   g. *The Glass Menagerie* (Williams)

5. Do a written analysis of a melodrama of your own choice, and prove that it is a melodrama or how it compromises the form. Here are some suggestions of categories: *Ladies in Retirement; The Cat and the Canary; The Asbern Papers; Rhinoceros; The Zoo Story.*

COMEDY

The most difficult of all the composite forms for a young director to understand is comedy. Tragedy is more a matter of feeling than of mind, and both the young director and the young actor can comprehend that form on the basis of their past emotional experiences in everyday life, though perception in depth requires experiences in depth. In contrast, comedy is more a matter of the mind than of the feelings. To find a joke funny one must perceive the incongruities that are presented in the joke: it amuses precisely because A is not congruent with B, but we must know both A and B intimately in order to note their incongruities.

The director is constantly confronted with the fact that if he and his actors are to make an audience laugh, they must first understand the jokes themselves. In this sense, comedy may seem to require greater maturity not only on the part of the director and the actors but also on the part of the audience, though the actors may have great capacities to communicate comic ideas and thus simplify comprehension on the part of the audience. What may be obscure on the printed page can appear both obvious and funny in the hands of comic actors—the instruments through which the incongruities are conveyed.

Though there are many levels of comedy that range from humor (the audience *likes* the trapped character and laughs with him) to satire (the audience looks objectively and closely at the trapped character, usually disliking him and laughing at him), comedy as a composite type has specific, identifiable emphases within the basic elements of dramatic form. A good comedy throws a strong emphasis on a character who is simplified in such a way that we can readily see the distortions that have made him a fool in other men's eyes; we can see them, that is, if we understand what is considered normal behavior in the society reflected in the comedy. Norms are, therefore, very important in comprehending comedy. Thus, the action in comedy consists of a string of incidents that reveal the fool in situation after situation where he always shows the same distortions, the same variations from what is considered normal behavior. Consequently, the fun of a comedy usually consists of the reactions of the other characters to the continuing stupidities of the principal character until he finally sees how distorted he is, or the others decide that it would be heartless to make him face his realities. In this sense, comedy is a social leveler because it shows average or less-than-average people caught in their own foolishness. It is based on the principle that no man knows what he is, that he cannot see his real mirror image but only what he wants to see.

Comedy thus produces laughter on the basis of distortion in character —a blind spot in the character's own view of his actions. Comedy can be gentle if the audience is led to sympathize with the behavior of the character, but it can be very cruel when a character gets no such sympathy and is laughed *at*.

The ideas behind this class of plays all concern man's adjustment to the social pattern in which he lives. They are literally plays of man against man. Given circumstances play an important part in setting up a comedy, for what may be funny in the context of restrictions of one social group may not be funny in another context at all. It also follows that the given circumstances place men and women on a fairly equal basis, for many of the ideas in comedy concern the struggle between the sexes, the age-old battle that never wants for an audience. Women are rarely the fools in comedy; it is the men who are the distorted ones in a world largely of their own making. Women are usually seen as creatures of common sense, while men are the creatures of nonsense in their confusion with what seems to them perfectly logical and so right that it can be taken for granted.

Dialogue is also given significant emphasis in comedy, for in this composite form, language can be one of the principal means of entertainment. In high comedy, we have conversation at its cleverest, its wittiest. Thus, language is not just a conveyor of action, but a delight in itself. We love word play because we all use language, but we all do not have the capability of putting it together in amusing ways. Yet, though the young director must be highly aware of the text in a comedy, what is truly funny in such a play cannot be revealed without the most careful delineation of the subtext. As with the other forms, comedy is still a matter of dramatic action.

A knowledge of comedy from a theoretical point of view is invaluable to a director, for he will sooner or later tangle with this composite form. Among the valuable principles he will learn is the one that always causes trouble if he does not know it: characters in comedy are all deadly serious about their points of view, and the principal fool is the most serious of them all. We laugh at characters in a comedy because they take themselves so seriously. The young director will learn that comedians do not pretend at being funny, but that they are so caught up in the distortions they are playing that they are absolutely convincing in every aspect of those distortions. Good comedians are thus not laughing at the characters they are playing but are *being* those characters, which makes us laugh. An actor who plays a comic role in such a way as to show that he finds the character funny is seldom funny to an audience.

Directing comedy, then, involves first knowing what is funny and then playing the actions very intensively. Life is comedic when we perceive the incongruities, and so it is on the stage. Comedy is all joke telling of an elaborate sort.

EXERCISES

1. Apply the basic description of comedy given above to the following plays by citing how the plays differ in structure and how they are alike:
   a. *The Frogs* (Aristophanes)
   b. *The Brothers* (Terence)
   c. *Volpone* (Jonson)
   d. *Tartuffe* (Molière)
   e. *The Way of the World* (Congreve)
   f *The School for Scandal* or *The Rivals* (Sheridan)
   g. *The Contrast* (Tyler)
   h. *Man and Superman* (Shaw)
   i. *The Show-Off* (Kelly)
   j. *The Circle* (Maugham)
   k. *Everything in the Garden* (Albee)

2. What is a comic fool? Cite specific examples from the plays above.

3. Analyze a recent joke you have heard. Exactly what makes it funny?

4. Do a detailed analysis of a comedy of your own choosing by citing all the points that prove it to be a comedy.

5. If the students in the class are prepared with background for advanced study, and if time is available, the following should be read, studied, and discussed comparatively: George Meredith's *An Essay on Comedy* and Henri Bergson's *Laughter*. Additional readings such as Northrup Frye's "The Mythos of Spring: Comedy" from *The Anatomy of Criticism* (Princeton, N.J.: Princeton University Press, 1957) pp. 163–186 can be most illuminating.

FARCE

Just as melodrama is a diluted form of the serious play, with the basic elements simplified and the emphasis placed on their external aspects, so farce is a diluted form of comedy, again with the basic elements of comedy simplified and the emphasis placed on the external aspects. In addition, just as tragedies may contain some scenes where melodrama takes over in the interest of intensive physical illustration (Shakespeare's *Macbeth* is a good example), so comedies may contain scenes where farce is used to intensify the illustration.

Farces are usually packed with laugh-getting situations and business, for the emphasis is thrown on simplified characters, ingenious involvements, and physical illustrations. Yet, though the characters are close to the realm of comedy by being distortions of life, they are meaner, more superficial, more puppetlike. It is precisely because they take life so seriously and can see no other avenue but their own that we find them funny. Excellent examples of farce are the moving-picture reels of Laurel and Hardy where both characters have below average intelligence, both are clumsy and awkward, both are sober and serious, both work industriously, with failure courting their every move. We can see ourselves in their farcical antics because we all have a certain amount of the same problems in everyday life; but at the same time, we can laugh at them not only because they are below average ("meaner") men, which brings out our own feeling of superiority, but also because we are distanced in a very specific way and made to see only certain things.

Farce takes on the look of exaggeration because of its simplified structural elements; we can see and easily recognize the incongruities in characters and actions because the actors hold them out to us in very clear ways. Although tragedy and comedy can be read from the printed page with a certain amount of reward, farces require acting to give them specific life because the funniest moments may be involvements with stage properties or machines or in physical contact among the characters. Only occasionally do we have farces that depend on language as one of the major emphases, and in these cases the fun is still in the acting, for it is the actor's sense of timing in line delivery that will provoke the best laugh.

Good stage farce is rare in our day because the movies and television are more capable of presenting the contrivances of farce. But however a director picks up his knowledge of the dramatic values in farce, if he understands well this composite form, he will be able to augment his sense of illustration in directing the higher form, comedy. Fools are fools, and in working with comedy, a significant moment of farce that is still in taste and in line with character can often bring audiences to clear understanding of the blocks in characters. Farce may be a lesser form of comedy but it has the great capacity of arousing audiences to explicit laughter by bringing them into the peculiar realm of fantasy that surrounds a farcical moment. An audience is simply lifted out of its sense of reality and led to believe in, if only for a few moments, the rarified world in which the farcical characters live.

EXERCISES

1. What is farcical in the following plays:
   a. *The Comedy of Errors* (Shakespeare)
   b. *The Doctor in Spite of Himself* (Molière)
   c. *She Stoops to Conquer* (Goldsmith). Is this play a comedy or a farce?
   d. *Box and Cox* (Morton)
   e. *The Importance of Being Earnest* (Wilde). Is this play a comedy or a farce?
   f. *Misalliance* (Shaw)
   g. *Boy Meets Girl* (Spewack)
   h. *The Bald Soprano* (Ionesco)

2. Why is the play of *Pyramus and Thisbe* in *A Midsummer Night's Dream* a farce?

3. Is Beckett's *Happy Days* a farce?

4. Do a written analysis of a farce of your own choice by proving from the structure that it is a farce.

OTHER COMPOSITE FORMS

Although there are a number of labels in use to describe other composite forms (tragicomedy, for instance), what they tend to do is to cross the lines of the major ones described above, thus delineating new composites by rearranging the emphases. At best, such labels are merely descriptive and offer nothing new in the way of help to a director. Once the director understands the nature of composite forms and how the principal forms are composed, he will realize that the game of close identification can be infinite, simply because there are so many possible arrangements of the pure composites. Serious plays, for instance, may contain comic moments just as comedies may contain serious moments. All labeling will, therefore, contain a certain amount of readjustment to this mingling of emphases, for few plays precisely conform to the strict definitions of the pure forms. If you keep in mind that one always deals with specific plays, because the major categories are abstractions, you will not get caught in the dangerous game of labeling plays, with the idea that you understand them because you have assigned them to categories. You must also keep in mind that changes in drama come about when playwrights break the narrow prescriptions of composite forms.

EXERCISES

1. How would you describe the following composite types? Try to use specific labels although they may be made by combining some of the four composite types already delineated.
   a. *The Bacchae* (Euripides)
   b. *The Second Shepherds' Play* (Anonymous)
   c. *Much Ado About Nothing* (Shakespeare)
   d. *The Misanthrope* (Molière)
   e. *A Month in the Country* (Turgeniev)
   f. *The Three Sisters* or *Uncle Vanya* (Chekhov)
   g. *The Plough and the Stars* (O'Casey)
   h. *Idiot's Delight* (Sherwood)
   i. *A Man for All Seasons* (Bolt)
   j. *The Boys in the Band* (Crowley)
   k. *Rhinoceros* (Ionesco). Comedy or what?

2. Make a list of as many plays from the modern repertoire you can think of that seem to cross the lines of the pure types. Why do we have so many today?

Searching for Style Through Backgrounds: The Director as Scholar

Although a detailed analysis of a play's structure is the only sure way of discerning its style simply because it necessitates a thorough probing of every aspect of the play, the study of some backgrounds surrounding authors and particular plays can often be helpful and even deeply revealing. After all, plays are composed by individuals who "write themselves" down, and the more we know about them as human beings living in particular and specific worlds, the more likely we are to understand what they are trying to say. Poetry is mysterious only if we make it so, for the best of its kind, though it may be subtle and half-concealed, is much clearer to us when we have a personal knowledge of the circumstances that gave it form. If "style is the man," as the sages say, knowing better the man who makes it cannot but sensitize our own perceptions.

Likewise, although it is dangerous to rely on historical sources in an attempt to understand those many plays that deal with history, simply because playwrights do not write history but use it only as background, the study of contextual history can provide a good basis for comprehension if it is only to permit us to see more clearly the points of departure taken by a particular playwright. A knowledge of history—and this knowledge includes backgrounds in our own times—is therefore an essential director's tool. A well-known American dramatic critic recently remarked that he could not see how directors could direct or critics could write about plays since 1920 without having a lively understanding of Marxist philosophy and all of the forces working out of it. Although he was no Marxist himself in any sense, he felt that political ideas involving either favorable attitudes toward it or condemnations of it were everywhere in modern drama, and a director or critic could easily miss them unless he was politically oriented. What this critic implied by his statement was that a director cannot modify or adapt historical drama to our own time and tastes without knowing a good deal about the historical background out of which the plays of that period were written, for knowing an author's bias or lack of bias toward what he took as historical fact can tell us much about the individual direction he may have taken in a play.

A director, then, is also a scholar, though he may think that label too pretentious. But whatever he calls himself, he certainly must do a great deal of probing into backgrounds if he is to understand the drama with which he works. If a playwright is still living and readily available, conversation with him can readily solve the problems about background, but if neither situation exists, a director will need to do a lot of spade work. To know an author and his sense of history, as well as to know the historical background of his plays, is to understand the circumstances in which the author's style took shape. Biography and history are therefore essential working tools in directing.

What follows are some specific points about each of these approaches to plays and playwrights.

BIOGRAPHY

Since playwrights tend to write about the things they feel strongest about, biographical research can often turn up directions in an author's own life parallel to the plays he writes. Understanding the playwright in

Jean Genet also requires comprehension of Genet as a thief, as a convicted and sentenced criminal, as a hunted and haunted man, and as a homosexual. The same necessity for inside awareness applies to Sartre, to Shaw, to O'Casey, to Brecht, to Saroyan, to O'Neill, to Hellman, and to any other playwright whose works a director wants to produce. Certainly, we can all be misled fairly easily by biography because at its base it is only an interpretation of someone's life, what the biographer thought it to be. Autobiographies are usually even more risky as dependable sources. But by reading such background materials carefully and by exercising your own sense of logic against the myth making or image making that may go on in any particular study, you can sift out significant points. More recent biographers have turned away from mere reporting of incidents and toward a sort of literary psychoanalysis; the traps in the present day approach may be more frequent because the projections are more speculative, but the insight is keener and more revealing, and is thus more illuminating to a director than was the older method.

What is perhaps most directly useful about biography is the context out of which a particular playwright works. If a biographer has done his job, not only do the social, economic, political, and religious worlds in which an author lives and works stand revealed, but also the way he may have participated directly in dealings outside of his life in the theatre. Playwrights are public personages, and, as such, they become involved in human relationships and commitments that reveal them as individuals. Consequently, what they write about for the theatre may be very closely tied to their everyday behavior and social participation. This interrelationship has been particularly true among twentieth-century dramatists, such as those listed in the previous paragraphs, but as we learn more and more about historical figures—Molière or Lope de Vega, for instance—we can see how they too were motivated in their writings out of the personal and public contexts in which they lived.

To be a director is to be highly curious about human beings. It follows that a director is not merely interested in the imaginary characters in the plays he mounts on the stage but is intensively sensitive to the revealing moments in the lives of the people with whom he works most closely, particularly his blood brother—the playwright.

HISTORY

Again it is necessary to point out that a director's pursuit of the historical background out of which a play is written can be very misleading, but with the exercise of great care, it can tell the director a good deal about a play.

Two aspects of historical review must be considered and clearly separated by a director. One is what the director accepts as historical fact *today,* and the other is what the playwright accepted as historical fact in his day. These two points of view may be in complete disagreement, and the director must keep them distinctly apart. We have been so influenced by nineteenth- and twentieth-century interpretations of history, many of them based on new scholarly discoveries, that we are all too ready to apply them to the thinking in other ages.

The safest approach to the study of historical backgrounds is to read contemporary (contemporary with the playwright) or earlier accounts of events used in plays that might have been available to the authors who wrote them. In this way, a director more easily can see what led to a playwright's interpretations of the events, and the resulting prejudices can stand revealed. Understanding Goldsmith's *She Stoops to Conquer,* for instance, can be much more lively if a director understands Goldsmith's immediate sense of history—his feelings about the new changes taking place in the late eighteenth-century society he wrote about—a class society confronted by humanist influences stemming from the revolutionary ideas associated with a slowly emerging philosophy of democracy. Reading historical accounts that Goldsmith might have known could more nearly reveal what he had in mind in his play beyond a simple plotting of "The Mistakes of a Night." There are many lines in this play that must be interpreted in the light of eighteenth-century thought and feeling if they are to get through to twentieth-century audiences with force, clarity, and good humor. Likewise, you will know a great deal more about Lope de Vega's *Fuente Ovejuna* if you try to answer the question of why the play seems to be filled with what we take to be democratic sentiments; or about Marlowe's *Doctor Faustus* if you ask yourself the questions Why was he so angry at the Roman Church? or just Why was he so angry? and then try to find some answers; or about Shaw's *Man and Superman* if you ask What is the difference between Jack Tanner's political philosophy and Straker's? or about Brecht's *Mother Courage* if you ask Did he warp historical fact to make his play apply to the war-torn Europe of the 1940s?; or about John Osborne's *Look Back in Anger* if you ask What was Osborne so mad about when he wrote the play in the mid-1950s?; or about Shakespeare's *Henry VI* if you ask What did he know about Joan of Arc beyond hearsay?

Wherever the search may lead a director, he must always keep in mind that his intention is not to infuse a play with his own interpretation of history, but to understand better an author's sense of what he was using as background. The intention is not to uncover an author's errors in historical fact, although that may be quite revealing, but to see fully what the author found dramatic and exciting in his vision of humanity placed in the historical context in which he chose to tell his story. Plays are largely about a *peripheral* situation surrounding historical events, but to see the periphery more clearly you must comprehend the core.

A director is not a historian or an archeologist in a technical sense, but he must have lively feeling for history and how it works in plays.

Finding Style by Examining Other Works of the Same Author

In the study of one particular play for production, if a director studies three or four additional plays by the same playwright—plays written in approximately the same time period—he will usually turn up most of the essential characteristics of that playwright's style. This is not to say that playwrights repeat themselves in content, although this can occasionally happen even with the better ones, but it does suggest that because style is a very personal thing, it can become inherent in a whole body of work.

Thus, we talk about "an Ibsen play," "a Chekhov play," "a Shaw play," "a Williams play," and by these designations mean a characteristic style associated with each writer. We mean that each playwright probably chooses his themes from a certain range; that the dramatic actions he devises are probably either serious or comic but seldom both, although each type may contain bits of the other; that the given circumstances he arranges probably deal with people from a certain class who hold attitudes inherent to that class, and with much pervious action or little previous action depending on the emphasis he, as a playwright, gives to environmental control; that the characters he draws in detail are commensurate with the action; that the dialogue he sets down has certain specific and individual markings always closely associated with his particular product, because dialogue is the expression of his subconscious self, despite his conscious use of techniques in its composition; that the moods and tempos he pulls out of all this particular usage will be individually marked in as positive and identifiable ways as the works of a musical composer. By looking closely in this manner at a playwright's individual characteristics, the examination of several of his plays written in approximately the same time period can establish the general style associated with his work, and from this general description the director can move to specific elements in the particular play he wants to produce. Comparative analysis is one of the surest ways of pinpointing style, for what goes for one play probably goes for another if their time of writing is fairly close together.

The period of composition, therefore, is a very important consideration because the works of some writers span several decades during which time their style changes. We can readily notice these changes in retrospective exhibitions of the work of painters that shows their lifetime contributions, for instance, the work of Rembrandt, who died in poverty because his buyer-patrons who had made him rich did not like his "new" style that now seems so marvelous to us and probably characterizes his best work. Close comparative study of art tells us much about style and its changing faces—a view of style we cannot possibly see in the performing arts (except in the moving picture) because we cannot place side-by-side performances that have occurred days, months, or years apart. We have a much better chance with playscripts because of their availability, but even though we can read and study several by the same playwright, the changing style is apt to elude us without careful examination because we cannot look at a playscript in one glance as we can a painting. The time-space aspect of drama that delineates it among the arts is scattered over several pages of print—and is, therefore, much more diffuse than it would be on the stage.

But if we are to understand changing style in a playwright, we must compare works from different periods of his writing as well as look at the plays immediately surrounding a particular drama. Ibsen's playwriting spanned half a century. To understand the body of his work, and, thus, to be able to place any one play, we must know that his earliest plays can be loosely characterized as romantic-historical dramas; that he followed this style with the allegorical dramatic poems of *Brand* and *Peer Gynt;* and that he followed these in turn with the Realistic plays dealing with the contemporary society he knew. Later, this middle-period style gave way in the late 1880s to a new style in which symbolism played a dramatic role, and finally in the last plays to a style some critics have termed Expressionistic. Thus, it would be quite wrong to define Ibsen's style only in terms of *A Doll's House* or *An Enemy of the People.* We can, perhaps, group all of Chekhov's plays together because they were written within a much narrower time span, although perceptive students of his dramas usually see differences between the early and the late plays.

Do playwrights consciously look for new ways and thus new styles to express themselves? Like the rest of us, they are strongly influenced by the real world, and it would be strange, indeed, if they did not move with the times. In one sense, this is what art means: the fresh revelation of man in the context of his times. When we say that the plays of a certain author mirror his society, we mean that he found an individual way—his style—of telling his audiences about themselves in such a way that they could see clearly what they were compelled, involuntarily, to watch and listen to; and, with study, we too can see that society clearly.

A director must be aware, therefore, of the shifts in style in a playwright's work, for in this way, he may discover points of style that run throughout the body of his plays as a whole. In addition, the more he knows about an author's other works—his poetry or fiction—the more easily the style can be detected and pinpointed. Of particular value are those usually brief discussions by playwrights of their theories of drama and the practice of playwriting. Like most working artists, playwrights resist telling us how they make plays because they recognize that creative art is subjective and that revealing the creative process in oneself is an extremely difficult, if not impossible, business.   Yet, when they do write critical comment, as have Jonson, Lope de Vega, Molière, Hugo, Shaw, Chekhov, Maugham, Anderson, Miller, Williams, and many others, they must be listened to with great attention, for what they have to say may be of great import to their plays when you contemplate production.

Translation Versus Adaptation

Strictly defined, a *translation* is a *literal* and *literary* carry-over of a playscript from one language to another, with the translator paying strict attention to accurate word or phrase *duplication*.   An *adaptation,* on the other hand, is a *loose* carry-over of a playscript in an attempt to recapture its spirit and feeling while reproducing the dramatic action (the subtext) in language more or less close to the original but inherently possessing the capability of reaching the audience for which it is intended.   In an adaptation, scene and line alteration is entirely possible because the intention is to transfer a play, not as a piece of literature but as a piece of theatre.   It is readily apparent that these two processes are very different in their intentions and thus in their final products.   The director's problem is to be able to perceive the quality of the transfer, no matter which method is used.

Whether you are dealing with a translation or an adaptation is a most important consideration in perceiving style, for as a director, you will be entirely at the mercy of those who carry over plays written in languages with which you do not have a firsthand acquaintance.   Since style is the inherent individuality in a work, how can you, as a director, possibly know what that individuality is unless you have either a firsthand command of the language in which a play is written, or great faith in the capabilities of a translator or adaptor.   Much attention has been given to this aspect of play production in recent years because, as the world has grown closer together, and as we have found great value and interest in one another's plays, theatre people have recognized that foreign-language plays do not transfer on the stage through words alone, but that far more intensive revelations of the works are necessary if the characteristic styles of the playwrights are to be captured.   The trend in the American theatre has been away from translation and toward free adaptation, not only of contemporary works but also of Greek drama and of French classical drama, on the premise that translators are usually only language oriented and adaptors are "playwrights" who are able to comprehend dramatic action and its theatricalities first, and then are able to find the appropriate language of the theatre to cover them.   But there may be poor adaptors, just as there are poor translators. In fact, some adaptors treat works in such a loose manner that the original work may be quite mutilated.

The process of adaptation is a most difficult one. After Lillian Hellman had adapted Jean Anouilh's *L'Alouette* for the American stage under the title of *The Lark,* she said she would never tackle an adaptation again because it was the most difficult dramatic composition she had ever done and had none of the compensations of free creativity. To note the kind of work she did, you will have to compare her version with Christopher Fry's "translation" of the same work for London production. You should note also that the New York production was a success, whereas the London production failed. (Why?) For a good look at what has been done with ancient Greek drama, you should compare a recent adaptation by William Arrowsmith with one by Gilbert Murray, also an adaptor, and compare both of these against a standard translation by Jebb, Coleridge, or Trevelyan.

The search for style, then, in foreign-language plays depends a very great deal on what a particular translator or adaptor has discerned about the style of the original. If either is both a perceptive playwright and a critic with the capability of looking closely and "telling the truth," a director may find the style close to the original; if either does not know how to make the transfer, the director who uses such translations or adaptations, in T. S. Eliot's disparaging phrase, will "make a fiction" of the original work.

In approaching foreign-language plays, then, a director should examine closely all of the translations and adaptations available to him as well as a text in the original language. This means careful comparison, sometimes of several works. Translations are frequently helpful because, though they may not be readily playable on the stage, they provide the keys to what adaptors have left out or changed. If possible, the director should work with a language consultant who can make fresh translations of contested passages or explain why translators or adaptors have chosen the language they use. In some cases, a new adaptation will result because the director sees in a playscript dramatic possibilities that other translators or adaptors have completely missed. At the very least, out of this comparative examination a director will learn the strength of the playscript with which he is dealing, and he will be able to penetrate the stylistic characteristics much more readily. Style is the man. And with foreign-language dramas, the director plays the role of detective even more intensively than he does with plays in his own language.

A word should also be said here about what to some people seems to be the curious phenomenon of plays written for the London stage, in English of course, which do not succeed with American audiences and vice versa. The difficulties encountered in this exchange of plays in the same language points up the very real problems in transferring drama from one language to another. Failures in the transfer can be explained only from the viewpoint that plays are deeply embedded cultural mirrors that require a sensitive understanding of the culture out of which they are written if they are to be comprehended at all. In particular, because contemporary drama looks so closely at cultural environments in its attempts to unravel psychological problems, unless an audience can feel the environment of the play through its own parallel and sympathetic environments, it remains insensitive to the dramatic action in a play except on a superficial level. This failure to feel environments has also happened to the European politically-oriented drama of commitment since 1920, such as that of Brecht, which passes by many American theatregoers because they cannot sense the dark intensity of the environments out of which these plays appeared. Likewise, the changes in English society, including the breakdown in the class structure, are unfamiliar and little understood by American audiences. Similarly, English audiences are subject to miscomprehension when it comes to looking at American plays. If you read the reviews of the London production of Arthur Miller's *Death of a Salesman*—reviews which obviously show a poor perception of intense American concerns—you will know more about the problems of cultural transfer.

EXERCISES

1. Compare available translations and/or adaptations of the following: *The Bacchae; The Trojan Women; Oedipus Rex; The Frogs; Medea.*

2. Compare the "A" text with the "B" text of Marlowe's *Doctor Faustus.* See: W. W. Greg's parallel text published by Oxford, 1950. Note the very great difference in content.

3. Compare several editions of Farquhar's *The Beaux' Strategem.* Note particularly the nineteenth-century acting edition.

4. Compare translations and/or adaptations of the following:
   a. Ibsen: *A Doll's House; The Lady From the Sea; The Master Builder; An Enemy of the People*
   b. Chekhov: *The Sea Gull; The Cherry Orchard*
   c. Strindberg: *The Father; The Ghost Sonata*
   d. Pirandello: *Six Characters in Search of an Author*
   e. Williams: *The Glass Menagerie.* Variant versions in this instance.
   f. Anouilh: *The Lark*

22

style-analysis reveals style:
the search for
inherent individuality

Now that you are more aware of the nature of style as the *individual emphasis in form,* you should be able to do a more intensive play-analysis. What you will soon see amounts to an analysis on another level. In Part I of this book, the intention of the discussion about play-analysis was to make you aware of the basic essentials that comprise form and their relationships to content, with the focus placed on Realistic drama. In the two chapters immediately preceding this one, we showed much more specifically how form and content are related to each other and how they relate directly to style. Further, we discussed the types of plays (tragedy, comedy, etc.) in order to show the options open to a playwright, all in the interest of revealing how he can begin to individualize a play's action by treating it in a certain way. And finally, we pointed out how a director can get inside a playwright's style through working with biographical and historical backgrounds, through close study of other works, and through the most careful selection of translations or adaptations.

At this point, we can go to the crux of this discussion, for now you are in a much better position to undertake *selection* in analysis: the sifting out of what you think an author has made emphatically his own—which of the seven elements of play-analysis he has given his greatest attention to and how he has developed them in detail—because his selective emphasis will inherently delineate his style. Furthermore, you should be able to see how this analytical approach can be applied to all plays and not just to those in the Realistic category.

Once you learn to do a play-analysis on this new level, you will no longer approach plays in a general way but will always look for the specifics of individualization. You will learn to characterize the plays of a certain author as you would characterize one of the persons he may draw in a play, and, further, you will learn to separate one play from another in the body of his work because you will be looking very closely at their specific characteristics. His plays will become personalities to you as readily identifiable one from the other as are your close friends. Once again, a director always directs a specific play, never a general play.

What to Look for in Analyzing Style

Style-analysis as a technique is based on play-analysis, but you must not undertake it until you have completed an intensive analysis of the form and content of a play—a play-analysis—in the usual manner. You will be tempted to try to do both analyses, the play-analysis and the style-analysis, simultaneously, but if you do, you will without question miss significant information about the play. If you think of the first analysis—the one outlined in Part I—as play description and the new one outlined here as style-analysis, you will better understand why the first analysis must be done before undertaking the second.

What immediately follows is a list of suggestions about what to look for in making a style-analysis. This list is not intended to be inclusive because style can range so widely that no list can ever cover the full possibilities. Nevertheless, the suggestions offered here include the basic points in the discovery of style. Once you learn to look at plays in these terms, you will expand enormously your comprehension of all drama, and probably for the first time will begin to look at plays as particular, individualized objects.

The points you are to look for are first discussed in detail. Near the end of this chapter (p. 323) you will find a work sheet for style-analysis that you should add to the form for play-analysis at the end of Chapter 6 (pp. 63–65). Used together, these two outlines cover all the major points of a play's form, content, and style.

SETTING A PLAY IN ITS CONTEXT:
SCHOLARLY BACKGROUNDS

1. Date the play both in its general historical period in relation to other plays and in the body of work by the specific author under consideration.

2. Study the author's background through biographical sources. Try to relate him to his time, and try to *see him as an individual* working in a general cultural and aesthetic pattern. Probe his personal life for reasons why he should write the sort of play he does.

3. Study at least three or four other plays closely associated in time to the principal play under study. If the playwright's career has been a long one, examine other plays separated by at least a decade or more before and/or after the principal play. Study other works by the playwright, such as his poems, novels, short stories, essays, and, if available, any dramatic criticisms he may have written either about the work of other playwrights or about his own. Criticisms of this sort are invaluable since they may illuminate the playwright's specific intentions in writing his plays whether he carried them out or not, or they may defend his work in a most revealing way. Introductions to plays often contain such inside views.

4. Carefully examine all available editions or, if a play derives from a foreign language, study the available translations and/or adaptations. Read any commentaries that accompany them in the attempt to understand what a particular editor, translator, or adaptor had in mind when he undertook the editing or the transfer of a work. These introductory essays frequently contain valuable insights into various aspects of play structure which, after your own study, you may accept or disregard for good reason.

The translations and/or adaptations should be studied for their actability in terms of the playwriting craftsmanship exercised in the transfer. Compare lines and speeches for economy in word usage, for imagery and poetic value, and for simple craftsmanship in technical details, such as building to the ends of lines and speeches. Examine comparatively the available translations or adaptations for mood values, for theatricality, and for all the dramatic values you think are commensurate with the play.

If a historical play in English is under consideration, you should look at all published editions, or, if available, to unpublished manuscripts. Not only do playwrights change their own work before publication, but editors often make extensive changes depending on where they obtained the work for publication. Many plays have been published—historical as well as modern—as acting editions; that is, they are versions

used by acting companies in actual stage production, and they consequently reveal any additions or cuttings that may have been made in
mounting a specific play. Such acting versions appear throughout English drama, from Marlowe's *Doctor Faustus* to Farquhar's *Beaux' Stratagem* to Williams' *Glass Menagerie*. Only by careful examination of all
available editions can you really know what sort of playscript you have
under study. This may leave you in some confusion as to what to do,
but at least you will be making your own decisions affecting style and are
not so apt to be misled by others.

5. Study the historical context of the specific play's setting. Where
did the author get his material? Are the sources available, as is Arthur
Miller's for *The Crucible?* If so, read the sources, and, while doing so,
try to decide why he selected the material he did and why he treated it
as he did. Bernard Shaw's *St. Joan* and Jean Anouilh's *The Lark* are
both about Joan of Arc and both draw largely from the same sources, yet
each is different. Shaw's play, by his own confession, is a direct interpretation of history. Anouilh is not very interested in history but is
greatly concerned with recapturing the poetic nature of the story and
Joan's spirit as a French symbol. Lillian Hellman, in adapting Anouilh's
play, made a third version: a melodrama that may well tell us more about
her feelings concerning the Spanish Civil War of the 1930s than it does
about the context of Anouilh's play—the confusion in France following
World War II—or about the historical fifteenth-century context of Joan.
What would you decide after reading the historical backgrounds?

Remember that you are not going to write your own notion of history
into a play. The sole purpose of such study is to understand as thoroughly as possible what an author thinks and feels about any background
material he may have used. Your own study must be pointed toward
revealing a playwright's awareness of history and how he approached his
use of it.

Historical-sociological research may also be of immense value in working with all kinds of plays, including fairly recent ones. How did people
live? What were the mores in real life, which the author mirrors, that
guided their actions and behavior? What is the play's context, in which
the author places his action? Note that the dramatic actions of many
plays depend on revolt against a society's existing requirements for behavior. If a director has a more lively understanding of moral, religious,
and social patterns, he will be better able to see the rigidities that must be
overthrown. And with comedy, how will a director know what is funny
unless he is knowledgeable about the patterns that make a character so
ridiculous in the eyes of his contemporaries?

6. Finally, when you have completed your other studies, you should
study the dramatic criticisms written about a play—what others have said

about it. This study should wait until you have made your own play-analysis, so that what others think a play to be does not interfere with your own critical view. But sooner or later you must make comparisons, if only to pit your own conclusions against other interpretations. Instead of weakening your own ideas, such countercriticisms should strengthen them because you now have a critical "audience" to fight with. Directing is setting out one's own interpretation with strength and decision, and it cannot help but advance on firm ground if weak and vague comprehensions are thrown out in the "critical battle" and the strong ones are given purpose and direction. A strong director—and the nature of his job says that he must be strong—is also a strong critic because he has faith in and has made a decision about his own interpretations or critical statements.

LOOKING INSIDE THE PLAY:
INHERENT STYLE-ANALYSIS

Again you must keep in mind that what follows is only a list of suggestions for helping to discover the emphasis a playwright may give to the basic elements in play-analysis. His style will be defined in his particular use of the elements he considers most expressive of his ideas. All plays will have all the elements, but individuality will reside in his "more-or-less" use of them and in the flavoring he gives to what he does use.

Given Circumstances. 1. *Environmental Facts.* What level of society does he write about—lower, middle, or upper? Does the author show strong interests in political or religious backgrounds? What are the mores issuing from these environmental factors, and how strongly does the writer impose them on his characters? Is environment assumed (the royal court in *Hamlet*), or does the writer specifically and intentionally set out a mass of detail (small-town life in *Ghosts*)?

2. *Previous Action.* Does the author use a minimum of previous action to tell his story (*Macbeth; Delicate Balance*), or is a great deal necessary (*Ghosts*)? Where does the playwright begin his story: near the beginning so that he can show all the incidents (*Hamlet*)? Or toward the end, just before the final major discovery (*Oedipus; Who's Afraid of Virginia Woolf; Cat on a Hot Tin Roof*)? Recent plays (since 1960) seem to have reduced previous action to a minimum in comparison to the way Ibsen and those who followed his techniques handled it. Departures from Realism tend to treat previous action only fragmentarily because the intention is not psychological development in depth but the unfolding of the action of the moment (*The Adding Machine; Our Town*).

3. *Polar Attitudes.*   This is a most important stylistic declaration because the points of view a playwright's characters will take toward the environment, will, in turn, tell us what that particular writer considers important in the society he mirrors, and out of that will come the actions of the play.   All plays are about revolt of some sort, about a character's overthrow of or submission to the restrictions that have fenced him in. Thus, the attitudes toward the environment at the opening of a play set up the initial pole in the major character, or characters if two are under consideration, which will be changed during the course of the action, resulting in a new attitude and thus a new pole at the end of the play. Plays take place between these two poles.   The style may be declared, then, by what sort of poles an author sets up, and, particularly, by how he has individualized them so that they are fresh and therefore have the potential to move audiences.   We are seldom moved by the trite; a writer's capability will lie in his devising of the polar structure.

Since the initial pole will initiate the action, what sort of pole an author chooses will declare a point of style.

Dialogue.   How a writer handles dialogue can certainly declare the outward appearances of style, but since dialogue also contains the action, the most careful scrutiny of this basic element is absolutely necessary.

Along with the usual study outlined in Part I, the director should pay particular attention to those idiosyncracies in line development that give the personal touch:

1. Look for specific choice of words, with close attention to repeated words that may contain strong moods or even symbolic values.
2. Look for choice in phrases, especially if the play is in the Realistic style, and the speech is intended to reproduce folk idiom.   Does the playwright use key phrases to set off the speech of certain characters in idiomatic fashion?
3. Look for poetic overtones in word and phrase choice declared by the use of imagery.   How elaborate are the images?   How frequently do they occur?
4. Is the dialogue *economic* as a container of the action?   How much room does it allow for acting?   Does it tend toward the literary?
5. Does the playwright intend textual dominance or does the play exist more on intensive illustration of the subtext (Shaw versus Saroyan)?
6. If the lines are in verse form, what is intended in the way of rhythm delivery?   Eliot, Fry, and Anderson, as well as recent versions of Greek plays and plays by Molière, among others, all require special handling because of the verse forms.   Are you sensitive to the styles?

7. Reread and restudy in Chapter 3 the section "Dialogue: The Facade of the Playscript" to insure that you are aware of the nature of dialogue.

Dramatic Action. Again you should be certain that you understand the basic characteristics of drama action set down in Chapter 4 before you proceed. Now look carefully for the following:

1. How complex is the action? Is it (in Aristotle's definition) simple or complex? Has the playwright written his play around a very simple unity of action or does he have a multiplicity of incidents affecting two groups of people (double plot) only casually related but who must be brought together in a final synthesis?
2. How are time and place handled?
3. Whose play is it? Only by an intensive analysis can you sometimes determine this question in plays where two or three people seem to play very strong roles. One character, however, must dominate. Therefore, it is essential that you decide which one, for the author's style will be exhibited in the subtlety with which he handles such characters, and the care with which he delineates them.
4. What is the type of the action? Here is a basic declaration of style. What sort of serious play or comedy does the author write? If you can describe it, you are describing a point of style. If the category is comedy, does he specialize in dialogue? In situations? In irony? In youthful caprice or in mature foolery? Is he a satirist? If you categorize him by the type of drama he writes, you will be able to pinpoint his style more clearly because you have assigned him a general area and you can look further for his distinguishing differences.
5. A major aspect of style lies in the sort of actions a playwright chooses to show on the stage. We say that drama is the showing of the strange, the unusual, the extraordinary, but what we mean by these words can differ greatly. We tend to regard as extraordinary those actions in real life in which we do not all participate: murder or violence, torture, sadistic cruelty, family destruction, and others. And it is possible to bring any or all of these onto the stage, although in some historical periods they were banned. But are they the extraordinary?

Much of modern drama converts peripheral action into the extraordinary, not the obvious we can all observe, but the subtle, marginal action we seldom pay attention to in moments of great stress. Thus, when we see an automobile accident in the street, a normal person's attention is apt to be caught up in the details at the center: the injured, the ambulance personnel, the police, the wrecked cars. Peripheral action in this instance would be the actions outside but near the core of the accident: someone in the crowd who reacts out of mental recall or guilt; someone not associated at all with the accident who reacts in a certain significant way. These are what good playwrights are apt to find most interesting. Thus, we do not need to see hard violence on stage because the truly exciting moments, the real violence, is on the edge of the violent activity, and it is this marginal activity that holds our attention in the theatre.

Here is the point: Authors declare themselves stylistically through the sort of actions they choose to record in the theatre.

6. How does the playwright make discoveries in the action? What characterizes the climaxes? Is the playwright truly theatrical?
7. Try to find the rhythm of the action. Here is a subtle delineation of style that is inherent in an author's work, and it can be most revealing of an author's individuality. If you can find his rhythm, you have pinned him down.

Character. A playwright is frequently known by the sort of characters he draws. One of the common truisms about Bernard Shaw is that his characters all sound alike, that they all seem to be talking as Shaw would talk. This is a generalization to describe a point of Shavian style: with few exceptions, the characters in Shaw's plays, no matter what level of society they come from, all talk in a dynamic, fully articulate way; there are no dunderheads, no inarticulate people, no low-energy types. Here is a point of style that a director must not only be aware of but learn to utilize to full advantage. In contrast, although Tennessee Williams' women might be grouped together as psychoneurotics—a point of style—the problem in style-analysis comes in trying to separate them to discover their special and distinctive psychoneurotic qualities. Like Ibsen, Williams has specialized largely in drawing female characters, but the life of each play will rest on the delicate shadings he gives to each character. Note Ibsen's specific attack. To describe his women as suffragettes or "new" women is to throw them all into a general stewpot, for Ibsen's women are all different. It is true that many of them are in revolt against a hard, Victorian, conformist world made by men, but you will find that they differ extensively once you examine them in depth. Ibsen's approach to playwriting often led him into drawing antipathies: once he had developed a character from one point of view in one play, he would follow it from just the opposite in another. Although they both drive men to their deaths, Hedda Gabler and Hilda Wangel (*The Master Builder*) are very different.

Style in characters, then, lies in the sort of people a playwright is interested in and wants to say something about, for he does not select his people at random and by accident but chooses them from among those he knows best, those he has studied in real life and can see clearly.   In this respect, there is no gap between William Congreve and Somerset Maugham, both of whom wrote comedies of manners about English society, because each wrote about the sort of people he saw about him.   To hold our attention, plays must reveal humanity; thus, it is the particular eyesight a playwright possesses that will or will not open up life to us. We are not talking about photographic reproduction here but about perception.   Style results in perceiving clearly, first by the playwright and later by the director, for the clearly perceived statement can be singled out from what is generalized and poorly observed.

What often holds our attention in the theatre is not the people we know but those we do not.   The new have something of an exposé quality about them, and, for this reason, new playwrights are always finding their way into the theatre: they are able to show us new people, new in the sense that they are freshly perceived.   The interest in folk plays in America during the 1920s and '30s may have been as much a reaction against middle-class drama as anything else.   Was the middle-class audience that primarily supported the theatre bored with looking at its own kind, and, consequently, found what seemed to be the simpler life of the lower class not only absorbing but also revealing, and therefore exciting theatre material?   But look what happened when playwrights began to tell the truth about the lower class: that it was poverty-ridden, that poverty could be terribly destructive, even disastrous; that the middle class was an actual enemy because it shut itself off from the lower class and forced its continuance?   Here was a shock drama that took seriously the characters caught in these given circumstances.   The movement of audiences away from such truthtelling is a matter of theatre history.

Here are some things to look for that concern style in character drawing:

1. Does the style lie in the desires of the characters—what they want?
2. Does the playwright deal with eccentric or rarely seen characters who hold audiences with great fascination?   (Genet in *The Balcony, The Blacks, The Maids;* Mart Crowley with his homosexuals in *The Boys in the Band;* Gerome Ragni and James Rado with the hippies in *Hair.*)
3. Is it possible, in controversion of Aristotle's *Poetics* and Maxwell Anderson's "The Essence of Tragedy," to write successful tragedies about evil people?   Who declares what evil is?   And once we see "evil people" in explained circumstances—what makes them think and behave in the way they do?—can we any longer see them in any other light but as human beings who may not agree with the way the majority thinks and feels?   Are gangsters Bonnie and Clyde the evil ones or is it the society that made them the villains?   The classical definition of evil seems to have altered, for in recent

times there seems to be no fence between good and evil. Humanity can be anything, and absolute goods become only what the majority at any one time says that they are.

Thus, the problem of human values can become a matter of style. Playwrights in revolt will give their characters those values necessary to achieve their ends. Consequently, the theatre in our times often holds our attention because age-old values people have long believed to be true are debated and even discarded. Our most energetic modern theatre concerns characters who are caught in this revolution in value judgments.

Idea. One of the crucial points about style in drama is that ideas in plays *become lost in time.* When we lose the context of a period, we also have great difficulty in reestablishing the ideas that made the plays of that period live in their day. Until fairly recently, the production of historical drama was approached only as storytelling drama with no other purpose than to show human motives and actions. In this sense, they were dead plays, because they were far removed from the heat and conflict of our own day—the quality in present-day drama that makes us pay attention. Nowadays, many directors approach the old drama quite differently because they have come to believe that such drama can also exist on the idea level if the ideas can somehow be pulled out of them; and also, that these plays are no different from modern plays but only seem so because we cannot feel the ideas easily. At the basis of this approach is the concept that plays always have underlying ideas and that *plays are written out of an assumed context which its audience takes for granted.* Thus, in this view, it is not that the historical dramas lacked ideas, but that we have lost the contexts in which they were written; and if we can only discover the contexts, we can find out what made them vivid and living experiences to the audiences who saw them, and consequently, we can bring them alive for audiences today.

The point of style, then—whether one is considering modern *or* historical plays—is what the playwright chooses to write about. What are the ideas in an author's plays that make him distinct from other playwrights?

The implication here is that no matter when a play was written, a director must search for the idea at its core if he is to fully comprehend that play. There is, of course, no reason why such ideas cannot be expressed in humanistic terms, but why an author chooses to write about specific ideas is very important. In today's approach to production, it is not the updating of plays that interests directors but why they were written in the first place. To discover the idea behind a play is to discover the need for producing it. Production that lacks this purpose will be diffuse and vague.

It is also true that many plays are unified primarily by idea—especially contemporary drama. *Hair,* the rock musical of the 1960s, for example, is not held together by a connected story but by a theme or concept. Often these plays do not have characters in the usual sense—the actors do not pretend to be someone else. They are agents of the play, and thus of the idea. Expressionistic, Brechtian, and Absurdist plays are also idea-unified on a different level.

Here are some suggestions about style in ideas:

1. If you want to understand Ibsen, read a play from each of his four periods and compare the ideas in each.
2. Perform a similar experiment with Chekhov, although you will find that his plays are written over a shorter time span. Why are the ideas in each of his plays harder to separate?
3. Now look at the ideas Edward Albee uses. How do they differ from Harold Pinter's? From Samuel Beckett's? From Bertolt Brecht's? From Eugène Ionesco's? (Note that each playwright in this group is characterized stylistically by the ideas each develops in his plays.)
4. What is the idea in Euripides' *The Bacchae?* Read some recent criticism of this play to compare with your own ideas about it. Do you have any comprehension of what Shakespeare wanted to do with *I Henry IV?* With *Othello?* With *As you Like It?* What was Molière's idea in *Les Précieuses Ridicules?*
5. Study the ideas in Brecht's *Mother Courage* and *The Good Woman of Setzuan.* How do they specifically mark his style?

Moods and Tempos. Although moods and tempos derive from the more basic elements of action and characters, they can explicitly mark style. The making of moods is the goal of the playwright, as it is also that of the director, and it is what we as an audience sense first. Some playwrights—Chekhov, Saroyan, and Williams, for instance—have such lyrical capabilities that the moods they create tend to dominate their plays, and we characterize them explicitly as mood dramatists, and by this designation mean that their most prominent mark of style lies in the quality of the moods they make. But all plays reach and hold audiences through the power of the moods they are able to evoke, with one fact quite clear: moods must be inherent in the playscript, for they cannot be overlaid on a script during production.

The first good reading of a play should tell you about its moods. Now is the time to note whether they are unusual and vigorous enough to declare a point of style. Later, after you have studied the play, you may find it more difficult to decide.

Tempos can be treated in the same way—by early discovery. Writers are characterized by their sense of rhythm. Can you recognize anything distinctive in a play you presently have under consideration? Do you sense the strong variations in tempos? Is your playwright musically-minded? What can be played very rapidly? What must move very slowly? Are there strongly marked differences in contrast throughout? Does the author have a marked sense of pause?

If you can detect the moods and tempos in several plays by the same author, you have probably found his basic rhythms. Some directors specialize in staging the plays of certain authors simply because they feel themselves in close harmony with an author's rhythm. But finding such rhythm is no easy matter. Because moods and tempos are more subjective than the other elements, it is often difficult to know, as a director, whether you have caught the style-rhythm of the author or are merely showing your own style-rhythm. A director has as many problems with letting his own personality show at the expense of a playscript as an actor has in trying to create a characterization.

Synthesis of Style: A Work Sheet for Style-Analysis

It is obvious that by summarizing all the points of style you have collected in this advanced level of play-analysis, you will be making not only a style-analysis of a playwright's work in general but also a style-analysis of a particular play. One point is very important: in working on this summary statement *you must do it in stylistic terms* and *not* in terms of basic play-analysis. In other words, style-analysis *assumes* a knowledge of form and content; if you have made a form-content description, doing a style-analysis will be relatively easy. Therefore, always study the play first in terms of form-content analysis before trying to set out the style-analysis. If you do not work in this order, you will miss important aspects of style because you will not understand the content well enough to collect all the elements.

The study of style in a particular play, then, is the study of its individuality. But before you could write a job recommendation for a person, you would first have to know a good deal about him; a style-analysis is a personal recommendation of a play in the most specific and heartfelt terms. "Style is the man," and you know the man well.

What follows is a suggested procedure for making a style-analysis. As you will note, it is a summary of the content of this chapter. Therefore, the purpose of the Work Sheet is to help you discover a play's style by pinning down its individuality. You must remember that you are new to play directing, and that later on, when you have acquired experience in style-analysis in depth, much of what you will find difficult to do here you will later do very easily and quickly. But now is the time to teach yourself efficient procedures for the careful scrutinizing that style-discovery requires.

Style-Analysis Work Sheet

1. A style-analysis should not be made until a play-analysis, as outlined on pages 63 to 65, has been completed because the content of this second analysis must be based on the accumulated content of the first. If you do a careful play-analysis in depth, you will have the facts neecssary for answering the questions introduced here.

2. Never force your play-analysis when you are looking for answers to the questions on style. If your proof is not readily available, it may not be in the text of the play. Be honest with both yourself and the play. Remember that the style of a playscript is based explicitly on what is there, not on what you imagine is there, though you may have to use your imagination extensively to pin down the explicit.

3. The order of development of a style-analysis is the same as for play-analysis. Stay with that order and you will better understand the relationships of the basic structural elements in a play.

4. Your intention in a style-analysis *is to look for the individualities* in a playscript. But remember that an author will share major aspects of style with his contemporaries. These major aspects are part of the statement of style and should be recorded as such. This approach is particularly essential in defining Realism where you will too easily take many stylistic devices for granted because they seem to fall within common usage. Therefore, be certain to look closely for variations on that usage.

5. The form of the style-analysis work sheet is arranged to cover the seven basic elements of play structure. The questions in each section are intended as suggestions and reminders of what to look for. The actual completion of such a work sheet may take the form of essay answers as long as they are brief, clear, and exactly stated. Do not use the questions as an end in themselves, but rather as a springboard to guide you to your own perception.

I. *Given Circumstances*

A. *Environmental Facts.* Is specific emphasis placed on any one of the categories? (Your answer here may well tell you the particular socio-political bent of your playwright and the play you are dealing with.)

B. *Previous Action.* How much is used? Is there a specific emphasis on a certain kind of previous action? How it is inserted into the play: all in the first part or sprinkled throughout? How expert is the author in presenting previous action through present dramatic action? Where does the dramatic action begin in relation to the previous action: near the beginning with a minimal previous action or near the end with much previous action? What sort of thing is recalled: situations, character delineations, psychological flavorings, and so forth.

C. *Polar Attitudes.* What sort of poles has the playwright set up? Are they fresh? Are they obvious? Is the principal character readily declared through your analysis of the poles? How many characters are given polar positions, that is, potential for change?

II. *Dialogue*

What is distinctive? Has the playwright a listening ear? Does he use words in an individual way? Beyond the basic dramatic actions, what marks the speeches? Does he use characterizing phrases and repeat them? Does he use monologues (Chekhov, O'Neill, Osborne)? What marks the length of the speeches? Is he witty? Of what does his wit consist? If it is other than prose, what characterizes the verse form? Does the playwright have genuine capability for using verse forms, or are they laid on? If a line were to be quoted, what would declare its individuality? Does the playwright have a poetic quality, a sense of mystery, in his dialogue? How obvious is the dialogue?

III. *Dramatic Action*

A. *Unities.* Does the author observe or violate the unity of time? Of place? Of action? How tight is the unity of action and what makes it so? Does observance of the unities give the play an artificial or a natural flavor? How far ranging is the action? Are there many minor plots or only a few? How tightly are the minor plots connected with the main plot or with each other?

B. *Type.* What is the type of action? How can you support this emphasis from the detailed action? If it is tragic, what specifically makes it so? If it is comic, what specifically makes it so? If the emphasis is divided, how is this division done? Why? Does the action declare the play a melodrama or is the action only melodramatic? Why? Is the action farcical or comedic with farcical moments? Why? If the action is tragic, how does it stand up against Aristotle's definition in the *Poetics?* If it is comic, how does it stand up against Henri Bergson's definition? Against George Meredith's? If you label the play serious, why?

C. *The Ending.* How is the ending of the action handled? Do the characters make discoveries about themselves? Is a *deus ex machina* used?

D. *Technical Development.* How are the *climaxes* handled? Are the methods of discovery logical and exciting? How quickly does the first action begin? How would you describe the surges in the play?

IV. *Characters*

A. *Choice.* What sort of people does the author write about? Why is the author interested in these types? How conventional are the characters? Are they conformist or relatively free? Are there any fantastic or allegorical characters? Why are they used?

B. *Development.* How finely drawn are the characters? Are they types or individuals? Why?

C. *Values.* What motivates the author in drawing his characters? Does he let them go free? Are they positive or negative people? Why or why not? If the play contains a hero (tragedy), what makes him one? If it contains a fool (comedy), what makes him one?

V. *Idea*

A. *Choice.* In comparing this play with others by the same author, what sort of ideas does he like to treat? Is the idea in this play fresh or worn? Why?

B. *Validity.* Is the author an original thinker in any way? Does the idea have validity today? Why or why not? Is the author moralistic in the presentation of his idea or purely objective?

C. *Motivation.* Does the author seem to care strongly about the idea in his play?

D. *Quality.* Is the idea poetic? Is it purely practical? What is the potential of the idea for survival?

VI. *Tempos*

Does the author have a musical sense? How can you prove the answer from the playscript? How sharp are the variations in tempo? Does the author tend to use erratic tempos, fast tempos, or are they slow and stately? What kind of music does the playscript suggest to you? How individual, how original is the author's musical sense? Is the rhythm of this play typical among the author's works? Can you describe his rhythm?

VII. *Moods*

Is the play a mood play; that is, is it distinctly marked by mood dominance?   Do moods tend to dominate logic?   How do the mood-arousing techniques used by this author differ from those of another?   How much does word choice have to do with mood arousal?   Does the author use theatricality or business for mood arousal or does he generate the moods directly from clashes in the dramatic action?   Are the moods odd or relatively usual?

VIII. *Summary of Style*

You should now make a summary statement of the style by noting the points in your analysis that you think have the greatest emphasis.   If you can integrate them in a conclusive statement of this sort, you will pin down your play as an individuality, for the summary is the epitome of your style-analysis.

EXERCISES

You will have to practice style-analysis extensively until you see clearly what must be done and why you are doing it.   The tendency at first will be to revert to the content of play-analysis because it is easier to deal with content readily perceived than to deal with it as an overview.   But with practice you will learn to separate the two levels of analysis and become much more articulate at the higher level.

The exercises that follow are intended to enrich your experience in style-analysis by leading you into divergent areas of play structure, beginning with the plays more familiar to you and progressing to the more difficult and removed ones.   As you will note, the exercises are presented more as challenges than as specific problems to be completed.

You must remember that although the exercises begin at the style-analysis level, it is expected that you will first complete a play-analysis before beginning at the second level.

1. Do a style-analysis of *Riders to the Sea.*   Can you see it as a play about three women instead of Maurya alone?   Is the play a tragedy?   If so, how does Synge get his tragic effect?

2. Do a style-analysis of *Ghosts.*   Is this a romantic story about the sins of a father, or is it an attack on a blind, middle-class morality upheld by a confused and weak clergy?   Is Pastor Manders a villain or a comic fool?

3. Do a style-analysis of Chekhov's *Uncle Vanya.*   Is it a comedy or a tragedy?   How can some critics say that there is very little dramatic action when every page seems crammed with it?   How does Chekhov handle dialogue?   How does he handle mood values?

4. Do a style-analysis of Shaw's *Man and Superman.*   How does Shaw handle dramatic action?   Why is there so little of it?   Is there great activity in the

dialogue? What sort of characters does Shaw deal with here? Why? Is the play all Shaw-talk, or are distinctive characters developed? Why is the play a comedy?

5. Do a style-analysis of Pirandello's *Six Characters in Search of an Author*. How does Pirandello tear apart the premises behind Realistic psychological drama? Is the play structurally classical in its use of the unities and denouement?

6. Do a style-analysis of Elmer Rice's *Adding Machine*. Why is it categorized as an Expressionistic play? What is the play's intention? How is dialogue and character handled? Is the play a comedy?

7. Do a style-analysis of Bertolt Brecht's *Mother Courage*. Why does the dramatic action seem to have no climax but seem to be joined end to end? What is the function of the songs? How does Brecht use given circumstances to make his play meaningful today?

8. Do a style-analysis of Ionesco's *The Bald Soprano*. Can you see it as a conventional, classical comedy with a well-developed, logical action, conventional character types, climax, and denouement? How can you be easily misled by the dialogue?

9. Do a style-analysis of Marlowe's *Doctor Faustus,* using the *B* text with the comic scenes. How did Marlowe violate classical notions of a tragedy? What characterizes Marlowe's poetic line? Did Marlowe intend an allegory on his own times, an attack on his own political confinement?

10. Do a style-analysis of Molière's *Les Présieuses Ridicules*. How does the translation or version you are using present Molière's style in comparison with that found in other versions? Why is this play a comedy? What was Molière's motivation in writing it? Does it have present-day meanings?

11. Do a style-analysis of Farquhar's *The Beaux' Strategem*. What does Farquhar intend beyond a simple story of high jinks? What can get through to an audience today? How does Farquhar devise dramatic action in this play? What characterizes Farquhar's style in dialogue?

12. Do a style-analysis of Goldsmith's *She Stoops to Conquer*. What characterizes Goldsmith's handling of dramatic action? Does the play contain satire? Why? How is it easy to dismiss this play today as only shenanigans? What are its strongest eighteenth-century qualities?

23

the director as stylist

When applied to play production, *form* means the *general shape* of the staging. This definition implies that a playscript has been physicalized on an available stage, that it has been given some sort of scenic investiture (not necessarily flat scenery), that it has been costumed and lighted (perhaps only with daylight), and that it has been acted, at least in a minimum way. All staged plays thus have form because they observe the basic premise that makes the theatre different from the other arts: a play is a story devised for presentation on a stage by actors before an audience. As we have pointed out earlier in this part of the book, the basic form in production has remained unchanged since the fifth century B.C. It is production style that has changed.

Style in production, as in playscripts, means "specific individuality," and it is thus a major step beyond form. Again, as we pointed out earlier, we use the word *style* to define not only the general characteristics of staging in any particular age but also the specific characteristics of an individual production. By the former definition, we simply mean the collective use of those conventions in staging that each age developed and kept in use for a period of time to enable it to express its own plays in a specific way (Elizabethan style; Restoration style, etc.). Which comes first—change in playwriting style or change in staging style—is very difficult to determine, but whichever brings the initial pressure, the fact remains that style does change and both playwriting and production are mutually affected, for each is trying to answer the needs of the other.

This chapter is concerned, however, only in part with historical production style. The major focus is on the director and how he is able to express himself through style. The subject we are discussing, then, is the director as stylist—perhaps his only reason nowadays for being in the theatre. Although we have only rare records as evidence, the stage manager as an organizer and assembly man must have existed throughout the history of the theatre, because someone with a knowledge of staging has always been needed to help arrange the basic form. Before stage managing became a specifically named job, the actor-manager of an average company probably worked out some details with the stage carpenter and his crew of painter-helpers and property men. If he wanted to go to the great expense of new scenery, he either turned the job over to the stage carpenter, who was also usually a painter, or he brought in a special architect-engineer-painter to do the job. The general style of a particular period was thus taken for granted. Theatre was something you did in a particular way and everyone did it much the same way.

The introduction of the scenic artist in the sixteenth century complicated the problem tremendously because here was a stylist—someone with a specific staging idea in mind. When presentation in the nineteenth century had advanced to the point where a new scenic background was needed not only for each play but also usually for several scenes in each play; when costumes of a like specificity were needed to go along with the scenery and had to be provided, not by the actor, but by a producer; when stage lighting became so controllable through the introduction of electricity that new effects never before seen on the stage became possible; when actors were hired, not for a stock season but for a single production— with all these changes a new type of theatrical manager was needed, and that manager was called the director. At first, he was largely a glorified stage manager hired for his knowledge of the theatre crafts and for his ability to help design the various aspects of a production and then to bring them all together into a single whole. With few exceptions, most directors made no pretense of being artists; they saw their jobs as practical craftsmen who assembled a production for their employer—the producer. The actors knew their jobs as actors, and, as long as the plays fell into similar patterns, there was no need to be anything else than a good craftsman who knew all of the jobs in the theatre.

The scenic revolution in Europe that came early in the twentieth century drastically changed this point of view, and out of it emerged the twentieth-century director as a stylist. In the "art-theatre," he was now expected to exert a strong artistic influence over the entire production. What an audience would see and hear would be first sifted through his eyes and ears and thus through his emotional responses. Historians of the American theatre have pointed out that the new director was responsible in many ways for the artistic surge in the theatre in the 1920s and 1930s, and that many of the best productions owed their unusual successes to talented directors. Many productions previously might have received only minimal attention in routine stagings, but because they were now staged in exceptional ways by directors of unusual theatrical vision they achieved both critical praise and box-office success.

The modern director, then, serves more than the function of effecting synthesis in play production. His job is to be a stylist—an individualist. But because the theatre has always been and always will be a group art, the director, if he is to be a stylist at all, must learn how to lead his fellow craftsmen to creativity beyond themselves and to making the unique production that he envisions.

A director can be a stylist only by being adventurous, but he must first be a born leader. He earns the name of director only when he is capable of both in a superior way.

Arts-and-Crafts Histories and Archeology as Background Studies

Because a great deal of a production style is expressed in visual languages, whether or not a director deals with modern or historical plays he must have a sensitive and detailed knowledge of the past. When objects or dress are new, the people who invent them use them naturally and freely because they have discerned their need and can take their functionalism for granted. But when we use historical objects or historical dress, if we are to prevent them from "using" the actors, a situation that never fails to draw attention to the objects or dress and away from the dramatic action, someone—and the someone is the director—must know their original need and thus their proper use. The same thinking applies explicitly to set design, whether it is a wall treatment, a furniture piece, a door, or a stairway that is being considered. Guessing is no substitute for knowing what is right.

This statement has never been more important than it is today when we frequently abstract historical places. The style of presentation may only suggest a specific locale; yet, the design must start from a reality since all true abstractions are firmly rooted in real-life usage. Conversely, side-by-side with the "theatre of suggestion" is the "theatre of realistic reproduction," a style that may continue for many decades, as we continue to live in an age of science where we are very much interested in explicit circumstances. Some settings we see on the stage today are almost as exact in their photographic realism as any that Antoine brought onto the stage in the 1890s during the height of Naturalism. The style of Realism as we have known it during the twentieth century is far from dead, and the director must be thoroughly familiar with real places if he is to exercise any control over the design of a production.

Of equal importance with scenic investiture is costume. The history of clothes is required knowledge not only for designing stage wear but also for acting in such wear because real clothes had and have movement of their own making. If you visit the Smithsonian Institute in Washington, D. C., you can see nearly two hundred years of women's evening dress in the wax museum of former presidents' wives. The fun in viewing this collection lies in imagining how these dresses moved and what their animate possibilities were. The large flowing skirts would have had much more activity than the confined dresses of the 1920s and 1930s. Such knowledge of dress can tell one much about decorum; and since decorum is style, directors can be sure to bring style onto the stage if their awareness of clothing is highly developed. A farce by Feydeau, for example, would be very poor without such awareness. Actors expect directors to have this information at hand, although they may pursue the subject on their own.

A background for the making of style, then, is the study of archeology, within which the study of portrait painting may be the most rewarding because painting explicitly mirrors the past. Everyday crafts also tell us much, as do studies of music and architecture. A director is constantly on the museum route, not in self-conscious search for what may later be useful but because he is naturally curious about the past. Much of play production is museumlike because its intention is to show the mirrors of the past ages. The director is also an avid reader of social, economic, and cultural history because he must know what a playwright takes for granted that his audiences will bring to the theatre without his explicit mention in the play. The actual style of production may well be far from exact *re*production, but such stagings all begin with a keen awareness of what real places and real clothes looked like.

Historical Play Production as Background

APPROACH AND USES

Historical play production as a term means the production of plays in their *original context* insofar as that context can be determined. As we have already suggested, we go to the real life of a historical period for source materials in stage design, but directors must also be highly knowledgeable about theatre history if they are to understand the old plays at all. Awareness of theatre architecture and how plays were produced is invaluable simply because playwrights have always taken for granted the stage machine for which they were writing, since they were making skeletons to be fleshed out and clothed by production. The study of the artifacts of theatre history can tell us much about the buildings and the productions in them.

Historical stage costume is much more difficult to ascertain accurately because few records exist to tell us explicitly what was worn. Until well into the nineteenth century, costumes for plays were usually devised by the actors themselves. They simply wore what they considered appropriate because coordination in design was not established as a premise in staging except in court masques. But it is the rarity of visual historical records that makes this study fascinating. As you continue with directing, you will learn to look everywhere for hints—at paintings of actors (not very reliable), at line drawings and etchings, at brief descriptions some viewer thought worth setting down. Your eye for such detail needs careful exercising.

WHAT TO LOOK FOR IN
HISTORICAL PLAY PRODUCTION

Since each period production style will differ in what it emphasizes in form, the study of any particular period will revolve around the basics of all production form: (1) stage shape and audience position; (2) scenic investiture; (3) properties; (4) costuming; (5) lighting; (6) makeup; (7) sound; (8) acting conventions. The intention in the following material is not to itemize what constitutes style in any one period—knowledge you can acquire only in an organized study of theatre history—but to show the general nature of historical style and the value of such knowledge. Too many students regard theatre history as a peripheral rather than as a central study in their work, a point of view that you simply cannot hold if you are to be a director.

The following list of what to look for is presented in the form of an inquiry sheet in order to point out the range of your necessary study, for you may apply these questions to any period in theatre history. As a continuation of the material included in Chapter 15 (pp. 202–204), this sheet encourages you to search out theatre history as explicitly as you can in the interest of discovering the nature of production style. You will certainly add to the list of questions here as you continue to make detailed historical studies on your own.

For class study, it is suggested that the question sheet be applied to at least two different periods of theatre history so that the production style of each can be seen in contrast. The general assignment can be broken down further by alloting each of the primary areas to a few students, who will then pursue the search in detail and report their findings to the class. Make a list of new questions raised in the general discussion.

A Check Sheet for Historical Play Production

1. *Stage*

   Where does the audience sit or stand in relationship to the stage? How close?

   Is the stage raised above the audience or lowered below it?

   Is the stage raked? How much?

   Is the stage roofed? If so, what purpose does the roof serve?

   What is the exact shape of the stage? Is there an apron?

   Is the stage floor trapped? Why?

2. *Scenery*

   Is the scenery a permanent architectural facade? If so, why? What purpose does such a facade serve? What does it do in terms of line and mass?

   How do actors gain entrance to the stage? How do entranceways affect the speed of entrance and the relationship to action already going on?

   Is the scenery fabricated and changeable? If so, what are the active functions of such scenery? What is done with line, mass, and color? How real is such scenery? How much of the stage is occupied by scenic investiture? Are the stage spaces above used?

   What are the acting areas and how effective are they?

3. *Properties*

   What is the quantity and extent of the set properties? If none are used, why not?

   How real are they?

   Are they carried onto the stage or previously set?

   How often do actors use hand properties in acting? (Confine your answer to historical use, not what you would do as a director.) What kind of properties do they use?

4. *Costuming*

   Why are costumes used? (Do not take the fact that costumes are used for granted, but try to pin down your answer.)

   Is what is worn costume or clothes?

How are line, mass, and color employed?

What is their potential for movement?

What is the silhouette for both men and women?

5. *Lighting*

Is daylight or artificial light used?   What would daylight accomplish? If artificial, what is the method?   What effects can be achieved?

Where does the light originate?

Is the audience lighted with the same light as the actors?   Why?

6. *Makeup*

What function does makeup serve?

What techniques are used?   How widely do they range?

7. *Sound*

What kind of sound effects are used?

How are sound effects made?

Are they live sounds or mechanically reproduced?

Is music used?   How?

8. *Acting*

How is movement employed?

What is the size and the scope of gesture?

What sorts of compositions are used?   Is the full stage used or only a portion of it?

How well is the actor heard?   How does he probably project his voice? Is speaking the primary theatricality?   Why?

Modern Designations of Style

Although theatre historians have tended to categorize theatre history into periods with the style designated along national or cultural lines (i.e., Greek, Roman, Medieval, English, Renaissance, Jacobean, Restoration, French classical, etc.), we have frequently followed the language of art used in designating styles in painting for naming modern production styles.   With the modern period now over a century old, we have accumulated a number of labels to specify style: Naturalism; Realism; Simplified Realism; Surrealism; Symbolism; Expressionism; Formalism; Theatricalism, and others.   These have been used as a means of grouping productions on the basis of the way staging has been done, for labels can be attached to a production style only after the style has appeared and has been recognized. Also, in large part these names apply usually to scenic investiture, although they occasionally describe costumes and makeup; only rarely are they applied to acting because acting is a human thing that cannot easily be forced into formalistic patterns without being self-conscious or quite non-human.

Once you have concerned yourself with style, you will quickly learn the jargon that accompanies modern stylistic description. Consequently, no specific expositions of these terms are given here. But for all practical purposes, there are only two major designations for modern production style that concern the director: (1) Realism and (2) Departures from Realism. These designations assume that Realism is the base from which other modern styles depart. Once you grasp this concept, you will have little difficulty in following what has happened to production styles since 1870.

Nor will you need to join the labelers of style at this time but can devote your energies to making descriptions in your own language on the basis of what you see and hear and thus what you comprehend. That labeling serves the function of separating differences is, of course, recognized, but the label alone will do no more than provide a general view because it must be attached to a group of like productions. Specific designations, on the other hand, must be based on analysis. By dividing all modern production, then, into the two major groups of Realism and Departures from Realism, you can proceed to specific labeling as you accumulate knowledgeable experience in production, not only through the actual process itself but also through diverse theatregoing experiences and through looking at photographs of productions. Do not let yourself be confused by the labeling, by the categorizing; learn to make style-analyses by yourself and leave the labeling to others until you are ready for it. Eventually, you should become familiar with the labels attached to departures from Realism since they are so widely used and may become confusing to you if you do not know one from another.

Again, the intention in this chapter is not to undertake a detailed breakdown of the differences in modern styles but to plant an approach to the problem so that you may pursue it and grow with it at your own speed. Of very great help are two major discussions on the subject that you should read: Mordecai Gorelik's *New Theatres for Old* and John Gassner's *Form and Idea*. Style is a complicated subject for the learning director, and only through study can he begin to formulate his own ideas about it. He may already have a strong, natural sense of style within himself, but he can learn how to exploit it only by becoming aware of what options lie open to him. Makers of style lead the way and others follow; but no stylist ever works in a vacuum.

What follow are brief descriptions of the two areas of concern in modern production: (1) Realism and (2) Departures from Realism. You must remember that the subject under discussion is style in play production and not style in dramatic writing, and you must also keep in mind that the former can take form only after the the latter has been studied and digested.

REALISM

The range of Realism has been so wide during the hundred years of its history that we cannot describe it easily as one style. But simply stated, it moves from exact photographic reproduction (Naturalism, or reproducing nature exactly as it is seen with the eye) to a form so simplified that many aspects are only suggested (for example, painted molding in place of real molding). Whatever the gradation may be, the intention is to show life as it actually appears to be. Realism is therefore a style to describe appearances. Because human beings live their lives surrounded by these appearances, it is assumed that we can understand them as individuals if we can see them in the midst of their specific, viewable surroundings.

That this point of view (aesthetic) is seriously open to question is revealed in the fact that no sooner had Realism been established as a style in the 1890s than the new stylists damned it as unpoetic, as noncommunicative, as inartistic, and as simply untrue to life. From that point on, we have had a steady stream of "departures from Realism," but not one has succeeded in completely replacing it.

DEPARTURES FROM REALISM

As this phrase implies, it includes all production styles that move away from the literal appearances of things. The basic intention of these styles is to communicate through essence rather than through appearance. The audience is given the feeling of something, and consequently, it is able therefore to receive the communication in direct terms. This aesthetic approach assumes that real objects do not communicate well because they are so familiar that most people do not perceive them, and thus cannot feel them. The artist, therefore, creates lines and masses that contain essences of real objects, and we are then able to *feel* them directly without the distractions of familiarity and everyday use. As viewers, we find these symbolizations exciting and illuminating not only because of their direct communication, but also because we may actually be perceiving the objects for the first time in our lives, not just seeing them. Art is an emotional experience and not an intellectual one.

One of the principal points about using such a label as *departures from Realism* for production designation is that it readily parallels departures from Realism in playwriting. We can see the two moving side by side since the 1890s. But it does not necessarily follow that the departures from Realism in plays will all require departures from Realism in production. Here is a crucial question about modern style: When can departures in production be used most effectively?

In the 1950s and 1960s, after several decades that thought dramaturgical style should be supported by the same sort of production style—that is, Realistic plays should have Realistic settings, and departure plays should have departure settings—what seemed to be thoroughly accepted has given way to a new style. Today, we have no confining rules about style because anything that will work with audiences goes. This flexibility means that Realistic plays can be effectively produced using departure approaches, and departure plays can be effectively produced using Realistic approaches. Thus, dramatic writing and production style are recognized as two separate and distinct areas of theatre as far as style is concerned. Approaches to production under this aesthetic will be treated in Chapter 25.

Adventure and Experiment

How much of an artistic gambler are you? Unless you are willing to venture as an idea man in the theatre, you will never become a stylist and thus will never fulfill your total function as a director. It should be perfectly clear to you by now that taking risks is not done for adventure's sake, but that it emerges out of the strongest integrity and the highest regard for limitations in the theatre. Yet, even with these apparent restrictions, you can move out alone and make something that can be called style.

A director's statement of style is the physicalization of a play in such a way that an audience is lifted into a fresh and exciting perception of it. Style excites because it communicates emotionally; it can never be dull because it is a very personal, very intimate statement.

If you are an adventurist, you are ready to proceed with the next game: The Making of Style.

24

the making of style: general problems

The making of style by a director is unlike that by a playwright, actor, or designer, for it is always a more or less self-conscious process. Ideas certainly come to him in a subjective way in his "dream moments" about a play during his early readings, but, sooner or later, he must use designers and actors to work out his dreams for him, and thus comes about the self-consciousness of communication to others. Because style is conveyed through physicalization, every aspect of the physical production comes under a director's close scrutiny and is turned toward making the production do what he wants it to do.

Certain problems of style must be met head on in the production of all plays. Those problems are discussed in this chapter.

Choosing the Dramatic Emphasis

The crucial point in style-making comes at the very beginning when the director makes a firm basic decision concerning the kind of statement he wants to make about a play. Every other move in this complex chess game will hinge on this decision. The director must, therefore, do his homework thoroughly so that he does not discover later in the rehearsal period, when it may be too late to redesign the production, that he has gotten off on the wrong track. As we have continuously pointed out in this book, a thorough play-analysis, which now includes style-analysis, can lead to sensitive decision making, for what your dramatic imagination may see in a play can be quite different from what someone else sees. Your individual seeing, then, will be the basis of your style.

Two very basic decisions must be made: (1) Whose play is it; that is, which character is dominant? (2) What is the spine of the action?

Before we are very aware of style, we are apt to assume that plays have limited basic meanings and that the principal characters are always declared. Thus, *Antigone* is about Antigone; *Macbeth* is about Macbeth; *Tartuffe* is about Tartuffe; *Ghosts* is about Mrs. Alving. This assumption may be true up to a point, but, beyond that, individual opinion comes into play, for we make the play we see and feel. All we have to do is to place a very strong actor in what appears to be the second role and we literally see a new play. Why cannot Cassius, instead of Brutus, dominate Shakespeare's *Julius Caesar*? (It is obvious that Caesar is only an instrument.) Or Mark Anthony? Cannot Creon become the principal role in *Antigone*? Lady Macbeth in *Macbeth*? Orgon in *Tartuffe*? Oswald Alving or Pastor Manders in *Ghosts*? Is Anouilh's *Becket or the Honor of God* about Becket or about the King? (Remember that Laurence Olivier switched from Becket to King Henry after playing the first role for many performances.)

Plays, you may argue, are about both the protagonist and the antagonist, and both must be given equal positions. But doing precisely that may weaken a play's structure considerably. It will be far better to settle on one character and give him prominence in every way. You then have not begged the issue but have presented a clear point of view. You may be prejudiced, but audiences can argue with your view or see something new in it. When Tyrone Guthrie cast a black actor as Horatio in his Minneapolis production of *Hamlet* in 1963, he greatly changed the significance of this supporting role and, along with it, the usual conception of Hamlet as a character. What would you make of the play on those terms?

Characters are, of course, *the result* of the action in a play, for we see what they are primarily on the basis of what they do. Therefore, character and action are intertwined in such a way that one declares the other; for once a character has been established, he cannot be artificially manipulated; that is, he cannot be made to do things in violation of his character without stretching our sense of logic to the breaking point. (Have you read Robert Ardrey's *Thunder Rock,* in which one character tries artificially to manipulate a set of characters he has imagined only to find out that it is impossible to do so?) Yet, it is possible to let actions lead our imaginations in certain directions by building up evidence in those directions. When Olivier made his film of *Hamlet,* he shocked critics and audiences alike with his strong emphasis on the Freudian aspects of the characters. Is Hamlet in love with his mother? Through a succession of scenes in which the camera probed Hamlet's subjective self, he built this point into a major emphasis. When the same actor played Othello as a full-blooded African Negro, with emphasis on Negroid physical features in face and body, he created another fresh view of a character in action—a fully declared style for the play. In an age when many people both fear and are intensely curious about miscegenation, he played on the full value of that fear-curiosity and thus startled his audiences into new vision. *Romeo and Juliet,* played by teenagers instead of mature actors as it was in Zeferelli's Old Vic production in 1961 and in his moving-picture version in 1969, gave audiences quite a new experience with the play. This was style.

What can be done with *Hedda Gabler?* Is there only one way to treat it or are there several possibilities? What happens with a production if:

1. Hedda is played as a Medea-like woman who revels in her dominance of others whom she craftily destroys?
2. Hedda is played as a nymphomaniac who brings about destruction of others because of the sexual denial of her marriage and the restrictions society has placed on her?
3. Hedda is played as a woman, perhaps homosexual, who hates and despises men because she considers them inferior and who goes under only when she finally meets an equal in Judge Brack?
4. Hedda is played as a masochist, as a suicidal paranoiac, who destroys everything about her, including a possible child before birth?
5. Hedda is played as a selfish, self-centered virgin who cannot stand violation of herself in any possible way?
6. Hedda is played as a "good" woman?

All these are options open to a director in his decision-making role. What his individual decision turns out to be will determine the style of his production.

Up to this point, serious plays have been under discussion, but you must be aware that decisions about comedies and farces may be even more difficult to make because the director must decide what is really funny in a play and how he can convey that joke to an audience. Comedy exists in the theatre only when a director and actors themselves understand the incongruities, for only then will they know how to reach an audience with the fun of a play. Deciding whose play it is and accordingly making gradations in the comedy are absolutely essential if a production is to have stylistic unity. Feydeau's *A Flea in Her Ear* cannot exist on its second-act chase scene alone but must be carefully constructed as both a comedy of manners and a comedy of characters in the first and third acts.

She Stoops to Conquer is not just about Tony Lumpkin's high jinks but must also be about Mrs. Hardcastle's pretensions, about Mr. Hardcastle's puritanism, and about Marlow's impotence with well-bred women.   If young Marlow is played straight—that is, as only a bashful young man —the principal comedy may not come through nearly as well as when he is played as an experienced London rake who moves unerringly among servant girls or among the demimonde but turns to rubber when confronted with middle-class "goodness."   If a director does not discover how to make *The Way of the World* or *The Importance of Being Earnest* "talk well," he might better not consider either for production, since both plays depend extensively on their verbal wit.   Is Sheridan's *School for Scandal* about Joseph Surface?   If he is made the central fool in a slippery, falsely pious way, not only can he be drolly amusing like Tartuffe, but he can also cause the other fools to stand out clearly.   Without solid building of character based on decision-making about character, comedy can never work, for we are amused primarily by the incongruities in human behavior and not by the situations in which characters are caught.

Whose play is it? then, is a decision of major importance, and you can make this decision only by making the most personal and intensive examination of the action in a playscript and the characters that grow out of it.   Once you know who will dominate and why, you can determine the specific line of action you want to emphasize, and in this way declare the *spine* of your production.   Each character will relate to this spine of action exactly as you intend him to relate to the principal character. You will now have a specific and personal way to tell the story of the play on the stage *as you see it.*

Although the Stanislavskian technique of declaring the spine by using the infinitive form of the verb is rather involved (see the essay by Elia Kazan, "Notebook for *A Streetcar Named Desire*," in *Directors on Directing* ed. Toby Cole and Helen Chinoy, Indianapolis: Bobbs-Merrill, 1963), you may find it useful to reduce your decision on the action to this highly abbreviated form of summarizing.   But whatever method you use, the purpose will be to make in your mind a tight unity of your own personal vision of the action so that you can easily hold onto this central drive that will declare at the base your style of production.

Style Derives
from the Director-Designer Relationship

THE METAPHOR

You will remember in the discussion of "the design process" in Chapter 19, it was suggested that one way of establishing director-designer contact was through a master image for a production—a metaphor. Many directors and designers build productions around such images because these images are, at the base, style oriented; that is, if the metaphor is a good one, it can have continuous application with many overtones throughout the areas of design, or will, at least, work well in one area. The production style can, therefore, flow from such an image. If the playscript of *The Beaux' Stratagem,* for example, is thought of as a clever chess game, with scene after scene of subtle maneuvering, it can be carried into production with a painted floorcloth made to look like a chessboard; scenic pieces can then be whisked on and off like moves in the game, with each new setup forcing a new play by the characters involved, and so on. An approach of this sort through a metaphor certainly has limitations, but it is possible for an exciting stylistic production to emerge. However, a director should never force a designer to work in this way unless he has been so trained. It is better for the director to create such an image for himself and then use it as he can.

DOMINANCE IN SCHEME-MAKING

Production style depends greatly on physical production—what it looks like and how it works. But since a play is always seen as a fluid progression, a tight interrelationship in the choice of stage, scenery, properties, light, costumes, makeup, and sound is absolutely necessary if a style is to emerge. What the director must bring about is a production scheme that works because it enhances the actor as the principal instrument in the storytelling. It is the director's job to decide what should be dominant in a production scheme and then to tie the other designs to that dominance.

The Mermaid Theatre's production of Henry Fielding's *Lock Up Your Daughters* (1969 version) used a marvelous stage machine—a high platform raised on a pedestal, with two swinging arms, each having platforms and steps, and the entire structure mounted on a turntable. This machine not only allowed multiple locations both on the stage level, on the steps, and above on the moveable platforms, but it also provided extensive possibilities for movement in a lively and vigorously busy play. *She Stoops to Conquer* (London, 1969) was played on a modified Elizabethan stage with a sharply raked forestage, side entrances, inner-below entrances, above positions, and a neutral area surrounding the whole as a place for the garden scene. By avoiding the usual eighteenth-century wing and backdrop stage, the play was seen in a fresh way on what amounted to an Elizabethan stage.

Mart Crowley's *The Boys in the Band* (1968–69) was also staged on a modified Elizabethan stage with the scene above (the bedroom) approached by means of a curving staircase. But even more stylistic was the use of a Serlian adaptation: real furniture was placed against wall units covered with photographic murals of real rooms with furniture. The effect was a super-Realism. Equally radical was the production of *Hadrian VII* (1969) which was staged in curtains, with the exception of one interior scene (the attic). *Hair* (1968) revolutionized the American musical by not using scenery except for a small scaffolding at the rear of a huge stage space and a few carry-on pieces, and by employing an unusually complex lighting design.

Many more examples of style can be given to illustrate how various directors and designers have seen plays in action and what they have chosen to dominate the physicalization. In the constant search for style, a new convention has appeared: the more limited the scenic investiture, the more important the lighting has become as emphatic design. This convention in turn has forced changes in what to do with the lighting. Should it be full of color, or should it be primarily white light? Should back lighting be employed as a basic principle? Should the quantity of light be an important factor in the style? All these questions directors will have to answer for themselves as each production is undertaken. In costume design, we are beginning to relearn past ways as we tackle the problems presented by the open stage with its strong sculptural demands.

The significant point in this discussion is to show once again the necessity for seeing interrelationships in design and how a director can make fresh theatre out of old devices. We no longer seem to be content in the theatre with the aesthetic of peeking in on humanity but now seem to want a theatrical theatre of high image-making potential in which the audience can more directly participate.

COUNTERPOINT IN SCHEME-MAKING

Once again, it is necessary to remind you of the *counterpoint principle* discussed in Chapter 15. If you reread this section (pp. 207–208) carefully, you will see how counterpoint is essential in the development of a production style. Designs that all proceed from a single impetus will lack contrast, and even necessary conflict. A director must see that each design fulfills its particular values in a production; only in this way, will each design exert the force of its own individuality, its contributing point of style. Although this approach takes more time, it may be better for a director to orient each designer separately, as is suggested in Chapter 19, than to meet with all the designers in a group, where the dangers of single emphasis are ever present.

THE RESULTS OF GOOD SCHEME-MAKING

A production must move. This is a basic fact about the theatre—a fact that no director can ignore. Pacing a play also means pacing the scheme of production, for the style will be the rhythm of the whole. In multiple stagings where several sets are used, the quick change, perhaps in front of the audience, is an absolute necessity. In this sense, we are back to the seventeenth-century masque tradition and its influence on moveable scenery: we want the change as part of the theatrical experience. To lower the curtain and take an intermission for changing scenery—the practice of the theatre of illusion—is no longer feasible in a theatre that places so much emphasis on things happening in a spirited tempo. Style will depend on a production scheme that works.

Tempo. Can all the designs be moved with the necessary speed to provide the appropriate tempo necessary for the style? The director must decide what the tempo should be and then see that the designing is done in accordance with it. A clearly defined tempo in a production scheme will give an audience both a sense of security and a sense of rhythm of the whole. Waiting for scene changes reduces audience attention and concentration, for once a production is set in motion, it must continue to move in a rhythmic way. If changes are made on a darkened stage, they must be made in a matter of seconds because waiting in the dark brings an audience back to its own reality, making it self-conscious. The major problem usually is scenery, but costume, light, and sound also require careful designing if the scheme is to work.

Effortless Scheme-Making. Graceful scene changes, if they are visible, are as essential in production as effortless acting. Whatever is done must seem right and inevitable, for the danger lies in making an audience self-conscious of the staging effects, a situation that will reduce their attention and concentration of dramatic action and character. Rhythmic changes tend to enhance the feeling of style because they have been made part of the overall rhythm of the play and thus are integrally associated with it.

The Theatricality of Change. Is the change interesting in itself? Without drawing attention to it, does the change provide the dramatic effect of suddenly presenting a new scene, or a new costume, or a new light? The purpose of scene changes is to provide new locales and new time settings—and thus new action. But does the change contain the element of surprise? The style of your production may depend on it. What is the mood contrast in the scene change? Can the dramatic difference be clearly pointed up with dynamic effect? Therein may lie declarations of the production style.

Style Derives from the Director-Actor Relationship

CASTING FOR EMPHASIS

The style of a production will depend significantly on how a play is cast because the idea of a play, and thus its emphasis, will be set out by the particular actors who play them. Casting is, therefore, the basis of interpretation, and it plays an intrinsic part in making style. Whoever plays a role will endow it with his specific personality, no matter how carefully the chosen actor works within the confines of the action, for, by nature, actors possess radiance, and that radiance will suffuse the action. Who the director selects, then, will declare the overall style more than any other factor.

Casting is such a delicate matching of weights and qualities, partly subjective, partly objective, that there can be no sure ways to go about it. Casting is projecting the future of a production—a gambling process in which a director tries to foresee what will happen by balancing certain actors with clearly defined qualities against other actors with different qualities equally well defined. It is all weights and measures. But if the director has done his homework, and if he exerts special care in the casting process, and if he has a fair choice of actors from whom to select, the style he envisions has a good chance of emerging. Success in this aspect of production, however, can come about only if a director has a firm idea in mind of what he wants; haphazard casting can only lead to confusion.

The following are suggestions for the casting process, all of which affect style in one way or another.

Orchestrate Voices. A cast with a variety of pitch differences will not only increase the hearability level but will readily declare character qualities. We take for granted that characters in operas are written for certain voices—tenors, sopranos, bassos, etc.; but we are apt to forget that characters in plays have similar pitch requirements, although the range when compared to opera castings can be much greater and is not so stereotyped. Hear the play "in concert" during a final casting session by not looking at the actors but only by listening to them if you want to know what it is apt to sound like four weeks hence.

Size-and-Shape Type Casting Versus Anti-Type Casting. Style in production often depends on the unexpected. Visual stereotypes may be necessary in some roles, particularly those that exert no particular force on the action and that act as instruments to the main action; but individualization in casting major roles may turn a worn play or a worn idea into a fresh and vitalizing experience. Anti-type casting is casting against what seems to be prescribed type. From modern psychological drama, we have learned one important principle that pertains to all drama: what people look like on the outside does not at all prescribe what they are like within. Consequently, in casting historical drama as well as modern plays, we have turned away from nineteenth-century type-casting and more toward anti-type casting.

Where does the truth lie? Bertolt Brecht, in describing the sorts of actors he would like to play his roles, specifies "potato faces" for his women, rather than conventional good-looks. He is suggesting that it is impossible to portray the peasantry who populate his plays with conventional types, that truth lies in the rugged edges actors bring to a play rather than in their physical attractiveness. Julian Beck, in his Living Theatre productions, takes the same position: truth, and therefore beauty, lies in the spiritual values one holds and not in the visible physical realities; therefore, what we take for physical ugliness may possess inherent beauty. Further, it is possible that only by being "turned off" by unsympathetic exteriors can we begin to see the beauty behind those exteriors. But whether or not you agree with Brecht or Beck, you will discover that a high potential in production style lies in anti-type casting just as you will find that certain plays—Feydeau's or Oscar Wilde's, for instance—cannot do at all without conventional beauty in its women as well as in its men.

Special Qualities Reveal Action. The discussion above already declares the necessity for a director to cast a play in such a way that it augments what he believes to be the emphatic action. Only then can he insure that his point of style will be preserved. A large variety of actors can play a specific dramatic action fairly convincingly, but only a few will possess those essential qualities that will endow the action with moving overtones. Leading actors in the professional theatre know this fact, and they avoid roles they feel they cannot fulfill in this special way. In the amateur theatre where the director has a great deal of control, he can usually cast the actor who can best illuminate the emphasis he has in mind.

The search for special qualities, then, is the major attack in the casting process. Actual selection may revolve around whether a role should be played by a cool or by a warm actor, for these qualities cannot be acted but will be inherent projections. Some actors can project more intellectuality than others; some pure animality and nothing else. Some actors have natural decorums in voice and gesture for projecting upper-class roles, whereas others simply cannot reflect such conformist qualities of behavior.

What can be achieved in style, then, will depend on what a director can project of his action-emphasis through the actors he selects in casting.

Overcoming Blocks. What stands between a director and adventurous, more exceptional casting, and thus clear declaration of style, are the blocks of (1) playing safe, (2) forming preconceptions about certain actors, (3) seeing and hearing too many actors in casting sessions, which results in a sort of blindness and deafness, (4) failing to make objective assessments before final decisions are made. There are others, but these are the most important ones.

To help you overcome your blocks you need to develop some specific techniques that will lead you away from subjective viewing and toward objective assessment. Get yourself into the habit of making for each actor a new tryout card, on which you can record his voice quality and speech pattern, his sense of the dramatic and the theatrical, his capability at improvisation, his dominant qualities as you can see them on the surface, and his capability as an actor in general. Read each actor in several roles, particularly the ones, at the outset, you think him least qualified for and make specific comments on his card. Use closed tryouts —one actor at a time—in the interest of keeping him from copying others reading in the same roles, and of relaxing him sufficiently to show you who he is; and hold group readings or improvisational sessions only after the individual assessments have been made. You also must arrange your early tryout plan in such a way that you are always seeing actors as individuals; later when you see and hear them in groups, you will be able to see how each actor affects the balance in the group—what he can bring that will be individual and, therefore, partly declarative of style.

A highly useful technique for sorting your actors with objectivity is that of casting sheets, on which you can list in numbered columns (1) the characters in the playscript, with the men and women collected separately; (2) a brief physical description of each character, along with any special qualities essential to the role; (3) the names of all the actors who can possibly play each role; (4) tentative decision 1; (5) tentative decision 2; (6) tentative decision 3; (7) final decision. You should gather all this information on two or three sheets of paper so that you can look at the entire situation easily and comparatively. Items four through six—tentative decisions—will indicate each reassessment you make as you progress through the casting period. Before you do number six you must take a long, hard look at your choices: Are they fresh in qualities and ideas? Can you hear their voices in your mind's ear, and are they the right ones? Are you being adventurous in leading young actors away from their tired stereotypes and toward sensitive and individual statements? Are the castings who are to play the protagonist and the antagonist in strong contrast? Are there possibilities for development of each actor as an actor during the rehearsal period?

The intention of all of these questions, as you can note, is to make you aware of what lies ahead—what an audience will eventually see and

hear. Above all, if you want to declare individuality in your productions
—style—you must be as adventurous in casting them as circumstances will
permit, for fresh statements are always the statements that communicate
to audiences most easily.

VIOLENCE, SIZE, AND ENERGY

A distinct mark of style in play production is the *violence level*. Most
young directors are afraid to open all the stops for fear it will result in
overplaying and thus make the illustration appear stagey. You should
take just the opposite point of view, while recognizing at the same time
that opening the stops does not necessarily mean playing at high volumes
but often just the opposite. Good actors move audiences precisely through
the intense level of illustration they give to the violent moments, the
climactic peaks of a play. And at these peaks, they expend enormous
energy by using their bodies as great and powerful instruments of communication. If we watch them closely, we also note that gesture has
either increased or decreased markedly, for illustrations of violence require size in acting.

How you show violence on the stage, then, will reveal your sense of
style. You must never fear overplaying, for it can happen only if the
actors do not believe their dramatic action or fail to act reciprocally.
Conversely, you should fear underplaying, because it will never move an
audience beyond itself, will not carry it into the astounding mysteries of
the passions of life. Nor must you think that violence, energy, and size
apply only to great drama, for they must be used in all drama, serious or
comic. Audiences come to the theatre to feel energy vicariously; this
identification is what actually thrills them because it makes them perceive that such energy is also possible in their own lives. If you miss this
inherent point about the need for acting, you will never touch audiences.

To make the theatrical moment, then, make it in big, bold strokes
(high volumes or low volumes; big movements or practically no movement at all), for you will grab an audience and thrill it only on this basis.

THE LIGHT TOUCH

Style is also revealed by getting a play acted with "a light touch."
Can you project violence fully, and still do it with a light hand? This
question is the paradox. A light touch depends partly on directing techniques but much more on a director's natural sense of taste, for it does
not at all mean a withdrawal from intensive dramatic moments nor a
backing away in any sense from the fact that the theatre is a robust,
knockabout business. What it does mean is that audiences are neither
deeply moved nor made to laugh in the theatre if the acting is too heavy,

too stolid, too predictable. Theatre is an art form that dances and sings, and is full of surprises; it is not a slugging battle between fighters but a sparring match between boxers. A light touch means a seeming lack of effort that permits the audience to relax into the play. Poorly performed plays never let you relax because they always seem in danger of going awry.

Building imagination, then, depends on a director's sense of taste, a quality that can be cultivated if he has an inclination to find out what it means. Good theatre always has taste, for acting at its best is not reality but ideality; because selection and emphasis are possible in theatre art, what can be *suggested* is usually more powerful than what we encounter in much of everyday life. A director who plays music and lets his actors dance—both seriously and joyously—can make his points of style with clarity and feeling.

TEMPOS

Finding the appropriate tempos for a production is to discover an inherent way to project style. Tempo is always a matter of feeling; it is, therefore, deeply embedded in the personal nature of style. How a production moves will declare its style because rhythm is the basis of comprehension: we vibrate empathically if we catch the rhythm, and only then do we believe a dramatic action to be right and true.

Actors are frequently excellent musicians, but the primary job of determining tempos lies with the director because only he can control multiple actor situations. As we noted in Chapter 5 (52–55) in the basic discussion of tempos, a play, because of its structure of action, has a surging effect, like surf rolling in on a seashore where the waves grow larger and larger until they finally culminate in a climactic wave, which then may be followed by a relative calm before the next surging begins. The director's job it to find these surges and to pinpoint their beginnings and endings.

The emergence of style, then, depends on whether a director can build the surges accumulatively with variations in tempo, with pauses, and with climaxes in such a way that a performance becomes a rhythmic whole. Each performance of the play must achieve this effect or the style will be lost. This is why plays that have long runs must be frequently redirected, with redirection actually the process of finding again the rhythm that has been lost. Topflight baseball players lose their rhythm from time to time, sometimes for weeks or months, and go into a batting slump. Their recovery depends on again finding the split-timing—the inherent rhythm—that first established them at the top of their trade. So it is with actors in an ensemble; once the rhythm is lost, it must be rediscovered or audience concentration will be lost.

STYLE AND THE AMOUNT OF

ACTOR ILLUSTRATION

If you were to see a production of Racine or Corneille at the Comédie Française in Paris, you would be struck by the quietude with which the actors perform their roles. This quietude is a point of style, for it assumes that French classical drama gains its greatest effects from line delivery and not from visual spectacle. Some plays like *Le Cid* are spoken in a hushed sound, only a few steps up from whispering, with the actors making very few movements or gestures. Such a style results in a dynamic and exciting theatrical experience because the verbal delivery is so unusual in the context of minimal visual illustration. Only at the Comédie will you hear a performance like this one, and you will be struck by its unique quality of style.

How much a director gives an actor to do or encourages him to develop will be a major point of style. American directors tend toward relatively heavy visual illustration, keeping the stage constantly busy. English directors do somewhat less, with a leaning toward economy and sparseness. French directors do least of all, in comedies as well as in serious plays, preferring their classical emphasis on the spoken play, whether it is modern or historical. How much visual illustration you use will depend on your inherent sense of rhythm, and what you think your particular audience needs to keep its attention and concentration at a high level. Overillustration may make a play seem choppy and insecure. Underillustration may make it seem vague and undeclared. The only way out of this dilemma is to use *appropriate* illustration. Therefore, each play will have its own rhythm of illustration built into it, and this quality the director must find and develop in his own terms and in those of his expected audience. For the most part, learning directors tend to underillustrate, or to emphasize small, detailed movements at the expense of larger, more dynamic surges. You will, of course, discover how to handle illustration only through experience, but you must recognize at this point that style will emerge only when you use appropriate illustration.

Style, then, will depend on the kind, the quality, and the quantity of illustration your production contains. You must learn to compose a play's illustrations so that there is always room for the bigger and better ahead. Quiet beginnings can lead to dynamic endings, whereas the reverse may result in boredom. Learn to build climactically; much of the secret of audience control will lie in this capability.

25

the making of style:
specific problems

"The Making of Style" has been divided into two chapters so that you can grasp the major problems facing directors in all situations—the contents of the previous chapter—before you try to tangle with the difficulties presented by specific kinds of plays. Consequently, Chapter 24 warned you that style would emerge only if you settled on a dramatic emphasis of your own choosing; if you then gave that emphasis expression by finding a focus in the scheme-making aspects of design, which could uncover the inherent tempos and appear effortless and rhythmical; if you selected a cast that would support and augment your chosen emphasis and would be rich in voice orchestration as well as in anti-types side by side with types; and if you found the "violence level," the "light touch," the "tempos," and the "appropriate" visual and oral illustrations in the acting.

Now that you have a grasp of the general problems of making style, you are in a position to deal with the specific ones you will face when you produce historical or modern plays. You have now reached the goal of this book: the staging of plays with individuality—with style. If you have mastered all that has gone before, you are ready to attack the problems outlined in this chapter.

Production Styles with Historical Drama

THE ADVENTUROUS DIRECTOR

No young director should tackle historical drama until he has a backlog of experience in modern play production; nor should he venture into this most difficult realm of staging until he has a lively concept of styles in both playwriting and production. Historical play production is not for the novice but for the experienced director simply because, as the previous chapters have pointed out, a mature understanding of play-analysis together with a strong sense of what composes individual expression (style) are basic requirements.

Yet, the peculiar paradox is that venturing into historical play production is one of the best ways to learn about the modern theatre, for most people are able to see clearly only through strong contrasts. Not until one has a sensitive historical perspective is it possible to see the changes and distinctions in modern styles in both playwriting and production because their differences are finely drawn, and one must first understand in depth the concept of style before he can see them clearly. This book, therefore, takes the position that although period play production *for a public audience* should wait on a director's experience with modern plays, training in directing cannot be complete without experimentation with historical drama as soon as a director is ready for it. Thus, laboratory production exercises that can be readily combined with critical discussion are suggested, for you will learn a very great deal, as with all the other aspects of directing, through personal discovery. Like the other arts, play production is discovered in the doing and not in talking about it. Even though such experimentation may turn out poorly, the conscientious student will learn how to fly as well as how to restrict himself.

It follows without question, however, that all such production experience must proceed in the pattern suggested in Part IV: first, a style-analysis of the play, then, and only then, a stylistic approach to production. In this sort of laboratory experience, the use of scenery, lighting, and costumes would not usually be available, but much can be done even with these limitations; for you still can decide on an appropriate stage, determine minimum lighting, design a ground plot, and, above all, work with actors. You must learn how to handle essentials before adding other determinants of style. It is quite enough to wrestle with the ideas in an antique play; with what translations or adaptations may be available; with the problems of verse forms; with acting problems of all sorts, including the all important one: highly sensitive line readings; with the choice of stage; and with the necessary choreography.   Visual designs can wait until later when you have much better ideas about how to use them. Actors like to experiment too; so, learn all you can from them.

THE RANGE OF CHOICE

The body of historical drama, as defined here, includes all drama before 1875.   This final date is, of course, a somewhat arbitrary one, but it is used here as it is in most modern drama studies in order to mark the beginnings of Ibsenite Realism, which closely relates to the dramaturgical patterns still dominating our stage.   The production of modern drama (since 1875), then, will be treated in the next section of this chapter.

Although the range of drama throughout the twenty-four hundred years before 1875 is extensive, the actual repertoire of such plays actively produced in America would probably be less than one hundred, of which only about half are produced regularly, and the other half sporadically. European theatres, because of their national dramas and state theatres, do much better.   The following list will give you some idea of the scope of producible historical drama.   In looking at this list, however, you must keep in mind that many historical plays are given individual productions when directors discover unexpected pertinence in them, and that this list contains only the most often produced plays.

Historical Plays Produced in America in the Professional and Educational Theatres

FAIRLY FREQUENTLY	RARELY
Oedipus Rex	The Agamemnon
Antigone	The Choephori
Medea	The Eumenides
The Trojan Women	Electra (Sophocles)
The Bacchae	Prometheus Bound
Lysistrata	Hippolytus
The Birds	Hecuba
	The Frogs
	The Menaechmi
The Second Shepherds' Play	The York or Chester Cycles
Everyman	Shakespeare: 10
Shakespeare: 15	Gammer Gurton's Needle
Doctor Faustus	The Dutchess of Malfi
The Shoemaker's Holiday	The White Devil
Volpone	'Tis Pity She's a Whore
The Alchemist	Fuente Ovejuna
	Cervantes: Short plays

The Beaux' Stratagem	*All for Love*
The Country Wife	*The Way of the World*
The Imaginary Invalid	*Love for Love*
The Bourgeois Gentleman	*The Misanthrope*
Tartuffe	*The School for Wives*
The Doctor in Spite of Himself	
The Highbrow Ladies	

She Stoops to Conquer	*Mary of Scotland*
The Rivals	*Faust I*
The Mistress of the Inn	*The Contrast*
The Servant of Two Masters	*The Critic*
	The School for Scandal

The Inspector General	*A Month in the Country*
Woyzeck	*Fashion*
	Uncle Tom's Cabin
	Ten Nights in a Barroom
	Across the Country
	Rip Van Winkle

Additional Plays Produced in Europe Either Frequently or Rarely and Only Occasionally in America

A few other Classical plays in Greece
Seneca
Mandragola
Shakespeare: All other plays
The Jew of Malta
Edward II
de Vega and Cervantes in Spain
Molière: All other plays
Corneille, Racine, Marivaux and Beaumarchais in France
Goldoni in Italy
Göethe and Schiller in Germany
Nathan der Weise (in Germany)
Hugo and de Musset in France
von Kleist in Germany

You should note from this list that France and Germany regularly produce a number of native playwrights whose works are little seen elsewhere; Italy and Spain occasionally revive plays by Goldoni and de Vega, respectively; Greece presents frequent revivals of the ancient Greek dramas; and England stages a variety of English plays. Only America has no regular productions of native historical drama. Except for *The Con-*

trast, Fashion, and *Uncle Tom's Cabin,* very few nineteenth-century American plays are staged except in the distorted form of travesties (*Ten Nights in a Barroom; The Drunkard,* etc.). As a result, America more than any other nation is heavily involved in producing the classics from the European repertoires; this is particularly so in educational theatres, where even Japanese Kabuki plays have been attempted. Thus, in search of tradition wherever they can find it, Americans borrow heavily from the English drama and make regular forays into the French, the German, the Italian, the Spanish, the Russian, and the ancient Greek. Shakespeare and Jonson are as much produced in America as in England, although their minor plays are less frequently tackled. Jacobean and Restoration dramas are not often produced, for in many ways these plays are deeply embedded in English culture and are thus more difficult to transfer. The English comedies of the eighteenth century are not infrequently produced, although not without the attendant problems of separated cultures. To see *Lock Up Your Daughters* or *The School for Scandal* in London, where one is surrounded by architectural and historical reminders of the eighteenth century, is quite a different matter from seeing these plays in New York or Chicago. Nevertheless, the body of producible plays is still a fairly large one, and the director's problems stem mainly from how to tackle each national drama.

THE DIRECTOR MUST HAVE SOMETHING TO SAY

Producing a historical play without having something specific to say can only result in vagueness and lack of unity. Audiences will turn away from such productions because they look like dead museum pieces caught up in costume and staging display. To make a historical play meaningful to an audience, a director must first find and pin down a core idea that is meaningful to him.

Having "something to say," however, does not mean overlaying a play with a director's own ideas, for his intention is not to act as a collaborative playwright but as an interpreter, which means that he wants to bring alive from the printed page what he feels to be moving or amusing in a play's content. The director's intention, then, is to put on an entertainment that a modern audience can respond to and to do it in such a way that that audience will be able to feel and think about what the director has felt and thought about in his association with the play. This challenge is very great because historical drama is truly inert drama—remote in ideas, archaic in language, even obscure in many actions—until someone comes along with a sensitive perception and a gift for style-making to breathe life into it. An individual view of a historical play as well as a strong personal reaction to it are imperative in production considerations. "Something to say" in this sense becomes a personal conviction, and out of such a conviction can come clarity and unity.

But once you feel strongly about a play, you must submit yourself to the next personal challenge: Will my ideas mean anything to average theatregoers who have not studied the play carefully? This is a rigorous, direct question because a director can easily be trapped, once he studies a play, by the historical context within that play and what surrounded its writing. He must not forget that the something to say must make sense to a present-day audience. The challenge is to say something for now and thus to place the play in a present-day context. Perhaps the challenge will be only that of showing the blind spots in our modern ways of looking at things, but more than likely, if a director searches deeply enough into a play, an idea can be found that will disturb us into new thinking about the world we live in. Great plays have the capability of revival because, somehow, they manage to say things about mankind that have been true in all ages. How to present those ideas so that they can be readily perceived by audiences today is the problem in production.

Here a director's acute sensitivity to his own times becomes a necessity, for he must find in these old plays those things that his audiences feel and know about their own culture. Of one thing he can be certain: playwrights throughout the history of the theatre have been writing about human beings for audiences who were intensely interested in the spectacle of another man's dilemmas and how he is trapped by them or escapes them. The form of drama as human spectacle has not changed, but only the immediate contexts in which such actions take place. A director's study of a historical drama, then, must proceed on the closest examination of the dramatic action *in the context of the given circumstances.* Once you comprehend this close relationship, the inner values of the play will become much more apparent to you.

In the 1960s, for instance, audiences could better understand violence and revolution in historical drama because of their own similar dilemmas. Not only was that decade actively making new plays that contained these feelings, but it revived a number of old plays that "came into meanings" not previously apparent. Jacobean drama, some of Greek drama, and even Shakespeare can be cited along with productions of such plays as *The Dutchess of Malfi, The Bacchae, The Trojan Women, Prometheus Bound,* and Shakespeare's history plays, including *Henry VI* and *Coriolanus.* These plays seemed to find audience comprehension on the level of feeling because directors found how to make them speak the *rhythm* of the 1960s. The premise that historical drama is acceptable to modern audiences whenever the *rhythms* are closely parallel to modern feelings makes excellent sense; such a theory implies that the dramatic actions in such plays are recognizable and meaningful on the subjective, emotional level.

But no matter why a play comes to meaning, a director must be certain to establish that it does have meaning and that he believes in its meaning as strongly as he would in that of a recent play based in his own context. Finding something to say is finding the first point of style on which all other production points will depend.

REACHING AUDIENCES
THROUGH STYLE IN STAGING

Once you have found a modern meaning for a historical play you are considering, you are in a position to decide on the physicalization. The problem is the same one confronting the director in finding something to say: the physical staging must somehow convey modern feelings if the play is to come alive on today's stage. Archeological reproduction, as we have already pointed out, has no life of its own, and finding other ways is quite necessary. Here are a few possibilities:

Adaptation of Historical Stages. One approach to the design problem is to devise a modern staging which uses the basic elements of the historical stage for which a particular play was written. In this approach, so the theory goes, a director still has the possibility of finding the inherent physical rhythm of a play because its production can proceed from its assumed environment. Although successful playwrights have always written for a specific stage, it does not at all mean that they did so consciously, for they probably took the popular stage form for granted; yet, it is precisely this subconscious assumption of stage "place" that will contain the patterns of the play. By adapting a stage to incorporate modern feeling in a direct way, a director can meet the inherent demands of a play in its original context and at the same time can reach his audience directly because it will "feel" the stage subconsciously as a part of its own world.

Such staging will involve the use of mass, line, and color in such a way that it will be in keeping with modern rhythms. Thus, the production will look very modern without the playscript actually being so. The use of modern lighting procedures can aid greatly in such staging.

Relocation of a Play in an Entirely Different Historical Context. Another approach in trying to reach modern audiences is to mount a play with settings and costumes from a completely different period from both the time in which it was first produced and from our own. When the American Shakespeare Festival staged *Troilus and Cressida* in Civil War costumes, as it did a number of years ago, the intention was to place the play in a context American audiences could understand, not that of their own day but that of America's past history. Such relocating has definite advantages, since it is possible for an audience to see a play imaginatively through its personal feelings about history. The something to say is thus historically placed, but because of the symbolism and mythology surrounding such history, an emotional reaction on the part of the audience becomes possible. (Note how Bertolt Brecht has used something very like this approach in his playwriting through his retelling, with modern overtones, of John Gay's eighteenth-century *The Beggar's Opera* under the

PLATE XXV   *Fuente Ovejuna* by Lope de Vega

Adaptation of a Historical Stage: Choice of stage: forestage-proscenium. Choice of scenery: architectural, fractionated. The intention here was to reproduce in kind what we know about the seventeenth-century stage in Spain. Thus, two entrances were provided on right-stage and leftstage, an above or balcony, and a below (the two large doors under the balcony open wide). The historical stage was modified, however, by using the stagehouse for flying the shuttered act curtain and by introducing a visible stairway connecting the balcony with the main acting area. The form of the play as Lope wrote it could thus be retained in the acting of the many scenes. Lope abhorred in his day the use of painted scenery then beginning to appear on European stages; so, the only device used in this production was the symbolic map of Spain hung from above. However, the use of large banners, as shown in the photograph, provided some of the same effects as painted scenery. Properties used were largely symbolic in accordance with offices performed, and lighting was modern directional. Costumes were adapted from High Italian Renaissance, as indicated in Plate XXIII, and makeup was conventional modern. Music used in this production was Spanish Renaissance guitar ensemble together with Spanish folk tunes played on guitars.

title *The Three Penny Opera* and Farquhar's *The Recruiting Officer* under the title *Fife and Drums.*)

Even though costumes and scenic pieces of the relocated period are used, modern lighting effects can still give the production a sense of belonging to the here and now. The challenge in this sort of symbolic transfer is to find an appropriate historical period that will reveal the play; but the director must remember that if he forces such a context, it can be both distracting and confusing.

The Use of a Neutral Stage. Another stylistic approach is an adaptation of a form of staging introduced by Jacques Copeau at the Vieux Colombier in Paris over half a century ago. At the base, his idea was architectural, for it required a single unit setting that could be rearranged in many different ways for the presentation of a wide range of drama. The intention was to provide a system of interlocking platforms and steps that could become locations for scenes without representing them in a realistic way. All recent architectural stages proceed on the same principle: a stage machine that can be easily manipulated.

The neutral stage has many advantages since it leaves the audience's imagination free to create its own places. Because this stage is functional, it offers extensive opportunities for variety in movement and in scene location. Period costumes on this stage are very effective because they provide "scenery" in a modern, dynamic way. Modern principles of stage lighting can also be used effectively—as Norman Bel Geddes first showed us in America—to give a seeming modernity to a production.

Modern Dress Production. This style can be very effective with highly selected historical plays. The intention is, of course, to make the play belong directly to us by giving it the look of contemporary life. Thus, the choice of stage is modern (perhaps open staging); the properties and costumes are of recent fashion; and the lighting and sound are what we would expect in a contemporary play. Such stagings are not easily accomplished in America because of the difficulties in finding gradations in dress that can readily delineate class differences, particularly those of royalty, required by historical playscripts. But even if parallels in dress can be found, forcing plays into this kind of staging may not help but hinder their communication. It might work for *Julius Caesar, Hamlet, Coriolanus,* or *As You Like It,* but *Othello* or *A Midsummer Night's Dream* might suffer badly, although some directors will try anything in the interest of more direct communication.

ACTING STYLES AND VERSE DIALOGUE

As we have already pointed out in previous discussions, one approach to acting—a usual one—is to take the given circumstances of a play literally, that is, to reproduce the exterior decorum we would expect the characters in the play to show us. Thus, an actor would illustrate the literal appearances of the social level of his character through his gesture, movement, speech, and use of his costume. And since decorum can mean either control or the lack of it, the actor would move through the action of a play with the literal range of the decorum specified by appearances. Our believability would in this way be satisfied on the basis of appearances. Those plays dealing with nobility would thus have a look of formality, with controlled gestures and movement; and other plays, particularly seventeenth- and eighteenth-century middle- and upper-class comedies, would have varied decorums but would still be near the formal pattern. But no matter how formal or informal the decorum might turn out to be, we would accept it as Realistic in style, as we would accept Ibsenite drama, because the appearances would be all of a piece. Thus, what has been called Realistic acting would support a Realistic interpretation of a play.

But quite a different approach to acting historical drama is to overlay the given circumstances, and thus the decorum, with Stanislavskian psychological acting, which means that the gesture, movement, and so on would be expressive of the inner character only and would not merely show the appearances of the literal decorum-character. This approach would allow a great increase in the range of illustration, for control or lack of control would not be determined by social level but only by motivation of the dramatic action. Consequently, another level of Realism in the acting would result, the level on which modern plays are now seen and heard—Inner Realism. Thus, the actors of the roles of Romeo and Juliet would not be bound by the decorum of the historical social level but would be free spirits in today's society. Or Hamlet would not be a "prince" first and a man with intense common feelings second, but vice versa. As you can readily see, quite a different play can result from the use of this style.

Consequently, we cannot say that historical drama is acted Realistically on our contemporary stage without defining the levels of Realistic style. You should be aware, however, that audiences have become so firmly rooted in expecting representational appearances in historical drama that any other stylistic-approach may seem a defamation of Shakespeare or of the Greek dramatists. But there is no question that the "modern acting" approach has genuine validity and may be the only way the old plays will continue to find audiences. Your decision of style here is a very crucial matter.

But whichever acting style you choose, you must not forget the absolute necessity for finding the *violence level* in the playing. Historical drama is written largely in verse forms in order to allow direct and intense expression of emotions. Character-mood-intensity thus becomes a matter of very great importance, for the poetic drama sings, surges, and reaches peaks we seldom find in plays written in prose. You must learn to exploit poetic forms and not to fight them.

But though you may learn fairly easily how to draw the subtext out of actors, getting out the text is quite another matter because much more emphasis has usually been placed in modern actor training on "getting across" the subtext. As a result, young actors tend to fight the verse line instead of recognizing that it is their best tool for reaching audiences. A director may need to reorient actors new to verse drama by emphasizing that the action in such plays *lies directly and literally in the lines* and not in the subtext as in modern psychological drama. At first, this may seem to them like a betrayal of modern approaches to acting, but they will soon see how effectively audiences can be held in tension on the force of the spoken word alone, that is, how they will see it if you really believe it yourself and sell it to them. Careful study of verse structure by a director is, therefore, essential if he is to get the most from his actors. Neglect of this technical approach can only result in a ragged production, for telling the subtext in verse plays is not nearly sufficient; it is the "way" it is told —the style of the spoken language—that makes the difference.

A director's training must therefore include a concentration on the study of verse dialogue and how to exploit it with actors. Such study will make a director aware that his first obligation to an audience is *letting* them hear such dialogue with ease and without *distraction;* if he does not, its effect and thus much of the action in a play will be entirely lost. This is a big order because verse dialogue, such as Shakespeare's or Marlowe's, often clouds our hearing with archaic words and phrases, lost allusions, inverted sentence structure, and frequent poetic imagery that cannot be received until the previous problems have been navigated. A director does not try to circumvent these problems by removing difficult lines from a playscript, but he faces them head on by paying close attention to such mechanics of verse structure as punctuation; emphatic words or phrases and where they fall in a line; placement of the caesura; cohesion within a single line or within several lines through proper breathing and the elimination of false pauses; and above all to the meter, for the discovery of a line's meaning by an audience may lie much more in its inherent rhythm when properly delivered than in its denotative word meanings. To convey to young actors a sense of meter is often like trying to teach tone-deaf people to sing; but without such a sense, an actor cannot deliver verse dialogue with meaning and excitement. Do you sense the musical form of such verse dialogue yourself? If you can "hear" it, you may be able to teach "hearing" to others.

Good verse delivery also means careful physical control by actors. As a director, you will learn to insist that actors keep their heads quite still when speaking; that they place the articulated sound as far forward in the mouth as possible; that they do not try to move across the stage when they are delivering a line; that they do not blast into lines with excessive volume, thus producing an in-and-out volume effect; that they keep fairly narrow ranges in pitch variation; that they relax the body and thus the voice to allow easy projection of the lines; that they articulate with great care; that they use pleasing vowel structure; that they place caesuras where they belong and do not introduce false pauses. Because verse plays contain high passions that tempt actors to "out-Herod Herod," you will also learn to insist that textual delivery must take precedence over all subtextual and visual illustration, for a passage unheard is a passage that bores an audience and prevents its comprehension of a play.

Production Styles with Modern Drama

STAGING "EARLY REALISM"

Much of the discussion above about producing historical drama applies to modern drama. A director must have the same gambler's sense of adventure; he must be highly motivated with something to say; and he must search for a physicalization that will fit his particular play. Style will emerge when he exerts his own individuality on the media of production.

Perhaps the biggest problem is that there are so few limitations in producing modern plays, for we are passing through an age of more diversified staging than that of any previous period. The problem lies in finding what will work best. This has become increasingly evident as we try to bring the Realistic plays written before 1920 into clearer focus for present-day audiences. Although these plays—by Ibsen, Strindberg, Chekhov, and Shaw early in his career—belong largely to the dominant modern style of Realism (Strindberg's departures excepted), their content and dramaturgical techniques appear dated to us. We can certainly produce them in the style of their first performances, but we may very well prefer to look at them in the same way we look at historical drama and to treat them as such. This means that a wide range of stylistic possibilities are open to a director in search of fresh meanings for present-day audiences— possibilities that may take him far from the box settings in which most of these early Realistic plays were originally played. Like the American playwright-adapters who have worked at transferring the plays of Ibsen, Chekhov, and Strindberg—Arthur Miller (*An Enemy of the People*), Thornton Wilder (*A Doll's House*), Stark Young (*The Cherry Orchard*), and Eva Le Gallienne (much of Ibsen)—American directors should search for fresh stagings. The historical approach is a good one because it recognizes that the major problem is audience communication, and it encourages a director to look always at this problem as the most important one he is constantly faced with. Overcoming it is his challenge and his job.

Among the problems in production communication is how to act early Realism. Inexperienced directors tend to shy away from the near melodramatic intensity of these plays, and by so doing, they underplay

PLATE XXVI *The Lady From The Sea* by Henrik Ibsen

Modern Adaptation: Ibsen's psychological drama could certainly have been staged in a representational manner with the probable use of box settings. This production, in an attempt to free Ibsen from the conventional style of Realism usually employed in staging with his plays, used a forestage-proscenium and both architectural and fractionated scenery. The photograph above together with Plate XXII will give you an idea of how the play was mounted. Note that both "outside" and "inside" locations are shown simultaneously, with the tall, curtained windows, flown from above behind the proscenium wall, not only providing a theatrical line to the setting but giving an openness, a symbolic search for freedom, to Ibsen's drama of human beings tied to confined patterns of monotonous daily living. The abstract forms provided as part of the architectural scenery were used as set properties and the hand properties were authentic realities. The costumes were adaptations of the period; the lighting was modern directional, deeply shadowed, and the music was that of a German band playing incessantly in this small Norwegian resort town.

the dramatic statements intended by the authors. It is important to remember that these plays appeared on the heels of a Romantic theatre, in which acting style by present standards was flamboyant and fully declared. Although the dramaturgy changed noticeably in style from that of Romantic drama, this does not imply that the acting style playwrights had in mind followed the identical pattern. An acting statement may, therefore, lie somewhere between the large, flamboyant acting style of the Romantic theatre and the small, behavoristic pattern of post-World War I Realism. If you look for a larger, more dynamic style for the acting (perhaps something like that in early silent movies) in contrast to what playscripts seem to suggest literally, you may find that these plays can grip audience attention where a more sedate, a more naturalistic style will not.

Another acting problem with these early Realistic plays is finding the decorum of the characters represented. After all, the people who populate these plays, whether they are drawn by Norwegians, Russians, or Frenchmen, are middle-class Victorians or Edwardians, and since the style is "observed Realism," a director and his actors must find that outer facade that allows the play to happen. You must never forget that an important part of the style of "observed Realism" is showing a facade that can be punctured, for the dramatic action in these plays is revealing what lies behind the exteriors—the skeletons in the closet, a game of hide-and-seek. You must, therefore, learn to build facades of manners just as you would for a seventeenth- or eighteenth-century comedy of manners, for you cannot break through them if they are not demonstrated. How actors walk, sit, stand, talk, laugh, greet others, wear their clothing-costumes, dress their hair, handle objects, and so on, thus becomes very important. The post-1920 American lower- to middle-class folk drama (everything from O'Neill and Odets to Paul Osborne, Williams, and Inge) has so disarmed us about a society in which class distinctions are taken for granted that young directors overlook the necessity of showing the mannered facades of the people in early Realism. These plays are about environment and how it forces action; you must, therefore, give intensive study when producing such plays to how you can reveal given circumstances with the greatest strength.

PENETRATING THE STYLES
IN MORE RECENT PLAYWRITING
AS THE BASIS FOR PRODUCTION STYLE

The problem facing the young director is always to force himself into a fresh approach for each play he undertakes. We tend to take plays written in the 1960s, for instance, too much for granted by assuming that because they appear to be similar on the outside, they must belong to the familiar Realistic category of earlier decades. You will, therefore, need to search out the difference between "outer" Realism and "inner" Realism. Once again, a director must always do a detailed style-analysis of every play he considers seriously for production, for only through this process can he be sure of a play's potential and thus be able to find a style to give it life on the stage.

A director must make an intensive structural examination of the wide range of plays written since 1915. You should be able to pinpoint the *departures from Realism* in the styles of Wedekind, Toller, Andreyev, Kaiser, Ghelderode, Ansky, Cocteau, Lenormand, Capek, Jarry, and Pirandello. Likewise, you should know O'Neill's experimental drama and what characterizes his style in such plays as *The Emperor Jones, The Hairy Ape, The Great God Brown,* and *Strange Interlude,* as well as his more Realistic style in *Desire Under the Elms, Mourning Becomes Electra, The Iceman Cometh,* and *The Long Day's Journey Into Night.* You must also know Odets, Rice, Sherwood, Behrman, Hellman, Saroyan, Howard, Wilder, Williams, Miller, just as you must know O'Casey, Synge, Maugham, Osborne, Bolt, and Behan. The Brechtian style will attract you but you will need to give it hard analysis to see how it works, just as you will need to study Sartre, Ionesco, Genet, Adamov, Beckett, Albee, and Pinter, and other European playwrights such as Frisch, Shafer, Dürrenmatt, and Betti. In other words, you must study all we consider the best of modern drama. You must know differences in order to see likenesses, but above all you must become aware of the nature of individuality, the nature of style in playwriting so that you have departure points for making style in production.

Your biggest problem, however, may be controlling production, not finding what to exploit in it. Flight must assuredly take place; but to a young director flight in production too often means making the audience self-consciously aware of the clever staging—an approach that can obliterate the text and all that flows from it. Departures from Realism (the core is, of course, the Expressionist drama of 1910 to 1930) are particularly prone to such treatment because they look so eccentric, so "out," that an inexperienced director goes all "out" in emphasizing eccentric aspects. You must learn, therefore, to recognize these plays for what they are: structured drama and not odd happenings; poetic prose or verse form that must be delivered carefully and with great attention to line dynamics; character "types" (types in contrast to the individuals in Realistic drama) that need much more than obvious demonstration of who they are; dramatic action that needs the fullest sort of illustration to bring out the basic conflicts; political and social points of view that need careful pointing in lines and character demonstration; moods and tempos that vary radically from those of Realism. You must learn to avoid gim-

PLATE XXVII   *The Chalk Circle* (Anonymous Chinese)

Adaptation of a Historical Stage: This production is shown as a
contrast to the following plate (Plate XXVIII) because, taken together, they illustrate both a historical Chinese play with a Chinese
setting and a modern play with an adapted modern Chinese setting.
The intention in staging *The Chalk Circle* was that of telling this
ancient play, dating from the fourteenth century, in the style of late
nineteenth-century Chinese opera.   The choice of stage is forestage-proscenium, although it probably should have been open-
thrust in line with the opera stages you can see in nineteenth-century
photographs.   However, the painted backwall has been retained,
along with the two entrance doors on either side of it, and painted
side panels.   The set properties are conventional tables and chairs,
as used in the opera, and the hand properties are symbolic (note the
white and the black flags to denote wind and snow).   The costumes
are taken from late nineteenth-century drawings of Chinese theatrical wear (note the property men in their blue suits).   Lighting was
modern conventional, and sound was that provided by a live
orchestra with Chinese instruments, gongs, and drums.   Unlike the
Western theatre of this period (late nineteenth century), which was
moving closer and closer to homogeneous staging of a representational nature, the Chinese theatre retained the ancient idea of mix-
ing the ingredients, partly representational, partly presentational,
partly symbolic.

mickry in setting out these plays, for if you fall victim to such methods, it undoubtedly means you have not uncovered the inner recesses and the potentials of these unusual plays.   Departures from Realism as a category is the modern theatre's poetic drama, and you can let it live only by treating it with integrity in production.   Let it fly, let it excite and thrill with its physicality, but let it come through on its own terms and not through gimmickry you may devise because you think that it is the only way you can help it survive.

PLATE XXVIII   *The Good Woman of Setzuan* by Bertolt Brecht

Modern Adaptation: If you will look at this plate in conjunction with Plates XIX and XXIV, you will see how it is possible to stage a modern play in the geographical setting a playwright calls for, while, at the same time, an audience is shown a location specifically familiar to it.   The curved line of the bridge, some suggestions in the costumes, the way of eating rice all provide a glimmer of something Chinese.   The set objects were employed intentionally to remind the audience of local poverty: the bedstead, .the ashcan, the corrugated roofing, the walls made of old newspapers and cardboard, the rubber tire, the window shutters, the cloth coverings over the doors.   Note that the lighting was designed to emphasize the textures, the plastic quality of the scenery and properties.   The music used in this production was Brechtian—the nostalgic sound of the vaudeville stage, though at the same time it was faintly reminiscent of Chinese music.   Thus, this production was counterpointed throughout the designs in the interest of revealing the confusion and complexity of modern life in the West.

STAGE LIMITATIONS AND AVAILABLE OPTIONS

The options in staging discussed in Chapters 16 through 18 of this book are the basis for all modern production. But although these options allow very great freedom, a director may find himself physically bound by a specific stage on which he must produce. Such is the case of the Broadway theatre in New York, where little attempt has been made, as it has in London in a few important theatres, to overcome the tight restrictions of the proscenium arch and its attendant curtain. But where this single form has been pushed aside in favor of multiple forms, as it has in the summer festival theatres, and in most educational theatres, directors have found new ways of meeting the problem of modern communication. Multiple production approaches are now possible as never before because we are overcoming the restrictions of theatre architecture and can think more and more in terms of stage-audience relationships and what they can do. Staging, thus, has become a matter of control of space with its focus on intensive communication—reaching out and touching. This new freedom has given directors more possibilities for creating dynamic and varied experience than any age has ever had. Whether or not the director can use it wisely and with sensitive imagination will probably declare his future need in the theatre.

The movement away from the proscenium has also made lighting a more dynamic staging tool. The problem is not one of merely illuminating actors on a stage but of *defining* space in a dramatic way. Thus, a new dimension in light has come about. Although no similar shift is apparent yet in costuming, the fact that costumes are now seen on many stages more "in-the-round," more as sculpture, than they ever have been before, makes it quite possible that stage wear may undergo pressures that will move it away from the representationalism that has largely confined it since the nineteenth century.

ACTING STYLE OF RECENT DRAMA

A major assumption of this book is that the prevailing acting style in America is still the style inspired by Stanislavski; that is, its primary attack is on the subtext and its conveyance with extensively detailed illustration to an audience. Perhaps the significant shift in the appearance of American acting since 1950 is an increase in the size and deliberateness of illustration, a move away from what can only be defined as the behavioristic acting of the 1930s and 1940s, that is, an acting style intended to reveal the exteriors of characters without intensive penetration within. In this sense, present acting styles have moved away from a literal interpretation of Stanislavsky. There has also been an increased emphasis on the text, undoubtedly under the pressure of the English tradition and the common necessity for actors to perform in historical drama where text concentration is necessary. Thus, this more highly developed process of illustration has brought us closer to the historical line of acting as we have watched it shift and change over the period of three hundred years for which we have records available.

The acting style for recent drama, then, could be defined as highly illustrated psychological projection of the subtext and of the text. This style demands the focus of primary attention on character-mood-intensity to bring about "violence levels" in appropriate tempos. The director's best instruction in acting, beyond his own active experimentation as an actor himself, lies in watching the best of contemporary acting—the prevailing general style—for only then will he begin to see how particular actors differ in the way they do things. Eventually, he will be able to answer for himself why the best actors are the most effective with audiences, that is, what makes them stylists in their acting.

DIRECTOR'S STYLE

The emphasis in what has preceded this point has been on how to bring out the individual work of others, that is, how to exploit the playscript, the actors, and the designers to their highest levels. We have thus defined director's style as the individual product he assembles out of this exploitation—what we defined earlier as theatrical art. It should now be clear to you that a director's style can only be what he is as a man: the strength of his artistic perception and taste; the strength of his will power in making decisions and in adhering to them; the strength of his capabilities in being a leader; the strength of his skills in theatre techniques and, above all, in using quiet, unassuming communication. The individual thing that he wants—the style of his production—can only emerge out of these qualities. Talent in a director, then, is possessing some part of each of them at the base but then in building them extensively through hard work and imagination.

Exercises in Production Style

EXERCISE 1

As was suggested earlier, learning directors should direct scenes from historical drama as a necessary part of their training, for the perception of modern drama and the scope of modern production can be greatly increased with this essential background. The student should, therefore, undertake the production of one or more ten-to-fifteen-minute scenes chosen from the standard repertoire of historical drama. Preparation and production procedures should follow those prescribed at the end of Parts II and III, and Chapter 22 (Style-Analysis).

One way to start is with a scene from a Greek play, for it will give you an excellent basis for comparison with other period plays in a chronological order. But if scenes from several period plays can be directed, much can be learned by working backwards: Do a scene from Ibsen first, then move to the eighteenth, seventeenth, sixteenth, Medieval, Roman, and Greek in that order. You will then see the relationship of modern drama to all the rest.

Make your choices wisely. Remember that historical drama requires focus on the text, which means the most extensive use of the actors' voices. Learn all you can about the power of big volume, about energy behind acting, about the physical demands on the actor's body.

Your designs for staging a scene from a historical play will give you a far better idea of how to get it acted. Do it with imagination and inventiveness. Remember that you must study the original forms of production in order to understand the playscript fully, but your obligation now is to an audience. "What can you do to make these old plays exciting now?" is the question you must proceed on.

EXERCISE 2

Concentration on plays from early Realism can accomplish a good deal for you simply because it will enable you to see what has happened to Realism as a style and in the departures from Realism since that time. You should, therefore, select a scene from Ibsen, Chekhov, Strindberg, or early Shaw. Stay with the masters to learn the most. Study the structure of their plays and isolate their individuality. Scenes from these plays done on the proscenium stage not only will tell you much about them as plays, but this procedure will also give you motivations for moving to other stages with later plays.

EXERCISE 3

Likewise, concentration on departures from Realism will give you a grasp of these styles. Do scenes from Wedekind, Pirandello, the German or American Expressionists, Brecht, Saroyan. Save the "absurdists" until you have done the earlier playwrights. And save Pinter and Albee until after you understand the others.

Experiment with these plays on *departure* stages. If it is at all possible, do a scene yourself, or watch closely scenes done by others (1) in arena style, on both raised and lowered stages; (2) in open-thrust style; and (3) in forestage-proscenium style. Finally, invent a stage that differs from all of these styles even though you may force the presentation of a scene by doing so.

EXERCISE 4

The first of two final projects (Exercise 5 is the second) is the full direction, designing, and mounting of a one-act play. If you can find a new one with the author on hand, you will profit more from this experience than with a published play without the author to talk with. At any rate, this project is similar to Exercise 4, p. 274, only this time you will carry through with the entire production. As in that project, you should use only your actors as crew personnel so that the entire burden for mounting the production comes from you. In this way, you can practice your skills in every possible way to understand how the designer and the technical director work. Evaluation should follow production as in Exercise 5, p. 275.

EXERCISE 5

Design and direct a full-length play. Here is the goal for the entire book. This time, although you will do the designs in order to learn all you can about the concept of coordination, you should have expert assistance in mounting the production.

Can you do it? This question is the challenge of your training in directing.

26

nonverbal theatricals
and the future of directing

The term *nonverbal theatricals* is used here as a designation for the sort of creative theatre-making that has developed in the last decade out of improvisational techniques. Such theatricals do not rely on the traditional dramatic form with structured dialogue containing given circumstances, dramatic action, characters, idea, moods, and tempos, and on production interpretation with trained actors and form in staging. Instead, it usually evolves from an improvisation, developed by a *group* under the direction of an "artist-leader," which conveys intensive dramatic ideas through the elements of visual and aural theatricality, through the variations and unexpected possibilities inherent in improvisation, and through a minimum of improvised words that may or may not employ the interchanges of dialogue. Thus, such theatricals are not open to interpretation by other directors and actors outside of the group because they are the improvised and unique products of the group and its leader who, in making them, stamp them with the only possible interpretation—the one they reveal to an audience. Since all the rules of improvisation apply, the participants are not actors in the traditional sense, nor is the staging in any way restricted to the conventions of established forms.

Concept

Nonverbal theatricals do not fall within the strict confines of this book because they are "beyond" interpretation, beyond the process of giving stage life through a director, actors, and designers to *someone else's* play. Yet, they are taking such an important part in the most recent developments in theatre-making in America that they must be mentioned here because they will undoubtedly influence the future of directing as we presently know it. What the immediate sources of this new direction in theatre may be are still being debated, but whatever they may prove to be, Gordon Craig's prophecy in 1905 that an artist-director would eventually bring about a Renaissance in the theatre seems to be coming partially true, even if the new artist-leader is not quite what Craig pictured him to be. If you will look at the quotation from Craig's essay "On the Art of the Theatre" recorded on the title page of Part IV, you will note the difference Craig saw between interpretation and the sort of creative theatre he thought could be made by an artist-director. In his view, the interpreter, the master-craftsman-director, first had to gain strength and move ahead strongly before it would be possible to move on to the major goal—the artist-director who would be the creator of the total theatrical experience, including the words. If Craig proves to be mostly right, and there is every reason now to believe that his prophecy has validity, then the interpretative director will have a serious rival in the theatre in the new artist-leader, a rival who may eventually take a permanent place alongside him.

Such a projection into the future is not at all impossible to envision. We have the *commedia dell'arte* before us as the prime example in theatre history of another such movement. From 1550 to 1700, the commedia flourished extensively across Europe, exciting audiences from the top to the bottom of the social scale with its spontaneity, its improvisational brilliance, and its intense personal vitality. That it was undoubtedly preferred by many people to the traditional theatre form affirms its strength as theatre experience. Thus, to assume, because we have had it so for several hundred years, that a play must be written down in words to assure an adequate dramatic content, is to rule out not only the commedia as valid theatre-making but also classical oriental theatrical forms as well. That the Indian dance theatre developed no language equivalent to our word *drama,* as we use it to define our Western literary form, helps to convince us that a people can also have, in addition to written drama, a highly developed and sophisticated expression in theatre without having to first establish it through formally written language. Consequently, Westerners have no cause whatsoever to look down on nonverbal Eastern theatre as a lesser form than their written drama, but, to the contrary, they should search as never before for those elements that have made it work so successfully for many centuries and for diverse national peoples that make up two-thirds of the world's population. Nonverbal theatre has had not only as long and vigorous a life as the verbal sort, but its possibilities for theatre experience, still unexplored to any great extent today in the West, may be not only equally satisfying but also artistically rejuvenating.

To think of nonverbal theatre as in any way a replacement for written-spoken (verbal) drama, however, is to endow it with supernatural powers. Traditional theatre has been entrenched far too long in the history of Western civilization to allow itself to be easily pushed aside. Thus, it seems certain that as long as a literary culture survives, so will written-spoken drama, and along with it, the actor, the designer, and the director or his equivalent. Man cannot stop talking no matter what a botch of the world's business he may make, and as long as man talks for public consumption, he will have verbal theatre. Consequently, rather than think of this new direction in the theatre as endangering the place of the old one, or in having to fight the old one for survival, it would be only sound sense to see a theatre in which both ways could exist healthily and compatibly side by side as they did in the seventeenth century. Moreover, nonverbal theatricals would seem to be limited in the complexity they can project. Silent movies had to resort to captions, and almost every nonverbal production today seems to find it necessary to provide program notes or some other statement of meaning, usually abstruse and conceptual.

But however this situation may be, directing seems to be evolving on two fronts, with the traditional interpreter—the master-craftsman-director—working in one part of the theatre and the creative artist-leader working in the other. It would seem unlikely, however, that the same person will be inclined by temperament as well as by training to work in both directions, even if he possesses the necessary talents for doing so, although both will certainly tend to strongly influence one another and to modify one another.

Making Nonverbal Theatre

"DIRECTOR" OR "ARTIST-LEADER"?

Although Craig used the term *artist-director* to describe his ideal theatre man of the future, it is quite misleading as a label to describe the new man in the theatre. Craig saw both the master-craftsman-director and the artist-director as theatre autocrats. His background was so buried in nineteenth-century thinking and aesthetics, with its emphasis in the arts on the individual and on the individual product, that he scarcely could have held any other view. As an artist-autocrat himself, he prescribed a director whose approach was individualistic to the point of dictatorship. Group dynamics as a concept was, therefore, entirely alien to his thinking.

It is to Constantin Stanislavski that we must turn for a new concept of the director and how he can be useful in a changing theatre. As a contemporary of Craig's, Stanislavski might certainly have held the same view, and for awhile possibly he did, but his long life as an actor had taught him the necessity of group work, and it was this point of view that wove itself into the fabric of his theory of directing. When Stanislavski's approach to actor training found its way to America in the 1920s and 1930s, along with it came the concept of the director as an artistic group leader—no dictator but a sensitive person who could arouse others, through his own sense of creative activity and through his capability in communication, to new dedication and to a higher level of artistic achievement. This position has continued to be modified, with today's director-interpreter holding the position of artistic leader not alone through his wide and deep knowledge of drama and theatre but primarily through his sensitivity in the process of communication.

Nonverbal theatricals cannot, therefore, be called "a director's theatre," as some critics have labeled it, because in practice it involves group improvisation, and such improvisation is not the product of one man's imagination, though that man may lead others into the improvisation and influence the shaping of it. What is made is that which emerges from interchanges within the group. The use of the word *director* as defined throughout this book therefore cannot apply. A much better designation is the one we have used—artist-leader—simply because it implies both a strong artistic background in theatre and in art as well as exceptional leadership capabilities. But above all, it implies that such a person does not *direct* the work of others, although he may play a significant role in bringing that work to the best group expression.

THE JOB OF THE ARTIST-LEADER

The intention here is not to discuss the techniques of making nonverbal theatricals because any techniques used in the process can be evolved only by a group itself in the process of effecting its own artistic goals. Therefore, they cannot be readily catalogued as can interpretive techniques. Furthermore, introducing present means when the range of possibilities can be very great would only confuse what is really important for a director in training to understand as clearly as possible: how the artist-leader differs in his work from the master-craftsman interpretive director.

There is no question that leadership of a very definite sort is involved in nonverbal theatricals.   In its earliest declarations this leadership has been based in a commitment to social, political, or religious ideas, or all three at the same time.   Thus, it is not just the leader's knowledge of the art and craft of the theatre that makes him a leader but his belief in a view of life, coupled with a dedication approaching that of a reformist— a dedication demanding that he reach and influence people with his ideas and points of view.   His intention, therefore, is not to propagate other people's ideas, such as the interpretive director does with the work of the playwrights he produces, but to arouse through a group statement the specific point of view he wants to inculcate.   His leadership necessarily involves collecting around him a group that sees eye to eye with his ideas and has a similar desire to propagate them.   Such commitment, however, may be only a passing phase in an emerging nonverbal theatre whose extent we cannot possibly yet imagine.   That such a theatre can move away from direct commitment seems only logical once the idea of such a theatre wins general acceptance.

And what has happened to acting?   In nonverbal theatricals, an actor is not necessarily an actor but a *performer* of tasks.   It does not necessarily matter who he is, for he is merely someone captured by police or someone who at a certain point carries something from here to there. His own appearance and manner may provide some characterization but of an incidental kind.   *Hair,* for example, does not ask for character except in very generalized terms.   *Frankenstein* (Living Theatre) uses a large cast of "doers" without any specific characterizations.   The shift in the conception of acting, it seems, is away from impersonation.

Along with this new approach to the creative process in theatre must go audience expectations: What can it expect in the future?   The traditional position of the audience as a spectator group that has looked on with a take-it or leave-it attitude may radically shift.   Whom is this sort of theatre for? seems to be a still unanswered question.   Is it primarily for the benefit of the actors who participate in it or for the audience that is also encouraged to participate in it?   Expression of audience opinion has been so curtailed in the twentieth century from the general participatory noise of the nineteenth and preceding centuries that more involvement seems inevitable.   And what will the spectators be expected to do?   Will they no longer be spectators but actors in the improvisation itself, as most "happenings" insisted that they be?   Will a new audience be found for it, a primarily youthful audience in contrast to the mature, middle-class audience of the established theatre?   Will the new audience demand immediate relevance and commitment?   As you can see, nonverbal theatricals leave us with many puzzling speculations about the theatre of the future.

And what will be the training of the artist-leader? Traditional backgrounds for work in the theatre still seem to be useful up to a point if only to develop the leader's feelings for the dramatic and the theatrical, but how far they can be used is still very much in question. Training in modern dance techniques, on the other hand, with its emphasis on the search for freedom through improvisation may play a much larger role than it previously has in leadership training, no matter which way it goes, because nonverbal theatricals in their present form seem to be more closely allied to the dance aspects of theatre than to the spoken aspects. Just as modern dance returned to primitive and oriental forms in trying to establish itself as a freshly conceived art form, so also may nonverbal theatre. If these two forms are in any way joined together, they may show us a new and dynamic theatre in the West—one very different from the interpretative theatre we have known continuously since the Renaissance.

It would appear, then, that in the future, anyone contemplating work in the theatre in a position of leadership will undoubtedly have some important decisions to make at the outset. But whatever route he decides to follow, he can be sure that although the director is scarcely a hundred years old, some sort of leader will be a necessary part in making theatre for a long time to come.

bibliography

What follows is a minimum list of books with which any advanced student of directing should be relatively familiar. It ranges from discussions of directing and directors at work, to the director's actor and designer relationships, to the theory of dramatic literature, and finally to background historical studies. You will accumulate a knowledge of many of these books as you work through your courses in theatre, but you will need to search out those works missed in the interest of giving you as complete a stance as possible for developing your own point of view about directing. Directing is not a virtuoso display of virtuosity but a highly developed craft firmly based in techniques and backgrounds.

About Directing

ARTAUD, ANTONIN, *The Theater and Its Double,* trans. Mary Caroline Richards. New York: Grove Press, Inc. 1958.

BAKSHY, ALEXANDER, *The Theatre Unbound.* London: Cecil Palmer, C. Q. Bailey Bros. Ltd. 1923.

BARRAULT, JEAN-LOUIS, *Reflections on the Theatre,* trans. Barbara Well. London: Rockliff Pub. Corp. Ltd. 1951.

BARRAULT, JEAN-LOUIS, *The Theatre of Jean-Louis Barrault,* trans. Joseph Chiari. New York: Hill and Wang Inc., 1961.

BENTLEY, ERIC, *In Search of Theatre.* New York: Alfred A. Knopf, Inc., 1953.

BLAU, HERBERT, *The Impossible Theater.* New York: The Macmillan Company, 1964.

BRECHT, BERTOLT and CASPAR NEHER, *Antigonemodell.* Berlin: Gebr. Weiss, 1948.

BROOK, PETER, *The Empty Space.* New York: Atheneum Publishers, 1968.

CHEKHOV, MICHAEL, *Director and Playwright,* compiled and written by Charles Leonard. New York: Harper & Row, Publishers, 1963.

CLAY, JAMES H. and DANIEL KREMPEL, *The Theatrical Image.* New York: McGraw-Hill Book Company, 1967.

CLURMAN, HAROLD, *Lies Like Truth.* New York: The Macmillan Company, 1958.

COLE, TOBY and HELEN KRICH CHINOY, eds., *Directors on Directing,* 2nd rev. ed. Indianapolis, Ind.: The Bobbs-Merrill Co., Inc., 1963.

ELIOT, T. S., "The Function of Criticism," in *Selected Essays.* New York: Harcourt Brace Jovanovich Inc., 1950.

FLANAGAN, HALLIE, *Dynamo.* New York: Duell, Sloan & Pearce, Inc., 1943.

GORCHAKOV, NIKOLAI, *Stanislavsky Directs,* trans. Miriam Goldina. New York: Funk & Wagnalls Company, 1954.

GRANVILLE-BARKER, HARLEY, *Prefaces to Shakespeare,* 2 vols. Princeton, N.J.: Princeton University Press, 1947.

GROTOWSKI, JERZY, *Towards a Poor Theatre.* New York: Simon and Schuster Inc., 1969.

GUTHRIE, TYRONE, *A Life in the Theatre.* New York: McGraw-Hill Book Company, 1959.

HOUGHTON, NORRIS, *Return Engagement.* New York: Holt, Rinehart & Winston Inc., 1962.

KNAPP, BETTINA, *Louis Jouvet, Man of the Theatre.* New York: Columbia University Press, 1957.

KOTT, JAN, *Shakespeare Our Contemporary,* trans. Boleslaw Taborski. Garden City, N.Y.: Doubleday & Company, Inc. Anchor Books Edition.

LABAN, RUDOLF, *The Mastery of Movement.* London: MacDonald & Evans Ltd., 1960.

OXENFORD, LYN, *Playing Period Plays.* London: J. Garnet Miller, Ltd., 1958.

PURDOM, C. B., *Harley Granville-Barker.* Cambridge, Mass.: Harvard University Press, 1956.

SAINT-DENIS, MICHEL, *Theatre: The Rediscovery of Style.* New York: Theatre Arts Books, 1961.

SHAW, BERNARD, *The Art of Rehearsal.* New York: Samuel French, Inc., 1928.

SPEAIGHT, ROBERT, *William Poel and the Elizabethan Revival.* London: William Heinemann Ltd., 1954.

STANISLAVSKI, KONSTANTIN, *My Life in Art,* trans. J. J. Robbins. New York: Theatre Arts Books, 1952.

————, *Stanislavsky on the Art of the Stage,* trans. David Margarshack. London: Faber & Faber Ltd., 1950.

————, *The Seagull Produced by Stanislavski,* ed. S. D. Balukhaty, trans. David Margarshack. London: Dennis Dobson, 1952.

YOUNG, STARK, *Theatre Practice.* New York: Charles Scribner's Sons, 1926.

Director-Actor Relationship

BOLESLAVSKY, RICHARD, *Acting; The First Six Lessons.* New York: Theatre Arts Books, 1949.

CHEKHOV, MICHAEL, *To the Actor on the Technique of Acting.* New York: Harper & Brothers, 1953.

COLE, TOBY, ed., *Acting: A Handbook of the Stanislavski Method.* New York: Crown Publishers, Inc., 1963.

HODGSON, JOHN, and ERNEST RICHARDS, *Improvisation.* London: Methuen & Co. Ltd., 1966.

LESSAC, ARTHUR, *The Use and Training of the Human Voice.* New York: DBS Publications, Inc., 1967.

McGAW, CHARLES, *Acting Is Believing.* New York: Holt, Rinehart & Winston, Inc., 1955.

MACHLIN, EVANGELINE, *Speech for the Stage.* New York: Theatre Arts Books, 1966.

PARRISH, WAYLAND MAXFIELD, *Reading Aloud.* Camden, N.J.: Thomas Nelson, Inc., 1933.

REDGRAVE, MICHAEL, *The Actor's Ways and Means.* London: William Heinemann Ltd., 1953.

SEYLER, ATHENE, and STEPHEN HAGGARD, *The Craft of Comedy.* New York: Theatre Arts Books, 1946.

SHAWN, TED, *Every Little Movement.* Brooklyn, N.Y. Dance Horizons, Inc., 1968.

SPOLIN, VIOLA, *Improvisation for the Theater.* Evanston, Ill.: Northwestern University Press, 1963.

STANISLAVSKI, KONSTANTIN, *An Actor Prepares.* New York: Theatre Arts Books, 1952.

————, *Building A Character,* trans. Elizabeth Reynolds Hapgood. New York: Theatre Arts Books, 1949.

STRASBERG, LEE, *Strasberg at the Actors Studio,* ed. Robert Hethmon. New York: The Viking Press, Inc., 1965.

The Design Process and Play Production

BABLET, DENIS, *Edward Gordon Craig,* trans. Daphne Woodward. New York: Theatre Arts Books, 1966.

BARTON, LUCY, *Historic Costume for the Stage.* Boston: Walter H. Baker Company, 1938.

————, *Appreciating Costume.* Boston, Mass.: Walter H. Baker Company, 1969.

BOYLE, WALDEN P., and JOHN H. JONES, *Central and Flexible Staging.* Berkeley, Calif.: University of California Press, 1956.

BURRIS-MEYER, HAROLD, and EDWARD C. COLE, *Scenery for the Theatre.* Boston: Little, Brown and Company, 1938.

————, *Theatres and Auditoriums.* New York: Reinhold Publishing Corporation, 1949.

CORSON, RICHARD, *Stage Makeup.* New York: Appleton-Century-Crofts, Inc., 1960.

CRAIG, EDWARD GORDON, *On The Art of the Theatre.* New York: Theatre Arts Books, 1957.

DAVENPORT, MILIA, *Book of Costume,* 2 vols. New York: Crown Publishers, 1948.

FUERST, WALTER R., and SAMUEL J. HUME, *Twentieth-Century Stage Decoration,* 2 vols. New York: Benjamin Blom, Inc., 1967.

GASSNER, JOHN, *Form and Idea in Modern Theatre.* New York: The Dryden Press, Inc., 1956.

GILLETTE, ARNOLD S., *Stage Scenery: Its Construction and Rigging.* New York: Harper & Brothers, 1959.

GRAVES, MAITLAND, *The Art of Color and Design.* New York: McGraw-Hill Book Company, 1951.

HAINAUX, RENÉ and YVES-BONNAT, *Stage Design Throughout the World Since 1950.* London: George G. Harrap & Co. Ltd., 1964.

JONES, ROBERT E., *The Dramatic Imagination.* New York: Theatre Arts Books, 1941.

LAVER, JAMES, *Costume in the Theatre.* New York: Hill & Wang, Inc., 1964.

McCANDLESS, STANLEY. *A Method of Lighting the Stage.* New York: Theatre Arts Books, 1958.

PARKER, W. OREN, and HARVEY K. SMITH, *Scene Design and Stage Lighting.* New York: Holt, Rinehart & Winston, Inc., 1968.

SIMONSON, LEE, *The Art of Scenic Design.* New York: Harper & Brothers, 1950.

SOUTHERN, RICHARD, *The Open Stage.* London: Faber & Faber Ltd., 1953.

Dramatic Literature

ANDERSON, MAXWELL, *The Essence of Tragedy.* Washington, D.C.: Anderson House, 1939.

BENTLEY, ERIC, *The Playwright as Thinker.* New York: Harcourt Brace Jovanovich, Inc., 1948.

BERGSON, HENRI, *Laughter,* ed. Wylie Sypher. Garden City, N.Y.: Doubleday & Company, Inc., 1956.

BRUSTEIN, ROBERT, *The Theatre of Revolt.* Boston: Little, Brown and Company, 1964.

BUTCHER, S. H., trans., *Aristotle on Music and Poetry.* New York: The Liberal Arts Press, 1956.

CLARK, BARRETT H., ed., *European Theories of the Drama.* New York: Crown Publishers, Inc., 1947.

CORRIGAN, ROBERT W., ed., *Comedy: Meaning and Form.* San Francisco: Chandler Publishing Co., 1965.

————, ed., *Tragedy: Vision and Form.* San Francisco: Chandler Publishing Co., 1965.

————, and JAMES L. ROSENBERG, eds., *The Context and Craft of Drama.* San Francisco: Chandler Publishing Co., 1964.

FREYTAG, GUSTAV, *Technique of the Drama.* Chicago: Griggs, 1895.

GASSNER, JOHN, *Masters of the Drama.* New York: Dover Publications, Inc., 1945.

MEREDITH, GEORGE, *An Essay on Comedy,* ed. Lane Cooper. Ithaca, N.Y.: Cornell University Press, 1956.

MILLER, ARTHUR, "The Family in Modern Drama," *Atlantic Monthly* 197 (April, 1956), 35–41.

QUINN, A. H., *A History of the American Drama: From the Beginning to the Civil War.* New York: Harper & Brothers, 1923.

————, *A History of the American Drama from the Civil War to the Present Day.* New York: F. S. Crofts & Co., 1936.

TENNANT, P. F. D., *Ibsen's Dramatic Technique.* New York: Humanities Press, Inc., 1965.

Historical Backgrounds

ARCHER, WILLIAM, *Masks or Faces?* New York: Hill and Wang, Inc., 1957.

BIEBER, MARGARETE, *The History of the Greek and Roman Theater.* Princeton, N.J.: Princeton University Press, 1961.

BOWERS, FAUBIAN, *Theatre in the East.* Camden, N.J.: T. Nelson, Inc., 1956.

CAMPBELL, LILY BESS, *Scenes and Machines on the English Stage.* New York: Barnes & Noble, Inc., 1960.

CLURMAN, HAROLD, *The Fervent Years.* New York: Hill and Wang, Inc., 1957.

COLE, TOBY and HELEN KRICH CHINOY, eds., *Actors on Acting.* New York: Crown Publishers, Inc., 1954.

COQUELIN, CONSTANT, HENRY IRVING, and DION BOUCICAULT, *The Art of Acting.* New York: Columbia University Press, 1926.

CRAIG, HARDIN, *English Religious Drama of the Middle Ages.* Oxford: Clarendon Press, 1955.

DUCKWORTH, GEORGE, *The Nature of Roman Comedy.* Princeton, N.J.: Princeton University Press, 1952.

DUERR, EDWIN, *The Length and Depth of Acting.* New York: Holt, Rinehart & Winston, Inc., 1962.

FRAZER, SIR JAMES, *The Golden Bough,* abr. ed. London: Macmillan Co. Ltd., 1959.

GASSNER, JOHN, *The Theatre in Our Times.* New York: Crown Publishers, Inc., 1954.

GORELIK, MORDECAI, *New Theatres for Old*. New York: E. P. Dutton & Co., Inc., 1962.

HODGES, C. WALTER, *The Globe Restored*. London: Ernest Benn Ltd., 1953.

KERNODLE, GEORGE, *From Art to Theatre*. Chicago: University of Chicago Press, 1964.

KOMISARJEVSKI, THEODORE, *The Theatre and a Changing Civilization*. London: John Lane, The Bodley Head Ltd., 1935.

LEWES, GEORGE HENRY, *On Actors and the Art of Acting*. New York: Henry Holt & Company, 1878.

NAGLER, ALOIS M., ed., *A Source Book in Theatrical History*. New York: Dover Publications, Inc., 1959.

NICOLL, ALLARDYCE, *The Development of the Theatre*. New York: Harcourt Brace Jovanovich, Inc., 1958.

PICKARD-CAMBRIDGE, ARTHUR, *The Dramatic Festivals of Athens*. Oxford: Clarendon Press, 1953.

ROWELL, GEORGE, *The Victorian Theatre*. London: Oxford University Press, 1956.

SIMONSON, LEE, *The Stage Is Set*. New York: Harcourt Brace Jovanovich, Inc., 1932.

SOUTHERN, RICHARD, *The Medieval Theatre in the Round*. London: Faber and Faber Ltd., 1957.

————, *The Seven Ages of the Theatre*. New York: Hill and Wang, Inc., 1961.

STEBBINS, GENEVIEVE, *Delsarte System of Expression*. Belmar, N.J.: Edgar S. Werner & Co., 1902.

SUMMERS, MONTAGUE, *The Restoration Theatre*. London: Kegan Paul, Trench, Trubner & Co., Ltd., 1934.

WATSON, ERNEST B., *Sheridan to Robertson*. New York: Benjamin Blom, Inc., 1963.

index